31st International Conference on Computational Linguistics (COLING 2025)

Systems Demonstrations

Abu Dhabi, United Arab Emirates
19-24 January 2025

ISBN: 979-8-3313-1357-9

Printed from e-media with permission by:

Curran Associates, Inc.
57 Morehouse Lane
Red Hook, NY 12571

Some format issues inherent in the e-media version may also appear in this print version.

Association for Computational Linguistics
209 N. Eighth Street
Stroudsburg, Pennsylvania 18360

Phone: 1-570-476-8006
Fax: 1-570-476-0860

acl@aclweb.org

Additional copies of this publication are available from:

Curran Associates, Inc.
57 Morehouse Lane
Red Hook, NY 12571 USA
Phone: 845-758-0400
Fax: 845-758-2633
Email: curran@proceedings.com
Web: www.proceedings.com

COLING 2025

The 31st International Conference on Computational Linguistics

Proceedings of the System Demonstrations

January 19 - 24, 2025

The COLING 2025 organizers gratefully acknowledge the support from the following sponsors.

Destination Partner

abu dhabi
Convention & Exhibition Bureau

Host Institution

Mohamed bin Zayed University of Artificial Intelligence

Diamond

TII Technology Innovation Institute

Winter School Sponsor

NYU Abu Dhabi

Platinum

Inception
A G42 company

Gold

Baidu 百度

Silver

Supporter

Message from the Program Chairs

This volume contains papers from the system demonstration session of the 31st International Conference on Computational Linguistics (COLING 2025) held in Abu Dhabi, UAE.

The demonstration session complements the conference's presentation and poster sessions and is focused on working software systems that are the tangible outcomes of research on computational linguistics. While the two previous COLINGs did not have a separate demo track, COLING 2025 has returned to having one, as was the case with COLING 2020 and earlier, and several of the other main NLP conferences.

There were 69 submissions, with 62 valid submissions reviewed. The program committee consisted of 149 members, with two chairs overseeing the reviewing. The acceptance criteria we followed during the selection process included the quality of work as well as the utility and demonstrability potential of the presented systems. We accepted 22 papers, giving an acceptance rate of 35

We thank the reviewers, the organizers of COLING, and everyone who submitted papers.

Mark Dras and Brodie Mather

COLING2025 Demonstration Program Co-Chairs

9 January 2025

Program Committee

Program Chairs

Brodie Mather, The Institute of Human & Machine Cognition, USA
Mark Dras, Macquarie University, Australia

Reviewers

Abdulaziz Alhamadani, Alessandra Zarcone, Alessandro Bondielli, Alex Fabbri, Alexander O'Connor, Alexandre Rademaker, Anais Ollagnier, Animesh Prasad, Anna Corazza, Antonio Moreno-Sandoval, Bang Liu, Bharat Ram Ambati, Boliang Zhang, Bonnie Webber, Brian Davis, Chao Shang, Chen Jia, Chen Wu, Chenchen Ding, Chenwei Yan, Chenyang Lyu, Chris Biemann, Christa Womser-Hacker, Dang Tuan Nguyen, Daniel Baumartz, Daniel Campos, Daryna Dementieva, Di Wang, Dimitar Dimitrov, Dimitar Shterionov, Dingzirui Wang, Eleri Aedmaa, Emily Allaway, Erica Kido Shimomoto, Evelin Amorim, Fangzhao Wu, Federico Ruggeri, Fiona Anting Tan, Flammie Pirinen, Francesca Frontini, Gael de Chalendar, Genta Winata, Georg Rehm, German Rigau, Giuseppe Abrami, Gosuddin Kamaruddin Siddiqi, Greta Damo, Guoxiu He, Hans Ole Hatzel, Hansi Hettiarachchi, Hui Lu, Huiqiang Jiang, Isao Goto, James Thorne, Ji-Ung Lee, Jiale Han, Joan Byamugisha, John Judge, Junhui Li, Juntao Yu, Kaili Huang, Kaja Dobrovoljc, Karina Halevy, Katsuhito Sudoh, Kaushik Roy, Kazunori Komatani, Kiet Nguyen, Koji Inoue, Lauriane Aufrant, Lei Shu, Liling Tan, Longyue Wang, Lucia Pitarch, Luis Morgado da Costa, Marco Turchi, Matthew Shardlow, Mikio Nakano, Mingxu Tao, Miquel Esplà-Gomis, Monjoy Saha, Muhammad Abdo, Muhua Zhu, Murali Raghu Babu Balusu, Muyun Yang, Naoki Otani, Nazia Nafis, Neelamadhav Gantayat, Nishat Raihan, Normaziah Aziz, Oier Lopez de Lacalle, Panupong Pasupat, Parnia Bahar, Paul Buitelaar, Paul Rayson, Peifeng Li, Peilin Zhou, Peng Li, Petra Bago, Philipp Koehn, Piji Li, Qihui Xu, Quzhe Huang, Rachele Sprugnoli, Robert Geislinger, Rodolfo Delmonte, Rodrigo Agerri, Roy Ka-Wei Lee, Rui Wang, Ruifan Li, Rémi Cardon, Sandeep Mathias, Sangha Nam, Seid Muhie Yimam, Seung-Hoon Na, Shiyi Han, Shuqing Bian, Simbiat Ajao, Siyou Liu, Smita Bailur, Sourabh Deoghare, Stefano Faralli, Sudeep Gandhe, Tafseer Ahmed, Tanel Alumäe, Taro Watanabe, Tharindu Ranasinghe, Thien Nguyen, Thomas Brovelli (Meyer), Timo Baumann, Tong Xiao, Torsten Zesch, Vibhu Mittal, Voula Giouli, Wang Xu, Wen Zhang, Wolfgang Menzel, Wuwei Lan, Xianchao Wu, Xin Zhang, Xinyuan Lu, Xixin Wu, Yinghui Li, Yo Ehara, Yu-Jung Heo, Yuanliang Meng, Yukun Ma, Yves Lepage, Zhongqing Wang, Ziwei Xu

Table of Contents

PolyMinder: A Support System for Entity Annotation and Relation Extraction in Polymer Science Documents
Truong Dinh Do, An Hoang Trieu, Van-Thuy Phi, Minh Le Nguyen and Yuji Matsumoto 1

Streamlining Biomedical Research with Specialized LLMs
Linqing Chen 9

LENS: Learning Entities from Narratives of Skin Cancer
Daisy Monika Lal, Paul Rayson, Christopher Peter, Ignatius Ezeani, Mo El-Haj, Yafei Zhu and Yufeng Liu 20

Loki: An Open-Source Tool for Fact Verification
Haonan Li, Xudong Han, Hao Wang, Yuxia Wang, Minghan Wang, Rui Xing, Yilin Geng, Zenan Zhai, Preslav Nakov and Timothy Baldwin 28

UnifiedGEC: Integrating Grammatical Error Correction Approaches for Multi-languages with a Unified Framework
Yike Zhao, Xiaoman Wang, Yunshi Lan and Weining Qian 37

Reliable, Reproducible, and Really Fast Leaderboards with Evalica
Dmitry Ustalov 46

BeefBot: Harnessing Advanced LLM and RAG Techniques for Providing Scientific and Technology Solutions to Beef Producers
Zhihao Zhang, Carrie-Ann Wilson, Rachel Hay, Yvette Everingham and Usman Naseem 54

AI-Press: A Multi-Agent News Generating and Feedback Simulation System Powered by Large Language Models
Xiawei Liu, Shiyue Yang, Xinnong Zhang, Haoyu Kuang, Libo Sun, Yihang Yang, Siming Chen, Xuanjing Huang and Zhongyu Wei 63

A Probabilistic Toolkit for Multi-grained Word Segmentation in Chinese
Xi Ma, Yang Hou, Xuebin Wang and Zhenghua Li 83

EasyJudge: an Easy-to-use Tool for Comprehensive Response Evaluation of LLMs
Yijie LI and Yuan Sun 91

LUCE: A Dynamic Framework and Interactive Dashboard for Opinionated Text Analysis
Omnia Zayed, Gaurav Negi, Sampritha Hassan Manjunath, Devishree Pillai and Paul Buitelaar 104

RAGthoven: A Configurable Toolkit for RAG-enabled LLM Experimentation
Gregor Karetka, Demetris Skottis, Lucia Dutková, Peter Hraška and Marek Suppa 117

MuRAR: A Simple and Effective Multimodal Retrieval and Answer Refinement Framework for Multimodal Question Answering
Zhengyuan Zhu, Daniel Lee, Hong Zhang, Sai Sree Harsha, Loic Feujio, Akash Maharaj and Yunyao Li 126

Human-Like Embodied AI Interviewer: Employing Android ERICA in Real International Conference
Zi Haur Pang, Yahui Fu, Divesh Lala, Mikey Elmers, Koji Inoue and Tatsuya Kawahara 136

CASE: Large Scale Topic Exploitation for Decision Support Systems
Lorena Calvo Bartolomé, Jerónimo Arenas-García and David Pérez Fernández 151

GECTurk WEB: An Explainable Online Platform for Turkish Grammatical Error Detection and Correction
Ali Gebeşçe and Gözde Gül Şahin 163

GR-NLP-TOOLKIT: An Open-Source NLP Toolkit for Modern Greek
Lefteris Loukas, Nikolaos Smyrnioudis, Chrysa Dikonomaki, Spiros Barbakos, Anastasios Toumazatos, John Koutsikakis, Manolis Kyriakakis, Mary Georgiou, Stavros Vassos, John Pavlopoulos and Ion Androutsopoulos 174

ViSoLex: An Open-Source Repository for Vietnamese Social Media Lexical Normalization
Anh Thi-Hoang Nguyen, Dung Ha Nguyen and Kiet Van Nguyen 183

CompUGE-Bench: Comparative Understanding and Generation Evaluation Benchmark for Comparative Question Answering
Ahmad Shallouf, Irina Nikishina and Chris Biemann 189

Autonomous Machine Learning-Based Peer Reviewer Selection System
Nurmukhammed Aitymbetov and Dimitrios Zorbas 199

CULTURALLY YOURS: A Reading Assistant for Cross-Cultural Content
Saurabh Kumar Pandey, Harshit Budhiraja, Sougata Saha and Monojit Choudhury 208

FEAT-writing: An Interactive Training System for Argumentative Writing
Yuning Ding, Franziska Wehrhahn and Andrea Horbach 217

Conference Program

PolyMinder: A Support System for Entity Annotation and Relation Extraction in Polymer Science Documents
Truong Dinh Do, An Hoang Trieu, Van-Thuy Phi, Minh Le Nguyen and Yuji Matsumoto

Streamlining Biomedical Research with Specialized LLMs
Linqing Chen

LENS: Learning Entities from Narratives of Skin Cancer
Daisy Monika Lal, Paul Rayson, Christopher Peter, Ignatius Ezeani, Mo El-Haj, Yafei Zhu and Yufeng Liu

Loki: An Open-Source Tool for Fact Verification
Haonan Li, Xudong Han, Hao Wang, Yuxia Wang, Minghan Wang, Rui Xing, Yilin Geng, Zenan Zhai, Preslav Nakov and Timothy Baldwin

UnifiedGEC: Integrating Grammatical Error Correction Approaches for Multi-languages with a Unified Framework
Yike Zhao, Xiaoman Wang, Yunshi Lan and Weining Qian

Reliable, Reproducible, and Really Fast Leaderboards with Evalica
Dmitry Ustalov

BeefBot: Harnessing Advanced LLM and RAG Techniques for Providing Scientific and Technology Solutions to Beef Producers
Zhihao Zhang, Carrie-Ann Wilson, Rachel Hay, Yvette Everingham and Usman Naseem

AI-Press: A Multi-Agent News Generating and Feedback Simulation System Powered by Large Language Models
Xiawei Liu, Shiyue Yang, Xinnong Zhang, Haoyu Kuang, Libo Sun, Yihang Yang, Siming Chen, Xuanjing Huang and Zhongyu Wei

A Probabilistic Toolkit for Multi-grained Word Segmentation in Chinese
Xi Ma, Yang Hou, Xuebin Wang and Zhenghua Li

EasyJudge: an Easy-to-use Tool for Comprehensive Response Evaluation of LLMs
Yijie LI and Yuan Sun

LUCE: A Dynamic Framework and Interactive Dashboard for Opinionated Text Analysis
Omnia Zayed, Gaurav Negi, Sampritha Hassan Manjunath, Devishree Pillai and Paul Buitelaar

RAGthoven: A Configurable Toolkit for RAG-enabled LLM Experimentation
Gregor Karetka, Demetris Skottis, Lucia Dutková, Peter Hraška and Marek Suppa

MuRAR: A Simple and Effective Multimodal Retrieval and Answer Refinement Framework for Multimodal Question Answering
Zhengyuan Zhu, Daniel Lee, Hong Zhang, Sai Sree Harsha, Loic Feujio, Akash Maharaj and Yunyao Li

Human-Like Embodied AI Interviewer: Employing Android ERICA in Real International Conference
Zi Haur Pang, Yahui Fu, Divesh Lala, Mikey Elmers, Koji Inoue and Tatsuya Kawahara

CASE: Large Scale Topic Exploitation for Decision Support Systems
Lorena Calvo Bartolomé, Jerónimo Arenas-García and David Pérez Fernández

GECTurk WEB: An Explainable Online Platform for Turkish Grammatical Error Detection and Correction
Ali Gebeşçe and Gözde Gül Şahin

GR-NLP-TOOLKIT: An Open-Source NLP Toolkit for Modern Greek
Lefteris Loukas, Nikolaos Smyrnioudis, Chrysa Dikonomaki, Spiros Barbakos, Anastasios Toumazatos, John Koutsikakis, Manolis Kyriakakis, Mary Georgiou, Stavros Vassos, John Pavlopoulos and Ion Androutsopoulos

ViSoLex: An Open-Source Repository for Vietnamese Social Media Lexical Normalization
Anh Thi-Hoang Nguyen, Dung Ha Nguyen and Kiet Van Nguyen

CompUGE-Bench: Comparative Understanding and Generation Evaluation Benchmark for Comparative Question Answering
Ahmad Shallouf, Irina Nikishina and Chris Biemann

Autonomous Machine Learning-Based Peer Reviewer Selection System
Nurmukhammed Aitymbetov and Dimitrios Zorbas

CULTURALLY YOURS: A Reading Assistant for Cross-Cultural Content
Saurabh Kumar Pandey, Harshit Budhiraja, Sougata Saha and Monojit Choudhury

FEAT-writing: An Interactive Training System for Argumentative Writing
Yuning Ding, Franziska Wehrhahn and Andrea Horbach

PolyMinder: A Support System for Entity Annotation and Relation Extraction in Polymer Science Documents

Dinh-Truong Do[1,2*] **Hoang-An Trieu**[1,2*] **Van-Thuy Phi**[2]
Minh Le Nguyen[1] **Yuji Matsumoto**[2]

[1]Japan Advanced Institute of Science and Technology, Ishikawa, Japan
{truongdo, antrieu, nguyenml}@jaist.ac.jp
[2]RIKEN Center for Advanced Intelligence Project, Tokyo, Japan
{truong.do, an.trieu, thuy.phi, yuji.matsumoto}@riken.jp

Abstract

The growing volume of scientific literature in polymer science presents a significant challenge for researchers attempting to extract and annotate domain-specific entities, such as polymer names, material properties, and related information. Manual annotation of these documents is both time-consuming and prone to error due to the complexity of scientific language. To address this, we introduce PolyMinder, an annotation support system designed to assist polymer scientists in extracting and annotating polymer-related entities and their relationships in scientific documents. The system utilizes recent advanced Named Entity Recognition (NER) and Relation Extraction (RE) models tailored to the polymer domain. PolyMinder streamlines the annotation process by providing a web-based interface where users can browse, verify, and refine the extracted information before obtaining the final results. The system's source code is made publicly available to facilitate further research and development in this field. Our system can be accessed through the following URL: `https://www.jaist.ac.jp/is/labs/nguyen-lab/systems/polyminder`.

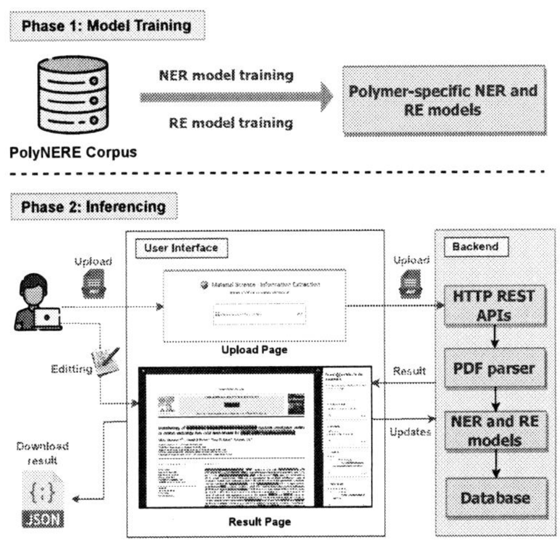

Figure 1: An overview of PolyMinder, showcasing its workflow from model training to entity/relation extraction and user interaction via the web-based interface.

1 Introduction

The study of polymers has gained significant momentum in recent years, driving advancements in diverse fields, including materials science, manufacturing, biomedical engineering, and environmental sustainability (Okolie et al., 2023; Sharma et al., 2021). Their versatility and wide-ranging properties make them indispensable in products such as plastics, rubbers, adhesives, and nanomaterials (Mohanty et al., 2022; AlMaadeed et al., 2020). As research in this area continues to grow, the volume of scientific literature on polymer structures, properties, and applications has grown substantially (Phi et al., 2024). Efficiently organizing and extracting valuable information from this vast corpus is crucial for both research and industry. However, manually extracting and annotating domain-specific entities like polymer names and material properties is challenging (Fagnani et al., 2022). The complexity of scientific language and the specialized expertise required make manual annotation time-consuming and error-prone.

While automated named entity recognition (NER) systems that use advanced neural networks have shown promise in the materials domain, including polymers (Oka et al., 2021; Phi et al., 2024; Cheung et al., 2024), existing solutions often accept only text-based inputs and output results in formats like JSON, lacking intuitive visualizations for users or annotators. They typically do not handle PDF inputs directly, despite PDFs being standard in the scientific community. Moreover, neural network

*Equal contribution

Proceedings of the 31st International Conference on Computational Linguistics: System Demonstrations, pages 1–8
January 19–24, 2025.

models are not infallible and can produce errors in entity extraction. Current systems lack features that allow annotators to efficiently refine or correct extracted data and parsing errors, necessitating manual adjustments without system support.

To bridge this gap, we present PolyMinder, an automated support system tailored specifically for the polymer domain. PolyMinder aids researchers by automatically identifying and extracting key information from scientific documents—such as polymer names, material properties—enabling the visualization and refinement of extracted data while significantly reducing manual effort. Figure 1 provides an overview of our system. In the training phase, we developed entity and relation extraction models using recent advanced techniques (Li et al., 2022; Zhou et al., 2021), trained on PolyNERE (Phi et al., 2024), a high-quality corpus for named entity recognition and relation extraction, covering a variety of entity and relation types. During inference, users can upload documents to the system, which extracts content from PDF files. The entity and relation extraction models process this content to identify relevant entities and relationships, which are then displayed in an intuitive web interface. Users can review and refine the automated extractions for accuracy before downloading the fully annotated output. In summary, our contributions in this paper are threefold: **(I)** we introduce PolyMinder, an automated support system that extracts and visualizes key polymer-related information from scientific texts, allowing annotators to review and refine the data; **(II)** we develop polymer-specific entity and relation extraction models utilizing state-of-the-art techniques tailored to the polymer science domain; and **(III)** we publicly release PolyMinder's source code[1] to support further research and development.

2 Related Work

Automated information extraction from scientific literature has advanced in fields like biomedical science, chemistry, and materials science (Yang et al., 2022). In polymer science, Oka et al. (2021) developed a system combining deep learning with rule-based methods to extract polymer data from tables in scientific articles. Similarly, Swain and Cole (2016) introduced ChemDataExtractor, a tool that processes chemical data using rule-based and supervised learning approaches. Weston et al. (2019) created MatScholar, which applies named entity recognition to extract key information from materials science literature. In biomedicine, the BENNERD system (Sohrab et al., 2020) targets COVID-19-related entity extraction, while Wadhwa et al. (2021) proposed a system for extracting fabrication knowledge in materials science, identifying key entities and relationships. More recently, Shetty et al. (2023) fine-tuned MaterialsBERT to extract material property records from large polymer corpora, significantly outperforming baseline models like BioBERT (Lee et al., 2020) and ChemBERT (Davronov and Adilova, 2023). Despite these advancements, the models used in these systems are still prone to errors, and current systems provide limited support for efficiently correcting them.

From the perspective of annotation tools, most existing solutions focus on entity recognition and relation extraction in plain text formats (Borisova et al., 2024). Tools like Brat (Stenetorp et al., 2012) and Doccano (Nakayama et al., 2018) offer a visual interface for annotating entities and relations in natural language texts, aiding manual curation. However, these tools lack direct interaction with PDF documents, the standard format for scientific research. PDFAnno (Shindo et al., 2018) addresses some of these limitations by enabling users to annotate entities and relations directly on PDF documents, preserving the original layout. Despite this, PDFAnno can become cluttered when annotating documents with numerous relations, as the visualization of arrows may overwhelm the interface and hinder the annotation process. This highlights the need for a more intuitive web-based interface that offers easy, clear annotation on PDF documents.

3 Method

3.1 Overview

Our proposed system, PolyMinder, is designed to extract polymer-related entities and their corresponding relationships from scientific documents (PDFs), followed by a visualization of these entities and relationships on a web interface for annotators to verify and refine (Figure 1). The process begins with training named entity recognition and relation extraction models using recent advanced methods, specifically ALTOP (Zhou et al., 2021) and W2NER (Li et al., 2022). Once the models are trained, we develop the web application, which includes both the frontend interface and the supporting backend infrastructure.

[1]`https://github.com/truongdo619/PolyMinder`

3.2 Entity and Relation Extraction Models

Entity extraction serves as the basis for identifying key polymer-related entities within documents. For this task, we employ the W2NER model (Li et al., 2022), which outperforms top-performing models on widely-used benchmark datasets on general, biomedical, and clinical domains. W2NER utilizes a word-to-span alignment approach, which allows it to handle three types of entity mentions (flat, overlapped, and discontinuous) effectively, a common challenge in scientific text. This model is trained on the PolyNERE corpus (Phi et al., 2024), a domain-specific dataset containing 750 polymer abstracts across 14 entity types. All entity types used in our system are summarized in Figure 2.

```
ENTITY
|------ MATERIAL_GROUP
|       |------ POLYMER_GROUP
|       |       |------ POLYMER
|       |       |------ POLYMER_FAMILY
|       |------ INORGANIC
|       |------ ORGANIC
|       |       |------ MONOMER
|       |------ COMPOSITE
|       `------ OTHER_MATERIAL
|------ PROP_NAME
|------ PROP_VALUE
|------ MATERIAL_AMOUNT
|------ CONDITION
|------ CHAR_METHOD
|------ SYN_METHOD
`------ REF_EXP
```

Figure 2: Ontology of material entities in PolyMinder, showing material types. Monomers fall under organic, while polymers may be organic or inorganic.

After identifying the entities, the next step is to establish their relationships. In polymer science, these relationships represent the essential connections between polymer-related entities. For instance, the entity POLYMER is related to the CHAR_METHOD entity through the characterized_by relationship. The details of all entities and their relationships in our system are illustrated in Figure 3. To extract these relationships, we tackle the RE task at the paragraph level, focusing on predicting relationships between entity pairs within the text. We utilize the ATLOP model (Zhou et al., 2021), designed for document-level or paragraph-level RE. By employing transformer-based attention mechanisms, ATLOP effectively captures complex, cross sentence relationships.

After training, the NER and RE models are integrated into PolyMinder's backend, generating JSON outputs. An example of output is as follows:

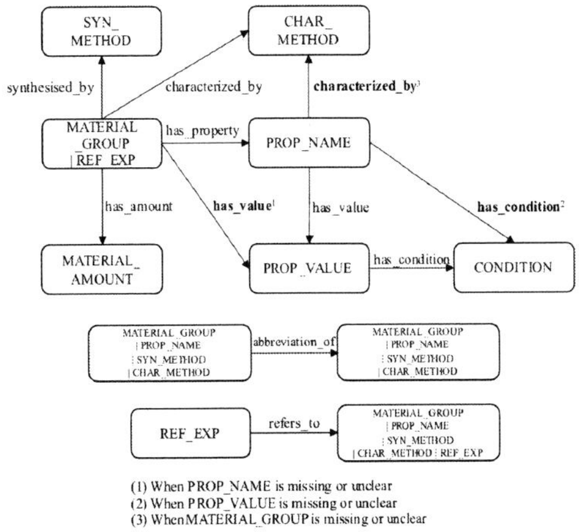

Figure 3: Illustration of the relationships between different polymer-related entities within PolyMinder.


```
{
  "text": "Sulfonated
      polyarylenethioethersulfone (SPTES
      ) copolymers with high ...",
  "entities": [
    [
      "T1",         #Entity ID
      "POLYMER",    #Entity Type
      [[0, 38]],    #Entity Position
      "Sulfonated
         polyarylenethioethersulfone"
                    #Entity Span
    ],
    [
      "T2",         #Entity ID
      "POLYMER",    #Entity Type
      [[41, 46]],   #Entity Position
      "SPTES"       #Entity Span
    ],
    ...
  ],
  "relations": [
    [
      "R1",                #Relation ID
      "abbreviation_of", #Relation Type
      [["Arg1", "T2"], ["Arg2", "T1"]]
            #Start and End Entities
    ],
    ...
  ]
}
```


3.3 PolyMinder System

PolyMinder is a web-based application designed to facilitate the extraction, visualization, and annotation of polymer-related information from scientific documents. It integrates a Python-based backend with a JavaScript-based frontend, seamless interaction between the user and the system. This section details the core components of the system and describes the data flow, as illustrated in Figure 4.

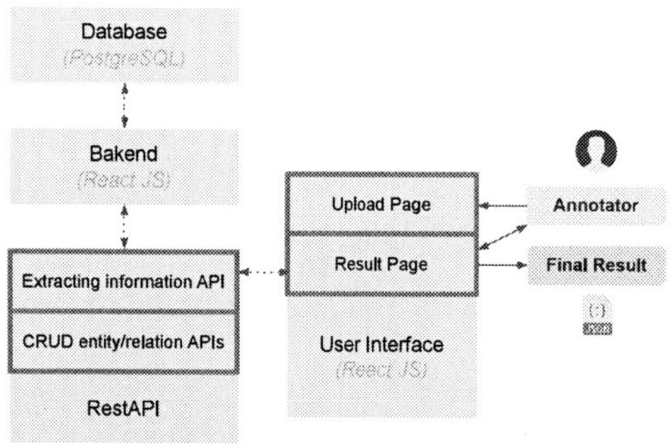

Figure 4: The architecture of the PolyMinder system, detailing its backend, RestAPI, and frontend.

3.3.1 Backend

The backend is implemented using the FastAPI framework[2] for its high performance and efficient development of RESTful APIs. These APIs handle communication with the frontend, supporting real-time data exchange and interaction. The backend's primary functions include document processing, data management, and facilitating user interactions.

When a PDF document is received, the backend employs PyMuPDF (McKie and Liu, 2020) to extract both text and its positional information within the document. PyMuPDF is particularly suited for this task because it supports the extraction of both text and bounding boxes, enabling accurate mapping of text to its location in the original PDF, which is crucial for visual annotations. The parsed text is then processed by pre-trained NER and RE models specifically tailored for polymer science, identifying and classifying relevant entities (e.g., polymer names, property names) and their relationships. For data management, the backend uses SQLAlchemy (Myers et al., 2015), an Object-Relational Mapping (ORM) tool that allows for flexible database selection, such as SQLite for lightweight applications or PostgreSQL for more demanding needs. The identified entities and relationships are stored in a structured, editable format, making it easy to retrieve and modify the data as needed. The backend also supports CRUD (Create, Read, Update, Delete) operations for entities, relationships, and PDF parsed text, enabling annotators to interact directly with the extracted data. Real-time updates are instantly reflected in the frontend through the REST APIs, ensuring a responsive and dynamic user experience that streamlines the annotation and correction process.

[2]https://fastapi.tiangolo.com/

3.3.2 Frontend

The frontend is developed using React[3] (JavaScript), along with HTML5 and CSS, to deliver an intuitive user interface. It allows users to upload polymer science PDFs for processing (Figure 5a) and visualizes extracted entities directly on the PDFs using overlays (Figure 5b), helping users see annotations in context. Relationships between entities are displayed in a Brat-like pop-up window (Stenetorp et al., 2012), offering clear insight into data connections (Figure 5c). To address potential errors from the PDF parser and NER/RE models, the frontend includes interactive tools allowing users to modify or correct parsed text and annotations, ensuring accuracy (Figure 5d). Upon completion, users can download the annotated documents for further analysis or use. Overall, the interface emphasizes ease of use and efficiency, streamlining annotators' workflows.

3.3.3 Data Flow

Figure 4 shows the typical workflow of the PolyMinder system. First, the user uploads a PDF document via the frontend interface. The backend processes the document using PyMuPDF to extract text and positional data. The extracted text is then sent to NER and RE models to identify relevant entities and their relations. The resulting data is stored in a database managed by SQLAlchemy, ensuring efficient retrieval and manipulation.

Next, the frontend accesses the extracted data via REST APIs and overlays the annotations on the original PDF, providing users with an intuitive visualization of the results. Users can review, refine, and edit the extracted entities, relationships, and parsed text using interactive tools. Any modifications made by the user are sent back to the backend through API calls, updating the database accordingly. If the parsed text data is edited, the system reprocesses the relevant components, generating and visualizing updated results. Once the user finalizes the annotations and is satisfied with the output, they can download the completed document, concluding the workflow.

4 Experiments on NER and RE models

4.1 Dataset for NER and RE Tasks

Our NER and RE system consists of two modules, forming a pipeline to identify entity mentions and extract relations between them. Both models are

[3]https://react.dev/

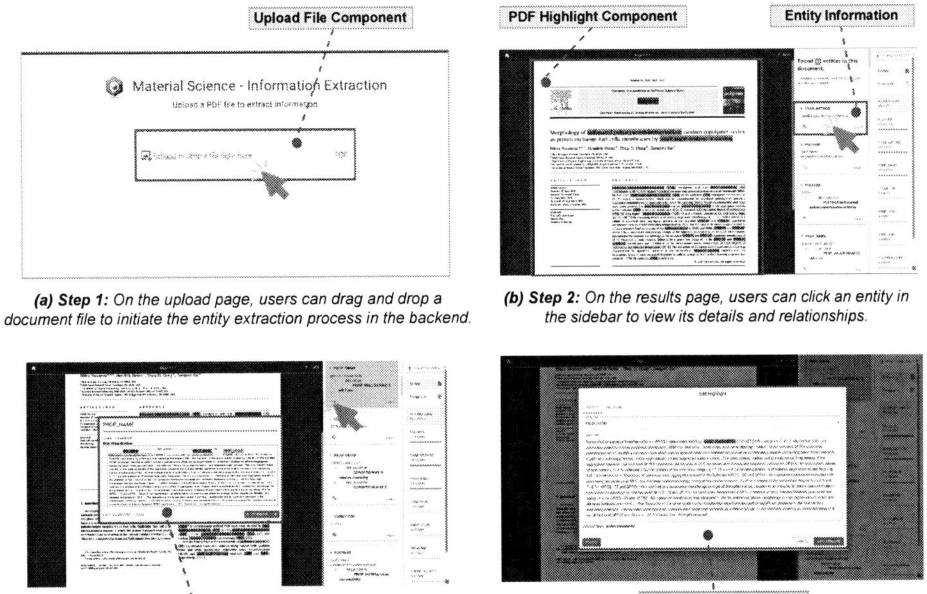

(a) Step 1: *On the upload page, users can drag and drop a document file to initiate the entity extraction process in the backend.*

(b) Step 2: *On the results page, users can click an entity in the sidebar to view its details and relationships.*

(c) Step 3: *On the results page, users can click the edit button next to an entity to open the editing panel for modification.*

(d) Step 4: *After editing, users can click the download button to save the final document.*

Figure 5: A step-by-step depiction of the typical user interaction flow within the PolyMinder interface, from document upload to entity editing and final result download. More guidelines are available on the demo website.

trained on the PolyNERE corpus (Phi et al., 2024) and are based on top-performing methods (Li et al., 2022; Zhou et al., 2021) in various configurations. For NER, most entities could be inferred from the context within the same sentence. Therefore, we focused on performing sentence-level NER to identify all possible entities in each abstract/paragraph. In contrast, extracting relationships between entities often requires cross-sentence reasoning, making it a paragraph or abstract-level task.

The PolyNERE corpus is split into 637 abstracts for training (85%), 38 for development (5%), and 75 for testing (10%). We report precision, recall, and F-score for both tasks. Models are developed and optimized using the training and development sets, with final evaluation on the test set.

4.2 Experimental Setup and Results

Named Entity Recognition. We conduct experiments using the W2NER model (Li et al., 2022), selected for its availability, efficiency, and ease of deployment. Furthermore, W2NER is particularly effective at identifying flat, overlapped, and discontinuous mentions, which are common in materials science texts where multiple entities are often discussed simultaneously. We utilize the AdamW (Loshchilov and Hutter, 2017) optimizer with a learning rate of 1e-3. For the BERT-BiLSTM encoder layer, the model features a distribution embedding size of 20 and an LSTM hidden size of 1024. Dropout rates of 0.5 are applied for both embeddings and convolutions. Training runs for up to 50 epochs with a batch size of 12, and the best checkpoint based on the development set is saved after training. We also experimented with different encoders to enhance NER performance.

Table 1: Results for NER on test set

Method	Encoder	P	R	F1
W2NER (Li et al., 2022)	BERT-large	77.78	73.55	75.61
	SciBERT	74.89	75.67	75.28
	MatSciBERT	**78.05**	**76.53**	**77.28**

Table 1 shows the evaluation of NER on the test set. Table 1 demonstrates that MatSciBERT (Gupta et al., 2022) yields better performance compared to the use of SciBERT (Beltagy et al., 2019).

Relation Extraction. We define the RE task as a cross-sentence relation extraction problem and evaluate it with pre-defined gold entities. An entity may have multiple mentions in the abstract, and a relation between two entities (e1, e2) exists if

Table 2: Results for RE on test set given gold entities

Method	Encoder	P	R	F1
ALTOP (Zhou et al., 2021)	BERT-large	84.35	73.59	78.60
	SciBERT	83.59	81.60	82.58
	MatSciBERT	**83.99**	**82.49**	**83.23**

expressed by any pair of their mentions. During inference, the goal is to predict relations between all possible entity pairs. To achieve this, we adapted the ATLOP method (Zhou et al., 2021), which aggregates contextual information using Transformer attention and employs an adaptive threshold for different entity pairs. Since ATLOP operates at the document level (or, in this case, at the paragraph level), a postprocessing step is used to convert the results into binary relations between entity mentions. Our model is optimized using AdamW (Loshchilov and Hutter, 2017) with a learning rate of 5e-5, a training batch size of 4, and a test batch size of 8, with a maximum of 30 epochs. We also experiment with different encoders.

As shown in Table 2, ATLOP achieves the highest F1 score of 83.23% using the MatSciBERT encoder. Overall, our system demonstrates strong performance and is well-suited for real-world use as an effective and practical RE system, addressing complex contexts in materials science papers, including flat, overlapping, and discontinuous entity mentions and relations across sentences. Additionally, the NER and RE models integrated into PolyMinder are modular and replaceable, allowing customization with advanced tools or adaptation to other domains beyond polymer science.

4.3 Efficiency and Processing Time Analysis

The PolyNERE corpus consists of 750 abstracts, each containing an average of 25.24 entities and 15.29 relations. Based on an estimated annotation time of 15 seconds per item[4], factoring in the annotator's familiarity with materials science and the task's complexity, manually annotating a single abstract would take approximately 10 minutes. This estimate could increase due to challenges like lengthy paragraphs, complex entity relationships, and maintaining context across multiple sections.

To assess the efficiency improvements introduced by PolyMinder, we applied our system to the 75 abstracts in the test set. The total processing time was 6.45 minutes, averaging 5.16 seconds per abstract. This represents a significant reduction compared to the estimated 10 minutes required for manual annotation. Although verification and refinement time are not included in this figure, the high precision and recall of our NER and RE models (as demonstrated in Tables 1 and 2) suggest that the need for extensive post-processing is minimized. Even if an additional 3–4 minutes per abstract is allocated for review, the overall time remains well below the manual annotation time, presenting a considerable efficiency advantage for researchers handling large volumes of literature.

[4]Estimate provided by the PolyNERE corpus author.

5 Threats to Validity

While PolyMinder shows promise in supporting entity and relation annotation for polymer-related documents, several limitations may impact its generalizability and performance.

Dataset Size, Diversity, and Annotation Quality. A key limitation is the system's reliance on the PolyNERE corpus for training NER and RE models. Though tailored to the polymer domain, it contains only 750 abstracts, which may not represent the full diversity of polymer science literature. Additionally, data imbalance and incomplete annotations for some entities may lead to biased models that underperform on less frequent or poorly labeled entities. Future work will focus on expanding the dataset with more diverse documents and improving annotation quality to boost robustness.

PDF Extraction Inconsistencies. Variations in PDF formatting, such as complex layouts, figures, and tables, create challenges. These inconsistencies can result in extraction errors, causing missed or incorrect entity annotations. Future work will investigate advanced extraction techniques to better handle diverse PDF structures.

6 Conclusion

In this paper, we introduced PolyMinder, a specialized support system that streamlines entity extraction and relation annotation in polymer science documents by leveraging advanced NER and RE models tailored specifically to the polymer domain. Our system automates the extraction of key polymer-related entities and their relationships, providing an intuitive web interface for users to efficiently browse, verify, and refine the information. Experimental results demonstrate high performance on the PolyNERE corpus, highlighting efficiency gains over manual annotation processes.

References

Mariam Al Ali AlMaadeed, Deepalekshmi Ponnamma, and Ali Alaa El-Samak. 2020. Polymers to improve the world and lifestyle: physical, mechanical, and chemical needs. In *Polymer Science and Innovative Applications*, pages 1–19. Elsevier.

Iz Beltagy, Kyle Lo, and Arman Cohan. 2019. SciBERT: A pretrained language model for scientific text. In *Proceedings of the 2019 Conference on Empirical Methods in Natural Language Processing and the 9th International Joint Conference on Natural Language Processing (EMNLP-IJCNLP)*, pages 3615–3620, Hong Kong, China. Association for Computational Linguistics.

Ekaterina Borisova, Raia Abu Ahmad, Leyla Garcia-Castro, Ricardo Usbeck, and Georg Rehm. 2024. Surveying the FAIRness of annotation tools: Difficult to find, difficult to reuse. In *Proceedings of The 18th Linguistic Annotation Workshop (LAW-XVIII)*, pages 29–45, St. Julians, Malta. Association for Computational Linguistics.

Jerry Cheung, Yuchen Zhuang, Yinghao Li, Pranav Shetty, Wantian Zhao, Sanjeev Grampurohit, Rampi Ramprasad, and Chao Zhang. 2024. POLYIE: A dataset of information extraction from polymer material scientific literature. In *Proceedings of the 2024 Conference of the North American Chapter of the Association for Computational Linguistics: Human Language Technologies (Volume 1: Long Papers)*, pages 2370–2385, Mexico City, Mexico. Association for Computational Linguistics.

Rifkat Davronov and Fatima Adilova. 2023. Bert-based drug structure presentation: A comparison of tokenizers. In *AIP Conference Proceedings*, volume 2781. AIP Publishing.

Danielle E Fagnani, Coralie Jehanno, Haritz Sardon, and Anne J McNeil. 2022. Sustainable green polymerizations and end-of-life treatment of polymers.

Tanishq Gupta, Mohd Zaki, NM Anoop Krishnan, and Mausam. 2022. Matscibert: A materials domain language model for text mining and information extraction. *npj Computational Materials*, 8(1):102.

Jinhyuk Lee, Wonjin Yoon, Sungdong Kim, Donghyeon Kim, Sunkyu Kim, Chan Ho So, and Jaewoo Kang. 2020. Biobert: a pre-trained biomedical language representation model for biomedical text mining. *Bioinformatics*, 36(4):1234–1240.

Jingye Li, Hao Fei, Jiang Liu, Shengqiong Wu, Meishan Zhang, Chong Teng, Donghong Ji, and Fei Li. 2022. Unified named entity recognition as word-word relation classification. In *proceedings of the AAAI conference on artificial intelligence*, volume 36, pages 10965 10973.

Ilya Loshchilov and Frank Hutter. 2017. Fixing weight decay regularization in adam. *ArXiv*, abs/1711.05101.

M. McKie and R. Liu. 2020. Pymupdf - python binding for mupdf. `https://pypi.org/project/PyMuPDF/`. Accessed: 2024-09-12.

Amar K Mohanty, Feng Wu, Rosica Mincheva, Minna Hakkarainen, Jean-Marie Raquez, Deborah F Mielewski, Ramani Narayan, Anil N Netravali, and Manjusri Misra. 2022. Sustainable polymers. *Nature Reviews Methods Primers*, 2(1):46.

Jason Myers, Rick Copeland, and Richard D Copeland. 2015. *Essential SQLAlchemy*. " O'Reilly Media, Inc.".

Hiroki Nakayama, Takahiro Kubo, Junya Kamura, Yasufumi Taniguchi, and Xu Liang. 2018. doccano: Text annotation tool for human. Software available from https://github.com/doccano/doccano.

Hiroyuki Oka, Atsushi Yoshizawa, Hiroyuki Shindo, Yuji Matsumoto, and Masashi Ishii. 2021. Machine extraction of polymer data from tables using xml versions of scientific articles. *Science and Technology of Advanced Materials: Methods*, 1(1):12–23.

Obinna Okolie, Anuj Kumar, Christine Edwards, Linda A Lawton, Adekunle Oke, Seonaidh McDonald, Vijay Kumar Thakur, and James Njuguna. 2023. Bio-based sustainable polymers and materials: From processing to biodegradation. *Journal of Composites Science*, 7(6):213.

Van-Thuy Phi, Hiroki Teranishi, Yuji Matsumoto, Hiroyuki Oka, and Masashi Ishii. 2024. PolyNERE: A novel ontology and corpus for named entity recognition and relation extraction in polymer science domain. In *Proceedings of the 2024 Joint International Conference on Computational Linguistics, Language Resources and Evaluation (LREC-COLING 2024)*, pages 12856–12866, Torino, Italia. ELRA and ICCL.

Shubham Sharma, P Sudhakara, Abdoulhdi A Borhana Omran, Jujhar Singh, and RA Ilyas. 2021. Recent trends and developments in conducting polymer nanocomposites for multifunctional applications. *Polymers*, 13(17):2898.

Pranav Shetty, Arunkumar Chitteth Rajan, Chris Kuenneth, Sonakshi Gupta, Lakshmi Prerana Panchumarti, Lauren Holm, Chao Zhang, and Rampi Ramprasad. 2023. A general-purpose material property data extraction pipeline from large polymer corpora using natural language processing. *npj Computational Materials*, 9(1):52.

Hiroyuki Shindo, Yohei Munesada, and Yuji Matsumoto. 2018. PDFAnno: a web-based linguistic annotation tool for PDF documents. In *Proceedings of the Eleventh International Conference on Language Resources and Evaluation (LREC 2018)*, Miyazaki, Japan. European Language Resources Association (ELRA)

Mohammad Golam Sohrab, Khoa Duong, Makoto Miwa, Goran Topić, Ikeda Masami, and Takamura Hiroya. 2020. BENNERD: A neural named entity linking system for COVID-19. In *Proceedings of the 2020 Conference on Empirical Methods in Natural Language Processing: System Demonstrations*, pages 182–188, Online. Association for Computational Linguistics.

Pontus Stenetorp, Sampo Pyysalo, Goran Topić, Tomoko Ohta, Sophia Ananiadou, and Jun'ichi Tsujii. 2012. Brat: a web-based tool for nlp-assisted text annotation. In *Proceedings of the Demonstrations at the 13th Conference of the European Chapter of the Association for Computational Linguistics*, pages 102–107.

Matthew C Swain and Jacqueline M Cole. 2016. Chemdataextractor: a toolkit for automated extraction of chemical information from the scientific literature. *Journal of chemical information and modeling*, 56(10):1894–1904.

Neelanshi Wadhwa, S Sarath, Sapan Shah, Sreedhar Reddy, Pritwish Mitra, Deepak Jain, and Beena Rai. 2021. Device fabrication knowledge extraction from materials science literature. In *Proceedings of the AAAI Conference on Artificial Intelligence*, volume 35, pages 15416–15423.

Leigh Weston, Vahe Tshitoyan, John Dagdelen, Olga Kononova, Amalie Trewartha, Kristin A Persson, Gerbrand Ceder, and Anubhav Jain. 2019. Named entity recognition and normalization applied to large-scale information extraction from the materials science literature. *Journal of chemical information and modeling*, 59(9):3692–3702.

Yang Yang, Zhilei Wu, Yuexiang Yang, Shuangshuang Lian, Fengjie Guo, and Zhiwei Wang. 2022. A survey of information extraction based on deep learning. *Applied Sciences*, 12(19):9691.

Wenxuan Zhou, Kevin Huang, Tengyu Ma, and Jing Huang. 2021. Document-level relation extraction with adaptive thresholding and localized context pooling. In *Proceedings of the AAAI conference on artificial intelligence*, volume 35, pages 14612–14620.

Streamlining Biomedical Research with Specialized LLMs

Linqing Chen, Weilei Wang, Yubin Xia, Wentao Wu, Peng Xu, ZilongBai,
Jie Fang, Chaobo Xu, Ran Hu, Licong Xu, Haoran Hua, Jing Sun, Hanmeng Zhong, Jin Liu,
Tian Qiu, Haowen Liu, Meng Hu, Xiuwen Li, Fei Gao, Yong Gu, Tao Shi, Chaochao Wang,
Jianping Lu, Cheng Sun, Yixin Wang, Shengjie Yang, Yuancheng Li, Lu Jin, Lisha Zhang,
Fu Bian, Zhongkai Ye, Lidong Pei, Changyang Tu
PatSnap Co., LTD. Suzhou, China
{chenlinqing, wangweilei}@patsnap.com

Abstract

In this paper, we propose a novel system that integrates state-of-the-art, domain-specific large language models with advanced information retrieval techniques to deliver comprehensive and context-aware responses. Our approach facilitates seamless interaction among diverse components, enabling cross-validation of outputs to produce accurate, high-quality responses enriched with relevant data, images, tables, and other modalities. We demonstrate the system's capability to enhance response precision by leveraging a robust question-answering model, significantly improving the quality of dialogue generation. The system provides an accessible platform for real-time, high-fidelity interactions, allowing users to benefit from efficient human-computer interaction, precise retrieval, and simultaneous access to a wide range of literature and data. This dramatically improves the research efficiency of professionals in the biomedical and pharmaceutical domains and facilitates faster, more informed decision-making throughout the R&D process. Furthermore, the system proposed in this paper is available at https://synapse-chat.patsnap.com.

1 Introduction

The development of Large Language Models (LLMs) has significantly transformed the landscape of natural language processing (NLP). Recent advancements, exemplified by models such as GPT (Radford et al., 2018), have decreased the reliance on extensive feature engineering, thereby simplifying the creation of complex NLP systems (Sarzynska-Wawer et al., 2021; Howard and Ruder, 2018). These models have demonstrated remarkable capabilities in understanding and generating nuanced text with minimal prompts. Unlike conventional computational methods, LLMs such as BioBERT (Lee et al., 2020) and ChemBERTa (Chithrananda et al., 2020) excel in deciphering specialized lexicons. Additionally, LLMs have begun integrating data from genomics, proteomics, and chemical databases to provide holistic insights into drug-target interactions (Zeng et al., 2016). For instance, models like Transformer-CNN (Karpov et al., 2020) illustrate the efficacy of combining LLM architectures with convolutional neural networks to enhance feature extraction in complex datasets.

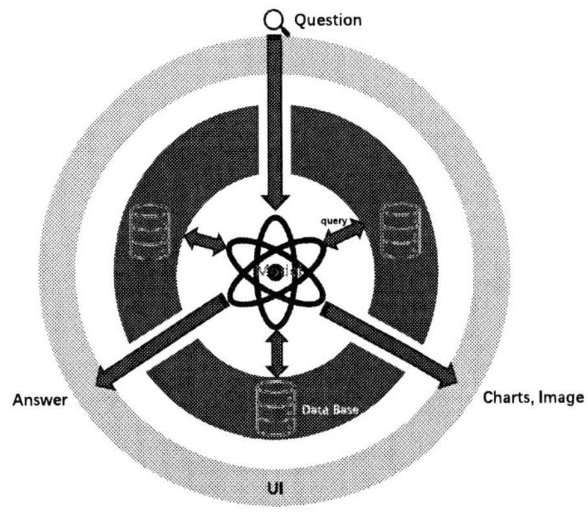

Figure 1: Synapse Chat System Architecture

Recently, we introduced PharmaGPT (Chen et al., 2024b), the foundational component of the Synapse Chat system. While general-purpose large language models (LLMs) have demonstrated impressive capabilities across a wide range of tasks, their applications in the biopharmaceutical domain have been relatively limited. Existing models often rely on incomplete or narrowly focused datasets, with many emphasizing clinical diagnosis or patient interaction (Luo et al., 2022; Singhal et al., 2023). These models lack comprehensive coverage of critical areas such as drug discovery, molecular biology, and regulatory affairs, which are essential for biopharmaceutical research and development. In contrast, PharmaGPT is specifically designed to possess extensive domain knowledge, ensuring full coverage across the biopharmaceutical lifecycle.

Proceedings of the 31st International Conference on Computational Linguistics: System Demonstrations, pages 9–19
January 19–24, 2025.

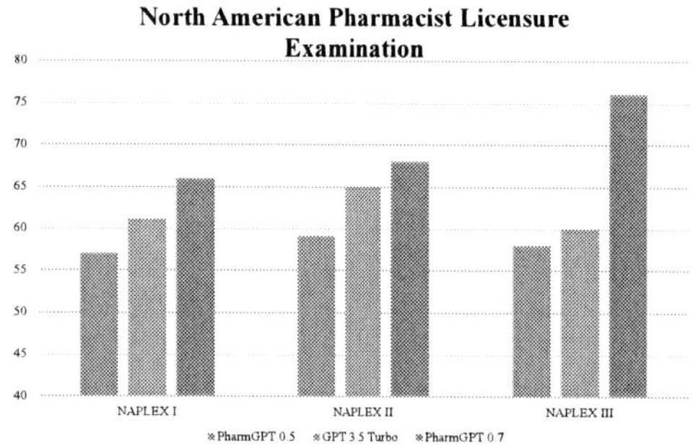

Figure 2: Test results of ChatGPT-3.5 Turbo and PharmaGPT models on the North American Pharmacist Licensure Examination (NAPLEX).

It integrates advanced capabilities such as natural language to SQL conversion, denoising, and reranking. A key feature of the system is its end-to-end reranking component, which enables the fusion of retrieval results from diverse sources with incomparable scoring mechanisms. This capability facilitates an ensemble approach that incorporates BM25, SQL-based, and vector-based retrieval methods, thereby enhancing the versatility and robustness of the system. Our experimental results demonstrate that PharmaGPT achieves notable improvements in denoising tasks, with relative gains of 2% to 4% over prior state-of-the-art general-purpose LLMs.

In this work, we present Synapse Chat, a comprehensive and enhanced system that builds upon the capabilities of PharmaGPT. Synapse Chat supports both asynchronous and real-time user interactions, enabling seamless dialogue, fact-checking, and open-domain question answering. Through extensive empirical evaluations, we demonstrate that Synapse Chat achieves state-of-the-art performance across these tasks within the biopharmaceutical domain. Notably, we introduce a approach that leverages a question-answering model to further enhance dialogue accuracy, significantly improving the system's ability to provide precise and contextually relevant responses. The Synapse Chat system is designed for a variety of use cases. It allows users to interact with the system at varying levels of verbosity, depending on their specific needs. Additionally, it enables users to cross-examine results across multiple tasks within the same system, providing a holistic and flexible approach to information retrieval and analysis.

2 System Architecture

The architecture of the Synapse Chat system, as depicted in Figure 1, is designed to facilitate seamless, real-time, and asynchronous interaction through a web-based interface. At its core, the system integrates multiple components—including a robust user interface (UI), a sophisticated data retrieval engine, and domain-specific large language models (LLMs)—to deliver comprehensive and contextually accurate responses. Users can query the system to retrieve information from various data sources, such as structured databases and unstructured documents, and the system intelligently combines the results through a multi-modal retrieval process. This process leverages an ensemble of retrieval techniques, including traditional keyword-based methods, SQL queries, and advanced vector-based retrieval, ensuring that the most relevant and high-quality information is surfaced. Our PharmaGPT model uses this combined information as input to generate a multi-modal response, assisted by APIs. The final output is then presented to the user in a clear and concise format, which may include text-based answers, charts, or images, depending on the nature of the query.

2.1 PharmaGPT

Large language models (LLMs) have significantly transformed Natural Language Processing (NLP) by reducing the reliance on intricate feature engineering. However, their application in highly specialized domains such as biopharmaceuticals and chemistry remains underexplored. These domains are characterized by highly specialized terminologies, complex knowledge structures, and a critical need for precision, areas in which general-purpose LLMs often exhibit limitations. In this work, we introduce **PharmaGPT**, a suite of domain-specific LLMs comprising 13 billion and 70-billion parameter models, meticulously trained on a comprehensive and domain-specific corpus tailored to the biopharmaceutical and chemical sectors. Our evaluation demonstrates that PharmaGPT consistently outperforms existing general-purpose models on domain-specific benchmarks such as the North American Pharmacist Licensure Examination (NAPLEX), showcasing its superior capability in addressing specialized tasks. Notably, this exceptional performance is achieved with models that utilize a fraction—sometimes as little as one-tenth—of the parameters of their general-purpose

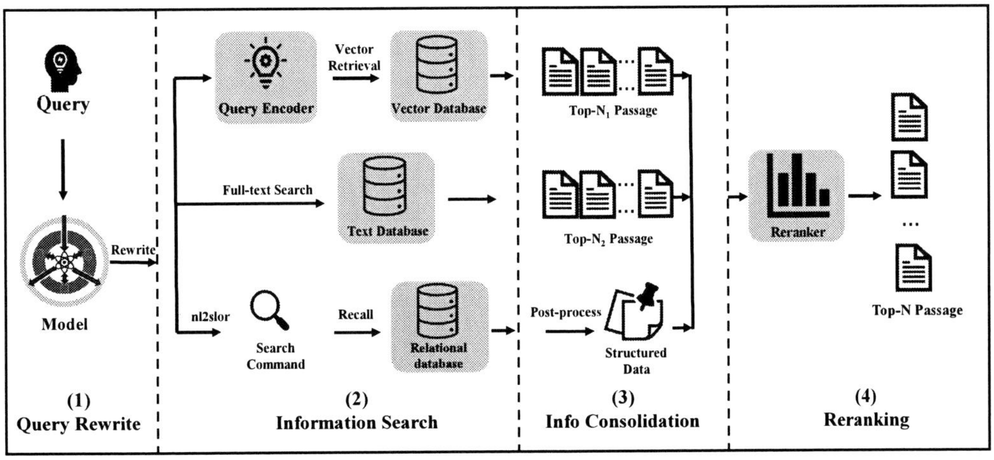

Figure 3: Pipeline of the SynapseChat Data Retrieval System

counterparts. This breakthrough establishes a new standard for LLMs in the biopharmaceutical and chemical fields, effectively filling the current gap in specialized language modeling. Moreover, it opens new avenues for research and development, paving the way for more accurate and efficient applications of NLP in these highly specialized areas.

Inspired by the work of Angel et al. (Angel et al., 2023), we conducted a comprehensive evaluation of our model, PharmaGPT, in comparison with other leading models using the North American Pharmacist Licensure Examination (NAPLEX) dataset. As shown in Fig. 2, this evaluation not only benchmarks the performance of PharmaGPT in a real-world, domain-specific examination but also highlights its applicability and potential in clinical and pharmaceutical scenarios. PharmaGPT consistently outperforms GPT-3.5 Turbo across several sections of the NAPLEX, underscoring its superior ability to understand and process biopharmaceutical knowledge.

As illustrated in Fig. 4, both versions of PharmaGPT (0.5 and 0.7) demonstrate strong performance across all four categories of the Chinese Pharmacist Examination. Achieving scores in the 70-80% range, PharmaGPT exhibits robust capabilities in pharmaceutical knowledge, regulations, and comprehensive skills. This consistent high performance indicates that PharmaGPT has been effectively fine-tuned on a large corpus of domain-specific biomedical and pharmaceutical literature, enabling it to excel in regionally and contextually diverse examinations.

As shown in Fig. 5, the translation performance

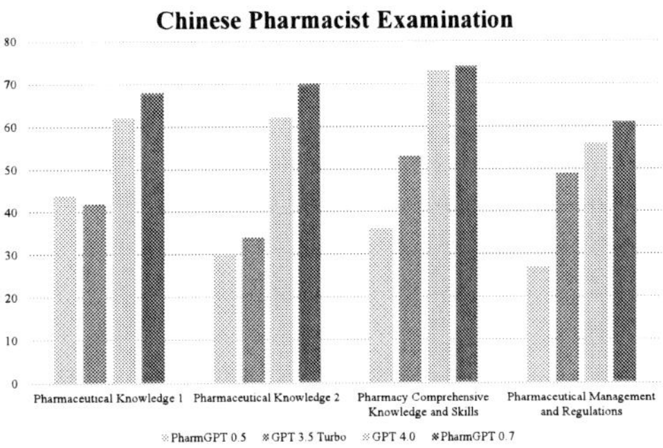

Figure 4: Test results of ChatGPT-3.5 Turbo, GPT-4, and PharmaGPT models on the Chinese Pharmacist Examination.

of four language models—PharmaGPT 0.7, GPT-3.5, CLAUDE3, and Google Translate—was evaluated across three levels of granularity: paragraph, sentence, and word. Translation quality was measured using BLEU scores (Papineni et al., 2002), with higher scores indicating better performance. PharmaGPT 0.7 demonstrates a clear advantage in translating biomedical papers. At the paragraph level, PharmaGPT 0.7 achieves a BLEU score of 30, outperforming GPT-3.5 (27), CLAUDE3 (26), and Google Translate (27). This trend continues at the word level, where PharmaGPT 0.7 scores 10, compared to GPT-3.5 (8), CLAUDE3 (9), and Google Translate (9). Even at the sentence level, PharmaGPT 0.7 excels with a score of 18, significantly higher than GPT-3.5 (15) and CLAUDE3 (16). These results highlight the superior ability of PharmaGPT 0.7 to handle the complexities of biomedical text translation, making it a highly effective tool for specialized domains.

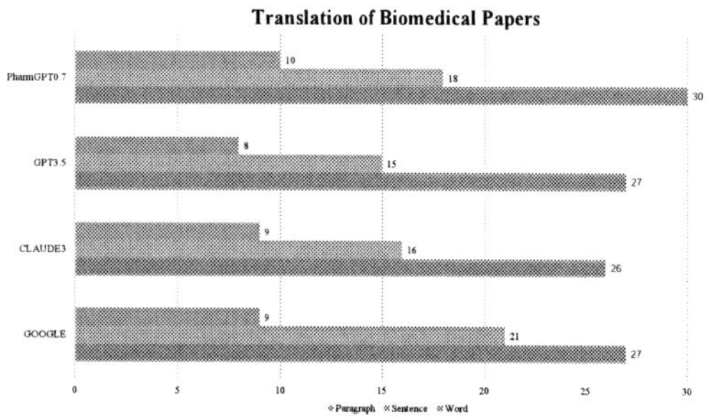

Figure 5: Test results of ChatGPT-3.5 Turbo, CLAUDE3, Google Translate, and PharmaGPT models on translation tasks for biomedical papers.

2.2 Multi-channel Retrieval System

To complement the domain-specific large language model (LLM) core tailored for the biopharmaceutical field, we have designed a robust and scalable multi-channel retrieval system. This system is a critical component in achieving our goal of developing a state-of-the-art question-answering platform for specialized biopharmaceutical queries. The retrieval system operates across three distinct data categories: structured data from our proprietary databases, unstructured textual data, and vectorized representations of documents.

As illustrated in Fig. 3, the unique nature of biopharmaceutical data necessitates a tailored approach to data retrieval. For instance, critical information such as drug development stages, approval statuses, and regulatory filings is stored as structured data in relational databases. This structured data can be efficiently queried using SQL-based methods. Meanwhile, vast corpora of research papers, patents, and clinical trial reports are better suited for vectorization and subsequent retrieval through vector-based search mechanisms. Given the rapid pace of advancements in the biopharmaceutical field, newly acquired or updated textual information is stored as unstructured text segments, which are indexed for full-text search.

The multi-channel retrieval system is designed to seamlessly integrate these three data types. Initially, a query from the user is rewritten by our model in case it is part of a multi-round dialogue. In this situation, our model completes the sentence to facilitate information retrieval. The rewritten query is then processed by the **Encoder**, which converts it into a suitable format for vector retrieval. The system performs parallel retrieval using both traditional full-text search for unstructured data and vector retrieval for vectorized documents. For structured data, we use nl2sql (Natural Language to SQL) to convert the user's query from natural language to SQL format. SQL queries are executed to extract relevant results. The top-N passages from each retrieval channel are combined, and a **Reranker** is applied to reorder the results based on relevance to the query. This reranked data is subsequently passed to the LLM core as reference material for generating precise and contextually accurate answers.

2.3 SynapseChat

As previously discussed, we have developed **PharmaGPT**, a robust large language model (LLM) specifically tailored for the biopharmaceutical domain. Leveraging its specialized training data, PharmaGPT possesses extensive and in-depth knowledge in biopharmaceuticals, consistently outperforming general-purpose models in domain-specific tasks such as professional examinations and scientific paper translation. PharmaGPT serves as the core "intelligence" of our system, efficiently accessing a vast array of proprietary databases containing biopharmaceutical, chemical, and genetic sequence data. It autonomously ranks, filters, and selects the most relevant information to generate precise, contextually accurate responses while also providing citation references to ensure transparency and reliability. However, to complete the full system, an intuitive and user-friendly interface is essential for facilitating user interaction.

The architecture of the final system is illustrated in Figure 1. Upon receiving a query from the user, PharmaGPT performs two key functions: (1) it interprets the query, retrieving and processing relevant data from multiple subfields and data types to generate a coherent textual response, and (2) it invokes APIs to dynamically generate visual content such as charts, images, and chemical structure diagrams for compounds, drugs, or gene sequences mentioned in the query. Notably, when the "deep search" mode is activated, PharmaGPT further enhances the output by automatically generating a mind map of the retrieved information, offering users an interactive and comprehensive view of the topic.

To further assess the system's performance, we conducted a comparative evaluation between

EN	Noise	SynapseChat(ac)	ChatGPT(ac)
	0.6	**92.33**	90.00
	0.8	**79.60**	76.00
ZH	Noise	SynapseChat(ac)	ChatGPT(ac)
	0.6	**89.33**	87.67
	0.8	**74.67**	70.67

Table 1: Comparative evaluation of SynapseChat and ChatGPT on information relevance discrimination.

SynapseChat and **ChatGPT** using publicly available datasets (Chen et al., 2024a)[1]. As shown in Table 1, regardless of the language (Chinese or English) and across different noise levels (0.6 or 0.8), SynapseChat consistently exhibits superior accuracy in discerning relevant information from irrelevant data. This enhanced ability to filter and utilize retrieved information effectively enables SynapseChat to provide users with more accurate and contextually appropriate responses, ultimately resulting in a better user experience. These findings underscore the robustness of SynapseChat in handling noisy data, which is a critical feature for real-world applications in the biopharmaceutical domain.

3 Applications for Enhancing Research

3.1 Domain-Specific Question Answering

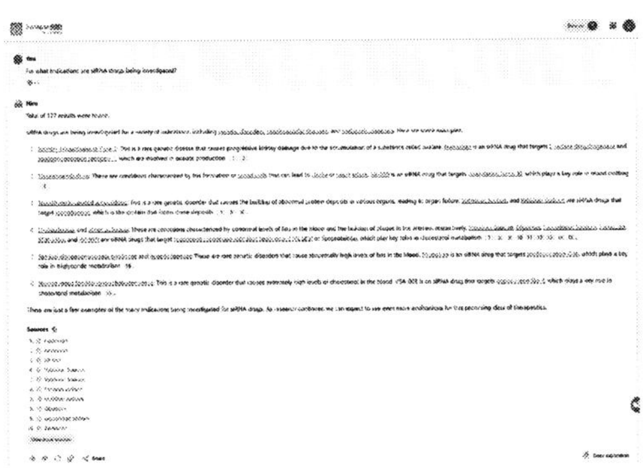

Figure 6: Drug-related Question Answering

In Figures 6, 10, 11, and 12, we demonstrate that our system integrates comprehensive and specialized databases encompassing drugs, clinical trial reports, chemical compounds, and regulatory information. This extensive data foundation enables the system to perform highly accurate, domain-specific question answering (QA) across these areas. The system not only retrieves precise answers but also provides detailed references, allowing users to navigate directly to the source material for further exploration. This capability ensures transparency and reliability in the information presented, which is essential for research purposes.

3.2 Compound Structure Recognition

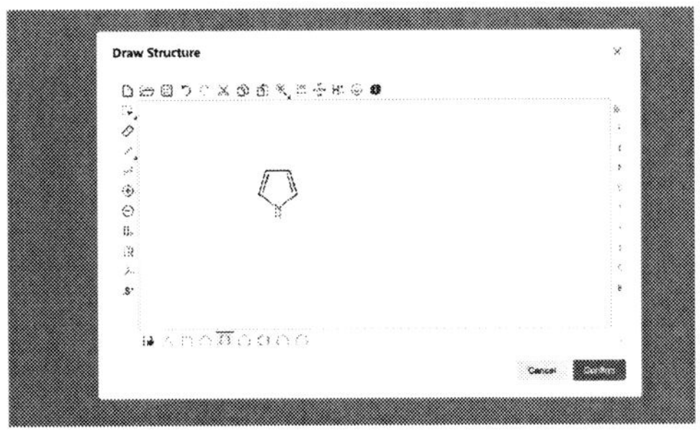

Figure 7: Compound Structure Editor

As illustrated in Figures 7 and 8, when a user inputs or draws a chemical structure, the system leverages a dedicated API to recognize the compound. The system then retrieves and synthesizes relevant compound-related data to provide a highly accurate and contextually appropriate response to the user's query. This functionality is particularly useful for chemical and pharmaceutical research, where understanding the properties and interactions of specific compounds is essential.

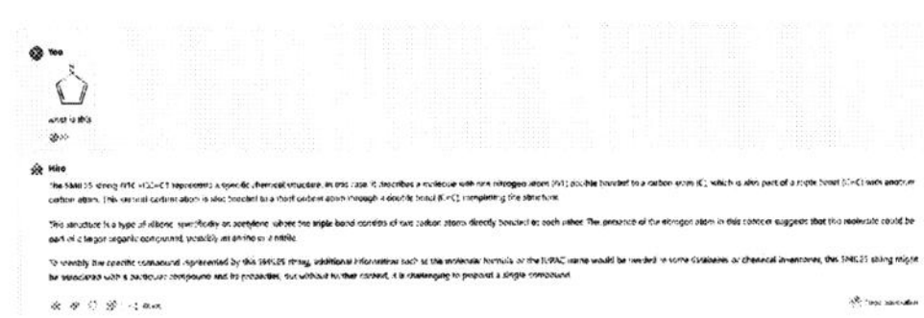

Figure 8: Compound Structure Question Answering

3.3 Deep Research Mode

For more in-depth analysis, users can activate the **Deep Research Mode**, as illustrated in Figures 9 and 13 (Appendix A). In cases where the standard response from SynapseChat lacks the necessary detail for complex research inquiries, this mode allows the system to retrieve a more comprehensive dataset, providing a thorough and integrated answer. Additionally, the system automatically generates a mind map based on the retrieved data,

[1]`https://github.com/chen700564/RGB/tree/master?tab=readme-ov-file`

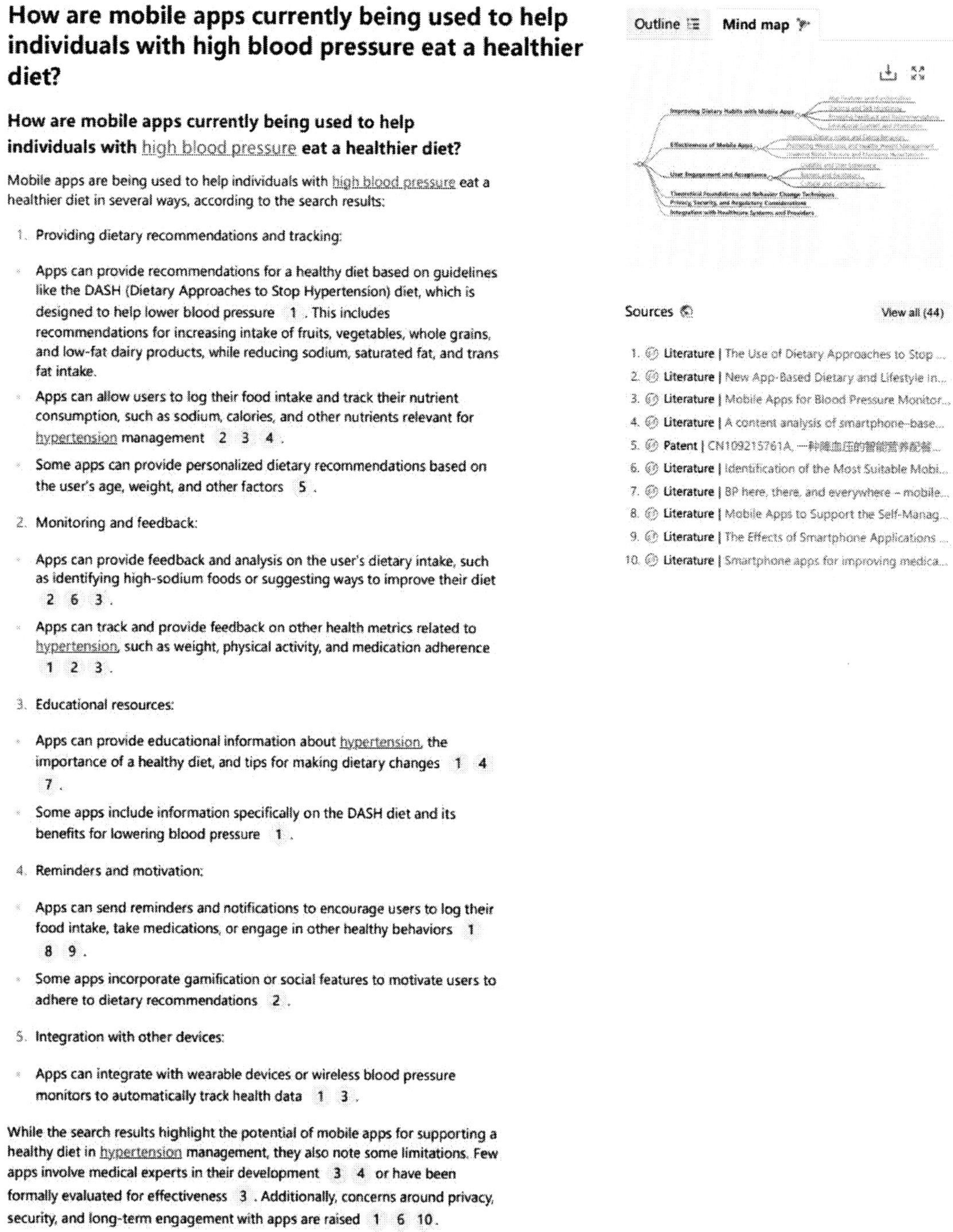

Figure 9: Deep Research Question Answering

visualizing the relationships between key entities and concepts. This feature enhances the user's ability to understand and explore the data, facilitating deeper insights and discoveries in fields such as drug development, chemistry, and clinical research.

4 Examples and Analysis

Table 2 (Appendix A) compares the performance of SynapseChat and GPT-4-turbo in the biomedical domain, specifically focusing on the clinical results of antibody-drug conjugates (ADCs) targeting gastric cancer. When provided with identical retrieved information, SynapseChat consistently demonstrates superior performance. With its enhanced domain knowledge, PharmaGPT is more effective at selecting data relevant to user inquiries. This improvement can be attributed to its specialized knowledge, enabling it to identify and utilize the most pertinent data more effectively, resulting in more accurate and contextually appropriate responses. This capability underscores SynapseChat's potential to deliver high-quality answers in specialized biomedical research environments.

5 Ethical Considerations

The deployment of large language models in the life sciences raises several ethical concerns. A primary issue is data privacy, especially when handling sensitive patient information that is essential for training these models. Ensuring data security and anonymity is crucial, given the serious implications a breach could have on individual privacy and research integrity. Furthermore, using large language models to synthesize new chemical entities or predict drug interactions requires rigorous validation to ensure reliability.

Data Privacy and Security: Implement advanced encryption, access controls, and differential privacy to protect sensitive user data.

Reliability and Validation of Predictions: Ensure rigorous validation of PharmaGPT across diverse datasets and maintain transparency about model limitations to prevent misuse.

Equitable Access: Partner with realated organizations and consider tiered pricing or open-source licensing to facilitate broader access, especially in low-resource settings.

These strategic measures can help mitigate risks and enhance the responsible deployment of PharmaGPT in the life sciences, ensuring safety, equity, and sustainability.

6 Conclusion

In this work, we presented **PharmaGPT**, a foundational large language model (LLM) specifically trained on biomedical domain knowledge. PharmaGPT is integrated into a multi-channel information retrieval system that seamlessly combines data from various sources, including proprietary databases on pharmaceuticals, research papers, patents, compounds, and clinical trials. By leveraging API calls and an advanced human-computer interaction (HCI) framework, the system provides users with a highly efficient tool for addressing complex research queries.

Our system delivers rapid and contextually accurate responses in specific biomedical domains, supported by reliable references. For users seeking more detailed or exploratory research, the system can generate hierarchical responses enriched with comprehensive content. This includes automated outlines and mind maps that visualize the relationships between key entities and concepts. Such functionality significantly enhances the system's utility for researchers, clinicians, and industry professionals who depend on timely and precise information to make informed decisions.

The comparative analysis (Table 2) demonstrates that **SynapseChat**, built upon PharmaGPT, significantly outperforms general-purpose models like GPT-4-turbo in domain-specific tasks. This is particularly evident in its ability to discern and apply the most relevant data from biomedical datasets. This advantage highlights the critical importance of domain specialization in large language models, especially in fields that require high levels of precision and expertise, such as biomedical research.

In summary, **PharmaGPT** represents a significant advancement in the application of large language models to the biomedical field, providing a robust and flexible solution for domain-specific question answering and research support. Future work will focus on expanding the model's knowledge base and enhancing its capabilities in other specialized areas of biomedicine.

References

Mirana Angel, Anuj Patel, Amal Alachkar, and Pierre Baldi. 2023. Clinical knowledge and reasoning abilities of large language models in pharmacy: A comparative study on the naplex exam. In *2023 Tenth International Conference on Social Networks Analysis, Management and Security (SNAMS)*, pages 1–4. IEEE.

Jiawei Chen, Hongyu Lin, Xianpei Han, and Le Sun. 2024a. Benchmarking large language models in retrieval-augmented generation. In *Proceedings of the AAAI Conference on Artificial Intelligence*, volume 38, pages 17754–17762.

Linqing Chen, Weilei Wang, Zilong Bai, Peng Xu, Yan Fang, Jie Fang, Wentao Wu, Lizhi Zhou, Ruiji Zhang, Yubin Xia, et al. 2024b. Pharmgpt: Domain-specific large language models for bio-pharmaceutical and chemistry. *arXiv preprint arXiv:2406.18045*.

Seyone Chithrananda, Gabriel Grand, and Bharath Ramsundar. 2020. Chemberta: large-scale self-supervised pretraining for molecular property prediction. *arXiv preprint arXiv:2010.09885*.

Jeremy Howard and Sebastian Ruder. 2018. Universal language model fine-tuning for text classification. *arXiv preprint arXiv:1801.06146*.

Pavel Karpov, Guillaume Godin, and Igor V Tetko. 2020. Transformer-cnn: Swiss knife for qsar modeling and interpretation. *Journal of cheminformatics*, 12:1–12.

Jinhyuk Lee, Wonjin Yoon, Sungdong Kim, Donghyeon Kim, Sunkyu Kim, Chan Ho So, and Jaewoo Kang. 2020. Biobert: a pre-trained biomedical language representation model for biomedical text mining. *Bioinformatics*, 36(4):1234–1240.

Renqian Luo, Liai Sun, Yingce Xia, Tao Qin, Sheng Zhang, Hoifung Poon, and Tie-Yan Liu. 2022. Biogpt: generative pre-trained transformer for biomedical text generation and mining. *Briefings in bioinformatics*, 23(6):bbac409.

Kishore Papineni, Salim Roukos, Todd Ward, and Wei-Jing Zhu. 2002. Bleu: a method for automatic evaluation of machine translation. In *Proceedings of the 40th annual meeting of the Association for Computational Linguistics*, pages 311–318.

Alec Radford, Karthik Narasimhan, Tim Salimans, Ilya Sutskever, et al. 2018. Improving language understanding by generative pre-training.

Justyna Sarzynska-Wawer, Aleksander Wawer, Aleksandra Pawlak, Julia Szymanowska, Izabela Stefaniak, Michal Jarkiewicz, and Lukasz Okruszek. 2021. Detecting formal thought disorder by deep contextualized word representations. *Psychiatry Research*, 304:114135.

Karan Singhal, Shekoofeh Azizi, Tao Tu, S Sara Mahdavi, Jason Wei, Hyung Won Chung, Nathan Scales, Ajay Tanwani, Heather Cole-Lewis, Stephen Pfohl, et al. 2023. Large language models encode clinical knowledge. *Nature*, 620(7972):172–180.

Haoyang Zeng, Matthew D Edwards, Ge Liu, and David K Gifford. 2016. Convolutional neural network architectures for predicting dna–protein binding. *Bioinformatics*, 32(12):i121–i127.

A Appendix

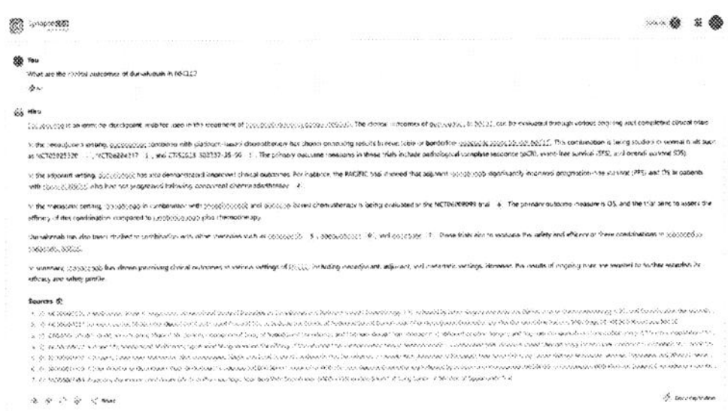

Figure 10: Clinical Trial-related Question Answering

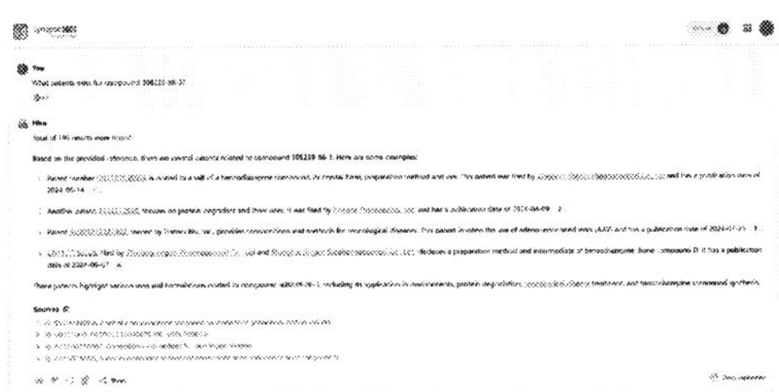

Figure 11: Compound-related Question Answering

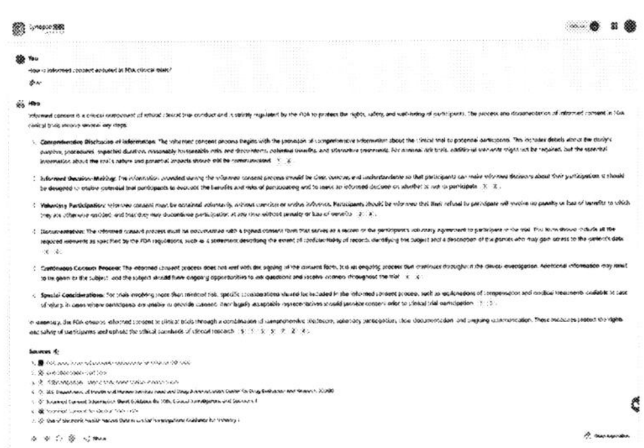

Figure 12: Regulatory and Policy-related Question Answering

B Case Study: Analysis of GPT-4-turbo and PharmaGPT Responses

In this case study (Table 2), we analyze the difference in the responses generated by GPT-4-turbo and PharmaGPT to the question: "The clinical results of ADC drugs targeting gastric cancer." Spccifically, wc focus on why GPT-4-turbo in cluded Reference [3], while PharmaGPT did not, and argue that PharmaGPT provided a more accurate and professional response in this context.

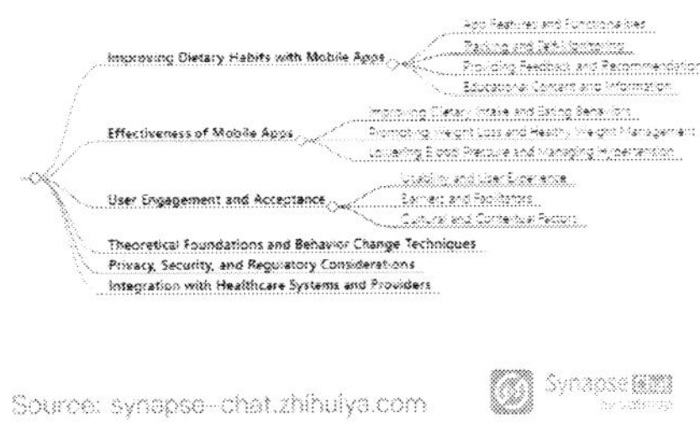

Figure 13: Automatically Generated Mind Map

B.1 Overview of the Question and Responses

The question asks for the clinical results of Antibody-Drug Conjugates (ADC) targeting gastric cancer. Both GPT-4-turbo and PharmaGPT provided responses summarizing the clinical results of ADC drugs such as Sacituzumab Tirumotecan, Disitamab Vedotin, and Fam-trastuzumab Deruxtecan-NXKI. While both models used References [1], [2], [4], and [5], a key difference was observed in their treatment of Reference [3].

Reference [3] describes a retrospective study involving the combination of trastuzumab deruxtecan (an ADC drug) and nivolumab (an immune checkpoint inhibitor) as a third-line or later treatment for HER2-positive advanced gastric cancer. GPT-4-turbo included Reference [3] in its response, while PharmaGPT did not. We argue that PharmaGPT's decision to exclude Reference [3] reflects a more appropriate and professional handling of the question's intent.

B.2 Analysis of GPT-4-turbo's Approach

GPT-4-turbo chose to include Reference [3] in its response, likely due to its broader interpretation of the question. Since trastuzumab deruxtecan is an ADC drug, GPT-4-turbo considered the study relevant, even though it involved a combination therapy with nivolumab, an immune checkpoint inhibitor. This approach suggests that GPT-4-turbo was more inclusive, focusing on any study where ADC drugs were part of the treatment, regardless of the involvement of other therapeutic agents.

While this inclusive approach offers a broader perspective, it introduces a significant issue: the focus on ADC drugs becomes diluted by the presence of immune checkpoint inhibitors, such as nivolumab. The study in Reference [3] does not strictly isolate the effects of the ADC drug, as the

Question	The clinical results of ADC drugs targeting gastric cancer.
Reference[1]	[1] "clinical register number": "NCT04152499", "clinical title": "Abstract CT038: Preliminary efficacy and safety results of anti-TROP2 ADC SKB264 (MK-2870) in patients (pts) with previously treated advanced gastric (G) or gastroesophageal junction (GEJ) cancer from a Phase 2 study", "phase": "Phase 2 Clinical", "conclusion": "The preliminary data suggests that pts with heavily pre-treated advanced G/GEJ cancer could achieve durable response and potentially prolonged OS from SKB264 monotherapy, with a manageable safety profile.", "drug name": "Sacituzumab tirumotecan", "indications": "Gastrooesophageal junction cancer", "target": "Tumor-associated calcium signal transducer 2", "mechanism of action": "Tumor-associated calcium signal transducer 2 modulator", "drug type": "Antibody drug conjugate (ADC)"
Reference[2]	[2] "clinical register number": "NCT04280341", "clinical title": "Disitamab vedotin (RC48) plus toripalimab for HER2-expressing advanced gastric or gastroesophageal junction and other solid tumours: a multicentre, open label, dose escalation and expansion phase 1 trial.", "phase": "Phase 1 Clinical", "conclusion": "Our findings suggested that RC48 plus toripalimab had a manageable safety profile and showed encouraging efficacy in pretreated patients with HER2-positive and low HER2-expressing G/GEJ cancer. The findings of our phase 1 clinical trial support further investigation of HER2-targeted ADC plus immunotherapy in HER2-expressing G/GEJ cancer and pancancer treatment in the future.", "drug name": "Disitamab Vedotin", "indications": "HER2-expressing Gastroesophageal Junction Adenocarcinoma", "target": "Tubulin, Receptor tyrosine-protein kinase erbB-2", "mechanism of action": "Microtubule inhibitor, receptor protein tyrosine kinase erbB-2 antagonist", "drug type": "Antibody drug conjugate (ADC)"
Reference[3]	[3] "clinical title": "Efficacy and safety of trastuzumab deruxtecan and nivolumab as third- or later-line treatment for HER2-positive advanced gastric cancer: A single-institution retrospective study.", "phase": "Not Applicable", "conclusion": "Conclusions:T-DXd and nivolumab had distinctive efficacy and toxicity profiles as third- or later-line treatment for HER2-positive AGC. Considering the distinct features of each regimen might help clinicians personalize the optimal treatment approaches for patients with HER2-positive AGC.", "drug name": "Fam-trastuzumab deruxtecan-NXKI", "indications": "HER2-positive gastric cancer", "target": "Receptor tyrosine-protein kinase erbB-2, DNA topoisomerase I", "mechanism of action": "DNA topoisomerase I inhibitor, receptor protein tyrosine kinase erbB-2 antagonist", "drug type": "Antibody drug conjugate (ADC)"
Reference[4]	[4] "clinical register number": "NCT04379596", "clinical title": "Phase 1b/2, open-label dose-escalation and -expansion study evaluating trastuzumab deruxtecan (T-DXd) monotherapy and combinations in patients (pts) with HER2+ and HER2-low gastric cancer (GC): DESTINY-Gastric03 (DG-03).", "phase": "Phase 1/2 Clinical", "drug name": "Fam-trastuzumab deruxtecan-NXKI", "indications": "HER2-Low Gastric Cancer", "target": "Receptor tyrosine-protein kinase erbB-2, DNA topoisomerase I", "mechanism of action": "DNA topoisomerase I inhibitor, receptor protein tyrosine kinase erbB-2 antagonist", "drug type": "Antibody drug conjugate (ADC)"
Reference[5]	[5] "clinical register number": "NCT05034887", "clinical title": "Phase 2 study of trastuzumab deruxtecan as neoadjuvant treatment for HER2-positive gastric and gastroesophageal junction adenocarcinoma (EPOC2003).", "phase": "Phase 2 Clinical", "conclusion": "T-DXd monotherapy showed modest single agent activity for locally advanced HER2-positive gastric or GEJ adenocarcinoma in this phase 2 study. An additional cohort combining perioperative T-DXd with capecitabine and durvalumab is planned, to assess whether treatment efficacy and outcomes can be enhanced.", "drug name": "Fam-trastuzumab deruxtecan-NXKI", "indications": "stomach adenocarcinoma, HER2 positive Gastroesophageal Junction Adenocarcinoma", "target": "Receptor tyrosine-protein kinase erbB-2, DNA topoisomerase I", "mechanism of action": "DNA topoisomerase I inhibitor, receptor protein tyrosine kinase erbB-2 antagonist", "drug type": "Monoclonal antibody, Antibody drug conjugate (ADC)"
gpt4-turbo	In the study of the clinical results of ADC (antibody-drug conjugate) drugs targeting gastric cancer, several drugs have shown varying degrees of efficacy and safety. The relevant clinical results of these drugs are detailed below: 1. **Sacituzumab tirumotecan** [1]: This drug targets the TROP2 receptor and is used for the treatment of heavily pre-treated advanced gastric cancer (G) or gastroesophageal junction cancer (GEJ). Preliminary data from a Phase 2 clinical study indicate that monotherapy with SKB264 (the clinical name for Sacituzumab tirumotecan) can lead to durable responses and potentially prolonged overall survival (OS) with a manageable safety profile. 2. **Disitamab Vedotin** [2]: In a Phase 1 clinical trial, Disitamab Vedotin combined with toripalimab was used for the treatment of HER2-expressing advanced gastric or gastroesophageal junction cancer, as well as other solid tumors. This combination therapy showed a manageable safety profile and encouraging efficacy in previously treated HER2-positive and low HER2-expressing G/GEJ cancer patients. 3. **Fam-trastuzumab deruxtecan-NXKI** [3][4][5]: Multiple studies on HER2-positive advanced gastric cancer have shown that both monotherapy and combination therapy with Fam-trastuzumab deruxtecan-NXKI exhibit good efficacy and acceptable safety profiles. Particularly in HER2-positive and HER2-low expressing gastric cancer patients, it has shown promising clinical effects in various treatment stages, including third-line or later treatments and perioperative therapy. These study results not only demonstrate the potential of ADC drugs in the treatment of gastric cancer but also emphasize the importance of continued research and development of ADC drugs targeting different receptors and combining different therapeutic mechanisms. ADC drugs, by linking antibodies with efficacious drugs (such as chemotherapy agents), can more precisely deliver the drugs to cancer cells, reducing the impact on normal cells, thereby enhancing efficacy and minimizing side effects.
pharma-gpt	The clinical results of ADC drugs targeting gastric cancer mainly come from the following studies: 1. **Preliminary efficacy and safety results of SKB264 (MK-2870)**: - **Clinical Study**: CT038 - **Clinical Results**: Preliminary data show that patients with heavily pre-treated advanced G/GEJ cancer can achieve durable responses and potentially prolonged OS with SKB264 monotherapy, with a manageable safety profile [1]. 2. **Study of Disitamab vedotin (RC48) combined with toripalimab**: - **Clinical Study**: NCT04280341 - **Clinical Results**: The results indicate that RC48 combined with toripalimab shows encouraging efficacy and a manageable safety profile in HER2-expressing advanced G/GEJ cancer patients. This finding supports further research into the use of HER2-targeted ADC combined with immunotherapy in G/GEJ cancer [2]. 3. **Studies of Trastuzumab deruxtecan (T-DXd)**: - **Clinical Study**: NCT04379596 (DESTINY-Gastric03) - **Clinical Results**: T-DXd shows certain efficacy in gastric cancer patients with low HER2 expression. Ongoing research aims to evaluate the combination effects of T-DXd with other treatment methods [4]. - **Clinical Study**: NCT05034887 (EPOC2003) - **Clinical Results**: T-DXd monotherapy shows moderate single-agent activity in locally advanced HER2-positive gastric or GEJ adenocarcinoma. Plans are underway to combine T-DXd with capecitabine and durvalumab to evaluate whether this can enhance treatment efficacy and outcomes [5]. In summary, ADC drugs have shown certain efficacy in the treatment of gastric cancer, particularly in patients with HER2 expression or HER2-positive gastric cancer. These drugs include SKB264, Disitamab vedotin, and Trastuzumab deruxtecan. However, the specific effects and safety of each drug still require further research and validation.

Table 2: Case study.

outcomes could be influenced by the addition of nivolumab. Therefore, including this reference in the context of a question specifically about ADC drugs may lead to misleading conclusions regarding the efficacy and safety of the ADC alone.

B.3 Analysis of PharmaGPT's Approach

In contrast, PharmaGPT's decision to exclude Reference [3] reflects a more focused and professional interpretation of the question. PharmaGPT appears to have recognized that Reference [3] deals with a combination therapy, where the effects of trastuzumab deruxtecan are intertwined with those of nivolumab, an immune checkpoint inhibitor.

Given that the question explicitly asks for the clinical results of ADC drugs, PharmaGPT likely excluded this reference to provide a more accurate and relevant response focused on studies where ADC drugs were the primary or sole intervention.

By excluding Reference [3], PharmaGPT avoids the potential confusion that could arise from including a study where the therapeutic outcomes cannot be solely attributed to the ADC drug. This decision demonstrates a more nuanced understanding of the clinical trial data and a stricter adherence to the question's request for ADC-specific results. Additionally, PharmaGPT's structured response, which includes detailed references to specific clinical trials (e.g., NCT04152499, NCT04280341, NCT04379596), allows for a more precise and reliable presentation of the data.

B.4 Professionalism and Accuracy in PharmaGPT's Response

PharmaGPT's approach demonstrates a higher level of professionalism and precision for several reasons:

- **Precision in Scope**: PharmaGPT interpreted the question narrowly and correctly, focusing solely on studies where ADC drugs were the primary treatment. This ensured that the results presented were directly relevant to the efficacy and safety of ADC drugs, without the confounding effects of additional therapies like nivolumab.

- **Structured and Detailed Response**: PharmaGPT provided a more structured and detailed response by clearly delineating the clinical trial results, including appropriate clinical trial identifiers (e.g., NCT numbers), target mechanisms, and study phases. This level of detail enhances the credibility of the response and allows researchers to trace the original studies easily.

- **Avoidance of Misleading Data**: By excluding Reference [3], which involved a combination therapy, PharmaGPT avoided presenting potentially misleading data that could overestimate or misattribute the efficacy of an ADC drug that was co-administered with an immune checkpoint inhibitor. This exclusion reflects a more careful and professional handling of clinical results.

B.5 Discussion of Interpretative Differences

The differing responses from GPT-4-turbo and PharmaGPT highlight two distinct approaches to interpreting the question:

- **GPT-4-turbo's inclusive approach**: GPT-4-turbo adopted a more inclusive interpretation, allowing studies where ADC drugs were part of a combination therapy. While this approach provided a broader overview, it lacked the precision necessary to isolate the clinical effects of ADC drugs alone, potentially leading to less accurate conclusions about ADC efficacy.

- **PharmaGPT's focused and professional approach**: PharmaGPT took a more precise and conservative approach, focusing on studies where ADC drugs were the primary treatment. By doing so, PharmaGPT delivered a more accurate and relevant response tailored to the specific nature of the question, demonstrating a higher level of professionalism in clinical data interpretation.

B.6 Conclusion

In this case study, we demonstrated that PharmaGPT's response was more accurate and professional compared to GPT-4-turbo's. PharmaGPT's decision to exclude Reference [3] reflects a more focused and precise interpretation of the question, ensuring that only relevant ADC-specific clinical results were included. Furthermore, PharmaGPT's structured and detailed format, along with its careful selection of references, indicates a deeper understanding of the nuances of clinical trial data. In contrast, GPT-4-turbo's broader, more inclusive approach diluted the focus on ADC drugs by including a combination therapy, which potentially misrepresents the efficacy and safety of ADC drugs alone. Therefore, PharmaGPT's response should be considered more reliable and professional in this context.

LENS: Learning Entities in Narratives of Skin Cancer

Daisy Monika Lal[1], Paul Rayson[1], Christopher Peter[2], Ignatius Ezeani[1], Mo El-Haj[1], Yufeng Liu[3], Yafei Zhu[4]
[1]School of Computing and Communications, Lancaster University, UK.
[2] National Institute of Mental Health and Neuroscience, Bengaluru, India.
[3] Linguistics and English Language, Lancaster University, UK.
[4] Shanghai International Studies University, China.
Correspondence: d.m.lal@lancaster.ac.uk

Abstract

Learning entities from narratives of skin cancer (LENS) is an automatic entity recognition system built on colloquial writings from skin cancer-related Reddit forums. LENS encapsulates a comprehensive set of 24 labels that address clinical, demographic, and psychosocial aspects of skin cancer. Furthermore, we release LENS as a pip package[1], making it easy for developers to download and install, and also provide a web application[2] that allows users to get model predictions interactively, useful for researchers and individuals with minimal programming experience. Additionally, we publish the annotation guidelines[3] designed specifically for spontaneous skin cancer narratives, that can be implemented to better understand and address challenges when developing corpora or systems for similar diseases. The model achieves an overall entity-level F1 score of 0.561, with notable performance for entities such as "CANC_T" (0.747), "STG" (0.788), "POB" (0.714), "GENDER" (0.750), "A/G" (0.714), and "PPL" (0.703). Other entities with significant results include "TRT" (0.625), "MED" (0.606), "AGE" (0.646), "EMO" (0.619), and "MHD" (0.5). We believe that LENS can serve as an essential tool supporting the analysis of patient discussions leading to improvements in the design and development of modern smart healthcare technologies.

1 Introduction

Social-media channels have unlatched the way to modern healthcare by promoting patient engagement, professional communication, accessibility, education, and awareness (Sinclair et al., 2015; Aceto et al., 2018). These forums often assist patients and carers (family member, partner, or friend) when seeking advice, exploration and information gathering, sharing lived experiences, peer support, discussions, etc. (Naslund et al., 2020; Bruce et al., 2024). Together with online health communities (HealthUnlocked[4], AskaPatient[5], MedHelp [6], Health24 (Ji et al., 2023)), dedicated social health platforms (Reddit, Facebook, Twitter, YouTube) have revolutionised research and paved a way for modern medicine (Griffiths et al., 2012; Aase and Timimi, 2013; Moorhead et al., 2013; Aase and Timimi, 2013; Gupta et al., 2022). Particularly, patients with chronic illnesses such as cancer use social-media to seek out practical, social, and emotional support (Fox and Purcell, 2010; Patel et al., 2015; Foufi et al., 2019). Illness narratives, in which patients and carers recount their actual experiences, often in a chronological sequence that includes their past, present, and future, are potent forms of expression that benefit the listener on an emotional, social, and physical level (Charon, 2001, 2022).

Non-Medical Language	Medical Terminology
lump or bump	Tumor or Mass
unexplained weight loss	Cachexia
feeling tired all the time	Fatigue
shortness of breath	Dyspnea
bloating	Abdominal distension
multicolored spots	Pigmented Lesion
lumps in neck or groin	Lymphadenopathy
small, firm, red or pink bump	Papule

Table 1: Non-Medical Language vs Medical Terminology (Cancer-Related Symptoms)

At almost 40% of all cancer cases, skin cancer is one of the most common types of cancer globally

[1]*Installation instructions* available at https://github.com/dml2611/LENS.
[2]*Web App* available at https://lens-demo.streamlit.app/.
[3]*annotation_guidelines.pdf* available at https://github.com/dml2611/LENS/tree/main/annotation

[4]https://healthunlocked.com/
[5]https://www.askapatient.com/
[6]https://www.medhelp.org

Proceedings of the 31st International Conference on Computational Linguistics: System Demonstrations, pages 20–27
January 19–24, 2025.

Entity Type	Labels
Clinical	Cancer Type (CANC_T), Staging and grading (STG), Treatment (TRT), Part of Body (POB), Result (RES), Symptom (SYM), Investigation (INV), Medication (MED), Adverse Effect (ADV_EFF), Etiology (EGY), Tumor size and shape (SIZE), Number (NUM), Duration (DUR), Mental Health Diagnosis (MHD), Diagnosis of other diseases (DIAG), Organization (ORG), People or Cancer care team (PPL)
Demographic	Age (AGE), Gender (GENDER), Age/Gender (A/G), Geopolitical Entity (GPE)
Psychosocial	Emotion (EMO), Metaphorical Expression (MET), Other Expressions (EXP)

Table 2: Named entities in skin cancer narratives.

(Whiteman et al., 2016; Apalla et al., 2017; Bray et al., 2018; Urban et al., 2021). It is recorded as 17th most common in males and 8th most common in females, in Europe (Ferlay, 2004; WCRF, 2022). Biomedical named entity recognition (NER) can be used to extract key concepts (such as diseases, signs/symptoms, medications, treatment, side effects, gender, and age) from illness narratives (Kumar, 2020; Hao et al., 2021). It is a powerful technique that has gained attention in medical research communities for detecting named entities from clinical documents (Wen et al., 2021; Kocaman and Talby, 2022). Even though NER is one of the most valuable tools for information extraction, the lack of open-source cancer NER libraries is bottleneck for healthcare text analytics.

The major contributions of this work include:

1. **MELNER Corpus:** An annotated corpus including 24 named entity markers for skin cancer narratives. MELNER provides a detailed set of entities (see Table 2), including skin cancer-specific (cancer type, treatment, symptoms, etiology, etc.), demographic (age, gender, geographical location), and psychosocial (emotions, metaphors, and other expressions).

2. **LENS:** An NER system trained using the MELNER corpus, for automatic extraction of named entities from colloquial texts, such as narratives of patients and carers. LENS is made publicly available for distribution via PyPI and pip, making it easy for developers to download and install.

3. **Web Interface:** A website interface will be available (the streamlit hosted version is being developed), making it useful for researchers and individuals with minimal programming skills, for analysing and downloading the tagged entities.

4. **Label Mapping:** The LENS tags are further mapped to SNOMED-CT[7] and MedCAT[8] codes (see Table 7), useful for researchers and professionals in the medical domain.

5. **Annotation guidelines:** The annotation process, involving a wide range of labels, required a significant amount of effort, with the guide being amended frequently in agreement with the annotators and domain specialists. This evolved in a standardized system for labelling entities in skin cancer narratives. They may serve as relevant training material and promote collaboration with other researchers.

2 Motivation

Although multiple NER tools are being developed by researchers, their application to social-media data is still hindered by the usage of non-clinical expressions rather than domain-specific terminology (Denecke, 2014; He, 2019). Patients often resort to the use of figurative language for describing their symptoms (see Table 1). Additionally, errors and misspellings are common hallmarks of colloquial communication. The grammatical and lexical variability of health-related natural language on social-media poses a significant challenge for the NER task (Babaian and Xu, 2024). One of the significant drawbacks of the current biomedical NER systems is their narrow coverage, focussing only on clinical entities with fewer labels. Moreover, information such as social or demographic factors that are also connected to a patient's health is not considered by these systems (Raza et al., 2022). Analysing the psychosocial burden of the disease provides a more complete understanding of the patient experience and can help design more personalized treatment plans taking into account both medical and emotional aspects of care.

[7] https://www.snomed.org/what-is-snomed-ct
[8] https://github.com/CogStack/MedCAT

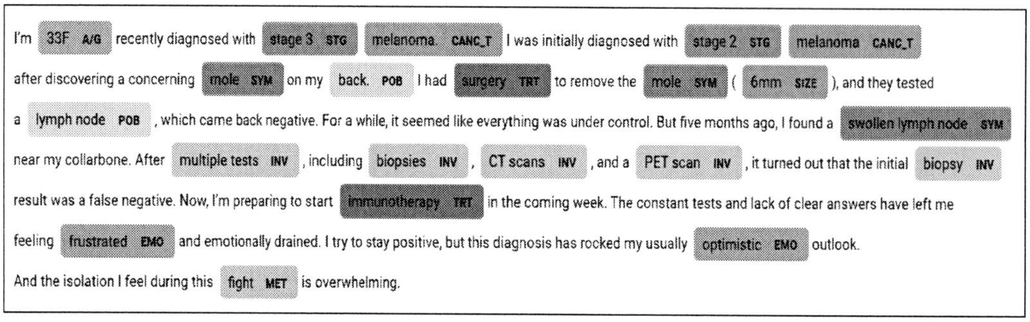

Figure 1: Extracting LENS entities from a narrative of skin cancer. For abbreviations see Table 2

3 Data Collection

Reddit supports a number of cancer-related forums that provide an anonymous environment for information sharing and discussions. As of January 2024, Reddit had 1.22 billion users globally, 73.1 million daily active users, and 36.7 million registered user accounts. There are roughly 100,000 active subreddits[9], with the cancer subreddit in particular having 58,380 subscribers[10].

We chose Reddit as the data source because, in addition to dedicated forums that reduce down manual searches for subjects of interest, it also allows for more structured text-based dialogue than other social media platforms. A finite number of 11 disease-specific subreddits relevant to skin cancer were empirically identified for analysis. These include, 'r/cancer', 'r/skincancer', 'r/cancersurvivors', 'r/cancerfamilysupport', 'r/cancercaregivers', 'r/melanoma', 'r/melahomies', 'r/melanomasupport', 'r/melanomaquestions', 'r/dermatology', and 'r/dermatologyquestions.'

4 Annotations

We retrieved around 1000 posts, which were manually annotated by four interdisciplinary annotators from NLP, Linguistics, and the medical domain. The posts were as long as 800 tokens. The annotation task was carried out using the NER text annotator for SpaCy[11]. To avoid duplicates, which can lead to model overfitting, we assigned each annotator a mutually exclusive subset for annotation. This resulted in developing the final training set with 9435 identified named entities from 24 label categories (see Table 2).

[9]https://www.statista.com/

[10]https://subredditstats.com/r/cancer

[11]https://tecoholic.github.io/ner-annotator/

4.1 Annotation Guidelines

Before starting, the annotators were introduced to the annotation rules, annotation software, and the types of texts to be annotated. In addition to comprehensive guidelines, the annotators were advised to follow generic rules (see Table 3 for examples): (1) *Consistency:* Similar expressions must be annotated with the same label throughout the entire document. 2) *Precision:* Annotate effectively by selecting expressions that are highly related to the label and avoiding overly general terms. (3) *No overlap:* Avoid entity overlap unless stated otherwise (nested entities are not permissible). (4) *Punctuation Exclusion:* Avoid including punctuation marks in the named entity provided they are part of the expression. (5) *Complete Coverage:* Ensure that all designated categories are included in the narrative, where applicable. (6) *Reddit Slang:* Reddit frequently accepts abbreviations such as "33M" or "33/F", which represent a user's age and gender. These shorthand expressions must be identified as unique entities. (7) *Medical Abbreviations:* Medical abbreviations like "WLE" for "Wide Local Excision" should be annotated consistently and not overlooked.

The annotation guidelines were periodically adjusted in response to issues encountered during the annotation process. The concerns were investigated with the guidance of domain experts, and rules were clarified with additional examples incorporated in the manual.

4.2 Inter-Annotator Agreement or IAA

The NER annotation is a sequence labeling task and bares numerous challenges, such as, (1) *Subjectivity:* Despite well-defined guidelines, annotations are susceptible to interpretation by the annotator and sometimes require a judgement call, leading to

Guideline	Correct ✓	Incorrect ✗
Consistency	*"chemotherapy"* → **TRT** (consistent across the document).	*"chemotherapy"* → **TRT** in one place, *"chemotherapy"* → **MED** elsewhere.
Precision	*"stage 2 melanoma"* → *"stage 2"* → **STG**, *"melanoma"* → **CANC_T**.	*"Stage 4 melanoma"* → **CANC_T** or **STG** without separating them.
No Overlap	*"swollen lymph node"* → **SYM** (without further annotation).	*"swollen lymph node"* → **SYM** for *"swollen lymph node"* and annotating *"lymph node"* separately as **POB** (overlapping).
Punctuation Exclusion	*"33 years old,"* → annotate "33 years old" as **AGE** (excluding the comma).	*"33 years old."* → annotating *"33 years old,"* including the period as part of the entity.
Comprehensive Coverage	*"PET scan showed mets in the brain and lungs"* → *"PET scan"* → **INV**, *"mets"* → **INV**, "brain" → **POB**, *"lungs"* → **POB**.	Missing annotations for *"brain"* and *"lungs"* as **POB**.
Reddit Slang	*"I am 33M"* or *"I am 26/F"* → *"33M"* → **A/G**, and *"26/F"* → **A/G**	Annotating *"33M"* or *"26/F"* as **AGE** → **GENDER**.
Abbreviations	*"WLE"* → **TRT** or *"BRAF/MEK"* → **MED**	Not tagging the abbreviation.

Table 3: General guidelines for LENS annotation. For abbreviations see Table 2

conflicts, (2) *Uneven annotations*: the annotators frequently identify varying number of entities, (3) *Spanning*: annotators might not agree on the same spans for the same entity (see Table 4), (4) *Unannotated tokens*: Annotators may overlook tokens.

Due to the granularity of annotations, mismatches, and unannotated regions, the inter-annotator agreement using conventional metrics is quite challenging (Jiang et al., 2022; Dhrangad hariya et al., 2023). For instance, Cohen Kappa, a standard IAA metric, has been frequently pointed out by researchers as being inappropriate for assessing agreement on NER annotations (Hripcsak and Rothschild, 2005; Deleger et al., 2012; Karimi et al., 2015; Brandsen et al., 2020). We adopted an analogous approach to (Karimi et al., 2015) to compute the IAA. The agreement, $IAA(i, j)$, between two annotators, i and j, is defined as the average of absolute match ($abs(A_i, A_j)$) and fuzzy match ($fuz(A_i, A_j)$) as follows:

$$IAA(i, j) = \frac{abs(A_i, A_j) + fuz(A_i, A_j)}{max(A_i, A_j)} \quad (1)$$

Here, A_i represents the set of all annotations by the annotator i, A_j represents the set of all annotations by the annotator j, $max(A_i, A_j)$ denotes the maximum of A_i and A_j. $abs(A_i, A_j)$ counts exact matches, while $fuz(A_i, A_j)$ counts fuzzy matches or overlaps as specified in Table 5.

To evaluate the IAA, we employed a separate sample of five skin cancer narratives consisting of 210 sentences and 3814 words. Each annotator was requested to tag the narratives applying the same

('27 years', 'DUR')	('for 27 years', 'DUR')
('stage 4', 'STG')	('late stage 4', 'STG')
('frequent headaches', 'SYM')	('headaches', 'SYM')
('brain covering.', 'POB')	('brain', 'POB')
('cauterize the wound', 'TRT')	('cauterize', 'TRT')
('a few weeks ago', 'DUR')	('few weeks ago', 'DUR')
('was cut out', 'TRT')	('cut out', 'TRT')
('incredibly shocked', 'EMO')	('shocked', 'EMO')

Table 4: Example of fuzzy agreement where annotators identify different spans for the same label.

annotation guidelines. The number of labels identified by annotators ranges between 260 and 340. We observed that the annotators have an absolute match of 48-69%, whereas the fuzzy match adds another 6-14%. The IAA between annotators varies from 0.58 to 0.78. Because of the large number of labels and the size of the assessment set, this score indicates moderate to good agreement among the annotators.

5 Model Training

LENS was trained using the pre-trained SpaCY model with built-in pipelines, *ner* and *transformer (bert-base-cased)*. Training was conducted on an NVIDIA Tesla T4 with the Adam optimizer with a learning rate of 0.0001 and L2 weight decay of 0.01. Further configurations include a dropout rate of 0.01, dynamically adjusted batch sizes, and the F1 score was computed every 200 steps. The assessment metrics (see Table 6) illustrate an overall entity-level F1 score of 0.561, with notable

	Criteria	Examples
Absolute Agreement (Same span, same label)	(start1 = start2) and (end1 = end2) and (label1 = label2)	("chemotherapy", TRT) ("chemotherapy", TRT)
Fuzzy Agreement (Different spans, same label)	(start1 = start2) and (end1 $\neq$ end2) and (label1 = label2) or (start1 $\neq$ start2) and (end1 = end2) and (label = label2)	("pain", ADV_EFF) ("chronic pain", ADV_EFF)
Absolute Disagreement (Same span, different labels)	(start1 = start2) and (end1 = end2) and (label1 $\neq$ label2)	("chemotherapy", TRT) ("chemotherapy", MED)
Fuzzy Disagreement (Different spans, different labels)	(start1 = start2) and (end1 $\neq$ end2) and (label1 $\neq$ label2) or (start1 $\neq$ start2) and (end1 = end2) and (label $\neq$ label2)	("tumor", SYM) ("tumor spread", INV) or ("mole", SYM) ("removed the mole", TRT)

Table 5: Criteria for computing agreement on labels. Here, start, end, and label, denote the start index, end index, and label of the identified named entity by respective annotators.

Label	P	R	F1
CANC_T	**0.708**	**0.790**	**0.747**
STG	**0.712**	**0.881**	**0.788**
POB	**0.721**	**0.707**	**0.714**
TRT	0.650*	0.601*	0.625*
INV	0.525	0.473	0.497
SYM	0.487	0.361	0.415
A/G	**0.833**	0.625*	**0.714**
DUR	0.389	0.092	0.149
ORG	0.381	0.276	0.320
MED	0.649*	0.568	0.606*
AGE	**0.705**	0.596	0.646*
ADV_EFF	0.083	0.020	0.032
SIZE	0.273	0.188	0.222
RES	0.375	0.150	0.214
NUM	0.393	0.250	0.306
EMO	0.664*	0.580*	0.619*
MET	0.100	0.043	0.061
PPL	**0.732**	0.676	**0.703**
MHD	0.667*	0.400	0.500
GENDER	**0.750**	**0.750**	**0.750**
DIAG	0.375	0.158	0.222
EGY	0.250	0.250	0.250
GPE	0.286	0.333	0.308
EXP	0.000	0.000	0.000
Overall	0.618	0.514	0.561

Table 6: LENS model performance with precision (**P**), recall (**R**), and F1 Score (**F1**). Here, **bold** represents scores ≥ 0.70, * represents scores ≥ 0.60 and ≤ 0.69.

performance for entities such as "CANC_T" (F1: 0.747), "STG" (F1: 0.788), "POB" (F1: 0.714), "GENDER" (F1: 0.750), "A/G" (F1: 0.714), and "PPL" (F1: 0.703). Other entities with significant results include "TRT" (F1: 0.625), "MED" (F1: 0.606), "AGE" (F1: 0.646), "EMO" (F1: 0.619), and "MHD" (F1: 0.5).

6 SNOMED-CT and MedCAT Mappings

To facilitate interoperability, standardization, and clinical relevance with clinical records and databases, LENS entities are mapped to standardized systematised nomenclatures of medicine, SNOMED-CT (Spackman et al., 1997; Stearns et al., 2001; Cornet and de Keizer, 2008; Lee et al., 2014) and MedCAT (Fodeh et al., 2013; Kraljevic et al., 2021). This bridges the gap between patient-reported experiences and structured clinical information. The mappings were manually curated by identifying the most appropriate medical or conceptual label in each ontology, corresponding to the description and definition of LENS tags (see Table 7). The mappings[12] were cross-checked by a domain specialist to ensure that both mappings accurately represented the corresponding LENS tag. One drawback was that there were no comparable formal codes for metaphors and expressions.

7 Limitations

Several limitations impacted the efficacy of LENS: **(1) Limited Data:** While LENS performs well for some entities, tags like ADV_EFF, MET, and EXP exhibit low F1, highlighting the need for more

[12] Mappings *lens2snomedct.json* and *lens2medcat.json* available at `https://github.com/4dpicture/LENS`

Terms	LENS	SNOMED-CT	MedCAT
28/F	A/G	[Age, Gender finding]	[Temporal Concept, Organism Attribute]
stage 4	STG	Tumor staging	Clinical Attribute
melanoma	CANC_T	Malignant neoplastic disease	Disease or Syndrome
neck	POB	Body part	[Body Part, Organ, or Organ Component, Body Location]
swollen lymph node	SYM	Sign	Sign or Symptom
spread	INV	Investigations	[Diagnostic Procedure, Finding, Laboratory or Test Result]
frustrated	EMO	Emotions	Mental Process

Table 7: Examples of LENS tags mapped to SNOMED-CT and MedCAT.

training samples. However, medical annotation is costly and labor-intensive, and focusing on a single subcategory like skin cancer, further narrows the data pool due to limited forums. **(2) Variability in Expression:** Patients describe similar experiences in varied ways, making entity identification difficult. For example, "depressed" for an individual could mean clinical depression, while for another, it may simply mean a temporary low mood, leading to inconsistent tagging. **(3) Defining Annotation Guidelines:** Patients may express anything from diagnosis to remission using a multitude of expressions. This makes it challenging to decide what should or should not be included in the annotation guidelines, where it fits, and how to correctly label it. The process is tedious and seems never-ending, as new expressions are ever evolving, complicating the annotation process. **(4) Overlapping Entity Boundaries:** Entity boundaries can be ambiguous, making it difficult to determine the span and label, resulting in inconsistent annotations that confuse the model and degrade performance.

8 Conclusion

In this work, we introduce LENS, an open-source library for learning entities from narratives of skin cancer. LENS is an easy-to-use, production-ready model trained on spontaneous clinical narratives assembled from Reddit forums related to skin cancer. This research aims to assist healthcare professionals and oncology researchers, in the fast retrieval of information. In addition to medical concepts, LENS identifies demographic and psychosocial entities, often overlooked by traditional biomedical NER systems, narrowing down a critical gap in medical research and patient care. This work provides opportunities for research and collaboration, including (1) developing NER models to automatically extract clinical information from non-technical unstructured language, (2) enhancing patient-care by learning about psychosocial behaviour and mental health conditions cancer patients, (3) studying the impact of the disease in different age groups and genders using demographic labels, (4) mapping informal vocabulary to formal medical concepts such as SNOMED-CT and MedCAT, (5) using rigorous annotation guidelines for developing corpora and systems for similar diseases, (6) addressing challenges when dealing with personal narratives on social-media platforms, such as slang and medical abbreviations.

9 Ethics Statement

The large-scale analysis of personal narratives on open or closed online forums, particularly related to sensitive topics such as cancer, requires ethical approval, and we have been granted approval for secondary data analysis of previously analysed datasets. The research presented in this paper is part of a larger multilingual multinational research project, and each partner will apply it in their organization or country to replicate our analysis. The overall aim of the research is to improve the cancer patient journey and ensure personal preferences are understood and respected during treatment discussions with medical professionals, thereby supporting treatment and care choices at each stage of disease or treatment.

Acknowledgements

This publication presents research from the 4D PICTURE project,[13] which is a collaboration of research teams from Austria, Belgium, Denmark, Germany, the Netherlands, Slovenia, Spain, Sweden, and the UK. The research leading to these results has received funding from EU research and

[13]https://4dpicture.eu/

innovation programme HORIZON Europe 2021 under grant agreement 101057332 and by the Innovate UK Horizon Europe Guarantee Programme, UKRI Reference Number 10041120.

References

Lee Aase and Farris K Timimi. 2013. Health care social media: Engagement and health care in the digital era. *Clinical Obstetrics and Gynecology*, 56(3):471–476.

Giuseppe Aceto, Valerio Persico, and Antonio Pescapé. 2018. The role of information and communication technologies in healthcare: taxonomies, perspectives, and challenges. *Journal of Network and Computer Applications*, 107:125–154.

Zoe Apalla, Aimilios Lallas, Elena Sotiriou, Elizabeth Lazaridou, and Demetrios Ioannides. 2017. Epidemiological trends in skin cancer. *Dermatology practical & conceptual*, 7(2):1.

Tamara Babaian and Jennifer Xu. 2024. Entity recognition from colloquial text. *Decision Support Systems*, 179:114172.

Alex Brandsen, Suzan Verberne, Milco Wansleeben, and Karsten Lambers. 2020. Creating a dataset for named entity recognition in the archaeology domain. In *Proceedings of the Twelfth Language Resources and Evaluation Conference*, pages 4573–4577.

Freddie Bray, Jacques Ferlay, Isabelle Soerjomataram, Rebecca L Siegel, Lindsey A Torre, and Ahmedin Jemal. 2018. Global cancer statistics 2018: Globocan estimates of incidence and mortality worldwide for 36 cancers in 185 countries. *CA: a cancer journal for clinicians*, 68(6):394–424.

Emmanuel Bruce, Zhao Shurong, John Amoah, Sulemana Bankuoru Egala, and Francis Kofi Sobre Frimpong. 2024. Reassessing the impact of social media on healthcare delivery: insights from a less digitalized economy. *Cogent Public Health*, 11(1):2301127.

Rita Charon. 2001. Narrative medicine: a model for empathy, reflection, profession, and trust. *Jama*, 286(15):1897–1902.

Rita Charon. 2022. Narrative medicine. In *Palgrave Encyclopedia of the Health Humanities*, pages 1–11. Springer.

Ronald Cornet and Nicolette de Keizer. 2008. Forty years of snomed: a literature review. *BMC medical informatics and decision making*, 8:1–6.

Louise Deleger, Qi Li, Todd Lingren, Megan Kaiser, Katalin Molnar, Laura Stoutenborough, Michal Kouril, Keith Marsolo, Imre Solti, et al. 2012. Building gold standard corpora for medical natural language processing tasks. In *AMIA Annual Symposium Proceedings*, volume 2012, page 144. American Medical Informatics Association.

Kerstin Denecke. 2014. Extracting medical concepts from medical social media with clinical nlp tools: a qualitative study. In *Proceedings of the fourth workshop on building and evaluation resources for health and biomedical text processing*, pages 54–60.

Anjani Dhrangadhariya, Roger Hilfiker, Karl Martin Sattelmayer, Nona Naderi, Katia Giacomino, Rahel Caliesch, Julian Higgins, Stéphane Marchand-Maillet, and Henning Müller. 2023. Robuster: A corpus annotated with risk of bias text spans in randomized controlled trials. *Journal of Medical Internet Research*.

J Ferlay. 2004. Globocan 2002: cancer incidence, mortality and prevalence worldwide. *IARC cancer base*.

Samah Jamal Fodeh, Maryan Zirkle, Dezon Finch, Ruth Reeves, Joseph Erdos, and Cynthia Brandt. 2013. Medcat: A framework for high level conceptualization of medical notes. In *2013 IEEE 13th International Conference on Data Mining Workshops*, pages 274–280. IEEE.

Vasiliki Foufi, Tatsawan Timakum, Christophe Gaudet-Blavignac, Christian Lovis, and Min Song. 2019. Mining of textual health information from reddit: Analysis of chronic diseases with extracted entities and their relations. *Journal of medical Internet research*, 21(6):e12876.

Susannah Fox and Kristen Purcell. 2010. *Chronic disease and the internet*. Pew Internet & American Life Project Washington, DC.

Frances Griffiths, Jonathan Cave, Felicity Boardman, Justin Ren, Teresa Pawlikowska, Robin Ball, Aileen Clarke, and Alan Cohen. 2012. Social networks–the future for health care delivery. *Social science & medicine*, 75(12):2233–2241.

Poonam Gupta, Asma Khan, and Amit Kumar. 2022. Social media use by patients in health care: a scoping review. *International Journal of Healthcare Management*, 15(2):121–131.

Tianyong Hao, Zhengxing Huang, Likeng Liang, Heng Weng, Buzhou Tang, et al. 2021. Health natural language processing: methodology development and applications. *JMIR medical informatics*, 9(10):e23898.

Zhe He. 2019. Understanding and bridging the language and terminology gap between health professionals and consumers using social media. *Social Web and Health Research: Benefits, Limitations, and Best Practices*, pages 103–121.

George Hripcsak and Adam S Rothschild. 2005. Agreement, the f-measure, and reliability in information retrieval. *Journal of the American medical informatics association*, 12(3):296–298.

Geonwoo Ji, Constantino Msigwa, Denis Bernard, Geon Lee, Jiyoung Woo, and Jaeseok Yun. 2023. Health24:

Health-related data collection from wearable and mobile devices in everyday lives. In *2023 IEEE International Conference on Big Data and Smart Computing (BigComp)*, pages 336–337.

Hang Jiang, Yining Hua, Doug Beeferman, and Deb Roy. 2022. Annotating the tweebank corpus on named entity recognition and building nlp models for social media analysis. *arXiv preprint arXiv:2201.07281*.

Sarvnaz Karimi, Alejandro Metke-Jimenez, Madonna Kemp, and Chen Wang. 2015. Cadec: A corpus of adverse drug event annotations. *Journal of biomedical informatics*, 55:73–81.

Veysel Kocaman and David Talby. 2022. Accurate clinical and biomedical named entity recognition at scale. *Software Impacts*, 13:100373.

Zeljko Kraljevic, Thomas Searle, Anthony Shek, Lukasz Roguski, Kawsar Noor, Daniel Bean, Aurelie Mascio, Leilei Zhu, Amos A Folarin, Angus Roberts, et al. 2021. Multi-domain clinical natural language processing with medcat: the medical concept annotation toolkit. *Artificial intelligence in medicine*, 117:102083.

A Kumar. 2020. Disambiguation model for bio-medical named entity recognition. *Deep Learning Techniques for Biomedical and Health Informatics*, pages 41–55.

Dennis Lee, Nicolette de Keizer, Francis Lau, and Ronald Cornet. 2014. Literature review of snomed ct use. *Journal of the American Medical Informatics Association*, 21(e1):e11–e19.

S Anne Moorhead, Diane E Hazlett, Laura Harrison, Jennifer K Carroll, Anthea Irwin, and Ciska Hoving. 2013. A new dimension of health care: systematic review of the uses, benefits, and limitations of social media for health communication. *Journal of medical Internet research*, 15(4):e1933.

John A Naslund, Ameya Bondre, John Torous, and Kelly A Aschbrenner. 2020. Social media and mental health: benefits, risks, and opportunities for research and practice. *Journal of technology in behavioral science*, 5:245–257.

Rajesh Patel, Tammy Chang, S Ryan Greysen, and Vineet Chopra. 2015. Social media use in chronic disease: a systematic review and novel taxonomy. *The American journal of medicine*, 128(12):1335–1350.

Shaina Raza, Deepak John Reji, Femi Shajan, and Syed Raza Bashir. 2022. Large-scale application of named entity recognition to biomedicine and epidemiology. *PLOS Digital Health*, 1(12):e0000152.

Wendy Sinclair, Moira McLoughlin, and Tony Warne. 2015. To twitter to woo: Harnessing the power of social media (some) in nurse education to enhance the student's experience. *Nurse education in practice*, 15(6):507–511.

Kent A Spackman, Keith E Campbell, and Roger A Côté. 1997. Snomed rt: a reference terminology for health care. In *Proceedings of the AMIA annual fall symposium*, page 640. American Medical Informatics Association.

Michael Q Stearns, Colin Price, Kent A Spackman, and Amy Y Wang. 2001. Snomed clinical terms: overview of the development process and project status. In *Proceedings of the AMIA Symposium*, page 662. American Medical Informatics Association.

Katelyn Urban, Sino Mehrmal, Prabhdeep Uppal, Rachel L Giesey, and Gregory R Delost. 2021. The global burden of skin cancer: A longitudinal analysis from the global burden of disease study, 1990–2017. *JAAD international*, 2:98–108.

WCRF. 2022. Skin cancer statistics. *https://www.wcrf.org/cancer-trends/skin-cancer-statistics/*.

Chaojie Wen, Tao Chen, Xudong Jia, and Jiang Zhu. 2021. Medical named entity recognition from unlabelled medical records based on pre-trained language models and domain dictionary. *Data Intelligence*, 3(3):402–417.

David C Whiteman, Adele C Green, and Catherine M Olsen. 2016. The growing burden of invasive melanoma: projections of incidence rates and numbers of new cases in six susceptible populations through 2031. *Journal of Investigative Dermatology*, 136(6):1161–1171.

Loki: An Open-Source Tool for Fact Verification

Haonan Li[1,2] **Xudong Han**[1,2] **Hao Wang**[1],
Yuxia Wang[1,2] **Minghan Wang**[3] **Rui Xing**[2,4] **Yilin Geng**[1,4]
Zenan Zhai[1] **Preslav Nakov**[2] **Timothy Baldwin**[1,2,4]
[1]LibrAI [2]MBZUAI [3]Monash University [4]The University of Melbourne

Abstract

We introduce LOKI, an open-source tool designed to address the growing problem of misinformation. LOKI adopts a human-centered approach, striking a balance between the quality of fact-checking and the cost of human involvement. It decomposes the fact-checking task into a five-step pipeline: breaking down long texts into individual claims, assessing their check-worthiness, generating queries, retrieving evidence, and verifying the claims. Instead of fully automating the claim verification process, LOKI provides essential information at each step to assist human judgment, especially for general users such as journalists and content moderators. Moreover, it has been optimized for latency, robustness, and cost efficiency at a commercially usable level. LOKI is released under an MIT license and is available on GitHub.[1] We also provide a video presenting the system and its capabilities.[2]

1 Introduction

In today's digital landscape, the rapid spread of misinformation has become a significant societal problem, with far-reaching consequences for politics, public health, and social stability (Pan et al., 2023; Augenstein et al., 2024). With the rise of online platforms, users are exposed to large volumes of information, often without the ability to assess its accuracy. While manual fact-checking is reliable, it is labor-intensive, time-consuming, and often requires domain expertise, creating a gap where misinformation can spread unchecked and cause harm before being addressed.

To address this problem, automated fact-checking systems have been proposed, but have mostly focused on full automation, which can negatively impact quality.

Here, we propose LOKI, which offers a semi-automated, human-in-the-loop approach to fact verification. Instead of completely eliminating human participation, LOKI assists users by breaking down the fact-checking process into five manageable steps, ensuring that human judgment remains integral to decision-making. This benefits users, such as journalists and content moderators, who need reliable tools to quickly and accurately verify information.

LOKI offers a five-step pipeline for fact verification: identifying claims, assessing their check-worthiness, generating queries for evidence retrieval, retrieving evidence, and verifying the claims. This modular framework ensures flexibility and adaptability. It supports fact-checking in multiple languages and integration with large language models (LLMs). Additionally, LOKI is optimized for practical use, with improvements in latency, robustness, and cost-efficiency, making it well-suited for commercial applications.

LOKI is implemented in Python and offers ease of use through multiple interfaces: a user-friendly graphical interface, command-line functionality, and the ability to be imported as a package into other projects. To demonstrate its utility, we compare LOKI against several recent fact-checking tools, and show that optimized system implementation and prompt engineering yields demonstrable improvements over other tools in terms of efficiency while achieving very competitive performance.

2 Related Work

Numerous automated fact-checking systems have been developed, including *RARR*, *FActScore*, *FacTool*, *Factcheck-GPT*, and *Longform SAFE* (Gao et al., 2023; Min et al., 2023; Chern et al., 2023; Wang et al., 2024a; Wei et al., 2024; Fadeeva et al., 2024). However, these tools are often inaccessi-

[1]https://github.com/Libr-AI/OpenFactVerification

[2]https://www.youtube.com/watch?v=L_3Dp41Lk_k

Proceedings of the 31st International Conference on Computational Linguistics: System Demonstrations, pages 28–36
January 19–24, 2025.

Fact-checking System	UI	Asynchronous	Multilingual	Multi-LLM	Granularity	Transparency	Open-source
RARR (Gao et al., 2023)	✗	✗	✗	✗	Document	✗	✓
FActScore (Min et al., 2023)	✗	✗	✗	✗	Claim	✗	✓
FacTool (Chern et al., 2023)	✗	✓	✗	✗	Claim	✗	✓
Factcheck-GPT (Wang et al., 2024a)	✗	✗	✗	✗	Claim	✓	✓
CoVe (Dhuliawala et al., 2024)	✗	✗	✗	✗	Claim	✗	✓
Longform SAFE (Wei et al., 2024)	✗	✗	✗	✓	Claim	✗	✓
FIRE (Xie et al., 2024)	✗	✗	✗	✗	Claim	✓	✓
Perplexity.ai	✓	✓	✓	unclear	Claim	✗	✗
OPENFACTCHECK (Iqbal et al., 2024)	✓	✓	✗	✗	Claim	✓	✓
LOKI (ours)	✓	✓	✓	✓	Claim	✓	✓

Table 1: Comparison of representative automatic fact-checking *pipelines*, DEMOS and products in the last two years from seven perspectives: (1) **UI** — the system has user interface supporting easy interaction with general users; (2) **Asynchronous** processing for retrieving evidence from web pages and calling LLM APIs; (3) **Multilingual** — the system is designed to support languages other than English; (4) **Multi-LLM** — flexibly calling different LLM APIs as fact verifiers; (5) **Granularity** — the smallest granularity of document decomposition and verification supported by the system; (6) **Transparency** — the system can show fine-grained snippets of evidence with the corresponding URL, and the relationship between the evidence and the claim (support, refute, or irrelevant); and (7) **Open-source** — the system is open-sourced.

ble to general users who may not have a Python environment to compile code and run verification processes. Although these systems can serve as backends for various services, they lack a user-friendly web interface that allows users to verify text inputs by simply typing or pasting text and clicking a check button. LOKI addresses this gap by providing an accessible, human-friendly user interface.

Each fact-checking system also has its own strengths. For instance, *Factcheck-GPT* offers a fine-grained framework encompassing all possible subtasks to enhance the fact-checking process. *FacTool* uses a low-latency evidence retriever through asynchronous processing, while *FActScore* introduces a scoring metric that calculates the percentage of true claims within a text, providing a quantitative measure of the input's credibility. LOKI integrates these advantages into a unified system (Wang et al., 2024b). Table 1 compares eight representative fact-checking pipelines, demos, or products (e.g., *Perplexity.ai*) with LOKI across seven dimensions. Of the systems surveyed, LOKI is the only one to support all seven listed system aspects.

3 Loki Fact Checker

In this section, we provide an in-depth overview of LOKI, focusing on its core functionalities and architectural design. We first outline the five-component fact verification pipeline and then discuss the architecture's flexibility that allows component substitution for different domains. After that, we explore how parallelism is employed to enhance the system's efficiency and reduce latency. Finally, we present the LOKI user interface, designed to provide a seamless and user-friendly user experience.

3.1 Fact Verification Pipeline

Previous work structures fact verification into a series of steps, commonly including text decomposition, checkworthiness identification, evidence retrieval and collection, stance detection, and correction determination (Wang et al., 2024a). In this work, we propose a five-step pipeline consisting of the following modules: Decomposer, Checkworthiness Identifier, Query Generator, Evidence Retriever, and Claim Verifier.

Decomposer breaks down long texts into smaller, atomic claims. It produces individual claims that can be verified independently. For a better user experience, we ensure the decomposed claims are traceable to the original text. During the result presentation, LOKI displays both the original and decomposed claims for contextual clarity.

Checkworthiness Identifier filters out unworthy claims that are vague, ambiguous, or opinion-based, ensuring only factual statements proceed for verification. For instance, claims like *MBZUAI has a vast campus* are deemed unworthy due to the subjective interpretation of *vast*.

Query Generator converts check-worthy claims into optimized queries for evidence retrieval, focusing on keyword-based retrieval.

Evidence Retriever gathers relevant information to support the verification process. Currently, LOKI retrieves evidence from online sources via search engine APIs.

Claim Verifier evaluates retrieved evidence to verify the claim, presenting supporting or refuting snippets for users to make informed judgments.

3.2 Implementation and Extensibility

LOKI is implemented in Python and can be easily integrated into other projects as an importable package. While the core functionality leverages the capabilities of LLMs, we also provide implementations using traditional NLP tools like NLTK or SpaCy.[3] This section introduces LOKI 's core implementation and its extensibility.

LLM-based Implementation LOKI employs LLMs in four of its five components: Decomposer, Checkworthiness Identifier, Query Generator, and Claim Verifier. Each component is implemented as a Python class with functions that interact with LLMs to perform core tasks. For instance, the Decomposer class includes functions to break down long texts into claims and map these claims back to the original text.

Each LLM-based function comes with a set of default prompts, typically including: (1) a brief task description, (2) input and output formats, and (3) few-shot examples to guide the LLM. To generate consistently parsable outputs, we prompt the LLMs to return results in a structured format, such as JSON.[4] This approach streamlines the integration of LLM outputs into subsequent steps of the pipeline. For each task, we hand-crafted 10 test cases and optimized the prompts to maximize LLM performance. An example prompt for the Decomposer is shown in Figure 1.

To maintain system reliability, all LLM function calls are wrapped with a retry mechanism that automatically retries in case of network issues or transient errors. We use the default hyperparameters for LLM inference and leave hyperparameter tuning to future work.

[3]Our evaluation shows that LLM-based implementations are generally more robust and accurate in practical scenarios.

[4]JSON output format is currently only well-supported in some models such as GPT4 (OpenAI, 2024). Switching the backend LLM to other models, such as Llama-3, may cause pipeline failures unless specifically designed to ensure a consistent output format.

```
Your task is to decompose the text into atomic claims.
The answer should be a JSON with a single key "claims", with the value of a list of strings, where each string should be a context-independent claim, representing one fact.
Note that:
1. Each claim should be concise (less than 15 words) and self-contained.
2. Avoid vague references like 'he', 'she', 'it', 'this', 'the company', 'the man' and using complete names.
3. Generate at least one claim for each single sentence in the texts.

For example,
Text: Mary is a five-year old girl, she likes playing piano and she doesn't like cookies.
Output:
{{"claims": ["Mary is a five-year old girl.", "Mary likes playing piano.", "Mary doesn't like cookies."]}}

Text: {doc}
Output:
```

Figure 1: An example of the prompt for the Decomposer. This is an template and the actual prompt is generated by replacing the placeholder {doc} with the input text.

Evidence Retriever Currently, LOKI uses the Google Search API (Serper API) for open-domain questions, retrieving web-based evidence to support or refute claims.[5] This module's design is flexible, allowing integration with alternative search engines or specialized databases to expand evidence sources. For each claim, LOKI generates three distinct search queries.[6] If the Google Search API returns a direct answer, it is captured as primary evidence. Otherwise, the top five search results are retained, and snippets are extracted. An optional Natural Language Inference (NLI) model can then be applied to rank snippets based on their relevance, prioritizing the most pertinent evidence.[7]

Extensibility LOKI's modular design enables high extensibility. Each component can be individually optimized or replaced with improved solutions as needed. For LLM-based functions, LOKI supports multiple LLM APIs as well as locally deployed models. Additionally, if users require only specific functionalities, each component can be imported and used independently.

3.3 Parallelism and Efficiency

LOKI uses parallelism to efficiently handle multiple verification requests at the same time. By using Python's `asyncio` library, the system can make asynchronous API calls, enabling concurrent processing without blocking the main thread.

[5]`https://serper.dev/`

[6]Using the claim itself as a query can lead to biased or irrelevant results, as false claims may mislead the search.

[7]Snippets classified as either entailment or contradiction are considered highly relevant.

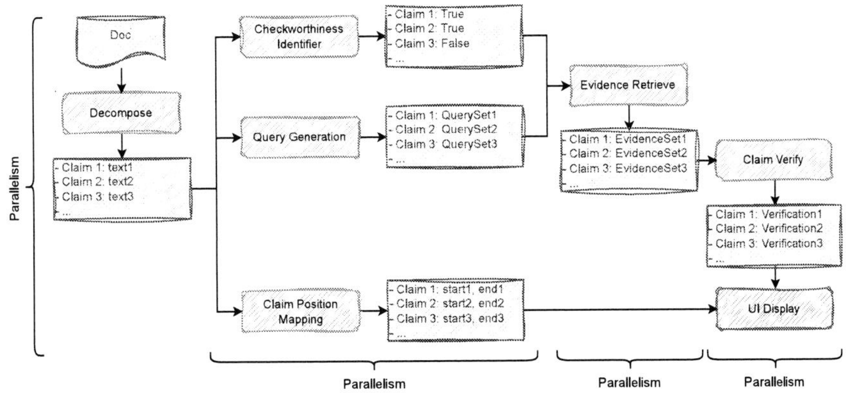

Figure 2: Parallel execution of independent components in the fact-checking pipeline. The entire process can be completed within the combined time of three LLM calls and one web query.

The LLM call function manages these calls and ensures compliance with rate limits with a user-defined maximum request per minute and request window. A traffic queue keeps track of active requests and removes old entries when they exceed the time window. This approach allows LOKI to process high volumes of fact-checking requests efficiently, improving overall system performance and scalability.

We also parallelize all independent components and functions, as shown in Figure 2. This modular design allows different parts of the fact-checking process, such as claim decomposition, query generation, and evidence retrieval, to be executed concurrently. Ideally, the entire fact-checking process can be completed within the time required for three LLM calls and one web query, significantly reducing the overall response time.

3.4 Multilingual Support

LOKI supports multilingual scenarios. Developers can easily adapt the system by modifying prompts for the target language and performing minimal testing. We provide a comprehensive development guide to facilitate this process. Currently, LOKI supports both English and Chinese, with the potential for easy adaptation to other languages.

3.5 Human-in-the-Loop Design

One of the key features of LOKI is its human-in-the-loop design, which prioritizes transparency and user engagement to enhance human decision-making rather than replace it.

Unlike fully automated solutions that aim to deliver a final verdict without intermediate steps, LOKI presents critical information and insights at each step, to assist users in making well-informed decisions. This approach is especially beneficial for users such as journalists and content moderators, who need reliable tools to verify information while retaining control over the final judgment.

To facilitate user understanding and engagement, LOKI offers information across four distinct levels:

Level 1 — Overall Credibility Score: At the highest level, LOKI provides a single percentage score representing the overall credibility of the input text, based on the proportion of claims verified as *well-supported*, *conflicting*, or *controversial*, offering a quick summary of the text's reliability.

Level 2 — Claim-Level Analysis: Claims are classified and displayed numerically beside the overall score, with visual cues highlighting each claim directly in the original text, allowing users to quickly identify areas requiring further scrutiny.

Level 3 — Evidence-Level Insight: For each claim, LOKI presents supporting or refuting evidence from various sources. It also provides contextual information to help users understand the broader background, enabling them to make informed judgments.

Level 4 — Detailed Evidence Breakdown: At the finest granularity, LOKI presents detailed information for each piece of evidence, including the source, relevant paragraphs, and the rationale for why the evidence supports or contradicts the claim.

Our interaction design is guided by three core principles: (1) Transparency and Trust — LOKI provides a clear breakdown of information at mul-

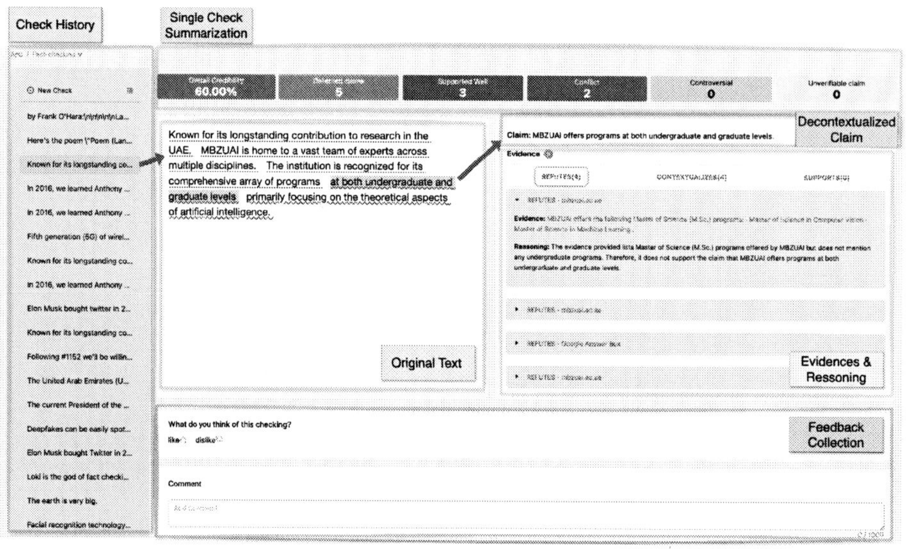

Figure 3: User interface of LOKI. The interface includes sections for Check History (left panel) showing past checks, and Single Check Summarization (top center) summarizing key metrics such as overall credibility and detected claims. Original Text (left center), and the Decontextualized Claim (top right) which isolates the specific claim being evaluated. The Evidence & Reasoning panel (right) provides detailed evidence that refutes, contextualizes, or supports the claim, sourced from various documents, while the Feedback Collection section (bottom) allows users to provide feedback.

tiple levels, allowing users to trace the decision-making process and build trust in the system's outputs. (2) Hierarchical Presentation — LOKI presents information in layers to avoid overwhelming users, enabling them to "zoom in and out" to different levels of detail for a seamless experience. (3) Assisting, not Replacing: LOKI does not aim to make judgments for the users, but rather to assist them with organized and structured information.

4 System Evaluation and Applications

We performed a comprehensive evaluation for LOKI across several key dimensions, including fact-checking accuracy (measured by precision, recall and F1-score), processing latency (execution wall time), and potential operation cost (number of tokens and queries consumed by API invocation).

Dataset Specifically, our experiments are carried out using two well-known automatic fact-checking evaluation datasets (FacTool-QA (Chern et al., 2023) and Factcheck-Bench (Wang et al., 2024a)), each covering a broad range of domains (see Table 3 for details). In addition to the prompts and LLM responses, these datasets also provide human-annotated claims for each response, along with their labels (`True` or `False`), enabling a more granular evaluation at the claim level rather than at the response level.

Baseline Systems We selected three fact-checking systems and a commercial retrieval-augmented generative model (Perplexity.ai) as baseline systems. While the three fact-checking systems share a similar pipeline, they differ in their components at various stages compared to LOKI, such as the LLM used in the verifier, data sources, and the retriever API being used. To ensure a comprehensive evaluation, we assess the baseline systems across multiple configurations of these components.

Evaluation Protocol To guarantee a fair evaluation across all fact-checking systems, we standardized the evaluation process by bypassing the step of extracting atomic claims from documents. As a result, all systems receive a claim as input and are expected to predict whether the claim is factual. Note that for frameworks like LOKI that predict a factuality score (ranging from 0 to 1), we apply a threshold of 0.8 to convert the score into a binary label.

All systems were evaluated on the same comput-

Framework	Verifier	Source/ Retriever	Factcheck-Bench Label = True P	R	F1	Factcheck-Bench Label = False P	R	F1	FacTool-QA Label = True P	R	F1	FacTool-QA Label = False P	R	F1
Random	–	–	0.79	0.43	0.56	0.18	0.52	0.27	0.79	0.56	0.66	0.28	0.54	0.37
Always True	–	–	0.81	1.00	0.88	0.00	0.00	0.00	0.76	1.00	0.86	0.00	0.00	0.00
Always False	–	–	0.00	0.00	0.00	0.19	1.00	0.33	0.00	0.00	0.00	0.24	1.00	0.39
FActScore	*LLaMA* 3-Inst 8B	Wiki/BM25	0.87	0.74	0.80	0.34	0.56	0.42	0.82	0.68	0.74	0.34	0.52	0.41
FacTool	*LLaMA* 3-Inst 8B	Web/Serper	0.88	0.80	**0.84**	0.40	0.56	0.47	**0.93**	0.38	0.54	0.32	**0.91**	0.47
FActScore	GPT-3.5-Turbo	Wiki/BM25	0.87	0.67	0.76	0.31	0.60	0.41	0.82	0.58	0.68	0.31	0.59	0.40
FacTool	GPT-3.5-Turbo	Web/Serper	0.89	0.74	0.81	0.37	0.62	0.46	0.92	0.59	0.72	0.39	0.84	0.53
Factcheck-GPT	*GPT-4*	Web/SerpAPI	0.90	0.71	0.79	0.52	0.80	**0.63**	0.88	**0.88**	**0.88**	**0.63**	0.63	**0.63**
FacTool	*GPT-4o*	Web/Serper	**0.91**	0.58	0.71	0.47	**0.87**	0.61	0.9	0.69	0.78	0.44	0.77	0.56
Perplexity.ai	Sonar-online	Web	**0.93**	0.73	0.83	0.40	0.76	0.53	0.82	**0.88**	0.85	0.50	0.38	0.43
LOKI	*GPT-4o*	Web/Serper	0.84	**0.83**	**0.84**	**0.63**	0.64	**0.63**	0.89	0.80	0.85	0.53	0.70	0.60

Table 2: The performance of fact-checkers for human-annotated claims in Factcheck-Bench, FacTool-QA, and FELM-WK, judging whether or not a claim is factually true or false with external knowledge (Wikipedia or Web articles) as evidence. *GPT-4* refers to `gpt-4-turbo-2024-04-09`, *GPT-4o* refers to `gpt-4o-2024-05-13`.

Dataset ↓	Domain	#True	#False	Total
FacTool-QA	History, geography, biology, science	177	56	233
Factcheck-Bench	Technology, history, science, sports	472	206	678

Table 3: The number of claim labels as well as the involved domain in FacTool-QA, FELM-WK and Factcheck-Bench.

Fact-Checker ↓	Web search (# queries)	# Prompt Tokens	# Completion Tokens	Time (s / sample)
FacTool	3.5 ± 2.3	1895 ± 911	283 ± 212	12.38 ± 46.84
LOKI	4.2 ± 2.6	6518 ± 4055	818 ± 565	8.32 ± 8.17

Table 4: Comparison between *FacTool* vs. LOKI (both are using *GPT-4o* and Serper for verification and retrieval) in terms of cost and latency. Metrics are presented in the form of their average and standard deviation ($\mu \pm \sigma$).

ing node of the M3 Cluster,[8] with the following configuration: 2 × Intel Xeon Gold 6330 CPUs, 200 GB of memory, and 2 A100 80GB GPUs.

Fact-checking Performance Experimental results for the evaluation of fact-checking accuracy on different systems are presented in Table 2. Although LOKI does not outperform all frameworks on every metric, its overall performance is comparable to the SOTA open-source baseline *Factcheck-GPT*. It's important to note that Factcheck-GPT uses the more advanced SerpAPI, which retrieves higher-quality documents, significantly improving its performance. However, the cost of SerpAPI ($0.015 per search) is much higher than Serper ($0.001 per search), making LOKI the more economical option in terms of cost-effectiveness. When compared to *FacTool*, which uses the same configuration, LOKI outperforms it in most of the metrics across three datasets, demonstrating the effectiveness of our design.

4.1 Cost and Latency

In Table 4, we provide a detailed comparison of the number of queries, token consumption during LLM API calls, and the average processing time per claim for both LOKI and *FacTool* across the two datasets. We did not include comparisons with other frameworks because only *FacTool* and OPENFACTCHECK support asynchronous processing, which results in significantly lower processing times than the other frameworks.[9] Since OPENFACTCHECK's fact-checking pipeline is largely derived from other frameworks, including *FacTool*, we consider *FacTool* sufficiently representative for comparison.

The results show that LOKI consumes more queries and more tokens than *FacTool*, primarily because LOKI retrieves and verifies a greater number of queries and evidence. This also explains why LOKI achieves superior fact-checking performance. Despite handling larger volumes of data, LOKI's efficient implementation ensures that its average processing time is substantially lower than that of *FacTool*, highlighting its better design, with the asynchronous processing pipeline.

5 Conclusion

In this paper, we present LOKI, a novel open-source Python tool that offers a human-centered approach to fact-checking. LOKI integrates a semi-automated five-step pipeline that balances efficiency with the need for human judgment, particularly for general users like journalists and con-

[8]https://massive.org.au/

[9]According to Wang et al. (2025), a cascade pipeline like *Factcheck-GPT* is normally 15.7× slower than an asynchronous pipeline.

tent moderators. Experimental results show that LOKI achieves competitive performance against state-of-the-art systems, offering an optimized and adaptable solution for tackling misinformation. As an open-source tool licensed under MIT, LOKI is accessible for further development, aiming to enhance fact-checking capabilities and support informed decision-making continuously.

References

Isabelle Augenstein, Timothy Baldwin, Meeyoung Cha, Tanmoy Chakraborty, Giovanni Luca Ciampaglia, David Corney, Renee DiResta, Emilio Ferrara, Scott Hale, Alon Halevy, Eduard Hovy, Heng Ji, Filippo Menczer, Ruben Miguez, Preslav Nakov, Dietram Scheufele, Shivam Sharma, and Giovanni Zagni. 2024. Factuality challenges in the era of large language models. *Nature Machine Intelligence 6, no. 8*, page 852–863.

I Chern, Steffi Chern, Shiqi Chen, Weizhe Yuan, Kehua Feng, Chunting Zhou, Junxian He, Graham Neubig, Pengfei Liu, et al. 2023. Factool: Factuality detection in generative ai–a tool augmented framework for multi-task and multi-domain scenarios. *arXiv preprint arXiv:2307.13528*.

Shehzaad Dhuliawala, Mojtaba Komeili, Jing Xu, Roberta Raileanu, Xian Li, Asli Celikyilmaz, and Jason Weston. 2024. Chain-of-verification reduces hallucination in large language models. In *Findings of the Association for Computational Linguistics: ACL 2024*, pages 3563–3578, Bangkok, Thailand. Association for Computational Linguistics.

Ekaterina Fadeeva, Aleksandr Rubashevskii, Artem Shelmanov, Sergey Petrakov, Haonan Li, Hamdy Mubarak, Evgenii Tsymbalov, Gleb Kuzmin, Alexander Panchenko, Timothy Baldwin, Preslav Nakov, and Maxim Panov. 2024. Fact-checking the output of large language models via token-level uncertainty quantification. In *Findings of the Association for Computational Linguistics ACL 2024*, pages 9367–9385, Bangkok, Thailand and virtual meeting. Association for Computational Linguistics.

Luyu Gao, Zhuyun Dai, Panupong Pasupat, Anthony Chen, Arun Tejasvi Chaganty, Yicheng Fan, Vincent Zhao, Ni Lao, Hongrae Lee, Da-Cheng Juan, and Kelvin Guu. 2023. RARR: Researching and revising what language models say, using language models. In *Proceedings of the 61st Annual Meeting of the Association for Computational Linguistics (Volume 1: Long Papers)*, pages 16477–16508, Toronto, Canada. Association for Computational Linguistics.

Hasan Iqbal, Yuxia Wang, Minghan Wang, Georgi Nenkov Georgiev, Jiahui Geng, Iryna Gurevych, and Preslav Nakov. 2024. OpenFactCheck: A unified framework for factuality evaluation of LLMs. In *Proceedings of the 2024 Conference on Empirical Methods in Natural Language Processing: System Demonstrations*, pages 219–229, Miami, Florida, USA. Association for Computational Linguistics.

Sewon Min, Kalpesh Krishna, Xinxi Lyu, Mike Lewis, Wen-tau Yih, Pang Koh, Mohit Iyyer, Luke Zettlemoyer, and Hannaneh Hajishirzi. 2023. FActScore: Fine-grained atomic evaluation of factual precision in long form text generation. In *Proceedings of the 2023 Conference on Empirical Methods in Natural Language Processing*, pages 12076–12100, Singapore. Association for Computational Linguistics.

OpenAI. 2024. Gpt-4 technical report. *Preprint*, arXiv:2303.08774.

Yikang Pan, Liangming Pan, Wenhu Chen, Preslav Nakov, Min-Yen Kan, and William Wang. 2023. On the risk of misinformation pollution with large language models. In *Findings of the Association for Computational Linguistics: EMNLP 2023*, pages 1389–1403, Singapore. Association for Computational Linguistics.

Yuxia Wang, Revanth Gangi Reddy, Zain Muhammad Mujahid, Arnav Arora, Aleksandr Rubashevskii, Jiahui Geng, Osama Mohammed Afzal, Liangming Pan, Nadav Borenstein, Aditya Pillai, Isabelle Augenstein, Iryna Gurevych, and Preslav Nakov. 2024a. Factcheck-bench: Fine-grained evaluation benchmark for automatic fact-checkers. In *Findings of the Association for Computational Linguistics: EMNLP 2024*, pages 14199–14230, Miami, Florida, USA. Association for Computational Linguistics.

Yuxia Wang, Minghan Wang, Hasan Iqbal, Georgi Georgiev, Jiahui Geng, and Preslav Nakov. 2025. Openfactcheck: Build, benchmark customized fact-checking systems and evaluate factuality of claims and llms. In *Proceedings of The 31st International Conference on Computational Linguistics (COLING 2025)*, Abu Dhabi, UAE. International Conference on Computational Linguistics.

Yuxia Wang, Minghan Wang, Muhammad Arslan Manzoor, Fei Liu, Georgi Nenkov Georgiev, Rocktim Jyoti Das, and Preslav Nakov. 2024b. Factuality of large language models: A survey. In *Proceedings of the 2024 Conference on Empirical Methods in Natural Language Processing*, pages 19519–19529, Miami, Florida, USA. Association for Computational Linguistics.

Jerry Wei, Chengrun Yang, Xinying Song, Yifeng Lu, Nathan Hu, Dustin Tran, Daiyi Peng, Ruibo Liu, Da Huang, Cosmo Du, and Quoc V. Le. 2024. Long-form factuality in large language models. *CoRR*, abs/2403.18802.

Zhuohan Xie, Rui Xing, Yuxia Wang, Jiahui Geng, Hasan Iqbal, Dhruv Sahnan, Iryna Gurevych, and Preslav Nakov. 2024. Fire: Fact-checking with iterative retrieval and verification. *arXiv preprint arXiv:2411.00784*.

A Usage of LOKI

Used as a Library LOKI can be integrated as a Python library, allowing developers to incorporate its functionalities directly into their applications. Figure 4 provides an example of how to use FactCheck as a library for verifying text within a Python script.

```
from factcheck import FactCheck

factcheck_instance = FactCheck()

# Example text
text = "Your text here"

# Run the fact-check pipeline
results = factcheck_instance.check_response(text)
print(results)
```

Figure 4: Using FactCheck as a Library

Used as a Web App LOKI can be deployed as a web application, providing a user-friendly interface for interacting with the tool. Figure 5 illustrates the command used to start the web application. The UI of open-source LOKI is introduced in Appendix B

```
python webapp.py --api_config demo_data/api_config.yaml
```

Figure 5: Running FactCheck as a Web App

Multimodal Usage LOKI supports multimodal input, enabling it to process and verify information from various sources, including text, speech, images, and videos. The system can be invoked using different modes specified by the `--modal` argument. Figure 8 demonstrates the usage of FactCheck across these different input modalities

```
# String
python -m factcheck --modal string --input "MBZUAI is the
↪ first AI university in the world"
# Text
python -m factcheck --modal text --input demo_data/text.txt
# Speech
python -m factcheck --modal speech --input
↪ demo_data/speech.mp3
# Image
python -m factcheck --modal image --input
↪ demo_data/image.webp
# Video
python -m factcheck --modal video --input demo_data/video.m4v
```

Figure 8: Multimodal Usage of FactCheck

B User Interface of LOKI

Figure 6 and Figure 7 show the user interface of LOKI (open-source version), which consists of two main pages: the submission page and the result page. The submission page allows users to input text for fact-checking, while the result page displays the decomposed claims, the evidence retrieved for each claim, and the overall credibility score of the text. The user interface is designed to be user-friendly, providing a clear and intuitive experience for users to interact with the system.

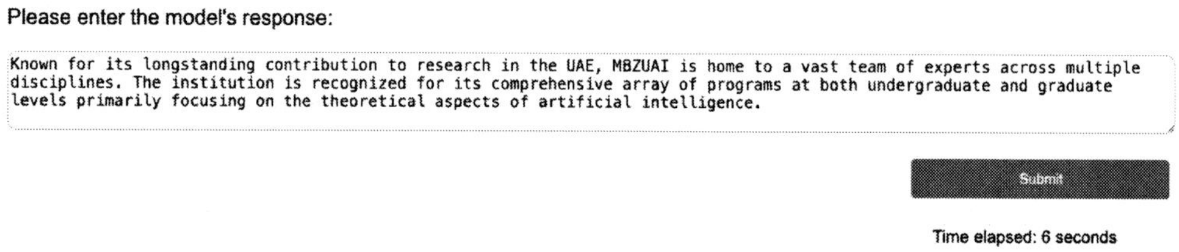

Figure 6: The user interface of LOKI, submission page.

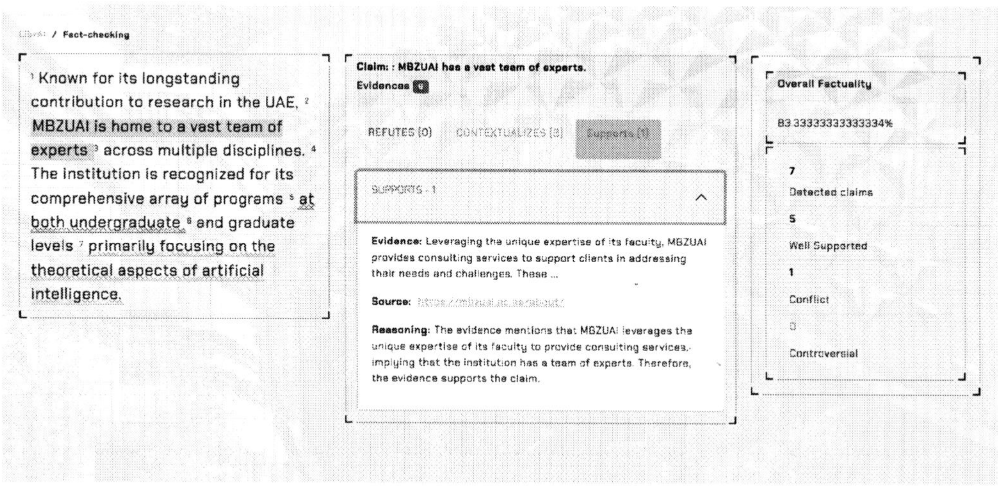

Figure 7: The user interface of LOKI, result page.

UnifiedGEC: Integrating Grammatical Error Correction Approaches for Multi-languages with a Unified Framework

Yike Zhao, Xiaoman Wang, Yunshi Lan*, **Weining Qian**
School of Data Science and Engineering, East China Normal University
Shanghai Engineering Research Center of Big Data Management
{ykzhao,xmwang}@stu.ecnu.edu.cn, {yslan,wnqian}@dase.ecnu.edu.cn

Abstract

Grammatical Error Correction is an important research direction in NLP field. Although many models of different architectures and datasets across different languages have been developed to support the research, there is a lack of a comprehensive evaluation on these models, and different architectures make it hard for developers to implement these models on their own. To address this limitation, we present **UnifiedGEC**, the first open-source GEC-oriented toolkit, which consists of several core components and reusable modules. In UnifiedGEC, we integrate 5 widely-used GEC models and compare their performance on 7 datasets in different languages. Additionally, GEC-related modules such as data augmentation, prompt engineering are also deployed in it. Developers are allowed to implement new models, run and evaluate on existing benchmarks through our framework in a simple way. Code, documents and detailed results of UnifiedGEC are available at https://github.com/AnKate/UnifiedGEC.

1 Introduction

Grammatical Error Correction (GEC), aiming to identify and correct grammatical errors in a sentence automatically, is an important research direction in the field of NLP. It has a wide range of applications in real life, including writing assistant, search engine, language learning education (Bryant et al., 2023; Grundkiewicz et al., 2020; Knill et al., 2019), which has attracted much attention in academic and industry fields. Existing GEC tools or commercial products such as Grammarly[1], QuillBot[2], ChatGPT[3] serve the customers with the close techniques. But we notice there is a need of an open and unified framework for more researches on GEC.

Through the investigation, we find there have been many datasets designed for GEC tasks in different languages (Zhao et al., 2018; Yannakoudakis et al., 2011; Ng et al., 2014; Zhang et al., 2022a; Náplava and Straka, 2019; Yamada et al., 2020; Boyd et al., 2014). Meanwhile, a lot of models have been proposed for GEC tasks, categorized into *Seq2Seq* models (Vaswani et al., 2017; Raffel et al., 2023; Zhang et al., 2022b) and *Seq2Edit* models (Omelianchuk et al., 2020; Gu et al., 2019). However, these models are designed with different architectures, and most of them are evaluated on only one or two datasets with different preprocessing pipelines, resulting in the lack of a unified comparison between these models. Furthermore, that makes it difficult for developers to implement these models on their own.

To tackle these issues, we propose UnifiedGEC, which is featured with several distinct characteristics: (1) **Modularization**: We decouple GEC methods with different architectures into modularized and reusable components, namely config, data, model, trainer, and evaluation components. We integrate them in a unified framework, which can be adapted to general GEC methods. (2) **Comprehensiveness**: We deploy datasets as well as dataloaders for different languages, models of different architectures, and mainstream evaluators for GEC tasks in our framework, which allows developers to run, evaluate and simply implement models. (3) **Extensibility**: UnifiedGEC toolkit provides user-friendly interfaces for various usages. The components in the unified framework are modeled as exchangeable modules, which makes it convenient for developers to develop their methods.

To validate the effectiveness and credibility of UnifiedGEC toolkit, we also conduct extensive experiments on GEC tasks via our toolkit, which achieves close results to the prior reports. Fur-

*Corresponding Author
[1]https://app.grammarly.com/
[2]https://quillbot.com/
[3]https://platform.openai.com/docs/api-reference/introduction

Proceedings of the 31st International Conference on Computational Linguistics: System Demonstrations, pages 37–45
January 19–24, 2025.

thermore, UnifiedGEC toolkit makes it easier to perform research on low-resource GEC, GEC with data augmentation and other cases. In this paper, we demonstrate extensive experiments on GEC tasks. We hope that our toolkit will help developers in GEC field to speed up their development on GEC tasks.

Our **main contributions** are as follows:

- We propose the first GEC-oriented toolkit, UnifiedGEC, which provides developers with a unified, extensible framework and allows them to implement models simply.
- We implement 5 GEC models and integrate 7 widely-used datasets and 3 mainstream GEC evaluators in our framework, including 2 *Seq2Edit* models, 3 *Seq2Seq* models, 2 Chinese datasets, 2 English datasets and 3 low-resource datasets, so that developers can run and evaluate these models through our framework easily.
- We design a data augmentation module and prompt module for low-resource tasks and research on LLMs.
- We conduct a comprehensive evaluation of integrated models and datasets, providing thorough conclusions and insights for developers in GEC field.

2 Related Works

In the perspectives of boosting text writing and language learning education, there are currently some toolkits or systems designed for different tasks and scenarios, such as OpenNMT (Klein et al., 2017) for machine translation tasks, TextFlint (Gui et al., 2021) for robustness text evaluation, Effidit (Shi et al., 2023) for writing assistant. Inspired by these works, we propose our toolkit UnifiedGEC for GEC tasks. To our knowledge, our UnifiedGEC is the first GEC-oriented toolkit that integrates GEC models of different architectures and datasets across various languages in a unified framework.

For GEC tasks, a lot of pre-trained models have been proposed and applied (Bryant et al., 2023). These models can be divided into two categories: *Seq2Seq* and *Seq2Edit*. *Seq2Seq* models treat GEC tasks as sequence generation tasks, directly generating tokens according to the context, such as Transformer (Vaswani et al., 2017), T5 (Xue et al., 2021) and SynGEC (Zhang et al., 2022b). Meanwhile, *Seq2Edit* models deal with GEC tasks in the form of sequence labeling tasks, and these models will predict labels of edits for the tokens, such as PIE (Awasthi et al., 2020) and GECToR (Omelianchuk et al., 2020). We have surveyed works in recent years and selected several representative models integrated in our framework. Moreover, there have been related works using data augmentation and LLMs in GEC tasks. We comprehensively integrate some augmentation methods and engineering prompts used in related work in our toolkit (Sottana et al., 2023; Song et al., 2023).

3 Framework Description

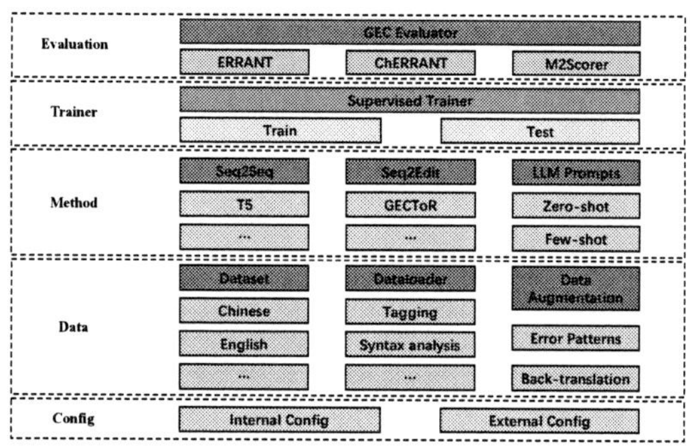

Figure 1: Framework of UnifiedGEC.

UnifiedGEC is a GEC-oriented toolkit based on PyTorch (Paszke et al., 2019), which integrates many models and datasets for GEC tasks. It allows developers to run models of different structures under a unified framework with only one single command. Meanwhile, developers are able to implement their own models through extensive and reusable modules integrated in our framework.

As depicted in Figure 1, our framework consists of five components: **Config** component, **Data** component, **Model** component, **Trainer** component, **Evaluation** component. Config component defines training parameters and records parameters of models to construct a complete configuration for the training process, which serves as the most basic part of our framework. Upon the configuration, data component processes data while model component allocates models for training or fine-tuning in the trainer component. Besides, we integrate several mainstream evaluators for GEC tasks in our evaluation component. Next, we will introduce each component in detail.

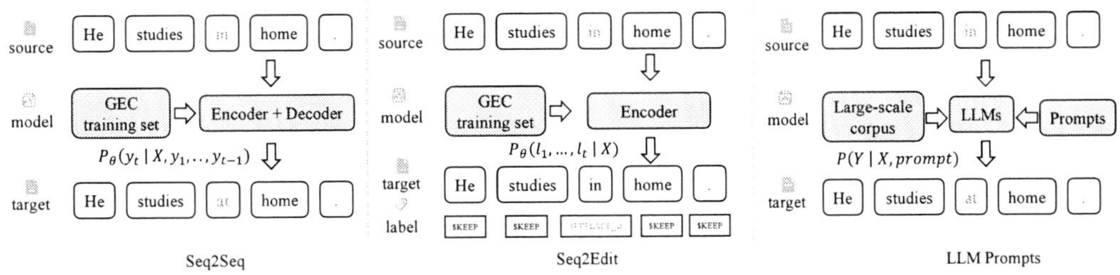

Figure 2: Illustration of different deployed method paradigms with examples. Noting that both *Seq2Seq* and *Seq2Edit* paradigms aim to fine-tune the models on the GEC training data set while the *LLM prompting* paradigm aims to conduct inference on an LLM.

3.1 Config Component

The config component is the preliminary component in which developers may customize the settings of datasets or models through related configuration files. There are two kinds of configuration files in our framework: *External Config* and *Internal Config*. The internal configuration file defines default configuration such as names of the model and dataset, learning rate and number of training epochs, while the external configuration file allows developers to modify some more detailed settings such as the parameters of a model.

3.2 Data Component

The data component plays a crucial role in our framework as it provides a unified approach for handling GEC datasets across diverse languages via various methods. As shown in Table 1, there are 7 GEC datasets integrated in our framework, including 2 Chinese datasets, 2 English datasets and 3 datasets in other languages. All the datasets deployed in our framework are open-sourced. Specifically, for MuCGEC[4] (Zhang et al., 2022a), we deploy its development set of as the test set in our framework because its official test set has not been published yet. Due to the different sources of datasets, unexpected variance my be involved for training. To bridge the gap, we integrate these preprocessing steps in our framework. This results in a standard and basic preprocessing pipeline, including *Dataset*, *Dataloader* and *Data Augmentation* modules.

Dataset module: Raw GEC data is initially read from a JASON file and converted into a *Dataset* class, which supports data splitting, noise removal and simple tokenization.

DataLoader module: After reading data, *Dataloader* module takes charge of preparing the data into batches in the configured format. Specifically, *Dataloader* module converts data into tensors based on the requirement of different model architectures. For example, the dataloader converts data into tagged text for GECToR (Omelianchuk et al., 2020) model, and the dataloader extracts the syntactic information of the dataset as additional input for SynGEC (Zhang et al., 2022b). We also provide *Abstract Dataloader* so that developers may inherit the abstract class and implement their dataloader class.

Data Augmentation module: We integrate *Data Augmentation* module in our framework, which can be launched via a single command line, which supports to augment training data with limited raw data. There are two methods implemented in this module, *error patterns* (Zhao et al., 2019; Ehsan and Faili, 2013), which will directly inject errors to original data to generate more sentence pairs, and *back-translation*, which generates parallel corpus through a bridge language (Madnani et al., 2012; Zhou et al., 2019).

3.3 Model Component

The model component consists of a variety of GEC models, which can be flexibly called to perform fine-tuning or inference. In this component, we introduce a unified paradigm for implementation. Each model should be pre-defined in terms of their initialized parameters, loss definition, and propagation procedures for training as well as testing. Hence, developers could simply focus on the development of the GEC model, trying different combinations and architectures for solving GEC tasks. In addition, since the basic modules such as Transformer are reusable to implement a new model, our

[4]https://github.com/HillZhang1999/MuCGEC/

Module		Component
Data	FCE (Yannakoudakis et al., 2011)	English dataset
	CoNLL14 (Ng et al., 2014)	English dataset
	NLPCC18 (Zhao et al., 2018)	Chinese dataset
	MuCGEC (Zhang et al., 2022a)	Chinese dataset
	COWSL2H (Yamada et al., 2020)	Spanish dataset
	Falko-MERLIN (Boyd et al., 2014)	French dataset
	AKCES-GEC (Náplava and Straka, 2019)	Czech dataset
Model	Transformer (Vaswani et al., 2017)	Transformer Encoder + Transformer Decoder
	T5 (Xue et al., 2021)	Pre-trained Encoder + Pre-trained Decoder
	SynGEC (Zhang et al., 2022b)	syntax analysis, DepGCN + Transformer Decoder
	Lev-T (Gu et al., 2019)	Transformer Encoder + Transformer Decoder
	GECToR (Omelianchuk et al., 2020; Zhang et al., 2022a)	tagging, Pre-trained Encoder
Data Augmentation	Error patterns (Ehsan and Faili, 2013; Zhao et al., 2019)	–
	Back-translation (Madnani et al., 2012; Zhou et al., 2019)	Pre-trained T5 model
LLM Prompts	prompts (Fang et al., 2023)	Chinese/English prompts for zero-shot/few-shot

Table 1: Deployed datasets and methods in `UnifiedGEC`, associated with their basic components. Here, "Lev-T" is the abbreviation of "Levenshtein Transformer".

`UnifiedGEC` also encapsulates these basic modules in a folder such that it is convenient for developers to build their models by reusing these basic modules. According to the paradigms of the methods, we categorize the deployed methods as *Seq2Seq*, and *Seq2Edit* and *LLM Prompts* paradigms.

Seq2Seq paradigm: This line of methods follow the autoregressive principle as shown in Figure 2, where the correct sentence is generated token by token. In detail, we have implemented Transformer (Vaswani et al., 2017), (m)T5 (Xue et al., 2021) and SynGEC (Zhang et al., 2022b) as the representative models of this type due to their good perforamnce on GEC tasks.

Seq2Edit paradigm: This line of methods have non-autoregressive architectures as shown in Figure 2. Instead of predicting the correct token, they first identify the operation labels, including keeping, substitution and deletion, then the model predicts the operation for each token in parallel. We implement Transformer(Vaswani et al., 2017) and Levenshtein Transformer(Gu et al., 2019) as baseline models for Seq2Edit models.

LLM Prompts paradigm: Due to the impressive capability of the Large Language Models (LLMs) in general tasks, we include LLM-based methods for solving GEC tasks and a *Prompt* module is integrated in our model component. We provide prompts for directly generating correct sentences in English and Chinese. In-Context Learning (Dong et al., 2023) is also supported in our *Prompt* module. Models integrated in our framework are shown in Table 1.

Our framework also provides developers with a unified interface through which they can either load any models or write their own instructions to prompt LLMs to correct erroneous sentences. Developers can specify the backbone model and dataset they use and the number of examples for in-context learning through command lines, and then our framework will extract demonstrations from the specified dataset randomly. In this way, the developers are able to test the capabilities of LLMs on various GEC datasets.

3.4 Trainer Component

To facilitate a more standard training and inference pipeline, we introduce a *Supervised Trainer* as the trainer component in our framework, which is mainly designed for GEC tasks. This component controls the training procedure with some tunable parameters such as learning rate and number of epochs. Developers can simply adjust the configuration file to modify related training setups. Furthermore, developers can choose to either conduct a full training process from scratch or load a pre-trained checkpoint to perform inference directly, based on their needs.

Similair as other components, we also provide an *Abstract Trainer* so that developers can inherit the class and implement their own trainer if there is any.

3.5 Evaluation Component

In the evaluation component, we implement a *GEC Evaluator* which can switch between different evaluation metrics based on the language of the dataset. For Chinese datasets, we use ChERRANT (Zhang et al., 2022a), and for other languages, we use ERRANT (Bryant et al., 2017). Following the majority of prior studies, our `UnifiedGEC` toolkit calculates average precision, recall and $F_{0.5}$ as the final evaluation results, known as *Micro PRF*.

In addition, we still integrate traditional evaluation metrics, known as *Macro PRF*, including mentioned ChERRANT and ERRANT, and M2Scorer (Dahlmeier and Ng, 2012) for specific datasets such as FCE (Yannakoudakis et al., 2011). These diverse evaluation methods enable a more comprehensive comparison of GEC models.

4 Usage

With our framework, developers are allowed to run existing models on integrated datasets and add a new model or a new dataset in a customized manner. This section illustrates the detailed usage and workflow of `UnifiedGEC`.

4.1 Basic Usage

Developers can simply run our toolkit through the following command:

```
$ python run_gectoolkit.py -m model_name -d
    dataset_name
```

Then, *Config* class will load *internal config* and *external config* to construct a complete configuration file that includes necessary information such as the language of the dataset and hyper-parameters of the model. Based on the configuration file, the *Dataset* class as well as the *Dataloader* class will be initialized to process the data. Subsequently, our `UnifiedGEC` toolkit initializes the model specified by developers and loads the pre-trained checkpoint if there is any. Next, it initializes the evaluation module and the *Trainer* class will be built upon the configuration file. Once everything is ready, the training process starts.

To set the configuration in a fast way, developers are allowed to modify detailed configurations through command lines, for example:

```
$ python run_gectoolkit.py -m model_name -d
    dataset_name --learning_rate 1e-5
```

During the process of initialization, our framework will parse arguments in the command line and overwrite original ones in *external config*. All the parameters in configuration files are allowed to tune through command lines, such as learning rate in *internal config* and dropout possibility in *external config*.

To implement a new model, we provide abstract options for models, so developers are able to add customized model modules by inheriting the *Model* class and defining their own functions. It is worth noting that possible parameters of the model are suggested to be stored in a configuration file in *properties* directory, as well as other required files such as a vocabulary or a configuration for the tokenizer, which makes it easy for developers to modify and manage these configuration files with a little efforts.

To add a new dataset, developers can simply incorporate new JSON files of datasets into the framework and create a corresponding configuration file in *properties* directory. Then, they can either call the existing components or implement their own *Dataset* class to process specific datasets in different languages.

4.2 Extended Usage

In addition to the aforementioned basic usage, we also deployed some commonly used functions in `UnifiedGEC` for extended usage.

To augment limited training data, developers can use the specified data augmentation strategy in experiments, as the *Data Augmentation* module can collaborate with any GEC models:

```
$ python run_gectoolkit.py -m model_name -d
    dataset_name --augment translation
```

`UnifiedGEC` toolkit will automatically detect whether the file of augmented data exists. If it does not exist, our framework will execute the corresponding augmentation function specified by developer's command line, and generate new data files in the *dataset* directory. Then our framework will directly use augmented data instead of generating them again. Eventually, the training process will then be conducted on the augmented data.

To conduct LLM prompting, developers can launch the *Prompt* module in the same way:

```
$ python run_gectoolkit.py -m model_name -d
    dataset_name --use_llm --example_num 4
```

When flag *use_llm* is detected, our framework will use provided prompts in *Prompt* module for the LLM specified by developers. Developers are able to specify the LLM through *model_name* parameter, such as *Qwen/Qwen1.5-14B-chat*. The argument *example_num* indicates the number of in-context learning examples. When the value of this

Models	CoNLL14 (EN)						NLPCC18 (ZH)					
	full data			10% of data	w/ EP	w/ BT	full data			10% of data	w/ EP	w/ BT
	R	P	$F_{0.5}$	$F_{0.5}$	$F_{0.5}(\Delta)$	$F_{0.5}(\Delta)$	R	P	$F_{0.5}$	$F_{0.5}$	$F_{0.5}(\Delta)$	$F_{0.5}(\Delta)$
Levenshtein Transformer	12.6	13.5	13.3	9.5	6.4(↓ 3.1)	12.5(↑ 3.0)	8.5	12.6	10.7	6.0	4.9(↓ 1.1)	5.9(↓ 0.1)
GECToR	21.7	52.3	40.8	14.2	15.1(↑ 0.9)	16.7(↑ 2.5)	20.9	30.9	28.2	17.4	19.9(↑ 2.5)	19.4(↑ 2.0)
Transformer	15.5	24.1	21.7	12.6	14.5(↑ 1.9)	16.6(↑ 4.0)	20.8	22.3	22.0	9.5	9.9(↑ 0.4)	10.4(↑ 0.9)
T5-large	39.5	36.6	37.1	31.7	32.0(↑ 0.3)	32.2(↑ 0.5)	21.1	32.5	29.4	26.3	27.0(↑ 0.7)	21.1(↓ 5.2)
SynGEC	51.8	50.6	50.9	47.7	48.2(↑ 0.5)	47.7(−)	36.8	36.0	36.2	32.4	34.9(↑ 2.5)	34.6(↑ 2.2)
zero-shot + LLM	49.1	48.8	48.8	–	–	–	38.3	24.7	26.6	–	–	–
few-shot + LLM	50.2	50.4	50.4	–	–	–	39.8	24.8	26.8	–	–	–

Table 2: Results of GEC models on CoNLL14 and NLPCC18 datasets implemented via `UnifiedGEC`. Here, "EP" and "BT" are abbreviations of error patterns and back-translation augmentation methods, respectively. The top section includes the setups with full and partial training data. The bottom section includes the setups with zero/few-shot data.

parameter is not 0, prompts designed for in-context learning will be used.

5 Evaluation

To validate our `unifiedGEC` toolkit, we conduct numerous experiments to evaluate 5 models in our toolkit on 7 GEC datasets of different languages. Furthermore, we also conduct experiments to evaluate our *data augmentation* module and *prompt* module. To be consistent with the evaluation settings in the original papers, different evaluation metrics are employed across various datasets in our experiments. We use M^2Scorer (Dahlmeier and Ng, 2012) for FCE, CoNLL14, NLPCC18, while ChERRANT (Zhang et al., 2022a) is utilized on MuCGEC. For other languages, we employ ERRANT (Felice et al., 2016; Bryant et al., 2017).

The results are shown in Table 2[5]. As we can see, most of the models integrated in our framework perform comparably to levels demonstrated in the original papers. The performance of GECToR on CoNLL14 dataset is slightly lower than that in the original paper, as we did not conduct cold epoch training. The performance of Transformer may also be lower than that in other papers because we only implemented the basic greedy decoding strategy instead of beam searching. According to Table 2, it can be observed that models tend to have better performances on Chinese and English datasets than on datasets of other languages. We believe this is because the amount of data in other languages is relatively limited in the GEC field, and most of the models we used have not been fine-tuned on corresponding languages. As an exception, the T5 model integrated in our framework performs well on all datasets, as we implement a multilingual version in our framework.

For evaluation of *data augmentation* module, we extract 10% data from the original datasets to simulate low-resource setting, and then conduct tests on two data augmentation methods. It is evident that our proposed approaches are effective in improving the performance of models in most cases.

For *prompt* module, we evaluate the performance of zero-shot and few-shot prompts. In the few-shot experiment, we randomly select examples from the training set and try different sets of number of examples. For Chinese dataset, we choose Qwen1.5-14B-chat[6](Bai et al., 2023) as an example, while for English dataset, we use LLaMA2-7B-Chat[7](Touvron et al., 2023), and we demonstrate the best performance achieved in our evaluation. Due to the page limitation, we put all the experimental results on our GitHub page[8].

6 Conclusions

We propose a developer-friendly, modularized and GEC-oriented toolkit `UnifiedGEC` in this paper. In our `UnifiedGEC`, we provide developers with multiple extensive modules so that they can implement their own models easily. We also integrate models of different architectures and datasets across various languages, which allows developers to evaluate their models simply. These features enable our our framework to help developers handle GEC tasks easily. Furthermore, we conduct a comprehensive evaluation on integrated models, which provides developers in GEC field with thorough conclusion and insights.

[5]We put results of experiments on more datasets on GitHub page.

[6]`https://huggingface.co/Qwen/Qwen1.5-14B-Chat`

[7]`https://huggingface.co/meta-llama/Llama-2-7b-chat`

[8]`https://github.com/AnKate/UnifiedGEC`

In the future, we will continue improving our framework and adding more GEC-related models, datasets and modules to the toolkit.

Acknowledgments

The authors would like to thank the anonymous reviewers for their insightful comments. This work is supported by the Young Scientists Project (No. 62206097) and the Funds for International Cooperation and Exchange of the National Natural Science Foundation of China (No. W2421085) .

References

Abhijeet Awasthi, Sunita Sarawagi, Rasna Goyal, Sabyasachi Ghosh, and Vihari Piratla. 2020. Parallel iterative edit models for local sequence transduction. *Preprint*, arXiv:1910.02893.

Jinze Bai, Shuai Bai, Yunfei Chu, Zeyu Cui, Kai Dang, Xiaodong Deng, Yang Fan, Wenbin Ge, Yu Han, Fei Huang, Binyuan Hui, Luo Ji, Mei Li, Junyang Lin, Runji Lin, Dayiheng Liu, Gao Liu, Chengqiang Lu, Keming Lu, Jianxin Ma, Rui Men, Xingzhang Ren, Xuancheng Ren, Chuanqi Tan, Sinan Tan, Jianhong Tu, Peng Wang, Shijie Wang, Wei Wang, Shengguang Wu, Benfeng Xu, Jin Xu, An Yang, Hao Yang, Jian Yang, Shusheng Yang, Yang Yao, Bowen Yu, Hongyi Yuan, Zheng Yuan, Jianwei Zhang, Xingxuan Zhang, Yichang Zhang, Zhenru Zhang, Chang Zhou, Jingren Zhou, Xiaohuan Zhou, and Tianhang Zhu. 2023. Qwen technical report. *arXiv preprint arXiv:2309.16609*.

Adriane Boyd, Jirka Hana, Lionel Nicolas, Detmar Meurers, Katrin Wisniewski, Andrea Abel, Karin Schöne, Barbora Štindlová, and Chiara Vettori. 2014. The MERLIN corpus: Learner language and the CEFR. In *Proceedings of the Ninth International Conference on Language Resources and Evaluation (LREC'14)*, pages 1281–1288, Reykjavik, Iceland. European Language Resources Association (ELRA).

Christopher Bryant, Mariano Felice, and Ted Briscoe. 2017. Automatic annotation and evaluation of error types for grammatical error correction. In *Proceedings of the 55th Annual Meeting of the Association for Computational Linguistics (Volume 1: Long Papers)*, pages 793–805, Vancouver, Canada. Association for Computational Linguistics.

Christopher Bryant, Zheng Yuan, Muhammad Reza Qorib, Hannan Cao, Hwee Tou Ng, and Ted Briscoe. 2023. Grammatical error correction: A survey of the state of the art. *Computational Linguistics*, 49(3):643–701.

Daniel Dahlmeier and Hwee Tou Ng. 2012. Better evaluation for grammatical error correction. In *Proceedings of the 2012 Conference of the North American Chapter of the Association for Computational Linguistics: Human Language Technologies*, pages 568–572.

Qingxiu Dong, Lei Li, Damai Dai, Ce Zheng, Zhiyong Wu, Baobao Chang, Xu Sun, Jingjing Xu, Lei Li, and Zhifang Sui. 2023. A survey on in-context learning. *Preprint*, arXiv:2301.00234.

Nava Ehsan and Heshaam Faili. 2013. Grammatical and context-sensitive error correction using a statistical machine translation framework. *Software: Practice and Experience*, 43(2):187–206.

Tao Fang, Shu Yang, Kaixin Lan, Derek F. Wong, Jinpeng Hu, Lidia S. Chao, and Yue Zhang. 2023. Is chatgpt a highly fluent grammatical error correction system? a comprehensive evaluation. *Preprint*, arXiv:2304.01746.

Mariano Felice, Christopher Bryant, and Ted Briscoe. 2016. Automatic extraction of learner errors in ESL sentences using linguistically enhanced alignments. In *Proceedings of COLING 2016, the 26th International Conference on Computational Linguistics: Technical Papers*, pages 825–835, Osaka, Japan. The COLING 2016 Organizing Committee.

Roman Grundkiewicz, Christopher Bryant, and Mariano Felice. 2020. A crash course in automatic grammatical error correction. In *Proceedings of the 28th International Conference on Computational Linguistics: Tutorial Abstracts*, pages 33–38, Barcelona, Spain (Online). International Committee for Computational Linguistics.

Jiatao Gu, Changhan Wang, and Jake Zhao. 2019. Levenshtein transformer. *Preprint*, arXiv:1905.11006.

Tao Gui, Xiao Wang, Qi Zhang, Qin Liu, Yicheng Zou, Xin Zhou, Rui Zheng, Chong Zhang, Qinzhuo Wu, Jiacheng Ye, Zexiong Pang, Yongxin Zhang, Zhengyan Li, Ruotian Ma, Zichu Fei, Ruijian Cai, Jun Zhao, Xingwu Hu, Zhiheng Yan, Yiding Tan, Yuan Hu, Qiyuan Bian, Zhihua Liu, Bolin Zhu, Shan Qin, Xiaoyu Xing, Jinlan Fu, Yue Zhang, Minlong Peng, Xiaoqing Zheng, Yaqian Zhou, Zhongyu Wei, Xipeng Qiu, and Xuanjing Huang. 2021. Textflint: Unified multilingual robustness evaluation toolkit for natural language processing. *Preprint*, arXiv:2103.11441.

Guillaume Klein, Yoon Kim, Yuntian Deng, Jean Senellart, and Alexander M. Rush. 2017. Opennmt: Open-source toolkit for neural machine translation. *Preprint*, arXiv:1701.02810.

Kate M Knill, Mark JF Gales, PP Manakul, and AP Caines. 2019. Automatic grammatical error detection of non-native spoken learner english. In *ICASSP 2019-2019 IEEE International Conference on Acoustics, Speech and Signal Processing (ICASSP)*, pages 8127–8131. IEEE.

Nitin Madnani, Joel Tetreault, and Martin Chodorow. 2012. Exploring grammatical error correction with not-so-crummy machine translation. In *Proceedings of the Seventh Workshop on Building Educational Applications Using NLP*, pages 44–53.

Hwee Tou Ng, Siew Mei Wu, Ted Briscoe, Christian Hadiwinoto, Raymond Hendy Susanto, and Christopher Bryant. 2014. The CoNLL-2014 shared task on grammatical error correction. In *Proceedings of the Eighteenth Conference on Computational Natural Language Learning: Shared Task*, pages 1–14, Baltimore, Maryland. Association for Computational Linguistics.

Jakub Náplava and Milan Straka. 2019. Grammatical error correction in low-resource scenarios. *Preprint*, arXiv:1910.00353.

Kostiantyn Omelianchuk, Vitaliy Atrasevych, Artem Chernodub, and Oleksandr Skurzhanskyi. 2020. GECToR – grammatical error correction: Tag, not rewrite. In *Proceedings of the Fifteenth Workshop on Innovative Use of NLP for Building Educational Applications*, pages 163–170, Seattle, WA, USA → Online. Association for Computational Linguistics.

Adam Paszke, Sam Gross, Francisco Massa, Adam Lerer, James Bradbury, Gregory Chanan, Trevor Killeen, Zeming Lin, Natalia Gimelshein, Luca Antiga, Alban Desmaison, Andreas Köpf, Edward Yang, Zach DeVito, Martin Raison, Alykhan Tejani, Sasank Chilamkurthy, Benoit Steiner, Lu Fang, Junjie Bai, and Soumith Chintala. 2019. Pytorch: An imperative style, high-performance deep learning library. *Preprint*, arXiv:1912.01703.

Colin Raffel, Noam Shazeer, Adam Roberts, Katherine Lee, Sharan Narang, Michael Matena, Yanqi Zhou, Wei Li, and Peter J. Liu. 2023. Exploring the limits of transfer learning with a unified text-to-text transformer. *Preprint*, arXiv:1910.10683.

Shuming Shi, Enbo Zhao, Wei Bi, Deng Cai, Leyang Cui, Xinting Huang, Haiyun Jiang, Duyu Tang, Kaiqiang Song, Longyue Wang, et al. 2023. Effidit: An assistant for improving writing efficiency. In *Proceedings of the 61st Annual Meeting of the Association for Computational Linguistics (Volume 3: System Demonstrations)*, pages 508–515.

Yixiao Song, Kalpesh Krishna, Rajesh Bhatt, Kevin Gimpel, and Mohit Iyyer. 2023. Gee! grammar error explanation with large language models. *Preprint*, arXiv:2311.09517.

Andrea Sottana, Bin Liang, Kai Zou, and Zheng Yuan. 2023. Evaluation metrics in the era of gpt-4: Reliably evaluating large language models on sequence to sequence tasks. *Preprint*, arXiv:2310.13800.

Hugo Touvron, Louis Martin, Kevin Stone, Peter Albert, Amjad Almahairi, Yasmine Babaei, Nikolay Bashlykov, Soumya Batra, Prajjwal Bhargava, Shruti Bhosale, Dan Bikel, Lukas Blecher, Cristian Canton Ferrer, Moya Chen, Guillem Cucurull, David Esiobu, Jude Fernandes, Jeremy Fu, Wenyin Fu, Brian Fuller, Cynthia Gao, Vedanuj Goswami, Naman Goyal, Anthony Hartshorn, Saghar Hosseini, Rui Hou, Hakan Inan, Marcin Kardas, Viktor Kerkez, Madian Khabsa, Isabel Kloumann, Artem Korenev, Punit Singh Koura, Marie-Anne Lachaux, Thibaut Lavril, Jenya Lee, Diana Liskovich, Yinghai Lu, Yuning Mao, Xavier Martinet, Todor Mihaylov, Pushkar Mishra, Igor Molybog, Yixin Nie, Andrew Poulton, Jeremy Reizenstein, Rashi Rungta, Kalyan Saladi, Alan Schelten, Ruan Silva, Eric Michael Smith, Ranjan Subramanian, Xiaoqing Ellen Tan, Binh Tang, Ross Taylor, Adina Williams, Jian Xiang Kuan, Puxin Xu, Zheng Yan, Iliyan Zarov, Yuchen Zhang, Angela Fan, Melanie Kambadur, Sharan Narang, Aurelien Rodriguez, Robert Stojnic, Sergey Edunov, and Thomas Scialom. 2023. Llama 2: Open foundation and fine-tuned chat models. *Preprint*, arXiv:2307.09288.

Ashish Vaswani, Noam Shazeer, Niki Parmar, Jakob Uszkoreit, Llion Jones, Aidan N Gomez, Ł ukasz Kaiser, and Illia Polosukhin. 2017. Attention is all you need. In *Advances in Neural Information Processing Systems*, volume 30. Curran Associates, Inc.

Linting Xue, Noah Constant, Adam Roberts, Mihir Kale, Rami Al-Rfou, Aditya Siddhant, Aditya Barua, and Colin Raffel. 2021. mT5: A massively multilingual pre-trained text-to-text transformer. In *Proceedings of the 2021 Conference of the North American Chapter of the Association for Computational Linguistics: Human Language Technologies*, pages 483–498, Online. Association for Computational Linguistics.

Aaron Yamada, Sam Davidson, Paloma Fernández-Mira, Agustina Carando, Kenji Sagae, and Claudia Sánchez-Gutiérrez. 2020. Cows-l2h: A corpus of spanish learner writing. *Research in Corpus Linguistics*, 8(1):17–32.

Helen Yannakoudakis, Ted Briscoe, and Ben Medlock. 2011. A new dataset and method for automatically grading ESOL texts. In *Proceedings of the 49th Annual Meeting of the Association for Computational Linguistics: Human Language Technologies*, pages 180–189, Portland, Oregon, USA. Association for Computational Linguistics.

Yue Zhang, Zhenghua Li, Zuyi Bao, Jiacheng Li, Bo Zhang, Chen Li, Fei Huang, and Min Zhang. 2022a. MuCGEC: a multi-reference multi-source evaluation dataset for Chinese grammatical error correction. In *Proceedings of the 2022 Conference of the North American Chapter of the Association for Computational Linguistics: Human Language Technologies*, pages 3118–3130, Seattle, United States. Association for Computational Linguistics.

Yue Zhang, Bo Zhang, Zhenghua Li, Zuyi Bao, Chen Li, and Min Zhang. 2022b. Syngec: Syntax-enhanced grammatical error correction with a tailored gec-oriented parser. *Preprint*, arXiv:2210.12484.

Wei Zhao, Liang Wang, Kewei Shen, Ruoyu Jia, and Jingming Liu. 2019. Improving grammatical error correction via pre-training a copy-augmented architecture with unlabeled data. In *Proceedings of the 2019 Conference of the North American Chapter of the Association for Computational Linguistics: Human Language Technologies, Volume 1 (Long and*

Short Papers), pages 156–165, Minneapolis, Minnesota. Association for Computational Linguistics.

Yuanyuan Zhao, Nan Jiang, Weiwei Sun, and Xiaojun Wan. 2018. Overview of the nlpcc 2018 shared task: Grammatical error correction. In *Natural Language Processing and Chinese Computing*, pages 439–445, Cham. Springer International Publishing.

Wangchunshu Zhou, Tao Ge, Chang Mu, Ke Xu, Furu Wei, and Ming Zhou. 2019. Improving grammatical error correction with machine translation pairs. *arXiv preprint arXiv:1911.02825*.

Reliable, Reproducible, and Really Fast Leaderboards with Evalica

Dmitry Ustalov
JetBrains / Belgrade, Serbia
dmitry.ustalov@jetbrains.com

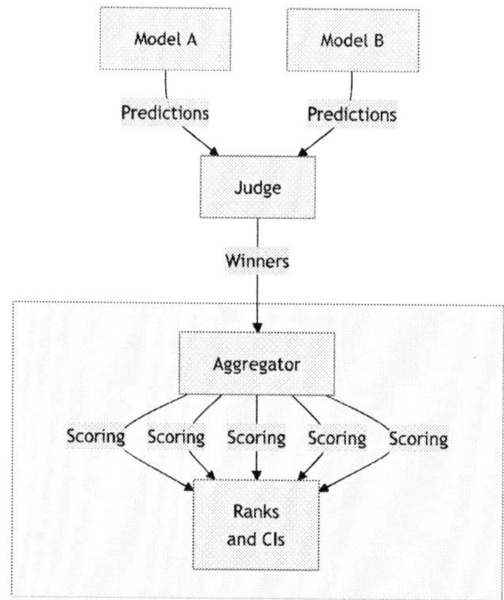

Figure 1: Evalica facilitates the highlighted aspects of leaderboard-making that involve aggregation of judgements, scoring the models with bootstrapped confidence intervals (CIs), and getting the final model ranks.

Abstract

The rapid advancement of natural language processing (NLP) technologies, such as instruction-tuned large language models (LLMs), urges the development of modern evaluation protocols with human and machine feedback. We introduce **Evalica**, an open-source toolkit that facilitates the creation of reliable and reproducible model leaderboards. This paper presents its design, evaluates its performance, and demonstrates its usability through its Web interface, command-line interface, and Python API.

1 Introduction

The emergent abilities, as exhibited by highly capable natural language processing (NLP) methods, such as instruction-tuned large language models (LLMs), urge the development of sound and reliable evaluation protocols. While the earlier methods could be reasonably evaluated on static datasets or individual benchmarks, modern methods require up-to-date benchmarks with live feedback from humans and machines (Faggioli et al., 2024). These benchmarks are often represented as pairwise comparison leaderboards (Figure 1), as popularized by LMSYS Arena (Chiang et al., 2024) and AlpacaEval (Dubois et al., 2024) projects.

As the NLP methodology evolves rapidly, today's evaluation methods are often implemented in computational notebooks and ad-hoc programs as an afterthought, which introduces errors, incompatibilities, and harms reproducibility and adoption. To improve the engineering aspect of benchmarking by reducing the number of methodological errors and simplifying the exchange and interpretation of the results, we present **Evalica**, an open-source evaluation toolkit that facilitates and speeds up the creation of reliable and reproducible NLP model benchmarks,[1] currently focused on the preference data. Based on our four-year experience in the development of production-grade tooling for quality control in crowdsourcing (Ustalov et al., 2024), we built Evalica with three practical goals in mind:

- *make the popular evaluation practices available* for a wide audience of users
- *ensure the performance and correctness* of the offered implementations
- *provide the best developer experience* possible

The remainder of this paper is organized as follows. Section 2 reviews the related work and its relationship with the declared goals. Section 3

[1] https://github.com/dustalov/evalica

Proceedings of the 31st International Conference on Computational Linguistics: System Demonstrations, pages 46–53
January 19–24, 2025.

shows Evalica's design and how it satisfies these goals. Section 4 describes the technical details of the Evalica implementation, including the means to ensure its correctness. Section 5 reports performance benchmarks against alternative implementations. Finally, Appendix A demonstrates a Web, a command-line , and a Python application programming interfaces (API) of Evalica.

2 Related Work

The research community has been developing various toolkits for ranking systems, such as Elo (1978) and TrueSkill (Herbrich et al., 2006). In our analysis, we distinguish several classes of them.

First, *dedicated leaderboard building tools*, such as IFEval (Zhou et al., 2023), LMSYS Arena (Chiang et al., 2024), Arena-Hard (Li et al., 2024), and AlpacaEval (Dubois et al., 2024). These toolkits were created by teams of researchers to implement a specific novel evaluation methodology. The code was generally written strictly tailored to the particular benchmark, requiring extra effort from the user to apply it to their own dataset and domain. Due to the high pace of today's scientific research, certain software engineering best practices were often omitted, such as test coverage, code documentation, continuous integration, and data format compatibility. At the same time, some implementations suffer from suboptimal computational performance on larger realistic datasets, which were out of scope of the original benchmarks.

Second, *ranking system implementations*, including Rust packages Propagon[2] and skillrating,[3] a Python package OpenSkill.py (Joshi, 2024), and others. As these packages are often written by skilled programmers in the best effort to bring correct implementations, these methods do not always match the ones used in current best practices in NLP evaluation. Also, the non-Python packages require an additional non-trivial effort to integrate with the existing Python code and notebooks.

Finally, *application-specific toolkits* like Elovation,[4] ArtistAssistApp,[5] and Crowd-Kit (Ustalov et al., 2024). These toolkits were built to accommodate user-generated content, usually in the form of crowdsourcing annotation, and often do not follow the methodology used in NLP evaluation.

[2]https://github.com/Refefer/propagon

[3]https://github.com/atomflunder/skillratings

[4]https://github.com/elovation/elovation

[5]https://github.com/eugene-khyst/pairwise-comparison

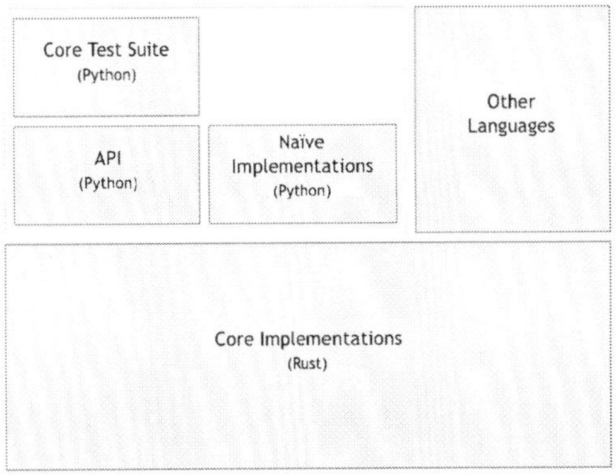

Figure 2: Evalica has a core in Rust that is covered by a comprehensive suite of tests in Python. We simplify prototyping and increase test reliability by keeping an independent implementation of each method in Python.

3 Design of Evalica

Evalica facilitates three tasks shown in Figure 1: it provides optimized single-threaded implementations of rating systems, simplifies the computation of confidence intervals for model scores, and offers convenient routines to prepare visualizations.

Figure 2 outlines the architecture of Evalica. In its *core*, there are performance-critical routines in Rust that process the raw data. These core routines are wrapped in convenient APIs for application developers in other languages. These APIs were responsible for transforming the representation into the indexed format as used by the core routines.[6] Examples of core routines are all the ranking algorithm implementations and helper routines for constructing win matrices.

We currently only support Python due to its popularity in machine learning. For the sake of reliability and ease of prototyping, we naïvely and implemented all the methods additionally in Python and built a comprehensive test suite that compares the Python implementations with the Rust ones. Other languages can be supported relatively easily (as long as there exists a bridge between Rust and that language), and improvements to the core implementations and tests will improve the state of all the derivative code.

We believe that these measures allowed satisfying the three goals mentioned in Section 1 ad-

[6]Models usually have names like `llama-3.1-405b-instruct` and `claude-3-5-sonnet-20240620`. Computers do not operate with strings *per se*, so we need to transform such names into the corresponding indices, e.g., `0` and `1`.

equately. Evalica accelerates popular evaluation practices by shipping the corresponding implementations in a high-performing compiled programming language, building on lessons learned from previously developed software to increase the developer's productivity.

4 Implementation Details

Evalica implements scoring approaches from popular benchmarks, such as Chatbot Arena and Arena-Hard: Elo (1978) and Bradley and Terry (1952), and average win rate. We ensured that they provided the same results as in these benchmarks. The package also contains implementations of the eigenvalue method (Bonacich, 1987), PageRank (Brin and Page, 1998), tie-aware method of Newman (2023), and trivial vote counting.

To invoke the implementation in Evalica (Listing 1), one needs to supply a vector of left objects (`xs`), a vector of right objects (`ys`), a vector of winner labels (`winners`), and, optionally, a vector of example weights (`weights`) for style control, as proposed in Li et al. (2024). Possible values of the winner labels are "X won," "Y won," and "tie." All methods are available in a lightweight and uniform functional API. We intentionally decided to avoid making assumptions about the tabular form of data as our experience in running Crowd-Kit (Ustalov et al., 2024) in production showed that it required an error-prone data transformation step that could have been avoided.

Internally, Evalica does not operate with model names, and core implementations require an index to compare the model name to the unique numerical identifier (as described in Section 3). Since this operation takes short yet non-negligible time, we provided the possibility to pass the already built index to save time during bootstrapping the confidence intervals and other routines that require resampling and recomputing the scores (Listing 2).

Besides the API, Evalica offers a built-in Web interface and a command-line interface, see Appendix A for illustrative examples. More specifically, the built-in Web interface follows a well-known input-output separation paradigm from Abid et al. (2019) and was created using the Gradio toolkit (Figure 4).[7] The command-line interface was developed using the pandas library for data manipulation (McKinney, 2010) and the tools available from the Python standard library (Figure 5).

[7] `https://www.gradio.app/`

After computing the scores and ranks, it is often useful to visualize the pairwise win rates for the compared models. Following Chiang et al. (2024), we applied the Bradley and Terry (1952) definition of such a quantity for all pairs of models i and j:

$$p_{ij} = \frac{s_i}{s_i + s_j},$$

where p_{ij} is the probability of model i winning against the model j, s_i is the score of model i, and s_j is the score of model j.

4.1 Correctness and Reliability

We applied a set of reasonable means to ensure correctness and reliability of the method implementations in Evalica. First, we implemented all the methods independently in two different programming languages, Rust and Python. We ensured that the outputs for the same inputs are the same between these implementations. Second, we employed property-based tests with the Hypothesis library (MacIver et al., 2019) for Python, which enumerated corner cases including empty or illegal inputs to break the program.[8] We covered all such cases and provide reasonable numerical fallbacks, where possible. Third, we compared the outputs against the canonical scores from external benchmarks. Fourth, we ensured that the test coverage is no less than 100%, and the test suite was executed on every revision in the repository.

4.2 Governance and Availability

We built Evalica using the trusted open-source ecosystem. The source code of Evalica was available under the Apache License 2.0 on GitHub.[9] Feature requests and code contributions were processed using the Issues and Pull Requests features on GitHub, correspondingly. We used continuous integration on GitHub Actions to invoke per-revision checks, including unit tests, linting, type checking, test coverage measurement, and computational performance testing. Public dashboards with test coverage and performance tests were available on Codecov[10] and Codspeed,[11] correspondingly. We used the trusted publishing approach to release Python packages to PyPI for the Linux, Windows, and macOS platforms.[12] Our compiled

[8] `https://github.com/HypothesisWorks/hypothesis`
[9] `https://github.com/dustalov/evalica`
[10] `https://codecov.io/gh/dustalov/evalica`
[11] `https://codspeed.io/dustalov/evalica`
[12] `https://pypi.python.org/pypi/evalica`

Setup	Time ↑
BT in Evalica	1.174 ± 0.009
Elo in Evalica	1.256 ± 0.019
Elo from Arena-Hard	3.778 ± 0.322
BT from Chatbot Arena	51.949 ± 1.797

Table 1: Performance of Evalica, Chatbot Arena, and Arena-Hard on the Chatbot Arena dataset. Time is in seconds; a 95% confidence interval is shown for ten runs. Smaller is better. BT means Bradley and Terry (1952), Elo means Elo (1978).

Algorithm	Rust	Python
Average Win Rate	0.005 ± 0.000	0.006 ± 0.000
Bradley–Terry	0.005 ± 0.000	0.012 ± 0.000
Counting	0.005 ± 0.000	0.009 ± 0.000
Eigenvalue	0.005 ± 0.000	0.006 ± 0.000
Elo	0.005 ± 0.000	0.484 ± 0.004
Newman	0.006 ± 0.000	0.010 ± 0.000
PageRank	0.005 ± 0.000	0.006 ± 0.000

Table 2: Running time comparison of core Rust and naïve Python implementations of methods in Evalica on the LLMFAO dataset. Time is in seconds; a 95% confidence interval for ten runs is shown for each implementation. Smaller is better.

packages were forward compatible with any version of Python newer than 3.8 due to the use of the stable CPython ABI. We also released Evalica on conda-forge for the users of Anaconda, a popular distribution of scientific computing tools.[13] Last but not least, we published the developer documentation on Read the Docs.[14]

5 Performance Tests

We performed two series of computational experiments to study the running time of algorithm implementations in Evalica after ensuring their correctness. First, we evaluated the difference in computational performance between the current implementations in a popular benchmark and the ones provided by Evalica. Second, we compared the performance of core and naïve implementations of all the methods inside Evalica. All the experiments were run using CPython 3.13.1, NumPy 2.2.0, and Evalica 0.3.2 on macOS 15.2 (Intel® Core™ i5-8500 CPU, 32 GB RAM). All confidence intervals were built using bootstrap with 10K samples and 95% significance level.

5.1 Chatbot Arena Experiment

We evaluated the performance of four setups in processing the August 14, 2024 version of the Chatbot Arena dataset (Chiang et al., 2024) that contained 1.7M pairwise comparisons of 129 models, ties were not excluded.[15] We compared four different setups: an implementation of the Elo (1978) ranking system in pure Python, as used in Chatbot Arena, an implementation of Bradley and Terry (1952) in Python with scikit-learn (Pedregosa et al., 2011), as used in Arena-Hard, and Rust implementations of these two methods in Evalica. For that, we ran every setup ten times to simulate the realistic problem of confidence interval estimation that does often appear in model leaderboards. As the results in Table 1 indicate, Evalica's implementations of ranking methods outperformed the current ones as used in the benchmarks by up to 46 times without any involvement of multi-threading processing. Although this was expected since Python is an interpreted language and Rust is a compiled language, we believe that the Evalica's combination of performance and ergonomics would allow running more experiments within the same time budget. At the same time, performing computation in multiple threads, e.g., processing one sampling round per thread, would allow one to better use of the modern multi-core CPUs and reduce the computation time by multiple times.

5.2 Rust vs. Python in Evalica Experiment

We evaluated the performance of all the methods implemented in Evalica's core in Rust against their naïve implementations in Python. Despite the name, these Python implementations were written using NumPy (Harris et al., 2020), a highly optimized library built on decades of successful performance engineering work for numerical computation in C and Fortran. We used the dataset from a smaller benchmark called LLMFAO (Ustalov, 2023), which had 9K pairwise comparisons for 59 LLMs, gathered in October 2023 using crowdsourcing. As the results in Table 2 show, the differences between core and naïve implementation were statistically significant, according to the permutation test ($p < 0.01$), but the effect size was not noticeable on that scale due to the efficient NumPy

[13] https://anaconda.org/conda-forge/evalica
[14] https://evalica.readthedocs.io/
[15] https://storage.googleapis.com/arena_external_data/public/clean_battle_20240814_public.json

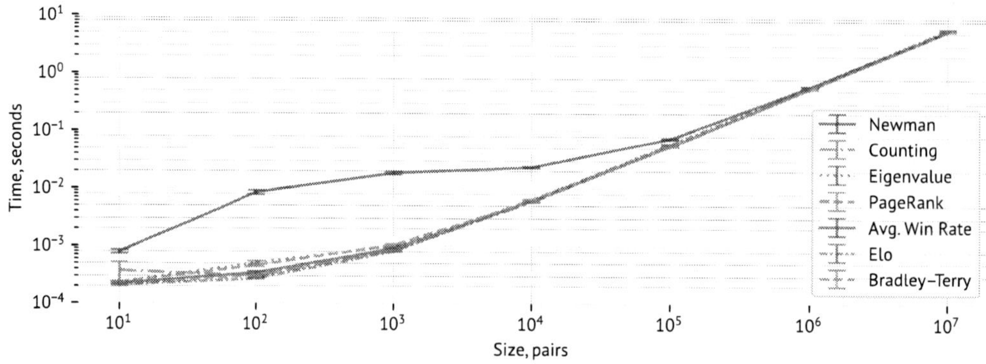

Figure 3: Performance scaling analysis of the Rust implementations in Evalica on the synthetic version of the Chatbot Arena dataset. Both scales are logarithmic. Time is in seconds, dataset size is the number of pairs; a 95% confidence interval is shown for ten runs. Lower is better.

routines used in the pure Python implementations. One important exception was Elo, whose equivalent implementation in Rust appeared to be more than 96 times faster than in Python due to the efficient compiler optimizations. At the same time, the Rust implementations had a smaller runtime variance and more predictable performance, which should be useful on larger-scale datasets.

5.3 Scaling on Synthetic Data Experiment

We analyzed the relationship between dataset size and computation time using Evalica on a synthetic dataset derived from Chatbot Arena as the original dataset was already larger than most existing preference-based NLP datasets. We selected seven dataset sizes, ranging from 10^1 to 10^7 pairs, with each size increasing by a factor of ten. For each size, we sampled the required number of pairs with replacement from Chatbot Arena ten times to study the time variance. Computation times were measured using Rust implementations of the methods available in Evalica, and we constructed 95% confidence intervals using bootstrapping. Figure 3 shows that the relationship between dataset size and computation time scales linearly for all methods, indicating good scalability. However, there are clear performance differences for small input sizes, with methods like Newman (2023) being slower initially but converging to similar trends as input size increases. Note that our analysis was limited by the number of models in the version of Chatbot Arena used in our experiments.

6 Conclusion

We believe that Evalica will foster the creation of reliable and reproducible benchmarks for future NLP systems. We define several potential directions of further work: (1) implementing a larger set of use cases widely used in practice, including confidence interval construction out of the box and additional ranking algorithms, (2) bringing additional performance and memory optimizations, and (3) supporting other popular programming languages with good interoperability with Rust, including JavaScript and Ruby. To the best of our knowledge, Evalica is the first attempt to offer drop-in accelerated preference-based benchmarks, which affects their computational performance and numerical reliability. We expect that a broader adoption of Evalica will result in faster iteration times, more useful experiments, and fewer model-selection mistakes.

Acknowledgements

We would like to thank three anonymous reviewers for their useful feedback. We are grateful to the early adopters of Evalica from the Vikhr team (Nikolich et al., 2024) and JetBrains AI team, whose kind feedback allowed improving the library. Note that the correct pronunciation of the library name is *eh-vah-lee-tsah*, which resembles a typical village name in the Balkans.

References

Abubakar Abid, Ali Abdalla, Ali Abid, Dawood Khan, Abdulrahman Alfozan, and James Y. Zou. 2019. Gradio: Hassle-Free Sharing and Testing of ML Models in the Wild. *Preprint*, arXiv:1906.02569.

Phillip Bonacich. 1987. Power and Centrality: A Family of Measures. *American Journal of Sociology*, 92(5):1170–1182.

Ralph Allan Bradley and Milton E. Terry. 1952. Rank Analysis of Incomplete Block Designs: I. The Method of Paired Comparisons. *Biometrika*, 39(3/4):324–345.

Sergey Brin and Lawrence Page. 1998. The anatomy of a large-scale hypertextual Web search engine. *Computer Networks and ISDN Systems*, 30(1):107–117. Proceedings of the Seventh International World Wide Web Conference.

Wei-Lin Chiang, Lianmin Zheng, Ying Sheng, Anastasios Nikolas Angelopoulos, Tianle Li, Dacheng Li, Banghua Zhu, Hao Zhang, Michael Jordan, Joseph E. Gonzalez, and Ion Stoica. 2024. Chatbot Arena: An Open Platform for Evaluating LLMs by Human Preference. In *Proceedings of the 41st International Conference on Machine Learning*, volume 235 of *Proceedings of Machine Learning Research*, pages 8359–8388. PMLR.

Yann Dubois, Percy Liang, and Tatsunori Hashimoto. 2024. Length-Controlled AlpacaEval: A Simple Debiasing of Automatic Evaluators. In *First Conference on Language Modeling*.

Arpad E. Elo. 1978. *The Rating Of Chess Players, Past & Present*. Arco Publishing Inc., New York.

Guglielmo Faggioli, Laura Dietz, Charles L. A. Clarke, Gianluca Demartini, Matthias Hagen, Claudia Hauff, Noriko Kando, Evangelos Kanoulas, Martin Potthast, Benno Stein, and Henning Wachsmuth. 2024. Who Determines What Is Relevant? Humans or AI? Why Not Both? *Communications of the ACM*, 67(4):31–34.

Charles R. Harris, K. Jarrod Millman, Stéfan J. van der Walt, Ralf Gommers, et al. 2020. Array programming with NumPy. *Nature*, 585(7825):357–362.

Ralf Herbrich, Tom Minka, and Thore Graepel. 2006. TrueSkill™: A Bayesian Skill Rating System. In *Advances in Neural Information Processing Systems 19*, pages 569–576. MIT Press.

Vivek Joshi. 2024. OpenSkill: A faster asymmetric multi-team, multiplayer rating system. *Journal of Open Source Software*, 9(93):5901.

Tianle Li, Wei-Lin Chiang, Evan Frick, Lisa Dunlap, Banghua Zhu, Joseph E. Gonzalez, and Ion Stoica. 2024. From Live Data to High-Quality Benchmarks: The Arena-Hard Pipeline.

David R. MacIver, Zac Hatfield-Dodds, et al. 2019. Hypothesis: A new approach to property-based testing. *Journal of Open Source Software*, 4(43):1891.

Wes McKinney. 2010. Data Structures for Statistical Computing in Python. In *Proceedings of the 9th Python in Science Conference*, SciPy 2010, pages 56–61.

Mark E. J. Newman. 2023. Efficient Computation of Rankings from Pairwise Comparisons. *Journal of Machine Learning Research*, 24(238):1–25.

Aleksandr Nikolich, Konstantin Korolev, Artem Shelmanov, and Igor Kiselev. 2024. Vikhr: The Family of Open-Source Instruction-Tuned Large Language Models for Russian. *Preprint*, arXiv:2405.13929.

Fabian Pedregosa, Gaël Varoquaux, Alexandre Gramfort, Vincent Michel, Bertrand Thirion, Olivier Grisel, Mathieu Blondel, Peter Prettenhofer, Ron Weiss, Vincent Dubourg, Jake Vanderplas, Alexandre Passos, David Cournapeau, Matthieu Brucher, Matthieu Perrot, and Édouard Duchesnay. 2011. Scikit-learn: Machine Learning in Python. *Journal of Machine Learning Research*, 12(85):2825–2830.

Dmitry Ustalov. 2023. Large Language Model Feedback Analysis and Optimization (LLMFAO). Dataset.

Dmitry Ustalov, Nikita Pavlichenko, and Boris Tseitlin. 2024. Learning from Crowds with Crowd-Kit. *Journal of Open Source Software*, 9(96):6227.

Pauli Virtanen, Ralf Gommers, Travis E. Oliphant, Matt Haberland, Tyler Reddy, et al. 2020. SciPy 1.0: Fundamental Algorithms for Scientific Computing in Python. *Nature Methods*, 17:261–272.

Jeffrey Zhou, Tianjian Lu, Swaroop Mishra, Siddhartha Brahma, Sujoy Basu, Yi Luan, Denny Zhou, and Le Hou. 2023. Instruction-Following Evaluation for Large Language Models. *Preprint*, arXiv:2311.07911.

A Usage Examples

```
>>> from evalica import elo, pairwise_frame, Winner
>>> result = elo(
...     xs=["pizza", "burger", "pizza"],
...     ys=["burger", "sushi", "sushi"],
...     winners=[Winner.X, Winner.Y, Winner.Draw],
... )
>>> result.scores
pizza      1014.972058
burger      970.647200
sushi      1014.380742
Name: elo, dtype: float64
>>> df_scores = pairwise_frame(result.scores)
>>> df_scores  # can be used for plotting the pairwise win rate
           pizza     sushi    burger
pizza   0.500000  0.500003  0.501499
sushi   0.499997  0.500000  0.501496
burger  0.498501  0.498504  0.500000
```

Listing 1: An example of computing Elo ranking and the corresponding pairwise win rates with Evalica. Other methods can be applied similarly with a trivial modification: `bradley_terry`, `average_win_rate`, etc. See `https://github.com/dustalov/evalica/blob/master/Tutorial.ipynb` for an executable example.

```
# index the compared models to save time by not re-indexing them at each round
*_, index = evalica.indexing(
    xs=df["model_a"],  # series with model A identifiers
    ys=df["model_b"],  # series with model B identifiers
)

bootstrap: list["pd.Series[str]"] = []  # assuming model names are strings

for r in range(BOOTSTRAP_ROUNDS):
    # for reproducibility, set the random seed equal to the number
    # of the bootstrapping round
    df_sample = df_arena.sample(frac=1.0, replace=True, random_state=r)

    # estimate the Bradley-Terry scores for the given sample
    result_sample = evalica.bradley_terry(
        xs=df_sample["model_a"],
        ys=df_sample["model_b"],
        winners=df_sample["winner"],
        index=index  # use the index built above to speed up
    )

    bootstrap.append(result_sample.scores)

# this is a data frame with BOOTSTRAP_ROUNDS rows,
# each row represents the score of each model at the r-th round
df_bootstrap = pd.DataFrame(bootstrap)

# this is a data frame with confidence intervals of scores
# for each compared model
df_bootstrap_ci = pd.DataFrame({
    "lower": df_bootstrap.quantile(.025),
    "rating": df_bootstrap.quantile(.5),
    "upper": df_bootstrap.quantile(.975),
}).reset_index(names="model").sort_values("rating", ascending=False)
```

Listing 2: An example of bootstrapping a 95% confidence interval of Bradley and Terry (1952) scores with Evalica and pandas (McKinney, 2010). Any other supported model can be applied after a trivial modification. For simplicity, we do not show an example with `scipy.stats.bootstrap` (Virtanen et al., 2020), yet it is possible. See `https://github.com/dustalov/evalica/blob/master/Chatbot-Arena.ipynb` for an executable example.

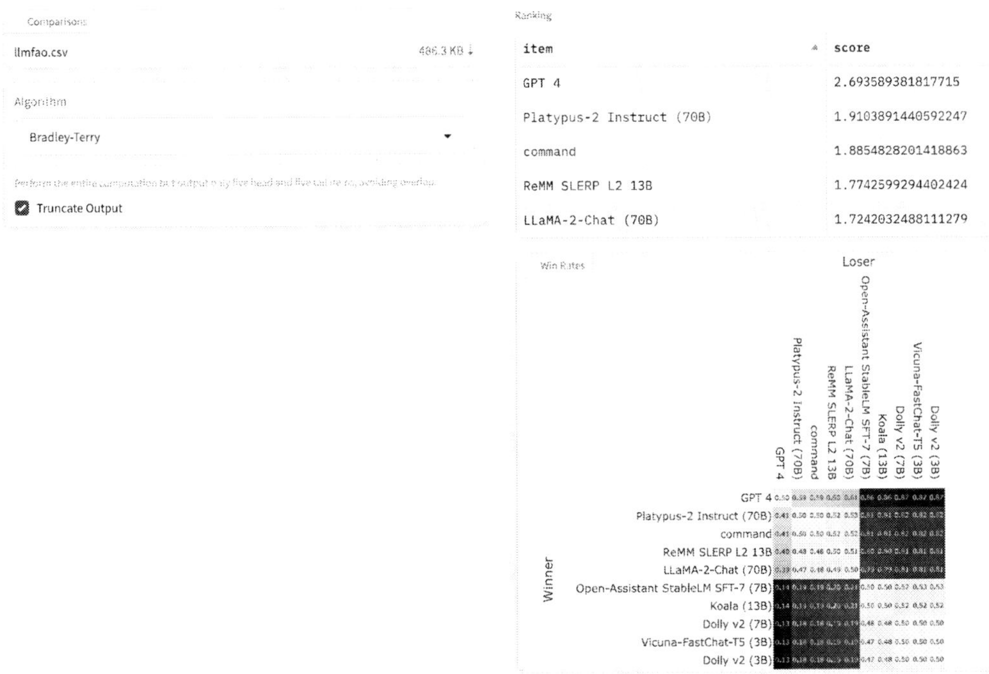

Figure 4: A screenshot of the Evalica's Web interface with the LLMFAO benchmark (Ustalov, 2023). On the left, there are the input file, algorithm choice, and additional parameters. On the right, there is a table with the ranking results and a win rate plot. For the sake of brevity, we showed only a truncated output, with no columns corresponding to the number of compared pairs and the current rank of the model. A live example can be accessed at `https://huggingface.co/spaces/dustalov/pair2rank`.

```
$ head -n6 food.csv | column -ts,
left    right  winner
Pizza   Sushi  left
Burger  Pasta  right
Tacos   Pizza  left
Sushi   Tacos  right
Burger  Pizza  left
$ evalica -i food.csv bradley-terry | column -ts,
item    score               rank
Tacos   2.509025136024378   1
Sushi   1.1011561298265815  2
Burger  0.8549063627182466  3
Pasta   0.7403814336665869  4
Pizza   0.5718366915548537  5
```

Figure 5: An example of using a command-line interface of Evalica to process a file in the comma-separated values format and print the item ranks and estimated scores.

BeefBot: Harnessing Advanced LLM and RAG Techniques for Providing Scientific and Technology Solutions to Beef Producers

Zhihao Zhang[1], Carrie-Ann Wilson[1], Rachel Hay[1], Yvette Everingham[1], Usman Naseem[2]
James Cook University, Australia[1], Macquarie University, Australia[2]
{zhihao.zhang, carrie.wilson1, rachel.hay, yvette.everingham}@jcu.edu.au
usman.naseem@mq.edu.au

Abstract

We propose **BeefBot**, a LLM-powered chatbot designed for beef producers. It retrieves the latest agricultural technologies (AgTech), practices and scientific insights to provide rapid, domain-specific advice, helping to address on-farm challenges effectively. While generic Large Language Models (LLMs) like ChatGPT are useful for information retrieval, they often hallucinate and fall short in delivering tailored solutions to the specific needs of beef producers, including breed-specific strategies, operational practices, and regional adaptations.There are two common methods for incorporating domain-specific data in LLM applications: Retrieval-Augmented Generation (RAG) and fine-tuning. However, their respective advantages and disadvantages are not well understood. Therefore, we implement a pipeline to apply RAG and fine-tuning using an open-source LLM in BeefBot and evaluate the trade-offs. By doing so, we are able to select the best combination as the backend of BeefBot, delivering actionable recommendations that enhance productivity and sustainability for beef producers with fewer hallucinations. Key benefits of BeefBot include its accessibility as a web-based platform compatible with any browser, continuously updated knowledge through RAG, confidential assurance via local deployment, and a user-friendly experience facilitated by an interactive website. The demo of the BeefBot can be accessed at `https://www.youtube.com/watch?v=r7mde1EOG4o`.

1 Introduction

The latest development of Large Language Models (LLMs) has advanced the field of Natural Language Processing (NLP), delivering a strong foundation for a wide range of potential applications. However, applying generic LLMs to solve domain-specific problems presents several challenges, such as understanding domain objects' uniqueness, aligning domain's diversity of constraints, and producing consistent domain-related contents (Ling et al., 2023). In the context of the beef industry within the agricultural sector, these challenges are particularly pronounced. With a generational shift in farming, many younger producers may not be fully versed in traditional practices, underscoring the importance of accessible, digital platforms that offer instant access to a wealth of historical and cutting-edge knowledge. Furthermore, the unique challenge of the beef industry lies in the rapid pace of development in agricultural technologies and innovations, coupled with frequent updates to government regulations and guidelines, necessitating a tool that can provide up-to-date, reliable advice.

To address these challenges, recent studies have pursued two primary methods of knowledge injection (Wang et al., 2021; Chen et al., 2022) in LLMs including fine-tuning and Retrieval Augmentation Generation (RAG) (Ovadia et al., 2024). While both approaches can improve LLMs' responses with precision and concision, fine-tuning incorporates additional domain knowledge into the model, whereas RAG prompts the model with external data (Balaguer et al., 2024). Given the variability in different domains, these methods have been applied accordingly in several areas for LLM applications, including health (Singhal et al., 2023), finance (Yang et al., 2023) and agriculture (Arora et al., 2020). Although both methods can be utilised for adopting LLMs in new domains, most of the existing models tend to utilise either fine-tuning or retrieval augmentation with prompting, and their respective advantages and disadvantages are not well studied. Furthermore, agriculture includes sub-fields like horticulture, arable farming, animal husbandry and forestry, which is still too general for direct industry application purposes. Additionally, the lack of easily accessible platforms also prevents the adoption of domain-specific LLM in industrial settings, often due to the required expertise in deep-learning and programming.

Proceedings of the 31st International Conference on Computational Linguistics: System Demonstrations, pages 54–62
January 19–24, 2025.

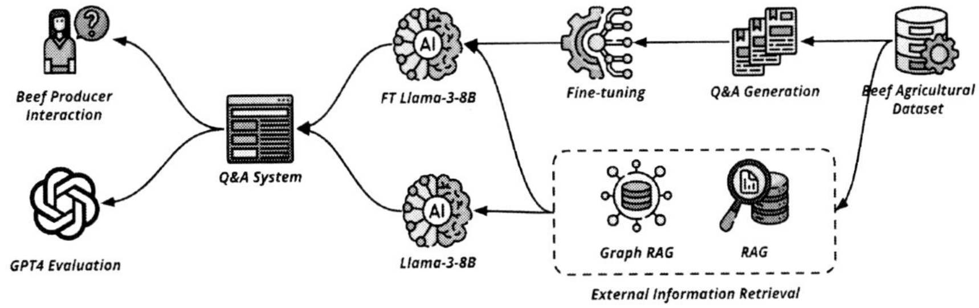

Figure 1: Overview of Beef Agriculture Pipeline for LLM

Contribution. With this in mind, we propose BeefBot, a LLM-powered web-based interactive chatbot, designed to support beef producers by providing immediate actionable recommendations and long-term strategies for their specific on-farm problems and goals. Its primary function is providing optimal solutions from the available knowledge in the beef industry, while taking into account farm-related variables such as economics, cattle breeds, grazing land management, and drought resilience strategies. More precisely, we first developed a pipeline to evaluate the impact of RAG and fine-tuning techniques on the performance of open-source LLM in the beef agriculture domain. The LLM was equipped with the optimal combination of these techniques, forming the complete architecture of BeefBot's backend. It can deliver answers through an interactive website similar to ChatGPT (Ouyang et al., 2022), with significantly reduced hallucination in out-of-knowledge response. This enhancement is designed to provide more precise and relevant responses for beef producers, thereby enabling them to focus more on implementation.

2 Beef Agriculture Pipeline for LLM

The pipeline is designed to utilize open-source LLMs to generate comprehensive responses for beef agriculture-specific questions. Its structure is shown in Figure 1. The beef agriculture dataset is gathered from trustworthy sources [1], comprising diverse content from text, podcasts, and videos. Following the data collection, we generate question-and-answer pairs for model fine-tuning and implement both original RAG and knowledge graph RAG. This aims to leverage different methods for improving the LLM responses in the beef agriculture domain.

2.1 Data Collection

We implemented a comprehensive data collection pipeline to extract and collect information from several trustworthy websites. This process includes two primary components: a web parsing algorithm and a resource downloading subroutine. The web parsing algorithm aims to scrape raw text data from source websites while removing any sensitive information, such as participants' names and business information in interviews or case studies. During web scraping, the algorithm identifies the webpage structure, removes trivial information such as web headers and social media links, but captures multimodal resources, including podcast and video content. The resource downloading subroutine targets those available multimodal contents and utilises open-source tools [2] [3] to download them. The downloaded multimodal content was further transcribed into text by the latest speech-to-text model Whisper (Radford et al., 2023). Both scrapped and transcript raw text are stored into plain text documents and indexed by their titles and source URLs. Together, this formed a comprehensive data collection, enabling us to provide the LLM agriculture pipeline with information and resources from the multimodal context in the beef industry domain.

2.2 Fine-tuning QA Generation

High-quality and contextually grounded questions that comprehensively reflect the collected text are essential for language model fine-tuning. Inspired by Alpaca (Taori et al., 2023), we utilize Llama-index [4] to transform the plain text into instructive question-answer pairs as the fine-tuning dataset. To

[1] Details on the specific websites utilised are withheld due to intellectual property concerns. It is important to note that all data collection and processing activities were conducted in compliance with ethical standards and considerations.

[2] https://github.com/yt-dlp/yt-dlp

[3] https://github.com/spotDL/spotify-downloader

[4] https://docs.llamaindex.ai

GPT-4

```
You are a Teacher/ Professor. Your task is to setup a quiz/examination. Using the provided
context, formulate 5 question-answer pairs that captures an important fact from the context.
<content> text chunk </content>

You MUST obey the following criteria:
- Restrict the question to the context information provided.
- Do NOT create a question that cannot be answered from the context.
- Phrase the question so that it does NOT refer to specific context and person. For instance, do
NOT put phrases like "given provided context" or "in this work" "How Jerry deal with" in the
question, because if the question is asked elsewhere it wouldn't be provided specific context.
Replace these terms with specific details.

- BAD questions:
What did the author do in his childhood
What were the main findings in this report
- GOOD questions:
What did the farmer do in his farm
What were the main findings in the original Transformers paper.

- Return your response in JSON format
Generate question:
Generate answer:
```

Figure 2: Fine-tuning QA Generation

achieve this, we split the long text documents into small text chunks of 2,000 characters and combine them alongside a carefully crafted prompt, following the Guidance framework [5]. For each text chunk, we utilise GPT-4 with the complete prompt to generate five specific question-answer pairs. This singular and unified process ensures the relevance and coherence of each question-answer pair given the source text. The prompt is shown in Figure 2, and the question-answer pairs are saved as instructive data instances in a JSON file. We divided the collected 24,057 instances into two sets: 19,245 for training and 4,812 for testing.

2.3 Model Fine-tuning

Model fine-tuning can inject factual knowledge into LLM parameters and provide promising results for completing in-domain tasks. We fine-tune the Llama-3 which is the latest generation of Llama model family. Llama (Touvron et al., 2023a) is an open-source autoregressive LLM based on the transformer architecture (Vaswani et al., 2023), comparable to GPT-3 (Brown et al., 2020). It leverages three main improvements over prior proposed models, including pre-normalisation (Brown et al., 2020), SwiGLU activation function (Chowdhery et al., 2023) and rotary embedding (Black et al., 2022). Llama-3 (Llama Team, 2024) is the third generation of Llama, which competes with ChatGPT (Ouyang et al., 2022). It features with twice context windows and more training data compared to the Llama-2 (Touvron et al., 2023b). These enhancements, along with grouped-query attention, enable Llama-3 to outperform many open-source LLMs such as Mistral and Gemma on reasoning, coding, and knowledge tests, indicating its capability in diverse tasks (Llama Team, 2024). Therefore, we fine-tune and validate the Llama-3-8B (Llama Team, 2024) model with the collected instruct data. The entire model is trained using paged AdamW for a single epoch, with a warm-up step of 100 and learning rate of 1e-5. Our implementation is based on HuggingFace Transformers (Wolf et al., 2020), following the instructions from Alpaca (Taori et al., 2023). To optimize the fine-tuning process, we deployed it with Fully Sharded Data Parallelism (FSDP) (Zhao et al., 2023), which allows the sharding of model weights, optimizer states, and gradients, enabling the efficient use of multiple GPUs in parallel. The entire fine-tuning process utilised 3 NVIDIA H100 GPUs over a duration of 5 hours.

2.4 Retrieval Augmentation Generation

Another method to improve the response from LLM is Retrieval Augmentation Generation (RAG) (Lewis et al., 2020). This method aims to extend LLM capability to precisely manipulate knowledge and handle out-of-knowledge queries to reduce hallucination in knowledge-intensive tasks. To prompt engineer the Llama-3 model with RAG system, there are three components involved in establishing: 1) vector database for knowledge con-

[5]https://github.com/guidance-ai/guidance

Llama-3-8B

```
You are an expert in the beef industry. Please provide
information on cattle breeds, production processes, environmental
impact, market trends, nutrition, regulations, and sustainable
practices in cattle farming.

Use the following context as your knowledge, inside
<context></context> XML tags to provide advice for the question.

<context>{context}</context>

When answer to user:
- If you don't know, ONLY say "I don't know".
- If you don't know when you are not sure, ask for clarification.
- Use step-by-step thoughts and make the answer more structural.
- Use `\\n\\n` to split the answer into several paragraphs.

Question: {input}
Your answer:
```

Figure 3: RAG Prompt

GPT-3.5

```
You are a data scientist working for a company that is building a knowledge
graph database. Your task is to extract information from data and convert it
into a knowledge graph database.
- Provide a set of Nodes in the form [head, head_type, relation, tail,
tail_type].
- It is important that the head and tail exists as nodes that are related by the
relation. If you can't pair a relationship with a pair of nodes don't add it.
- When you find a node or relationship you want to add try to create a generic
TYPE for it that describes the entity you can also think of it as a label.
- You must generate the output in a JSON format containing a list with JSON
objects. Each object should have the keys: "head", "head_type", "relation",
"tail", and "tail_type".
Be Concise.

Examples: {examples}

For the following text, extract entities and relations as in the provided
example.
Text: {input}
```

Figure 4: Graph RAG Prompt

text reference, 2) model serving for instant inference, and 3) prompt designing for hallucination reduction.

Vector Database. We utilise Chromadb [6] to build a large-scale vector database with all the available documents collected from trustworthy sources. This vector database is constructed by truncating and embedding the collected document from Section 2.1 into text blocks, with a maximum of 500 tokens per block for context-related reference. The vector database can be continuously updated with the latest external resources, and we index all documents with unique IDs along with their original source URLs in the vector database to maintain the traceability of each text block.

Model Serving. The fine-tuned model is served via Ollama [7], with a temperature of 0.1 and a repeat penalty of 1.15, to respond to in-coming queries with external context. Unlike traditional deep-learning pipelines that require complex dependencies and initial model loading for the first launch, Ollama serves the model as a system-wide service via a Docker-like container, making model inference simpler and faster.

Prompt Designing. As shown in Figure 3, we integrate LangChain [8] prompt templates within the RAG system by sending the most relevant text excerpts from the vector database, along with the queries, to the model. This approach allows the model's responses to include both its internal knowledge and external in-domain knowledge with proper references. To minimise hallucination, we prompt the model with a static response "I don't know" for queries beyond its knowledge scope.

2.5 RAG with Knowledge Graph

RAG with knowledge graph or Graph RAG (Edge et al., 2024) is a updated version of RAG, which enhances the model capability to answer global questions requiring the understanding of an entire document. Based on the original RAG, there are two extra stages involved: 1) deriving an entity-based knowledge graph from source document and 2) related entities' community summaries pre-generation. Apart from these changes, the model serving remains the same for consistency.

Knowledge Graph Derivation. Collected documents are spited into manageable text chunks and each text chunk is further processed to identify and extract their entities and relationships. To ensure a comprehensive extraction while maintaining cost-effectiveness, we utilise GPT-3.5-turbo with multipart prompts, demonstrated in Figure 4. The extracted entities and relationships are then summarised into single descriptive blocks for each graph element. We incorporate Neo4j [9] to store the graph elements and build an undirected weighted graph, where entities are transformed as nodes and relationships are transformed as edges.

Community Summaries Pre-generation. For each community in the Neo4j graph database, report-like summaries are generated, which provides an overview of communities' semantics. When a question is received, relevant community summaries are retrieved for answering the question based on the relevance. The final answer is then generated by summarising all the summaries to provide a comprehensive response.

2.6 Pipeline Evaluation

To better understand the benefits of each method for LLM in the beef agriculture domain, we evaluated

[6] https://www.trychroma.com/
[7] https://ollama.ai/
[8] https://www.langchain.com/
[9] https://neo4j.com

Llama3-8B	Relevance	Groundedness	Helpfulness
OG	75.12	78.74	**74.49**
OG-RAG	76.14	78.35	72.76
OG-GRAG	**76.46**	**79.37**	73.31
FT	**78.19**	**80.39**	**74.49**
FT-RAG	68.11	73.54	63.78
FT-GRAG	69.76	76.14	66.46

Table 1: Evaluation results. "OG" represents Original Llama3-8B model. "FT" represents Fine-Tuned Llama3-8B model. "GRAG" represents Graph RAG.

different combinations using the same evaluation metric. The combinations include both the original Llama-3 and fine-tuned Llama-3, with and without RAG and Graph-RAG systems. Since human evaluation is expensive and non-experts cannot determine the correctness of the technical answers, we utilised GPT-4 as an evaluator by providing the ground-truth answers as guidance.

Evaluation Setup. Following the similar idea in Section 2.2, we applied GPT-4 to generate 200 question-answer pairs from the collected beef agriculture documents. The detailed evaluation generation prompts is shown in Appendix. After filtering out the duplicate topics, there is a total number of 127 question-answer pairs that can represent the ground-truth dataset. We prompt the models with the questions and provide GPT-4 with the ground truth answers and model generated answers for evaluation.

Evalution Metrics. To better reflect the application in the industry domain, we introduce three different evaluation metrics: **1) Relevance**: How closely the model answer addresses the specific question. **2) Groundedness**: The correctness of the answer compared with the ground truth. **3) Helpfulness**: The usefulness the answer can be utilised or implemented by a beef farmer. For each metric, GPT-4 will provide a score from 1 to 10, where 1 is the worst and 10 is the best. We take the mean value of each combination and linearly scale up the scores to 100 for evaluation.

Evaluation Result. The evaluation results are summarise in Table 1. Compared with original Llama3-8B model, both RAG system and fine-tuned model have better performance in relevance and groundedness. The Helpfulness are slightly worse in RAG system and remains the same in fine-tuned models. This might due to the technical knowledge injection into the model, which lead to more technical language during question answering. For original Llama3-8B model, Graph RAG improve its answer in all three metrics comparing with original RAG. For fine-tuned Llama3-8B model, it's worth noting that the integration of RAG and Graph RAG decrease the performance of the model. This might be caused by catastrophic forgetting where model can loss its major reasoning capability while acquiring new domain knowledge (Luo et al., 2024). However, we observe that even under this circumstance, Graph RAG still outperform RAG in all three metrics. We also compare the performance with the proprietary models, although their performance are better than the open-source models, the concerns about privacy and cost-efficiency preventing deploying them into real-world application.

3 BeefBot Architecture

According to the observation from the beef agriculture pipeline, we propose a chatbot named BeefBot. It offers beef producers a well-designed, interactive Graphic User Interface (GUI) accessible through the web browser. Therefore, we designed both back-end and front-end of the system to ensure accuracy and efficiency of answering relevant beef production questions. This equips beef producers to tackle specific agricultural challenges with technology and scientific insights. Its design is shown in Figure 1, and the backend and front-end are described in the following sections.

3.1 Backend System

To streamline the application and simplify deployment, BeefBot's backend is constructed using a Flask HTTP server [10] with API calls. More specifically, the Llama3-8B model is hosted on RunPod [11] with Ollama API exposure. The Graph RAG database is stored on a Neo4j database, and the retrieval information is available during Ollama API calls. Langchain fuses the backend logic and provides a textual response to post via the Flask HTTP server. When there is a user query, Langchain retrieves the Graph RAG context and sends it to the Llama3-8B model along with the original query via an Ollama API call. The returned model response is extracted and formatted as a markdown text for the Flask HTTP server for front-end posting.

[10] https://flask.palletsprojects.com/

[11] https://www.runpod.io/

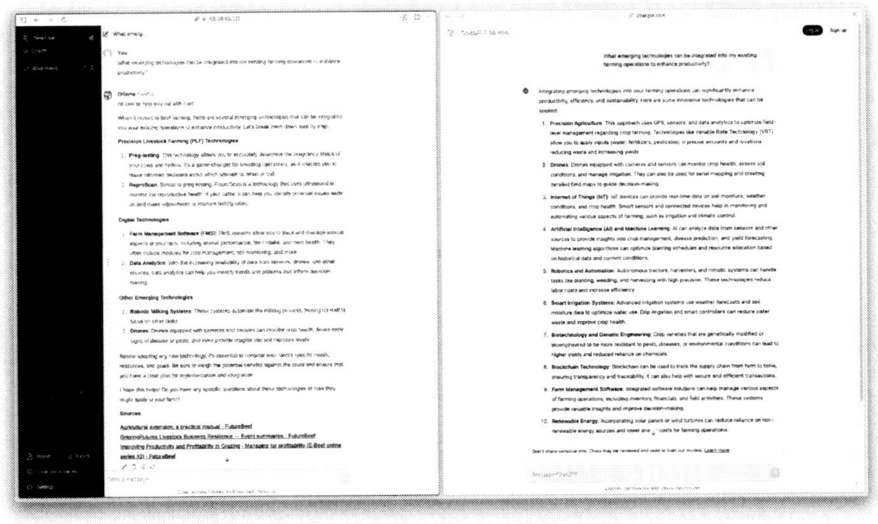

Figure 5: Comparison between front-end responses from BeefBot and ChatGPT for the same question. BeefBot (left) features responses tailored to the beef industry domain, while ChatGPT (right) offers generic responses.

3.2 Interactive Front-end Website

BeefBot offers an interactive web front-end built on the ollama-webui lite [12]. As shown on the left side of Figure 5, beef producers can interact with BeefBot by typing their questions into the text bar located at the bottom of the webpage. By integrating the BeefBot with external resources through the Graph RAG, its responses include all the source URLs referred to in the context. These clickable links guide beef producers to the websites of the mentioned techniques, helping them find the optimal solution for their specific problems without extensive web browsing. The conversations are searchable from the sidebar, which helps the user to find the previous information efficiently. To ensure privacy, all chat history is stored in the random access memory (RAM) of the host machine. Therefore, exiting each web session or clicking "Clear conversations" in the sidebar wipes out the entire conversation with BeefBot. We also provide a method that allows the user to export or import their conversations for continuous usage.

3.3 Case Study Comparison

As demonstrated in Figure 5, we compare the responses from BeefBot and ChatGPT to the same questions likely to be asked by beef producers. Even though the question does not specifically mention the beef industry, BeefBot tailors its response in that direction with actionable suggestions, such as Preg-testing technology, ReproScan technology, and Farm Management Software. These actionable suggestions align with our 'helpfulness' metric, as they reflect practical solutions that beef producers can implement, which evaluates the utility of answers in real-world applications, ensuring they are actionable and tailored to user needs. In contrast, ChatGPT tends to provide general answers within the broader agriculture domain, some of which are only high-level concepts, including artificial intelligence, robotics, and blockchain. Moreover, ChatGPT's responses rely solely on its internal knowledge without any external references, making it challenging to verify their correctness.

4 Conclusion

We propose BeefBot, a web-based interactive chatbot powered by a LLM, designed to offer precise, immediate, and long-term solutions to beef producers by leveraging the available knowledge in the beef industry. BeefBot's architecture, including its RAG system, model serving with Ollama, and frontend interface, is largely domain-independent and can be reused across sectors. Domain adaptation primarily requires collecting domain-specific data, generating high-quality Q&A datasets, and finetuning the LLM accordingly. This process would typically involve moderate effort depending on the data availability and complexity of domain-specific tasks.

[12]`https://github.com/ollama-webui/ollama-webui-lite`

References

Bhavika Arora, Dheeraj Singh Chaudhary, Mahima Satsangi, Mahima Yadav, Lotika Singh, and Prem Sewak Sudhish. 2020. Agribot: A natural language generative neural networks engine for agricultural applications. In *2020 International Conference on Contemporary Computing and Applications (IC3A)*, pages 28–33.

Angels Balaguer, Vinamra Benara, Renato Luiz de Freitas Cunha, Roberto de M. Estevão Filho, Todd Hendry, Daniel Holstein, Jennifer Marsman, Nick Mecklenburg, Sara Malvar, Leonardo O. Nunes, Rafael Padilha, Morris Sharp, Bruno Silva, Swati Sharma, Vijay Aski, and Ranveer Chandra. 2024. Rag vs fine-tuning: Pipelines, tradeoffs, and a case study on agriculture. *Preprint*, arXiv:2401.08406.

Sid Black, Stella Biderman, Eric Hallahan, Quentin Anthony, Leo Gao, Laurence Golding, Horace He, Connor Leahy, Kyle McDonell, Jason Phang, Michael Pieler, USVSN Sai Prashanth, Shivanshu Purohit, Laria Reynolds, Jonathan Tow, Ben Wang, and Samuel Weinbach. 2022. Gpt-neox-20b: An open-source autoregressive language model. *Preprint*, arXiv:2204.06745.

Tom B. Brown, Benjamin Mann, Nick Ryder, Melanie Subbiah, Jared Kaplan, Prafulla Dhariwal, Arvind Neelakantan, Pranav Shyam, Girish Sastry, Amanda Askell, Sandhini Agarwal, Ariel Herbert-Voss, Gretchen Krueger, Tom Henighan, Rewon Child, Aditya Ramesh, Daniel M. Ziegler, Jeffrey Wu, Clemens Winter, Christopher Hesse, Mark Chen, Eric Sigler, Mateusz Litwin, Scott Gray, Benjamin Chess, Jack Clark, Christopher Berner, Sam McCandlish, Alec Radford, Ilya Sutskever, and Dario Amodei. 2020. Language models are few-shot learners. In *Advances in Neural Information Processing Systems 33: Annual Conference on Neural Information Processing Systems 2020, NeurIPS 2020, December 6-12, 2020, virtual.*

Xiang Chen, Ningyu Zhang, Xin Xie, Shumin Deng, Yunzhi Yao, Chuanqi Tan, Fei Huang, Luo Si, and Huajun Chen. 2022. Knowprompt: Knowledge-aware prompt-tuning with synergistic optimization for relation extraction. In *WWW '22: The ACM Web Conference 2022, Virtual Event, Lyon, France, April 25 - 29, 2022*, pages 2778–2788. ACM.

Aakanksha Chowdhery, Sharan Narang, Jacob Devlin, Maarten Bosma, Gaurav Mishra, Adam Roberts, Paul Barham, Hyung Won Chung, Charles Sutton, Sebastian Gehrmann, Parker Schuh, Kensen Shi, Sasha Tsvyashchenko, Joshua Maynez, Abhishek Rao, Parker Barnes, Yi Tay, Noam Shazeer, Vinodkumar Prabhakaran, Emily Reif, Nan Du, Ben Hutchinson, Reiner Pope, James Bradbury, Jacob Austin, Michael Isard, Guy Gur-Ari, Pengcheng Yin, Toju Duke, Anselm Levskaya, Sanjay Ghemawat, Sunipa Dev, Henryk Michalewski, Xavier Garcia, Vedant Misra, Kevin Robinson, Liam Fedus, Denny Zhou, Daphne Ippolito, David Luan, Hyeontaek Lim, Barret Zoph, Alexander Spiridonov, Ryan Sepassi, David Dohan, Shivani Agrawal, Mark Omernick, Andrew M. Dai, Thanumalayan Sankaranarayana Pillai, Marie Pellat, Aitor Lewkowycz, Erica Moreira, Rewon Child, Oleksandr Polozov, Katherine Lee, Zongwei Zhou, Xuezhi Wang, Brennan Saeta, Mark Diaz, Orhan Firat, Michele Catasta, Jason Wei, Kathy Meier-Hellstern, Douglas Eck, Jeff Dean, Slav Petrov, and Noah Fiedel. 2023. Palm: Scaling language modeling with pathways. *J. Mach. Learn. Res.*, 24:240:1–240:113.

Darren Edge, Ha Trinh, Newman Cheng, Joshua Bradley, Alex Chao, Apurva Mody, Steven Truitt, and Jonathan Larson. 2024. From local to global: A graph rag approach to query-focused summarization. *Preprint*, arXiv:2404.16130.

Patrick S. H. Lewis, Ethan Perez, Aleksandra Piktus, Fabio Petroni, Vladimir Karpukhin, Naman Goyal, Heinrich Küttler, Mike Lewis, Wen-tau Yih, Tim Rocktäschel, Sebastian Riedel, and Douwe Kiela. 2020. Retrieval-augmented generation for knowledge-intensive NLP tasks. In *Advances in Neural Information Processing Systems 33: Annual Conference on Neural Information Processing Systems 2020, NeurIPS 2020, December 6-12, 2020, virtual.*

Chen Ling, Xujiang Zhao, Jiaying Lu, Chengyuan Deng, Can Zheng, Junxiang Wang, Tanmoy Chowdhury, Yun Li, Hejie Cui, Xuchao Zhang, Tianjiao Zhao, Amit Panalkar, Wei Cheng, Haoyu Wang, Yanchi Liu, Zhengzhang Chen, Haifeng Chen, Chris White, Quanquan Gu, Jian Pei, and Liang Zhao. 2023. Domain specialization as the key to make large language models disruptive: A comprehensive survey. *Preprint*, arXiv:2305.18703.

AI@Meta Llama Team. 2024. The llama 3 herd of models. A detailed contributor list can be found in the appendix of this paper.

Yun Luo, Zhen Yang, Fandong Meng, Yafu Li, Jie Zhou, and Yue Zhang. 2024. An empirical study of catastrophic forgetting in large language models during continual fine-tuning. *Preprint*, arXiv:2308.08747.

Long Ouyang, Jeffrey Wu, Xu Jiang, Diogo Almeida, Carroll L. Wainwright, Pamela Mishkin, Chong Zhang, Sandhini Agarwal, Katarina Slama, Alex Ray, John Schulman, Jacob Hilton, Fraser Kelton, Luke Miller, Maddie Simens, Amanda Askell, Peter Welinder, Paul F. Christiano, Jan Leike, and Ryan Lowe. 2022. Training language models to follow instructions with human feedback. In *Advances in Neural Information Processing Systems 35: Annual Conference on Neural Information Processing Systems 2022, NeurIPS 2022, New Orleans, LA, USA, November 28 - December 9, 2022.*

Oded Ovadia, Menachem Brief, Moshik Mishaeli, and Oren Elisha. 2024. Fine-tuning or retrieval? comparing knowledge injection in llms. *Preprint*, arXiv:2312.05934.

Alec Radford, Jong Wook Kim, Tao Xu, Greg Brockman, Christine McLeavey, and Ilya Sutskever. 2023. Robust speech recognition via large-scale weak supervision. In *International Conference on Machine Learning, ICML 2023, 23-29 July 2023, Honolulu, Hawaii, USA*, volume 202 of *Proceedings of Machine Learning Research*, pages 28492–28518. PMLR.

Karan Singhal, Tao Tu, Juraj Gottweis, Rory Sayres, Ellery Wulczyn, Le Hou, Kevin Clark, Stephen Pfohl, Heather Cole-Lewis, Darlene Neal, Mike Schaekermann, Amy Wang, Mohamed Amin, Sami Lachgar, Philip Mansfield, Sushant Prakash, Bradley Green, Ewa Dominowska, Blaise Aguera y Arcas, Nenad Tomasev, Yun Liu, Renee Wong, Christopher Semturs, S. Sara Mahdavi, Joelle Barral, Dale Webster, Greg S. Corrado, Yossi Matias, Shekoofeh Azizi, Alan Karthikesalingam, and Vivek Natarajan. 2023. Towards expert-level medical question answering with large language models. *Preprint*, arXiv:2305.09617.

Rohan Taori, Ishaan Gulrajani, Tianyi Zhang, Yann Dubois, Xuechen Li, Carlos Guestrin, Percy Liang, and Tatsunori B. Hashimoto. 2023. Stanford alpaca: An instruction-following llama model. https://github.com/tatsu-lab/stanford_alpaca.

Hugo Touvron, Thibaut Lavril, Gautier Izacard, Xavier Martinet, Marie-Anne Lachaux, Timothée Lacroix, Baptiste Rozière, Naman Goyal, Eric Hambro, Faisal Azhar, Aurélien Rodriguez, Armand Joulin, Edouard Grave, and Guillaume Lample. 2023a. Llama: Open and efficient foundation language models. *CoRR*, abs/2302.13971.

Hugo Touvron, Louis Martin, Kevin Stone, Peter Albert, Amjad Almahairi, Yasmine Babaei, Nikolay Bashlykov, Soumya Batra, Prajjwal Bhargava, Shruti Bhosale, Dan Bikel, Lukas Blecher, Cristian Canton Ferrer, Moya Chen, Guillem Cucurull, David Esiobu, Jude Fernandes, Jeremy Fu, Wenyin Fu, Brian Fuller, Cynthia Gao, Vedanuj Goswami, Naman Goyal, Anthony Hartshorn, Saghar Hosseini, Rui Hou, Hakan Inan, Marcin Kardas, Viktor Kerkez, Madian Khabsa, Isabel Kloumann, Artem Korenev, Punit Singh Koura, Marie-Anne Lachaux, Thibaut Lavril, Jenya Lee, Diana Liskovich, Yinghai Lu, Yuning Mao, Xavier Martinet, Todor Mihaylov, Pushkar Mishra, Igor Molybog, Yixin Nie, Andrew Poulton, Jeremy Reizenstein, Rashi Rungta, Kalyan Saladi, Alan Schelten, Ruan Silva, Eric Michael Smith, Ranjan Subramanian, Xiaoqing Ellen Tan, Binh Tang, Ross Taylor, Adina Williams, Jian Xiang Kuan, Puxin Xu, Zheng Yan, Iliyan Zarov, Yuchen Zhang, Angela Fan, Melanie Kambadur, Sharan Narang, Aurelien Rodriguez, Robert Stojnic, Sergey Edunov, and Thomas Scialom. 2023b. Llama 2: Open foundation and fine-tuned chat models. *Preprint*, arXiv:2307.09288.

Ashish Vaswani, Noam Shazeer, Niki Parmar, Jakob Uszkoreit, Llion Jones, Aidan N. Gomez, Lukasz Kaiser, and Illia Polosukhin. 2023. Attention is all you need. *Preprint*, arXiv:1706.03762.

Ruize Wang, Duyu Tang, Nan Duan, Zhongyu Wei, Xuanjing Huang, Jianshu Ji, Guihong Cao, Daxin Jiang, and Ming Zhou. 2021. K-adapter: Infusing knowledge into pre-trained models with adapters. In *Findings of the Association for Computational Linguistics: ACL/IJCNLP 2021, Online Event, August 1-6, 2021*, volume ACL/IJCNLP 2021 of *Findings of ACL*, pages 1405–1418. Association for Computational Linguistics.

Thomas Wolf, Lysandre Debut, Victor Sanh, Julien Chaumond, Clement Delangue, Anthony Moi, Pierric Cistac, Tim Rault, Remi Louf, Morgan Funtowicz, Joe Davison, Sam Shleifer, Patrick von Platen, Clara Ma, Yacine Jernite, Julien Plu, Canwen Xu, Teven Le Scao, Sylvain Gugger, Mariama Drame, Quentin Lhoest, and Alexander Rush. 2020. Transformers: State-of-the-art natural language processing. In *Proceedings of the 2020 Conference on Empirical Methods in Natural Language Processing: System Demonstrations*, pages 38–45, Online. Association for Computational Linguistics.

Hongyang Yang, Xiao-Yang Liu, and Christina Dan Wang. 2023. Fingpt: Open-source financial large language models. *Preprint*, arXiv:2306.06031.

Yanli Zhao, Andrew Gu, Rohan Varma, Liang Luo, Chien-Chin Huang, Min Xu, Less Wright, Hamid Shojanazeri, Myle Ott, Sam Shleifer, Alban Desmaison, Can Balioglu, Pritam Damania, Bernard Nguyen, Geeta Chauhan, Yuchen Hao, Ajit Mathews, and Shen Li. 2023. Pytorch fsdp: Experiences on scaling fully sharded data parallel. *Preprint*, arXiv:2304.11277.

A Appendix 1

```
Generate 5 question and answer pairs for the following content in the
<content></content> tag:

<content> {content} </content>

Follow these steps to ensure the questions and answers are practical,
detailed, and suitable for farmers and industry professionals:

1. Understand the Context: Ensure each question and answer is relevant to the
northern Australian beef industry and addresses real-world concerns of
farmers.

2. Use Simple Language: Write in clear, straightforward language that a beef
producer would use and understand. Avoid technical jargon unless it is
commonly known in the industry.

3. Cover a Wide Range of Topics: Include questions from the topic list below
to ensure comprehensive coverage.

4. Ensure Practicality: Each answer should provide actionable advice or
information that can be directly applied by farmers in the Australian beef
industry.

5. Reference Provided Knowledge Set: Base your answers on the documents
provided as the ground truth dataset. Ensure the answers are directly
supported by and verifiable within these documents.

6. Reflect Real-World Concerns: Craft questions that mirror the actual
problems and scenarios beef producers encounter. This includes daily
operational issues, long-term planning, and unexpected challenges.

Instructions for Generation:

Step 1: Start with a broad topic from the list.

Step 2: Identify a specific issue or common question within that topic.

Step 3: Formulate a clear and concise question a farmer might ask.

Step 4: Provide a detailed, actionable answer directly supported by the
ground truth dataset.

Step 5: Repeat the process, ensuring no duplication of questions or answers.
```

Figure 6: Evaluation Prompt

AI-Press: A Multi-Agent News Generating and Feedback Simulation System Powered by Large Language Models

Xiawei Liu[1†], Shiyue Yang[1†], Xinnong Zhang[2†], Haoyu Kuang[1], Libo Sun[1], Yihang Yang[1], Siming Chen[1], Xuanjing Huang[3], Zhongyu Wei[1,4‡]

[1]School of Data Science, Fudan University, China

[2]Institute of Science and Technology for Brain-Inspired Intelligence, Fudan University

[3]School of Computer Science, Fudan University, China

[4]Research Institute of Intelligent Complex Systems, Fudan University, China

{liuxw24, shiyueyang24, xnzhang23}@m.fudan.edu.cn

{simingchen, xjhuang, zywei}@fudan.edu.cn

Abstract

The rise of various social platforms has transformed journalism. The growing demand for news content has led to the increased use of large language models (LLMs) in news production due to their speed and cost-effectiveness.

However, LLMs still encounter limitations in professionalism and ethical judgment in news generation. Additionally, predicting public feedback is usually difficult before news is released.

To tackle these challenges, we introduce AI-Press, an automated news drafting and polishing system based on multi-agent collaboration and Retrieval-Augmented Generation. We develop a feedback simulation system that generates public feedback considering demographic distributions. Through extensive quantitative and qualitative evaluations, our system shows significant improvements in news-generating capabilities and verifies the effectiveness of public feedback simulation.

1 Introduction

Powerful Large Language Models (LLMs) like ChatGPT (OpenAI, 2024) are emerging as potential game changers in the press industry (van Dalen, 2024).

Journalists hold diverse attitudes and technological acceptance of LLMs (Gómez-Calderón and Ceballos, 2024).

Some of them are concerned that LLMs pose a potential threat to their profession (Carlson, 2015). They strongly defend their authoritative role in information dissemination and emphasize the necessity of their active participation when LLMs are integrated into news production (Milosavljević and Vobič, 2019).

As it is generally acknowledged that LLMs offer advantages in enhancing the objectivity, timeliness, and efficiency of content production (Simon, 2024), more and more editorial offices, including news studios and journal publishers, are utilizing LLMs to boost efficiency and effectiveness during their working pipeline (Whang, 2024) by issuing application guidelines or recommendations for the use of LLMs (Miller et al., 2023; Victor et al., 2023; Hamm et al., 2024).

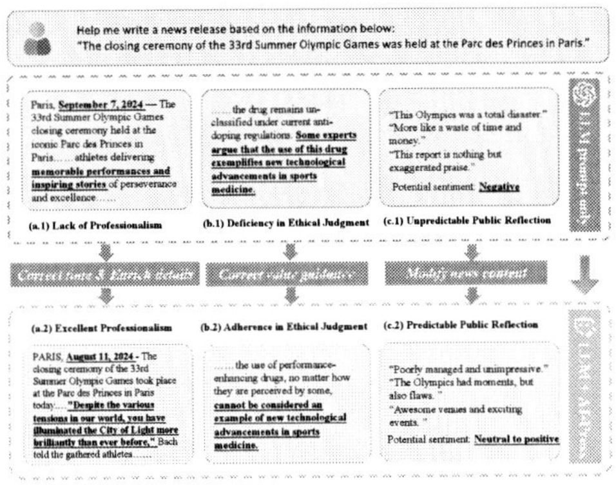

Figure 1: AI-Press overcomes the challenges faced by the prompt-only LLM method.

While LLMs can generate a press release in seconds, the quality of the generated content is not yet satisfying for journalists. We conduct further research and reveal three main challenges that need to be addressed to achieve full integration of LLMs into the news industry.

LLMs lack professionalism in drafting press releases. They have significant limitations that conflict with journalistic norms and values (Nishal and Diakopoulos, 2024). Additionally, LLMs may experience "hallucination" issues when generating long texts. This is particularly problematic in the press industry, which demands high accuracy and trustworthiness (Desrochers et al., 2024), as shown in Figure 1 (a).

LLMs exhibit limitations in making ethical judgments within complex news contexts. Rely-

†These authors contribute equally to this work.

‡Corresponding author

Proceedings of the 31st International Conference on Computational Linguistics: System Demonstrations, pages 63–82
January 19–24, 2025.

ing solely on LLMs for ethical decisions in these scenarios can result in inaccurate or inappropriate outcomes (Li et al., 2024). Therefore, ethical oversight in machine-generated journalistic content is crucial. Integrating LLMs with critical supervision from human editors is essential (Whang, 2024). Figure 1 (b) highlights this deficiency in ethical judgment, emphasizing the necessity for human intervention.

Journalists struggle to accurately predict public trends following a news release. This difficulty arises from the inherently complex and dynamic nature of public feedback, which is influenced by multifaceted factors. The diversity and heterogeneity of the audience further complicate predictions, making it challenging to foresee how different individuals and groups will react to specific news content. Figure 1 (c) illustrates the same event with different styles of narration may cause varied and unpredictable public reactions.

Therefore, we propose a framework that combines both human involvement and automated agent collaboration for news production, namely, **AI-Press**[1]. This framework leverages Retrieval-Augmented Generation (RAG) through interactions between intelligent agents to automatically draft and polish news. Additionally, we develop a simulation method based on demographic distribution to reflect public feedback accurately in real-world scenarios. This allows journalists to modify content accordingly before its release. By comparing the scores of AI-Press-generated texts and prompt-only language models,

we found that our system significantly enhances the newswriting capabilities of language models. Moreover, the simulated comments effectively mirror real-world public feedback on the news.

To sum up, the main contributions of our system are as follows:

- We develop an automated news drafting and polishing system that employs multi-agent collaboration and RAG. This system facilitates both the coarse-grained and fine-grained processing of new content.
- We implement a true-to-life news feedback simulation system that enables customized audience demographic distributions for targeted news delivery.
- We perform a thorough evaluation of our system, incorporating both quantitative and qualitative experiments to assess the quality of the news and the effectiveness of the simulation. The overall results fully demonstrate that the AI-Press successfully overcomes the challenges and achieves impressive performance.

2 Related Works

2.1 Retrieval-Augmented Generation

The primary characteristic of any information becoming 'news information' is accuracy (Anatassova, 2004). However, LLMs pose a risk of generating false or misleading information in the process of news generation due to their potential illusions (Vatani Nezafat, 2024). Retrieval-augmented generation (RAG) addresses this issue by combining external knowledge sources with LLMs to improve the quality and accuracy of the output. This method shows promise in reducing the errors associated with LLMs and ensuring the accuracy of generated news (Chen et al., 2024).

2.2 Multi-Agent Framework

Journalism work is teamwork, which is the main reason for choosing the 'multi-agent' method. By leveraging the diverse capabilities and roles of individual agents within a multi-agent framework, it can tackle complex tasks through collaboration (Han et al., 2024; Anatassova, 2004). MetaGPT provides a meta-programming framework that integrates efficient human workflows with LLM-based multi-agent collaboration (Hong et al., 2024). The multi-agent framework is widely applied in areas such as healthcare (Fan et al., 2024), law (Cui et al., 2024; Yue et al., 2023) and has yielded remarkable results.

2.3 Role-Playing Agents

Employing LLMs to build role-playing agents (RPAs) can effectively simulate typical representatives ranging from individuals to demographic groups (Li et al., 2023). RPAs have wide applications in fields such as entertainment[2], psychotherapy (Stade et al., 2024), economics (Fu et al., 2023), and social research (Grossmann et al., 2023). Major implementation approaches include refined prompts and fine-tuning on datasets tailored to specific roles (Sun et al., 2024).

[1] *license*: https://www.apache.org/licenses/LICENSE-2.0
video link: https://youtu.be/TmjfJrbzaRU

[2] https://character.ai

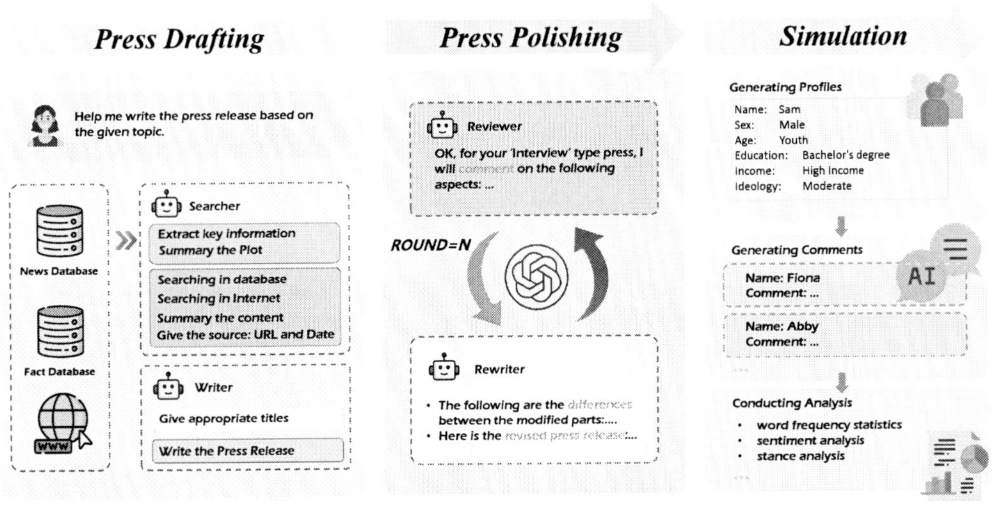

Figure 2: AI-Press System Framework

3 AI Press System

In this section, we will introduce the framework design for the AI-Press System.

3.1 Framework Design

The news workflow is referred to as 'news flow'. In terms of the horizontal production process of Reuters news products, the basic steps include *collection*, *processing*, *publishing*, and *feedback* (Shen et al., 2008). Based on the above 'news flow', we design the entire framework for the AI-Press System, as shown in Figure 2.

To highlight 'human-in-the-loop' in the news flow, we adopt a modularized workflow instead of an end-to-end one.

Among the three modules, the **Press Drafting Module** is designed for the collection and coarse-grained processing of news material and information, the **Press Polishing Module** aims at the fine-grained processing of news content, and the **Simulation Module** simulates the process of publishing and feedback.

3.2 Press Drafting Module

The primary task of the Press Drafting Module is to conduct multidimensional information retrieval and draft press releases based on provided topics or materials. We have designed two types of agents, **Searchers** and **Writers**, to assist journalists in information collection and drafting. The user interface is shown in Appendix A.1.

The core function of Searcher is information retrieval and collection. To enhance accuracy and effectiveness, the Searcher first extracts key information and organizes events from the given topics and materials before initiating retrieval. To maintain a balance of professionalism, accuracy, and timeliness, we utilize three sources for retrieval: *the news database*, *the fact database*, and *the Internet*. The prompts for searchers are detailed in Appendix C.1.

Both the news database and the fact database are built on local vector databases. The news database contains a dataset of 200,000 high-quality articles from authoritative news websites, covering four major themes: *politics*, *economy*, *sports*, and *entertainment*, as well as three major genres: *news*, *commentary*, and *features*. To avoid extracting irrelevant or incorrect information, Writers will only refer to the framework and writing style of the news in news database, see Appendix C.2.

The search results are then forwarded to the Writers for title and press drafting, completing the coarse-grained processing of the news release. Given that different news genres require unique writing frameworks and emphases, we have established specific writing guidelines for Writers to ensure professional outputs, as detailed in Appendix C.2.

3.3 Press Polishing Module

The Press Polishing Module aims to refine the initial news draft through multiple rounds of editing to achieve optimal results. We design two types of agents: **Reviewers** and **Rewriters**, to collaborate and handle the fine-grained processing of press releases. The Reviewer provides targeted modification suggestions based on the specified news release genre, and the Rewriter implements changes according to these suggestions. The prompts are shown in Appendix D.

We emphasize the active role of journalists in this module. Journalists can set the number of modification rounds to achieve the desired news release quality. And the collaboration between Reviewer and Rewriter agents will be visually displayed. The user interface is depicted in Appendix A.2.

3.4 Simulation Module

The Simulation Module functions as a sandbox for news publishing and feedback. To enhance the authenticity of the simulation, we annotate nearly 10,000 anonymized real user data from social media platforms, creating a user profile pool with demographic tags. The real user data and the annotation method are detailed in Appendix F. The user profile pool will be used to generate audiences for news delivery.

Users can customize various demographic factors of the news audience and the system automatically draws samples from the user profile pool to create specific audience. Upon delivering news to a targeted audience, their corresponding comments will be simulated. Subsequently, a word cloud map, sentiment scores, and a statistical analysis of stances will be presented. The corresponding user interface is presented in Appendix A.3. The prompts for simulated comments generating are shown in Appendix E.

4 Experimental Setup

4.1 Experiment on Press Generating

Task Definition. We compare the press releases generated by our framework with those generated by prompt-only LLM (see Appendix B for prompts) to prove our AI-Press framework is efficient. Although the AI-Press System emphasizes 'human-in-the-loop', to avoid biases caused by human factors on the evaluation results, human participation is strictly excluded during the experiment, ensuring that the agents automatically complete the entire process.

Data. To demonstrate that our system can achieve good quality in different news categories and fields, we use 300 press releases as our test data, including three genres: news, profile, and commentary. The types cover various fields, and the sources include internationally renowned news organizations such as *Reuters*[1], *BBC*[2], and *New York Times*[3], as shown in Appendix G.2. We use the abstract of the original press release as the initial material to generate press articles. Meanwhile, to avoid data leakage and potential bias, the local news database used by the AI-Press System does not include press articles for testing.

Baselines. Considering the potential bias caused by different model bases, we employ GPT-3.5[4] (Openai, 2022), GPT-4o[5] (OpenAI, 2024), Claude-3.5[6] (anthropic, 2024), Gemini-1.5-pro[7] (Team, 2024) and Qwen-2.5[8] (Yang et al., 2024)as baseline models.

Evaluation metrics. To comprehensively evaluate the quality of press releases of different genres, we design a set of evaluation metrics for three types of articles. These metrics are designed to capture the unique characteristics of each genre and quantify multiple key attributes of the articles. For example, we use richness, depth, uniqueness, inspiration and readability to evaluate the quality of a profile. We choose GPT-4o as a grading assistant through specific prompts to objectively score the generated articles, which is shown in Appendix G.1.

4.2 Experiment on Simulation

Task Definition. Our expectations for the simulation are to achieve two core objectives. First, there is a significant difference in the feedback of the simulated population. Second, the behavior of the simulated population possesses realism. We designed two experiments to verify whether our simulation achieved the above objectives.

- *Simulation Variance Experiment* will verify that simulated populations with different distributions will exhibit significant differences in sentiment and stance towards the same news, thereby proving that changes in the distribution of simulated populations can accurately and sensitively affect the direction of

[1] https://www.reuters.com
[2] https://www.bbc.com
[3] https://www.nytimes.com
[4] `gpt-3.5-turbo-16k`
[5] `gpt-4o-2024-05-13`
[6] `claude-3-5-sonnet-20240620`
[7] `gemini-1.5-pro`
[8] `qwen-plus-latest`

Metric Dimensions	Original Press	GPT3.5	GPT3.5 AI-Press	GPT4o	GPT4o AI-Press	Qwen2.5	Qwen2.5 AI-Press	Claude3.5	Claude3.5 AI-Press	Gemini1.5pro	Gemini1.5pro AI-Press
News											
comprehensiveness	3.67	2.88	3.43	3.50	**3.83**	3.76	3.78	3.10	3.69	2.74	3.17
depth	3.00	2.11	2.63	2.71	**3.16**	2.89	2.89	2.32	2.99	2.20	2.51
objectivity	4.29	3.90	3.97	4.23	4.38	4.43	**4.48**	4.16	4.31	3.92	4.09
importance	3.87	3.72	4.00	4.00	4.04	4.02	**4.09**	3.88	4.04	3.49	3.88
readability	4.53	4.56	4.55	4.82	4.77	4.87	**4.91**	4.66	4.83	4.25	4.68
Profile											
richness	3.09	2.20	2.76	2.86	3.04	3.25	**3.68**	2.56	2.72	2.74	2.72
depth	2.74	1.96	2.43	2.46	2.61	2.73	**3.00**	2.21	2.32	2.60	2.32
uniqueness	3.15	2.51	3.07	2.96	3.13	3.15	**3.36**	2.88	2.86	3.19	2.86
inspiration	3.64	3.09	3.74	3.69	3.79	4.01	**4.19**	3.40	3.40	3.25	3.40
readability	4.09	3.87	4.10	4.08	4.16	4.31	**4.63**	3.98	4.06	4.03	4.06
Commentary											
comprehensiveness	**4.28**	3.19	3.52	3.89	4.13	3.83	4.02	2.39	3.22	3.71	3.73
clarity of opinions	3.87	3.99	4.01	4.46	**4.50**	4.27	4.33	3.37	3.83	4.38	4.26
sufficiency of evidence	**4.60**	2.87	3.14	3.59	3.97	3.58	3.87	2.42	3.31	3.36	3.52
relevance	4.62	4.31	4.57	4.88	**4.93**	4.84	4.92	3.08	4.42	4.75	4.77
readability	3.89	3.95	4.04	**4.41**	4.38	4.30	4.35	4.01	4.05	4.32	4.23

Table 1: Press Generating Evaluation Results. The **bold** number represents the best results, and the underlined number represents the second-best results. The scores of all metrics are range from 0 to 5.

public feedback.

- *Simulation Consistency Experiment* will verify that the sentiment and stance reactions of simulated populations with the same distribution are close to those of real populations, thereby proving that the public feedback trends obtained through simulation can accurately predict the real public feedback trends.

Data. We selected *New York Times* as our news source and gathered representative articles with over 100 comments in three areas: politics, economy, and conflict.

Additionally, we collected real user comments from these articles. More informations about the selected news article and the number of comments is displayed in Appendix G.3. To understand the distribution of the commenting group, we meticulously labeled users by GPT-4o based on the content of their comments. The prompt is detailed in Appendix F.2.We manually verify these labels to ensure their accuracy and take them as the real population distribution.

Evaluation metrics.

To enhance the accuracy of our simulation, we utilize the high-performance GPT-4o for user label annotation and the simulation process of two experiments. In *Simulation Variance Experiment*, we use GPT-4o to assess the sentiment and stance of comments from different distributions.

In *Simulation Consistency Experiment*, we use GPT-4o to score the sentiment of real comments and simulated comments based on real population distribution, with a score range of [-1,1].

The prompts are shown in Appendix G.4. And we use kernel density estimation (KDE) to evaluate the simulation effect.

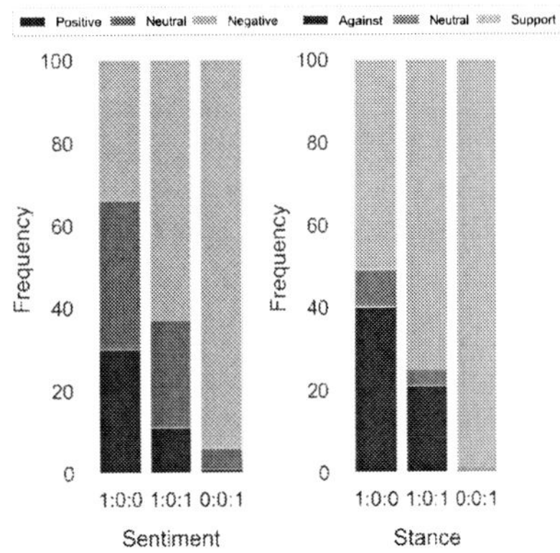

Figure 3: Simulation Variance Experiment Results. The sentiment tendencies and stances of people with different ideological distributions towards the same news. The distribution ratio of ideological inclinations is: Conservative: Moderate: Liberal = 1:0:0, 1:0:1, 0:0:1.

5 Results

5.1 Analysis on Press Generating Evaluation

The specific evaluation metrics and scoring results are summarized in Table 1.

News genre. In the news genre, the models show varying levels of performance across different indicators but overall, it can be observed that the models integrated with AI-Press generally demonstrated enhanced performance compared to their

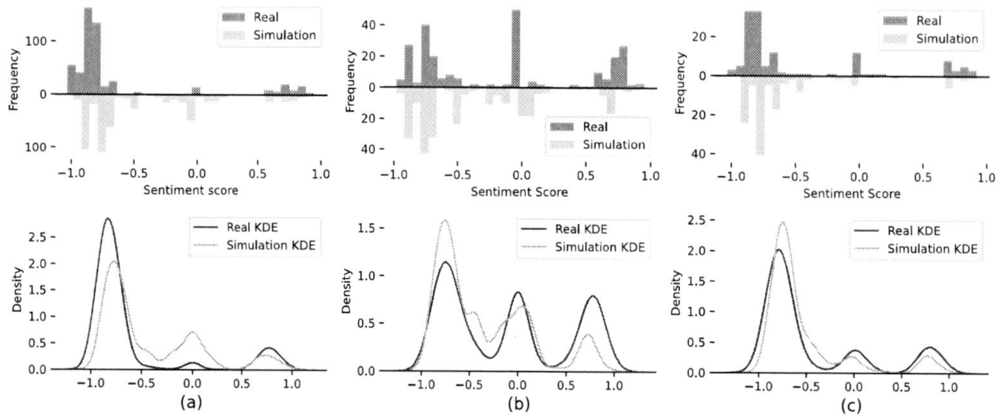

Figure 4: Simulation Consistency Experiment Results. Frequency statistics and KDE of sentiment scores for real and simulated comments. News (a) focuses on questions regarding Trump's age and capacity. News (b) delves into the challenges of offshore wind. News (c) reports on the conflict between Israel and Hezbollah.

counterparts without it. GPT4o+AI-Press stands out in terms of comprehensiveness and depth, while Qwen2.5+AI-Press excels in objectivity, importance, and readability.

Profile genre. In the profile genre, Qwen2.5+AI-Press achieves the highest scores in all five indicators. Similar to the news genre, the integration of AI-Press significantly enhances the performance of the models in the profile genre as well.

Commentary genre. In the commentary section, Qwen2.5+AI-Press and GPT4o+AI-Press exhibit the most optimal performance in different aspects. The participation of AI-Press still greatly improves the quality of news. It should be noted that the content of the commentary section is typically complex and requires subject initiative. Consequently, LLMs still find it challenging to surpass articles penned by professional journalists in terms of comprehensiveness and the sufficiency of evidence.

5.2 Analysis on Simulation Evaluation

We have verified whether changes in the distribution of the simulated population can significantly influence the simulated public feedback trends. We set the ratios of conservative, moderate, and liberal in the simulated population to 1:0:0, 1:0:1, and 0:0:1, respectively, and then release news[1].

We subsequently analyze the sentiment and stance distributions of the comments under different population distributions. As shown in Figure 3, there is a notable increase in comments with Negative sentiment and Support stance as the proportion of liberals increases.

News\Round	0	1	2	3	4	5
(a)	4.0	4.2	4.2	4.2	4.2	4.2
(b)	4.2	4.2	4.4	4.4	4.4	4.4
(c)	3.6	3.6	4.0	3.6	3.6	4.0

Table 2: Average Socre of the News with Different Polish Rounds.

The consistency between simulated and real feedback is a crucial metric for gauging the success of a simulation. We conduct a study comparing the feedback of simulated and real populations to the same news items under identical distribution conditions. Figure 4 illustrates the sentiment distribution of simulated and real comments for three news articles (a)[1], (b)[2], and (c)[3], where the KDE of the two are remarkably similar.

5.3 Ablation Study on Polish Round

We utilized the same three pieces of news mentioned in §5.2 to assess the impact of polish round N. As presented in Table 2, with the increment of the number of Polish rounds, the quality of the news first improves and then tends to remain unchanged. The appropriate number of rounds for polishing is 2.

[1]As Debate Looms, Trump Is Now the One Facing Questions About Age and Capacity

[2]Offshore Wind Slowed by Broken Blades, Rising Costs and Angry Fishermen

[3]Israel Strikes Hezbollah as Nasrallah Vows Retribution

6 Conclusion

This paper contributes to both the automated news-generating pipeline and the simulation of public feedback following news dissemination. In our work, we introduce **AI-Press**, a news auto-drafting and polishing system based on multi-agent collaboration and RAG.

Furthermore, we design a public feedback simulation system for news dissemination, which can generate corresponding feedback by setting simulated population distributions. Finally, we conduct extensive and comprehensive evaluations of both the news-generating system and the feedback simulation, including quantitative experiments based on news genres and qualitative experiments with comments' sentiments and stances as indicators. The results of both experiments fully demonstrate the effectiveness of our work.

Acknowledgement

This research is supported by National Key R&D Program of China (2023YFF1204800) and National Natural Science Foundation of China (No. 62176058). The project's computational resources are supported by CFFF platform of Fudan University.

Limitations

Due to the variety of news genres and their significant differences, we still need to further investigate genre characteristics to make our system applicable to more genres. Also, we will evaluate the performance using different models with more comprehensive metrics, and human evaluations will also be included.

Ethics Statement

We are committed to protecting individuals' privacy and rights in all aspects of our work. User data from social media platforms are anonymized for privacy. Moreover, all sourced historical data are public content, and their use complies with relevant privacy regulations. The news articles utilized in our databases or evaluations are sourced exclusively from reputable and authoritative news organizations, ensuring the integrity and reliability of our data. We take great care to ensure that these articles do not contain sensitive or harmful content.

References

V Anatassova. 2004. Journalistic multi-agent system. In *2004 2nd International IEEE Conference on'Intelligent Systems'. Proceedings (IEEE Cat. No. 04EX791)*, volume 3, pages 86–91. IEEE.

anthropic. 2024. Claude 3.5 sonnet.

Matt Carlson. 2015. The robotic reporter automated journalism and the redefinition of labor, compositional forms, and journalistic authority. *DIGITAL JOURNALISM*, 3(3, SI):416–431.

Jiawei Chen, Hongyu Lin, Xianpei Han, and Le Sun. 2024. Benchmarking large language models in retrieval-augmented generation. In *Proceedings of the AAAI Conference on Artificial Intelligence*, volume 38, pages 17754–17762.

Jiaxi Cui, Munan Ning, Zongjian Li, Bohua Chen, Yang Yan, Hao Li, Bin Ling, Yonghong Tian, and Li Yuan. 2024. Chatlaw: A multi-agent collaborative legal assistant with knowledge graph enhanced mixture-of-experts large language model. *Preprint*, arXiv:2306.16092.

Sarah Desrochers, James Wilson, and Matthew Beauchesne. 2024. Reducing hallucinations in large language models through contextual position encoding.

Zhihao Fan, Jialong Tang, Wei Chen, Siyuan Wang, Zhongyu Wei, Jun Xi, Fei Huang, and Jingren Zhou. 2024. Ai hospital: Benchmarking large language models in a multi-agent medical interaction simulator. *Preprint*, arXiv:2402.09742.

Yao Fu, Hao Peng, Tushar Khot, and Mirella Lapata. 2023. Improving language model negotiation with self-play and in-context learning from ai feedback. *Preprint*, arXiv:2305.10142.

Igor Grossmann, Matthew Feinberg, Dawn C. Parker, Nicholas A. Christakis, Philip E. Tetlock, and William A. Cunningham. 2023. Ai and the transformation of social science research. *Science*, 380(6650):1108–1109.

Bernardo Gómez-Calderón and Yaiza Ceballos. 2024. Journalism and artificial intelligence. the treatment of the chatbots in the spanish press. *index.comunicación*, 14(1):281–300.

Bernd Hamm, Luis Marti-Bonmati, and Francesco Sardanelli. 2024. Esr journals editors' joint statement on guidelines for the use of large language models by authors, reviewers, and editors. *EUROPEAN RADIOLOGY*.

Shanshan Han, Qifan Zhang, Yuhang Yao, Weizhao Jin, Zhaozhuo Xu, and Chaoyang He. 2024. Llm multi-agent systems: Challenges and open problems. *arXiv preprint arXiv:2402.03578*.

Sirui Hong, Mingchen Zhuge, Jonathan Chen, Xiawu Zheng, Yuheng Cheng, Jinlin Wang, Ceyao Zhang, Zili Wang, Steven Ka Shing Yau, Zijuan Lin, Liyang

Zhou, Chenyu Ran, Lingfeng Xiao, Chenglin Wu, and Jürgen Schmidhuber. 2024. MetaGPT: Meta programming for a multi-agent collaborative framework. In *The Twelfth International Conference on Learning Representations*.

Guohao Li, Hasan Abed Al Kader Hammoud, Hani Itani, Dmitrii Khizbullin, and Bernard Ghanem. 2023. Camel: Communicative agents for "mind" exploration of large language model society https://www.camel-ai.org. In *ADVANCES IN NEURAL INFORMATION PROCESSING SYSTEMS 36 (NEURIPS 2023)*, Advances in Neural Information Processing Systems. 37th Conference on Neural Information Processing Systems (NeurIPS), New Orleans, LA, DEC 10-16, 2023.

Miao Li, Ming-Bin Chen, Bo Tang, ShengbinHou ShengbinHou, Pengyu Wang, Haiying Deng, Zhiyu Li, Feiyu Xiong, Keming Mao, Cheng Peng, et al. 2024. Newsbench: A systematic evaluation framework for assessing editorial capabilities of large language models in chinese journalism. In *Proceedings of the 62nd Annual Meeting of the Association for Computational Linguistics (Volume 1: Long Papers)*, pages 9993–10014.

Kathy Miller, Emilie Gunn, Angela Cochran, Hal Burstein, Jonathan W. W. Friedberg, Stephanie Wheeler, and Paul Frankel. 2023. Use of large language models and artificial intelligence tools in works submitted to <i>journal of clinical oncology</i>. *JOURNAL OF CLINICAL ONCOLOGY*, 41(19):3480+.

Marko Milosavljević and Igor Vobič. 2019. Human still in the loop: Editors reconsider the ideals of professional journalism through automation. *Digital journalism*, 7(8):1098–1116.

Sachita Nishal and Nicholas Diakopoulos. 2024. Envisioning the applications and implications of generative ai for news media. *arXiv preprint arXiv:2402.18835*.

Openai. 2022. Introducing chatgpt.

OpenAI. 2024. Gpt-4 technical report. *Preprint*, arXiv:2303.08774.

Miao Shen, Mengruan Huang, and Zhengmao Zhan. 2008. Research on the production process management system of reuters news. *Today's Mass Media*, (02):71–73.

Felix Simon. 2024. Artificial intelligence in the news: how ai retools, rationalizes, and reshapes journalism and the public arena.

Elizabeth Stade, Shannon Stirman, Lyle Ungar, Cody Boland, H. Schwartz, David Yaden, João Sedoc, Robert DeRubeis, Robb Willer, and Johannes Eichstaedt. 2024. Large language models could change the future of behavioral healthcare: a proposal for responsible development and evaluation. *npj Mental Health Research*, 3.

Libo Sun, Siyuan Wang, Xuanjing Huang, and Zhongyu Wei. 2024. Identity-driven hierarchical role-playing agents. *Preprint*, arXiv:2407.19412.

Gemini Team. 2024. Gemini 1.5: Unlocking multimodal understanding across millions of tokens of context. *Preprint*, arXiv:2403.05530.

Arjen van Dalen. 2024. Revisiting the algorithms behind the headlines. how journalists respond to professional competition of generative ai. *Journalism Practice*, pages 1–18.

Mohammad Vatani Nezafat. 2024. *Fake News Detection With Retrieval Augmented Generative Artificial Intelligence*. Ph.D. thesis.

Bryan G. Victor, Rebeccah L. Sokol, Lauri Goldkind, and Brian E. Perron. 2023. Recommendations for social work researchers and journal editors on the use of generative ai and large language models. *JOURNAL OF THE SOCIETY FOR SOCIAL WORK AND RESEARCH*, 14(3):563–577.

Yunhee Whang. 2024. Chatgpt for editors: enhancing efficiency and effectiveness. *SCIENCE EDITING*, 11(1):84–90.

An Yang, Baosong Yang, Binyuan Hui, Bo Zheng, Bowen Yu, Chang Zhou, Chengpeng Li, Chengyuan Li, Dayiheng Liu, Fei Huang, Guanting Dong, Haoran Wei, Huan Lin, Jialong Tang, Jialin Wang, Jian Yang, Jianhong Tu, Jianwei Zhang, Jianxin Ma, Jianxin Yang, Jin Xu, Jingren Zhou, Jinze Bai, Jinzheng He, Junyang Lin, Kai Dang, Keming Lu, Keqin Chen, Kexin Yang, Mei Li, Mingfeng Xue, Na Ni, Pei Zhang, Peng Wang, Ru Peng, Rui Men, Ruize Gao, Runji Lin, Shijie Wang, Shuai Bai, Sinan Tan, Tianhang Zhu, Tianhao Li, Tianyu Liu, Wenbin Ge, Xiaodong Deng, Xiaohuan Zhou, Xingzhang Ren, Xinyu Zhang, Xipin Wei, Xuancheng Ren, Xuejing Liu, Yang Fan, Yang Yao, Yichang Zhang, Yu Wan, Yunfei Chu, Yuqiong Liu, Zeyu Cui, Zhenru Zhang, Zhifang Guo, and Zhihao Fan. 2024. Qwen2 technical report. *Preprint*, arXiv:2407.10671.

Shengbin Yue, Wei Chen, Siyuan Wang, Bingxuan Li, Chenchen Shen, Shujun Liu, Yuxuan Zhou, Yao Xiao, Song Yun, Xuanjing Huang, and Zhongyu Wei. 2023. Disc-lawllm: Fine-tuning large language models for intelligent legal services. *Preprint*, arXiv:2309.11325.

A User Interface

A.1 Press Drafting Module

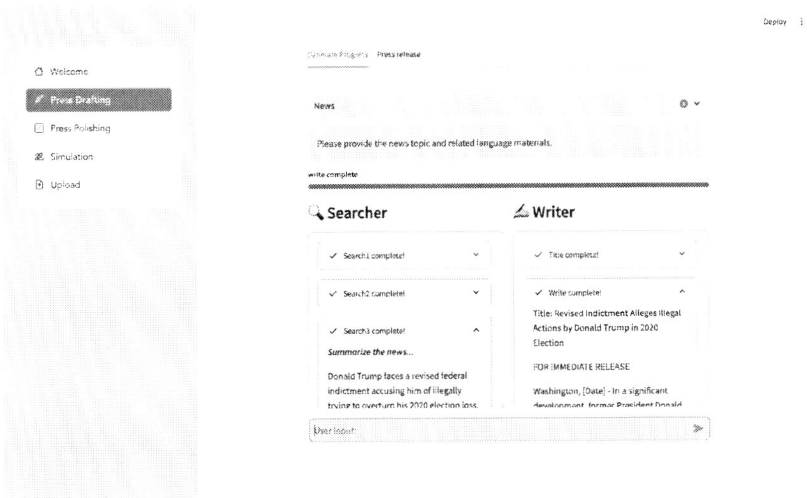

Figure 5: A screenshot displays a sample press-drafting interface, showcasing the output results generated by the searching and writing agents.

A.2 Press Polishing Module

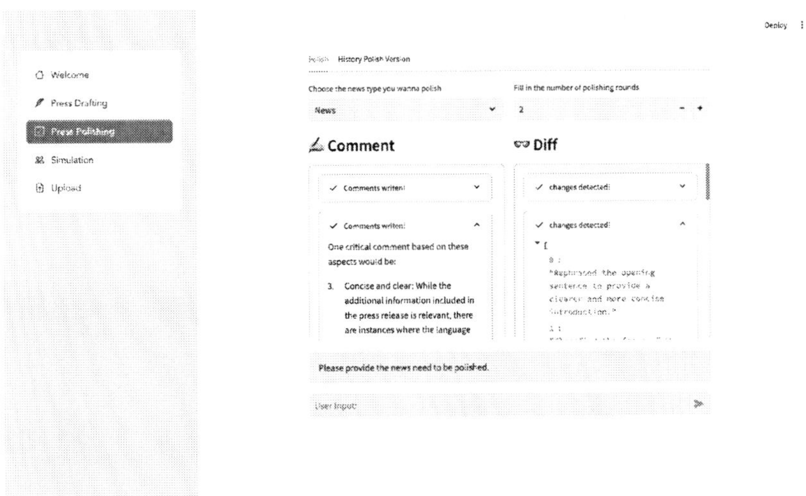

Figure 6: A screenshot presents a sample press-polishing interface, illustrating the output results produced by the reviewing and rewriting agents.

A.3 Simulation Module

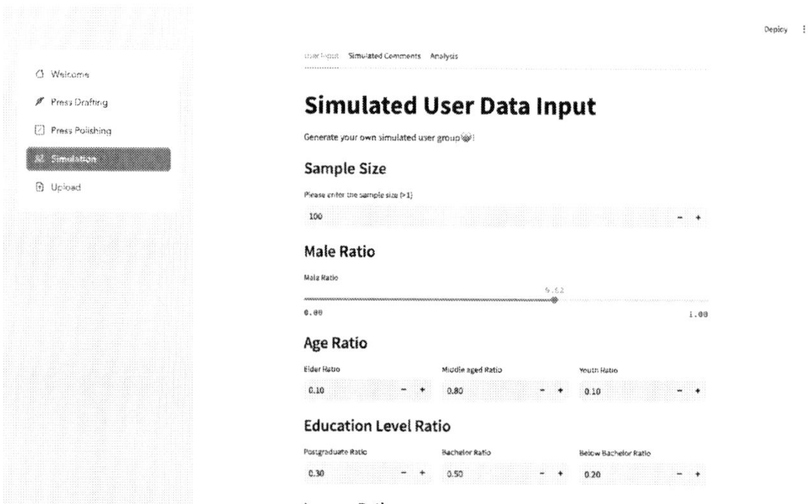

Figure 7: A screenshot illustrates the user interface for generating a specific population distribution, utilizing customized demographic indicators.

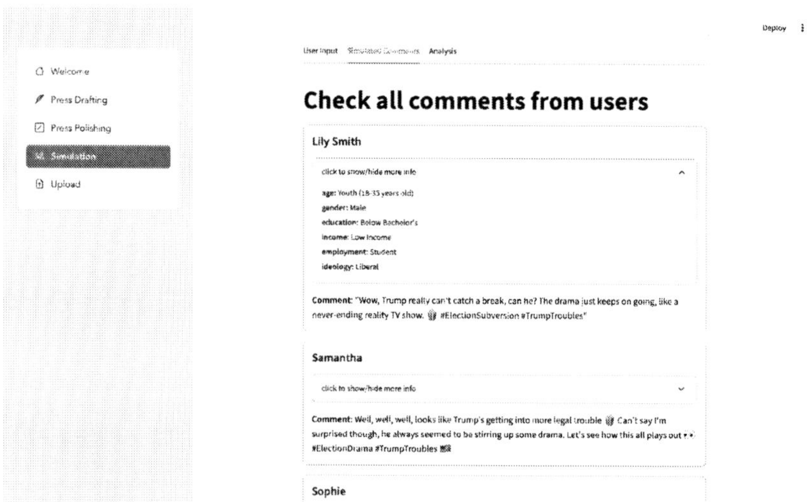

Figure 8: A screenshot presents the generated simulated comments. The specific demographic indicators of the simulated commenters are also displayed.

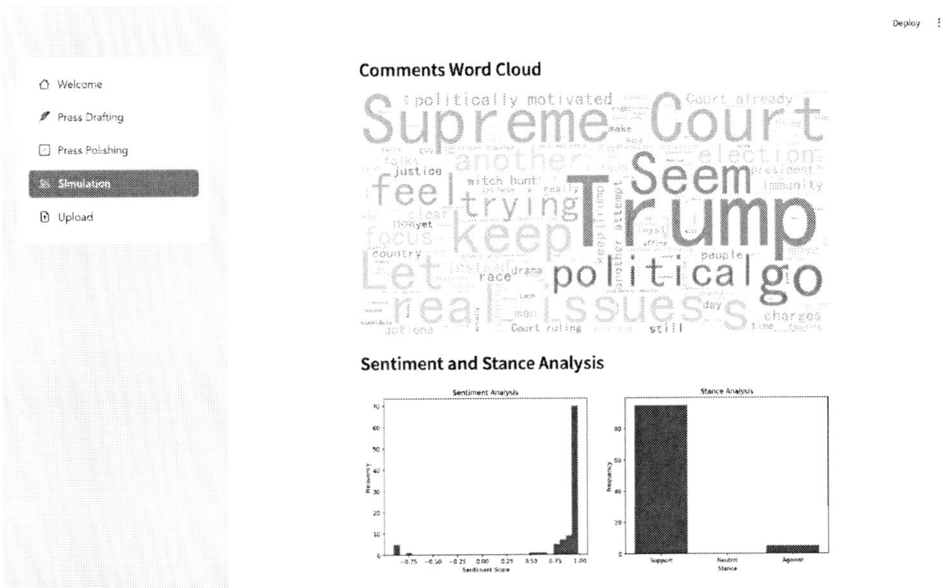

Figure 9: The screenshot shows the analysis interface of simulated feedback, which displays the word cloud of comments and the frequency statistics of sentiments and stances.

B Prompts for LLMs

Genres	Prompts
News	Write a news release with a genre NEWS based on the following content. News reports on current events with timeliness and objectivity. content:{content}.
Profile	Write a news release with a genre of PROFILE based on the following content. Profile journalism offers in-depth looks at people or topics. content:{content}.
Commentary	Write a news release with a genre of COMMENTARY based on the following content. Commentary provides analysis and opinion on current events. content:{content}.

Table 3: Prompts for LLMs. {content} is news corpus.

C Prompts for Agents on Press Drafting Module

C.1 Prompts for Searchers

Searchers	Prompts
Searcher1	{content} Based on the above corpus, extract the core elements of the event, including time, place, key people, etc. Here are the detailed instructions: Identify the exact date and timeframe of the event. Identify the exact location of the incident, including the city, region, or even a specific place. Identify the key people involved, such as the dominant person, the victim, or the relevant authority.
Searcher2	{content} Sort out the passage of time timeline and key plot points based on the provided news corpus. Describe the course of events and record important steps and twists in time sequential order. Extract key episodes and details, e.g. flashpoints, important decisions, or actions. For example, at YYYY-MM-DD, some events happened, etc.

Table 4: Prompts for Searchers. {content} is news corpus, the same as the ones in Table 3.

C.2 Prompts for Writers

Writers	Prompts
Title	{content} Based on the content of UserRequirement, extract the core elements, process, key plot of the event, and the collected background information and impact. Propose 3-5 headlines for the news. Please return the result based on the following JSON structure: [{{"title": str}}].
Content of News	{content} Select the most suitable title from the Title. A good news headline should be accurate, concise, and attractive. Complete the writing of the press release and present a complete, professional, excellent, and directly publishable press release. Requirement: - Refer to the language style, article structure, and narrative techniques of [News Database], maintain objectivity and neutrality, and present the occurrence, development, and results of events in a clear structure. Use concise and clear language, avoiding lengthy and complex sentences as well as obscure vocabulary. - You can refer to the factual basis that may be used in the [Fact Database] (or not) to correct the misinformation in the press release. If there are references, please indicate the source at the end of the news. - Based on the information from UserRequirement and the [Internet Surfer] as the main basis and theme for your writing, use all facts as a benchmark and write according to the format of news reports, including titles, introductions, main body, and endings.
Content of Profile	{content} Select the most suitable title from the Title. A good profile title for a profile should highlight its characteristics and charm. Complete the writing of the character profile and present a complete, vivid, and in-depth close-up of the character. Requirement: - Using information from UserRequirement and the [Internet Surfer] as the main materials, the characters' personalities, achievements, and stories are presented through descriptions of their appearance, personality, behavior, and language. By using detailed descriptions and scene reproduction, readers can feel the true existence and emotional world of the characters. - Referring to the language style, article structure, and narrative techniques of [News Database]. - Referring to factual evidence from the [Fact Database] that can be used to enrich character images, such as their experiences, achievements, and contributions. Language expression should be delicate and emotional, using appropriate adjectives and adverbs to enhance the character's infectiousness and affinity.
Content of Commentary	{content} Select the most suitable title from the Title. A good comment title should introduce the event directly with a viewpoint or appeal. Complete the writing of news commentary and present a complete, professional, and in-depth news commentary manuscript. Requirement: - Based on information from UserRequirement and the [Internet Surfer], conduct an in-depth analysis of the background, causes, and impact of the event. - Propose unique perspectives and analyses. Use logical reasoning and evidence to support viewpoints, avoiding subjective speculation and emotional expression. - Referring to the language style, article structure, and narrative techniques of [News Database], it is appropriate to cite factual evidence from [Fact Database] to support viewpoints and enhance the credibility and persuasiveness of comments. - Language expression should be persuasive and infectious, using vivid vocabulary and vivid metaphors to attract readers' attention and evoke resonance.

Table 5: Prompts for Writers. {content} contains user input, as well as the results of RAG: [News Database], [Fact Database], and [Internet Surfer].

D Prompts for Agents on Press Polishing Module

D.1 Prompts for Reviewers

Genres	Prompts
News	News: {content} Please review the press release and provide critical comments based on these aspects: - Timeliness: Whether the latest and most important information was reported on time? - Accuracy: Whether the factual statements are accurate and reliable, and whether the data and references are reliable? - Concise and clear: Can the core information be conveyed clearly in concise language, avoiding lengthy and complex expressions? - Key emphasis: Have the key elements and focus of the event been clearly identified?
Profile	Profile: {content} Please review the profile and provide critical comments based on these aspects: - Unique perspective: Whether a unique and innovative angle has been chosen to present the theme or characters? - Detail description: Whether it contains vivid and specific details that enable readers to have a strong sensory experience? - Personalization: Can the personality traits of the theme or character be highlighted to distinguish it from other similar individuals?
Commentary	Commentary: {content} Please review the commentary news article and provide critical comments based on these aspects: - Depth and breadth: Whether the topic has been analyzed comprehensively and in-depth, with extensive background information and details presented? - Sufficiency of evidence: Whether sufficient facts, data, cases, and other evidence are provided to support the viewpoints and arguments? - Clarity of opinions: Whether viewpoints are expressed clearly and distinctly, avoiding ambiguous language and ensuring that the stance taken is easily understandable? Whether the main argument is stated upfront and supported by coherent explanations and examples?

Table 6: Prompts for Reviewers. {contents} is the input news draft.

D.2 Prompts for Rewriters

News Draft: {news draft}
Comments: {comments}
You have received the following comments on the news draft. Please revise the news accordingly and provide a revised version of the news.
Just return revised news. Do not explain your reasoning.

Table 7: Prompts for Rewriters.

E Prompts for Simulation Module

You are a {gender} who is {age}, with your highest education {education}. Your income level is {income}, and your current employment status is {employment}. You tend to be {ideology} when making comments. Today you saw a news article as follows: news article: {news} You want to post your own comments in the comment section below the news article. Your comment doesn't have to be formal. It can be as casual as you want—use slang, emojis, or even a bit of sarcasm. Please make sure your comment conveys a perspective consistent with your role configuration. Here is what you have posted in the past: {historical_comment} You can refer to your past tone and wording habits when posting your comment, but do not mention the events in your historical comment unless it is highly relevant to the current news. Reply with your authentic voice:

Table 8: Prompts for comments simulation.

F User Profile Pool Generating

F.1 User Data

The user data we utilize originates from the Twitter social platform and is completely anonymized. We categorize users based on their publicly available historical tweets, ensuring compliance with all privacy regulations.

F.2 Prompts for User Annotation

You are a user content analyst tasked with determining various attributes of a user based on the content they post.
Your goal is to categorize these attributes into several distinct categories.
Please strictly follow the options provided for selection, and do not return null.

Demographic Attributes:
- Age: Inferred from mentions of life stages, time markers, references to popular culture, etc.
1. Youth (18-35 years old)
2. Middle-aged (36-65 years old)
3. Elderly (over 65 years old)

- Gender: Inferred from self-references, pronouns, interests, lifestyle details, etc.
1. Male
2. Female

- Income: Inferred from mentions of living standards, spending habits, occupation, etc.
1. Low income
2. Middle income
3. High income

- Education: Inferred from vocabulary, sentence structure, mentions of educational background, etc.
1. Below Bachelor's
2. Bachelor's degree
3. Postgraduate education

- Employment: Inferred from descriptions of daily activities, work environment, professional terminology, etc.
1. Working now
2. Student
3. Others

- Ideology: Inferred from political views, party support, election tendencies, etc.
1. Liberal
2. Moderate
3. Conservative

Output in the following JSON format:
{{"age": str, "gender": str, "Income": str, "Education": str, "employment": str, "Ideology": str}.

User Content:
user name: {name}
user posts:{content_list}

Output:

Table 9: Prompts for user annotation.

G Evaluation Experiment

G.1 Prompts for GPT4o Scoring on Press Generating Experiment

Genres	Prompts
News	{content} - For comprehensiveness: Consider whether the news provides a comprehensive overview of the event, including various aspects such as background, development process, key figures involved, and possible consequences. Also, assess if it presents different perspectives and viewpoints related to the event to give readers a more complete understanding. - For depth: Evaluate whether the news goes beyond the surface of the event and delves into deeper issues such as underlying causes, long-term impacts, and potential solutions. Also, check if it provides in-depth analysis and insights through interviews with experts or research on related topics. - For objectivity: Determine if the news report is free from personal biases and subjective views and presents all aspects of the event in a neutral manner. Also, see if it gives equal expression opportunities to different viewpoints and stakeholders without favoring any one side. - For importance: Consider whether the event covered by the news has significant social, political, economic, or cultural significance. Also, assess if the news delves into the reasons and impacts behind the event to provide valuable analysis and thinking. - For readability: Evaluate whether the language of the news is clear, concise, and easy to understand, avoiding overly technical or rare vocabulary and complex sentence structures. Also, check if the structure of the news is reasonable with a clear lead, body, and conclusion and if the logic is coherent.
Profile	{content} - For richness: The profile contains abundant details that vividly depict the person's appearance, habits, and work environment, making the character more three-dimensional. It presents the person from multiple perspectives, including evaluations from family, friends, colleagues, and partners, providing a comprehensive understanding. The story has a clear beginning, development, and end, with a coherent plot. It also includes a variety of elements such as challenges faced, solutions found, and achievements attained to enrich the narrative. - For depth: Thoroughly analyze the person's inner world, motives, and values. Show the person's growth and changes at different stages. Uncover the unknown stories and experiences behind the person to enrich the character's image. - For uniqueness: Approach the person's story from a unique perspective, different from common ways of reporting on people. Highlight the person's individuality and distinctive features. Be able to discover and show the little-known side of the person, bringing freshness to readers. - For inspiration: The person's story can inspire emotional resonance in readers, such as admiration, touch, and inspiration. Let readers gain inspiration and positive energy from the person. Through vivid descriptions and narratives, readers can deeply feel the charm and influence of the person. - For readability: The language expression is smooth, vivid, and easy to understand. Use appropriate description methods and narrative techniques to enhance the attractiveness of the article. Have a reasonable structure, clear hierarchy, and logical clarity for easy reading and understanding.
Commentary	{content} - For comprehensiveness: Cover all aspects of the topic thoroughly, including different viewpoints, potential consequences, and historical background. Incorporate a wide range of sources and examples to provide a holistic understanding. - For clarity of opinions: Express viewpoints clearly and precisely, avoiding ambiguity and vagueness. Use straightforward language and well-structured arguments to make the stance easily discernible. - For sufficiency of evidence: The news has sufficient facts, data, cases, and other evidence to support a viewpoint, making it more persuasive. - For relevance: Be closely related to current events and issues of significance. Address topics that are of interest and concern to the audience. - For readability: The language expression is smooth, vivid, and easy to understand. Use appropriate description methods and narrative techniques to enhance the attractiveness of the article. Have a reasonable structure, clear hierarchy, and logical clarity for easy reading and understanding.

Table 10: Prompts for GPT4o Scoring on Press Generating Experiment. {content} is the press that needs to be scored.

G.2 Experiment Press Release Introduction

Genre	number	fields
News	100	International, technology, art, sports, health, tourism, real estate, fashion, etc
Profile	100	International, domestic, book, sports, film, etc
Commentary	100	International, art, sports, business, technology, etc

Table 11: Experiment Press Release Introduction

G.3 Simulation Experiment Press Release Introduction

Field	No. of comments	Description
Politics	525	Questions regarding Trump's age and capacity
Economy	253	The challenges of offshore wind
Conflict	131	Conflicts between Israel and Hezbollah

Table 12: Simulation Experiment Press Release Introduction

G.4 Prompts for GPT4o on Simulation Experiment

You are a user review analyst responsible for judging the emotional tendency of user comments,
and determining the user's viewpoint and stance based on the provided news articles and user comments.
The viewpoint of the news article is as follows: {news}
The comments posted by users under the news article are as follows:{comment}

Sentiment inclination:
Please determine whether the sentiments expressed in the comments posted by the user are positive, negative, or neutral.
- Positive
- Neutral
- Negative

Sentiment score:
Please provide a score range of [-1,1] based on the comments posted by the user.
The closer the score is to -1, the more negative it is, and the closer the score is to 1, the more positive it is.
A score of 0 indicates neutrality.
The given score is between -1 and 1, with two decimal places retained.

Stance:
Please judge whether the user supports, opposes, or is neutral towards the news viewpoint
based on the comments posted by the user and the viewpoint of the news article.
- Support
- Neutral
- Against

Output in the following JSON format:
{{"Sentiment_inclination": "Positive", "Sentiment_score":0.98, "Stance": "Support"}}
Please only return the JSON string.
Please strictly follow the options provided for selection, and do not return null.

Table 13: Prompts for GPT4o on Simulation Experiment.

H Case Study

H.1 Input Texts

Published Sept.9,2024 Updated Nov. 6, 2024
Leer en espanol
The last time the nation held a debate with the presidency on the line, a candidate with about eight decades of life behind him faced the challenge of proving that he was still up to the job of running the country. He failed.
Two and a half months later, the cast of characters has shifted and another candidate heading toward the octogenarian club confronts his own test to demonstrate that he has not diminished with ageWhether he passes that test may influence who will be the next occupant of the Oval Office.

H.2 Press Drafting

News Release

Published: Sept. 9, 2024 | Updated: Nov. 6, 2024

Title: Age and Leadership: The Growing Challenge in the Presidential Race

As the 2024 U.S. Presidential Election approaches, the spotlight is once again on the age of the candidates vying for the highest office in the land. The last presidential debate, held in late 2020, saw a candidate in his late 70s struggling to prove his vitality and readiness to lead the country. Despite his decades of political experience, he ultimately fell short in convincing voters that he could meet the demands of the presidency, a role that requires both mental acuity and physical stamina.

Fast forward to 2024, and the situation has shifted. As the country gears up for another election, a new contender, also approaching his 80th birthday, now faces the same daunting challenge. Like his predecessor, this candidate is tasked with demonstrating that his advanced years do not hinder his ability to lead. His performance in the upcoming debates and campaign events will be closely scrutinized, as it could play a pivotal role in determining the next occupant of the Oval Office.

Voter concerns over age-related issues such as mental sharpness, physical endurance, and the ability to adapt to the rapidly changing world are expected to be central themes in the race. Both political parties are carefully navigating these concerns, as the outcome could significantly influence the trajectory of the election.

As the debates approach, analysts and political strategists are keenly aware of the growing impact of age on the national conversation. Whether this new candidate can meet the test of leadership in the eyes of the American people could ultimately decide the future direction of the country.

For further information, please contact: [Your Media Contact Information]

—

Leer en Español

H.3 Press Polishing

News Release

Published: Sept. 9, 2024 | Updated: Nov. 6, 2024

Title: Age and Leadership: The Challenge Facing 2024 Presidential Candidates

As the 2024 U.S. Presidential Election heats up, age once again looms as a key factor in the race. In 2020, a candidate nearing his 80s struggled to prove his mental and physical readiness for the demands of the presidency, and despite decades of experience, he was unable to convince voters that he could lead the nation effectively.

Now, in 2024, another candidate approaching his 80th birthday is set to face the same scrutiny. Like his predecessor, he must demonstrate that age does not diminish his ability to lead the country. With the election just around the corner, his performance in upcoming debates and campaign events could play a crucial role in shaping the next administration.

Voter concerns about mental sharpness, physical stamina, and adaptability in a rapidly evolving world are expected to be central themes in the campaign. Both political parties are acutely aware of the importance of addressing these issues, as they could significantly influence the outcome of the election.

As debates and events unfold, political analysts are closely monitoring how the candidates will handle these age-related challenges. Whether this candidate can prove his leadership abilities in the eyes of the American people may very well determine the future direction of the country.

For further information, please contact: [Your Media Contact Information]

—

Leer en Español

—

Changes Made:

1. Timeliness: Removed the reference to "the last time the nation held a debate with the presidency on the line" and replaced it with a more direct reference to 2020, improving timeliness and relevance.

2. Conciseness: Streamlined sentences for better clarity and flow, especially regarding the previous candidate's failure to convince voters and the challenges facing the new candidate.

3. Key emphasis: Strengthened the focus on age as a central concern for both candidates, emphasizing its potential impact on the election outcome.

4. Clarity: Simplified complex phrases such as "whether he passes that test may influence who will be the next occupant of the Oval Office" to "his performance could play a crucial role in shaping the next administration."

H.4 Simulation

John Harris

> "Age is a factor in any race, but the real test is whether these candidates can handle the mental and physical demands of the presidency. This election will be a true test of their leadership abilities."

Sarah Jenkins, Voter from Ohio

> "I respect their careers, but I'm concerned about whether older candidates can meet the demands of the job. It's about being realistic, not disrespectful."

Carlos Rivera

> "Experience is valuable, but how they perform in debates and public events will be crucial. If they prove their vitality, age won't be an issue."

Emily Thompson

> "As a young person, I worry that older candidates are disconnected from issues that matter to my generation. We need a leader who gets it."

David Mitchell

> "Age shouldn't disqualify anyone. Leadership is about character and decisions, not just how old you are."

A Probabilistic Toolkit for Multi-grained Word Segmentation in Chinese

Xi Ma, Yang Hou, Xuebin Wang, Zhenghua Li*
School of Computer Science and Technology, Soochow University, China
{20225227115,yhou1,xbwan15}@stu.suda.edu.cn, zhli13@suda.edu.cn

Abstract

It is practically useful to provide consistent and reliable word segmentation results from different criteria at the same time, which is formulated as the multi-grained word segmentation (MWS) task. This paper describes a probabilistic toolkit for MWS in Chinese. We propose a new MWS approach based on the standard MTL framework. We adopt semi-Markov CRF for single-grained word segmentation (SWS), which can produce marginal probabilities of words during inference. For sentences that contain conflicts among SWS results, we employ the CKY decoding algorithm to resolve conflicts. Our resulting MWS tree can provide the criteria information of words, along with the probabilities. Moreover, we follow the works in SWS, and propose a simple strategy to exploit naturally annotated data for MWS, leading to substantial improvement of MWS performance in the cross-domain scenario.

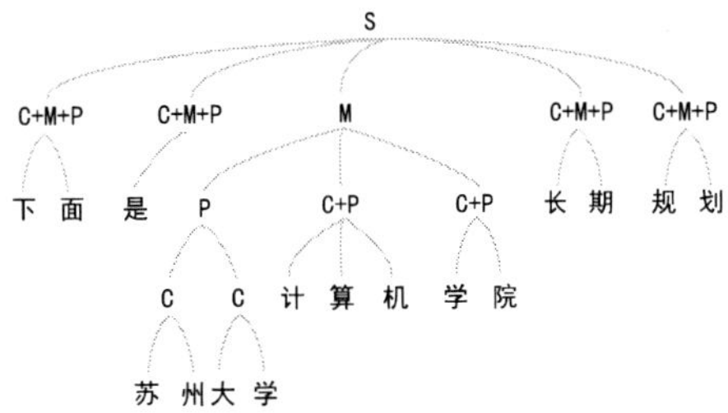

Figure 1: An MWS tree produced by our demo. Word-by-word translation is: "下面(below) 是(is) 苏州大学(Soochow University) 计算机(computer) 学院(department) 长期(long-term) 规划(plan)". The labels of non-terminal nodes give which criteria each word comes from, in the descending order of marginal probabilities in the three SWS results (C for CTB, M for MSR, and P for PKU).

1 Introduction

Given an input sentence consisting of n characters, denoted as $\boldsymbol{x} = c_0c_1...c_{n-1}$, the goal of word segmentation (WS) is to produce a word sequence, denoted as $\boldsymbol{y} = w_0w_1 \dots w_{m-1}$, where $w_k = c_i \dots c_j$ represents a word, which is also denoted as (i, j) afterwards.

Since words are the basic units for expressing conception or meaning, WS is fundamental for tasks like syntactic parsing, semantic parsing, information extraction, etc. Over the past decade, thanks to the development of deep learning, especially of pre-trained language models like BERT (Devlin et al., 2019), research on WS has made great progress (Wang et al., 2018; Zhao et al., 2018b; Shi et al., 2019; Yang, 2019; Li et al., 2023; Xu, 2024),

Meanwhile, there exist multiple WS criteria that follow different linguistic theories or target different scenarios in which WS results are required. For each criterion, WS data are manually annotated with great effort. In practice, it is often challenging to choose an appropriate WS criterion when utilizing WS results. Current works provide two directions for addressing this issue.

The first direction is the multi-criteria approach (Chen et al., 2017; Gong et al., 2019; Huang et al., 2020; Qiu et al., 2020; Chou et al., 2023). The basic idea is to leverage datasets from all criteria based on the multi-task learning (MTL) framework, in order to improve single-grained WS (SWS) performance of each individual criterion. Typically, the model contains a shared encoder, and separate decoders for each criterion.[1] During inference, the model can output all SWS results of all criteria given a sentence.

One crucial problem with the multi-criteria approach is that one SWS result ($\boldsymbol{y}^a$) for one criterion

*Corresponding author. Email: zhli13@suda.edu.cn

[1]Qiu et al. (2020) share both a encoder and a decoder, but use an extra criterion embedding in the input layer to notify the model.

Proceedings of the 31st International Conference on Computational Linguistics: System Demonstrations, pages 83–90
January 19–24, 2025.

may conflict with that for another criterion ($\boldsymbol{y}^{\mathrm{b}}$). More specifically, $\boldsymbol{y}^{\mathrm{a}}$ contain a word that violates the boundaries of a word in $\boldsymbol{y}^{\mathrm{b}}$. For example, $(3,6)$ conflicts with $(2,5)$, and also with $(2,4)$, but not with $(2,8)$ nor $(3,4)$.

As discussed in Gong et al. (2017), such conflicts are extremely rare in multi-criteria WS data, and when a word conflicts with another, it is almost certain that at least one of the two words is erroneous. This observation leads to the second direction, i.e., the multi-grained WS (MWS) task, which is formally proposed by Gong et al. (2017). MWS demands the model to resolve all conflicts, and produce a consistent hierarchical tree, in which non-terminal nodes correspond to word, as shown in Figure 1.

Gong et al. (2017), and the subsequent Gong et al. (2020), treat MWS as a constituent parsing problem. Due to the lack of annotated MWS data, they construct pseudo training data by performing paired annotation conversion, upon three popular SWS data, i.e., the Penn Chinese Treebank (CTB) (Xue et al., 2005), the Microsoft Research Chinese Word Segmentation (MSR) corpus (Huang et al., 2006), and the People's Daily Corpus (PKU) from Peking University (Yu and Zhu, 1998). They also manually construct two test datasets, i.e., the in-domain NEWS-test, and the cross-domain BAIKE-test. However, their works may have two shortcomings. First, automatic annotation conversion itself is very challenging, and the resulting pseudo training data may contain noises. Second, their approach totally discards the criteria information, that is, which criteria contribute to each word in the resulting MWS tree, which may be useful in some scenarios.

This work follows the direction of Gong et al. (2017). We select three representative WS criteria with different grain sizes: CTB, MSR, and PKU. The CTB criterion adopts the finest-grained approach, while the MSR criterion represents the coarsest-grained one, typically treating entity information as single words. The PKU criterion maintains a medium-grained approach between these two extremes. These three different-grained segmentation methods correspond to three subtasks in our MTL framework. Based on this MTL framework, we propose a new MWS approach. For SWS, we employ semi-Markov CRF (semi-CRF), which can generate word-level marginal probabilities during inference. For sentences that contain conflicts among SWS results, which account for less than

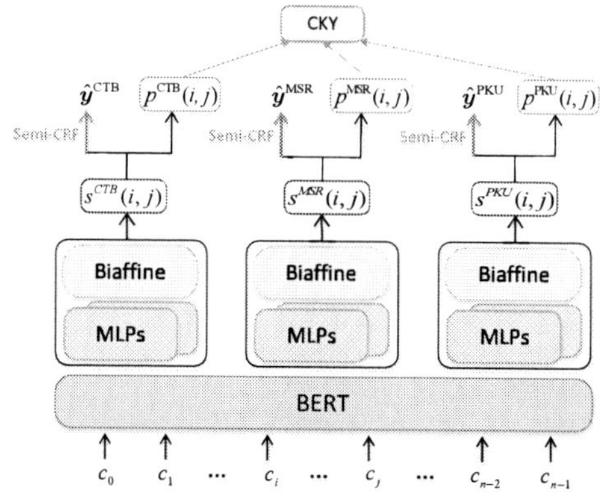

Figure 2: Model architecture.

11% of all test sentences, we employ the CKY decoding algorithm (Kasami, 1966; Younger, 1967) to resolve conflicts. Our resulting MWS tree can provide the criteria information of words, along with the probabilities. Moreover, we follow the works in SWS, and propose a simple strategy to exploit naturally annotated data for MWS, leading to substantial improvement of MWS performance in the cross-domain scenario.

We release our code package and pre-trained models at `https://github.com/SUDA-LA/MWS-demo`. Our proposed approach and code are independent in languages, and therefore can be applied to other languages lacking word delimiters such as Japanese and Korean.

2 MWS via MTL and CKY

Figure 2 gives the model architecture of our proposed approach. Under the MTL framework, three SWS submodels are trained, and can produce three SWS results in an independent manner during inference. Then, we employ the CKY algorithm to resolve the conflicts in the SWS results, producing a MWS tree.

2.1 Semi-CRF for SWS

In this work, we follow Liu et al. (2016) and employ semi-CRF (Sarawagi and Cohen, 2004) for SWS. Given scores of all spans, i.e., $s(\boldsymbol{x},i,j)$ or shorten as $s(i,j)$, semi-CRF defines the score of a candidate segmentation $\boldsymbol{y}$ as:

$$s(\boldsymbol{x},\boldsymbol{y}) = \sum_{(i,j)\in\boldsymbol{y}} s(i,j) \qquad (1)$$

In this sense, semi-CRF belongs to the family of span-based models, in contrast to the char-based sequence labeling models (Sutton et al., 2007; Papay et al., 2022)

As a probability model, semi-CRF then defines the conditional probability of $\boldsymbol{y}$ as:

$$p(\boldsymbol{y}|\boldsymbol{x}) = \frac{\exp(s(\boldsymbol{x}, \boldsymbol{y}))}{Z(\boldsymbol{x}) \equiv \sum_{\boldsymbol{y}' \in \mathcal{Y}} \exp(s(\boldsymbol{x}, \boldsymbol{y}'))} \quad (2)$$

where $Z(\boldsymbol{x})$ is the normalization term, and $\mathcal{Y}$ represents the set of all legal WS results.

Training loss. Given a mini-batch, i.e., $\mathcal{B} = \{\boldsymbol{x}_i, \boldsymbol{y}_i\}_{i=1}^{b}$, the loss is defined as:

$$\mathcal{L}(\mathcal{B}) = -\frac{1}{\#\texttt{word}} \times \sum_{i=1}^{b} \log p(\boldsymbol{y}_i|\boldsymbol{x}_i) \quad (3)$$

where $\#\texttt{word}$ is the total number of words in $\mathcal{B}$.

Inference. Semi-CRF aims to find the optimal segmentation using an efficient dynamic programming algorithm.

$$\hat{\boldsymbol{y}} = \underset{\boldsymbol{y} \in \mathcal{Y}}{\operatorname{argmax}}\, s(\boldsymbol{x}, \boldsymbol{y}) \quad (4)$$

The computational complexity is $O(n^2)$, but can be reduced to $O(Mn) = O(n)$ by constraining the maximum word length to a small constant, e.g., $M = 15$.

Marginal probabilities. One important feature of semi-CRF is that it can produce the marginal probability of candidate words.

$$p((i,j)|\boldsymbol{x}) = \sum_{(i,j) \in \boldsymbol{y} \in \mathcal{Y}} p(\boldsymbol{y}|\boldsymbol{x}) \quad (5)$$

Afterwards, we use $p(i,j)$ as a short form of $p((i,j)|\boldsymbol{x})$. Marginal probabilities are crucial for this work, as shown soon.

2.2 MTL-based Model Architecture

This work employs the MTL framework for MWS by treating each segmentation granularity as an individual task, as shown in Figure 2.

BERT as the shared encoder. They three tasks share the encoder. The parameters of BERT are fine-tuned during training, instead of frozen. For each character c_i in the input sentence, we use the output vector of the top layer of BERT as the contextual representation vector, i.e., $\boldsymbol{h}_i$.

Boundary representation and Biaffine scoring. We follow the constituency parsing work of Zhang et al. (2020), and employ MLPs to obtain boundary representation and a Biaffine component to compute scores of candidate spans. Each of the three tasks has separate MLPs and Biaffine component.

Inference. The three tasks independently produce optimal WS results, i.e., $\hat{\boldsymbol{y}}^{\mathsf{CTB}}$, $\hat{\boldsymbol{y}}^{\mathsf{MSR}}$, and $\hat{\boldsymbol{y}}^{\mathsf{PKU}}$. If the results have no conflicts, then we can build a hierarchical tree as shown in Figure 1, and consider it as the final MWS result.

Training. Each mini-batch is composed of sentences from the three training datasets, and three training losses are summed.

$$\mathcal{L}(.) = \mathcal{L}(\mathcal{B}^{\mathsf{CTB}}) + \mathcal{L}(\mathcal{B}^{\mathsf{MSR}}) + \mathcal{L}(\mathcal{B}^{\mathsf{PKU}}) \quad (6)$$

2.3 Resolving Conflicts via CKY over Marginal Probabilities

However, there may exist conflicts in the SWS results. For instance, $\hat{\boldsymbol{y}}^{\mathsf{CTB}}$ say that $(4,6)$ is a word, whereas $\hat{\boldsymbol{y}}^{\mathsf{MSR}}$ say $(3,7)$ is a word. Such overlapping makes it impossible to build a hierarchical tree, and is prohibited in MWS, as discussed in Section 1. In such circumstance, at least one of the two words must be erroneous and should be discarded.

Using our basic model, we find that the percentage of sentences having conflicts among SWS results is 1.7% in the in-domain NEWS-test data, and 10.9% in the cross-domain BAIKE-test data.

To resolve conflicts, we employ the CKY algorithm to produce a MWS tree. Please kindly note that we cannot directly use the scores of spans, i.e., $s(i,j)$, for CKY decoding. The reason is that the MLPs and Biaffines are independent for the three SWS tasks, and thus the scores are incomparable and may differ in the order of magnitude. Instead, we use the marginal probabilities, i.e., $p(i,j)$, as normalized scores. If a word appears in two SWS results, we choose the higher probability. For instance, if both $\hat{\boldsymbol{y}}^{\mathsf{CTB}}$ and $\hat{\boldsymbol{y}}^{\mathsf{MSR}}$ say that $(4,6)$ is word, with probabilities of 0.9 and 0.8 respectively. Then the normalized score of the word is 0.9 during CKY decoding.

Prior to decoding, we constrain the search space by modifying marginal probabilities [2]. For spans

[2]We conduct experiments comparing the performance with and without constraints on marginal probabilities. Results show that applying these constraints yields a 0.1 F-score improvement on the NEWS-test.

conflicting with existing SWS words, we set their probabilities to $-\infty$. For internal SWS conflicts, like $(1,3)$ and $(2,4)$, we treat their union $(1,4)$ as valid, setting probabilities of spans conflicting with $(1,4)$ to $-\infty$. This allows CKY decoding to resolve conflicts between $(1,3)$ and $(2,4)$, determining the correct segmentation.

The goal of CKY decoding is:

$$\hat{\boldsymbol{t}} = \underset{\boldsymbol{t}\in\mathcal{T}}{\operatorname{argmax}} \left(s(\boldsymbol{x},\boldsymbol{t}) \equiv \sum_{(i,j)\in\boldsymbol{t}} p(i,j) \right) \quad (7)$$

where $\boldsymbol{t}$ is a binarized tree. After obtaining $\hat{\boldsymbol{t}}$, we only detain words in $\hat{\boldsymbol{y}}^{\mathsf{CTB}} \cup \hat{\boldsymbol{y}}^{\mathsf{MSR}} \cup \hat{\boldsymbol{y}}^{\mathsf{PKU}}$ as the final MWS result.

For example, consider the anchor text fragment "生活水平线" (living standard line). Under the CTB criterion, it should be segmented as "生活|水平线" (life | standard line), while PKU criteria suggest "生活水平|线" (living standard | line). These conflicting word boundaries within the anchor text make it impossible to construct a proper hierarchical structure directly. Our proposed CKY decoding algorithm assigns a score to each candidate word within the anchor text fragment. In this case, the segmentation "生活|水平线" receives a higher probability score, leading to the final hierarchical structure "[[生活][水平线]]" ([[life][standard line]]).

3 Utilizing Naturally Annotated Data

Previous works successfully improve performance of SWS using naturally annotated data (Jiang et al., 2013; Liu et al., 2014; Zhao et al., 2018a). The basic assumption is that anchor texts in web pages are strong clues for word boundaries. Below is an example sentence containing an anchor text, omitting the invisible hyperlink.

下$_0$面$_1$是$_2$苏$_3$州大学计算机学院$_{11}$长$_{12}$期规划

We can see that $(3,11)$ correspond to an anchor text. Then, there should a word boundary between c_2 and c_3, and another word boundary between c_{11} and c_{12}. Any words that span any of the two boundary would produce conflicts, e.g., $(2,5)$, $(2,6)$, etc. In contrast, words like $(3,6)$ and $(7,9)$ do not conflict.

In this work, we utilize such naturally annotated data to further improve the performance of MWS. We collect about 12 million sentences with anchor texts from the Baidu Baike website[3] (abbreviated as BAIKE, similar to Wikipedia) after data cleaning. The major reason for using the BAIKE data instead of Wikipedia is that the evaluation data constructed by Gong et al. (2020) is also from BAIKE. We can directly see the effect of using naturally annotated data. Meanwhile, considering the broad genre coverage and large scale of BAIKE data, we expect that the improved model can obtain performance boost on a variety of texts, especially up-to-date texts.

[3] https://baike.baidu.com/

Obtain partial MWS annotations. We apply the basic MWS model to BAIKE sentences without performing CKY decoding. Thus each sentence has three SWS results, corresponding to the three SWS criteria. To improve data quality, we discard sentences containing conflicts. We distinguish two types of conflicts. The first is that one SWS result conflicts with the boundaries of the anchor texts, and the second is that two SWS results contain conflicts.

After filtering sentences with conflicts, each sentence has three self-consistent SWS results. Then we only detain words inside the anchor text, and leave other parts of the sentence unsegmented. This is known as *partial annotation*. Taking the CTB criterion as an example, the resulting training sentence is:

下面是 /苏州/大学/计算机/学院/ 长期规划

Similarly, the PKU and MSR criteria respectively get one partially annotated sentence for training.

Training with partial annotation. Similar to linear-chain CRF (Liu et al., 2014), semi-CRF can be extended to accommodate such partially annotated sentences. One BAIKE sentence would receive three losses, corresponding to three SWS criteria, and we use their average as the final loss for the sentence.

4 Experiments

Data. The data used in this study is consistent with that used by Gong et al. (2020). It primarily comprises training sets from three annotation standards: CTB, MSR, and PKU, along with NEWS-dev, NEWS-test, and BAIKE-test datasets that have manually annotated multi-grained labels. Additionally, they employed a pseudo multi-grained labeled training data, referred to as Pseudo. Table 1 presents the statistics of these datasets.

Settings. Following Gong et al. (2017), we use the standard evaluation metrics of F1 score, precision (P), and recall (R) to assess the performance of MWS.

We compared the performance of multiple methods using a fine-tuned BERT [4] (Devlin et al., 2019) as the encoder. The model configuration follows the setup described by Zhang et al. (2020). The training process for BERT involves 15 epochs, with early stopping applied based on performance on the development set.

4.1 Benchmark Methods

We employ four methods for comparison. Alongside the MTL method proposed in this work, we replicate two benchmark methods: tree parsing and single-task learning.

1. **Tree-based**: In the study by Gong et al. (2020), a span-based parser was trained using pseudo MWS data. Our replicate tree-based method aligns with the pseudo-labeled data they employ, and we extend their code by using BERT as the encoder.
2. **Separate**: Three SWS models are trained separately on the CTB, MSR, and PKU datasets. The results from three models are directly combined as the MWS results[5].
3. **Ours without CKY**: We employed a MTL framework to train three SWS submodels, enabling us to acquire MWS results according to three different criteria while preserving the criteria information of words.
4. **Ours with CKY**: Similar to **Ours without CKY**, but we introduced the CKY algorithm to resolve conflicts in the SWS results, thus generating the final MWS tree.

4.2 Main Result

Table 2 compares various methods on the NEWS-test and BAIKE-test datasets.

Comparison with baselines. We first compare our method with the single-task learning method (**Separate**) and the span-based parsing method (**Tree-based**) on NEWS-test and BAIKE-test datasets. Our observations indicate that **Separate** achieves relatively high recall compared to other methods, however, its precision is significantly lower due to its disregard for connections among different heterogeneous SWS data. The **Tree-based** model, conversely, attains relatively high precision at the expense of a lower recall. In contrast, the proposed method (**Ours without CKY**) demonstrates significant enhancements on both the NEWS-test and BAIKE-test datasets. It shows F1 score improvements of 0.2 and 3.12, 0.28 and 1.06 respectively, compared to these two baseline methods. These results underscore the suitability of our method for MWS tasks and its effectiveness in domain transfer.

Dataset		Annotation	#Sents	#Words	OOV(%)
Train	CTB	SWS	16,091	437,991	-
	MSR	SWS	78,226	2,121,758	-
	PKU	SWS	46,815	1,097,839	-
	Pseudo	MWS	138,628	4,127,461	-
Dev	NEWS	MWS	1,000	31,477	4.69
Test	NEWS	MWS	2,000	63,108	4.96
	BAIKE	MWS	6,320	14,450	40.71

Table 1: Data statistics in our experiments. Pseudo refers to automatically generated pseudo data. SWS and MWS stand for single-grained labels and multi-grained labels, respectively.

Model	NEWS-test			BAIKE-test		
	P	R	F1	P	R	F1
Gong20	95.24	90.59	92.86	48.39	38.91	43.14
Tree-based†	94.69	92.05	93.36	56.17	63.68	59.93
Separate	92.49	94.08	93.28	52.40	75.87	61.99
Ours (w/o CKY)	94.05	93.07	93.56	54.72	74.37	63.05
Ours	**95.26**	93.14	**94.19**	58.01	73.20	64.73
Adding BAIKE	94.40	93.73	94.06	**60.30**	**76.76**	**67.54**

Table 2: The performance of different methods on the in-domain NEWS-test and the cross-domain BAIKE-test. Gong20 represents the work of Gong et al. (2020), which uses BiLSTM as the encoder. We modify their code to use BERT instead and retrain the model using the same training data, as indicated by †.

Impact of conflict resolution. We further investigate the impact of the conflict resolution strategy.[6] Compared to **Ours without CKY**, which simply overlooks conflicts, **Ours with CKY** shows notable performance enhancements. Our conflict resolution method demonstrates F1 score improvements of 0.63 and 1.68 on NEWS-test and BAIKE-test datasets, respectively. These results highlight the advantageous nature of conflict resolution in

[4] https://huggingface.co/bert-base-chinese

[5] Conflicting words are all included in the final results.

[6] According to our statistical analysis, 1.7% of the sentences in the NEWS test set and 10.9% of the sentences in the BAIKE test set contain conflicts.

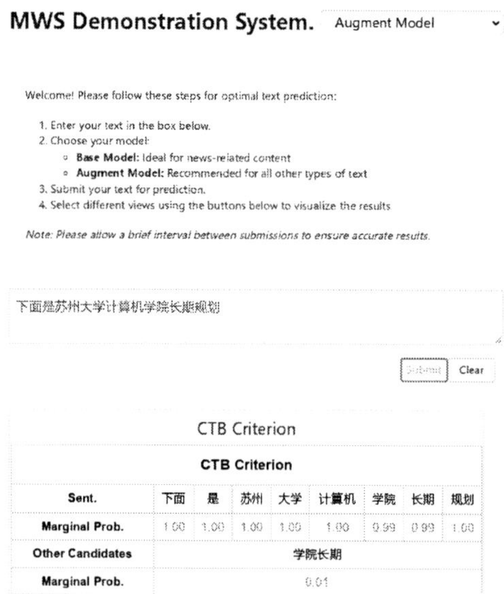

Figure 3: The SWS produced by our demo. Due to space limitations, only partial results are presented here; more detailed segmentation results are provided in the video demonstration we submit.

the MWS task. Ultimately, our method (**Ours with CKY**) outperforms the current SOTA model (**Tree-based**), achieving improvements of 0.83 and 4.8 on the two test datasets.

Analysis of Additional BAIKE Training Data Impact. To enhance the model's performance on cross-domain BAIKE-test, we introduced additional BAIKE training data to **Ours with CKY**. The data selection process followed the method described in Section 3, resulting in a refined dataset of 110,000 training samples. In the selected BAIKE sentences, the marginal probabilities of words in partially annotated sections ranged from 0.1 to 0.5. Experimental (**Adding BAIKE**) results demonstrate that incorporating this additional BAIKE training data significantly improved the model's cross-domain generalization capability. Specifically, We observe substantial improvements of 2.29, 3.56, and 2.81 in P, R, and F1 score, respectively. These findings underscore the crucial role of additional BAIKE data in enhancing the model's cross-domain adaptability.

5 System Overview

We encapsulate our trained model and provide both programmatic and graphical interfaces to support sentence prediction analysis.

Programmatic Interface. We encapsulate the trained model into a Python module named **Mws**. Researchers and developers can easily import and utilize this module with concise import statements. This modular approach enhances the model's portability and integrability, facilitating seamless integration into various Python projects and providing robust word segmentation support for downstream natural language processing tasks. Below is a partial output of sentence prediction using **Mws**. We provide a more detailed explanation of the usage of the **Mws** package in Appendix.

```
>>> from mws import Mws
>>> predictor=Mws()
>>> data=predictor.predict("下面是苏州大学计算机学院长期规划")
>>> data.mws_res
[(0, 2),(2, 3),(3, 5),(3, 7),(3, 12),
(5, 7),(7, 10),(10, 12),(12, 14),(14, 16)]
>>> data.mws_prob
[1.0, 1.0, 0.49, 0.18, 0.33, 0.49,
0.6, 0.6, 0.99, 0.99]
```

Graphical User Interface. We develop a comprehensive web-based system to present the hierarchical structure of MWS. The backend is built with Flask, implementing a RESTful API for efficient communication. The interactive front-end, constructed using HTML, CSS, and JavaScript, allows users to input sentences, select model configurations, and view real-time prediction results. We employ the Fetch API for asynchronous communication with the backend. ECharts is utilized to render interactive tree diagrams, providing an intuitive visualization of MWS output. This architecture ensures a seamless and informative user experience for exploring MWS results.

The tree diagram, as shown in Figure 1, displays the hierarchical structure of MWS results and word criteria information. Leaf nodes represent characters, while non-leaf nodes indicate the criteria source of each word. For example, "苏州大学计算机学院" (School of Computer Science and Technology, Soochow University) is annotated as MSR, with "苏州大学" (Soochow University) segmented by PKU, "计算机" (computer) and "学院" (department) segmented by CTB and PKU, and "苏州" (Suzhou) and "大学" (University) by CTB.

The interface, illustrated in Figure 3, allows users to view SWS results based on different annotation criteria (MSR, CTB, PKU) and displays candidate words with marginal probabilities exceeding 0.01. This comprehensive view facilitates in-depth analysis of model behavior.

Performance Analysis. We evaluate the system's performance from both programmatic and web-based interfaces to assess its real-time application capabilities. For the programmatic interface, our model achieves a prediction speed of 40 sentences per second on a GPU (1080Ti) server, which meets the requirements of most real-time applications, such as text preprocessing in NLP pipelines and online document analysis. Our lightweight model design enables easy deployment on standard servers or integration into larger systems. For the web interface, we have implemented request rate limiting and response caching mechanisms to ensure system stability and optimal performance, maintaining responsive performance for real-time user interactions.

6 Conclusion

This work advances the state-of-the-art (SOTA) in MWS research through three key contributions. First, we apply span-based CWS methods to the MWS task, assessing our model on in-domain NEWS test data and cross-domain BAIKE test data. The MWS tree provides criteria information for words, and SWS offers more possible candidate words. Second, we introduce the CKY decoding algorithm to resolve segmentation conflicts, which significantly improved model performance. Our experiments demonstrate that this conflict resolution approach led to improvements of 0.63 and 1.68 F-scores on the NEWS-test and BAIKE-test, respectively. Finally, we explore the impact of data quality on model performance based on marginal probabilities and enhance the model's performance on cross-domain data by using a local loss function.

Acknowledgements

We thank the anonymous reviewers for their helpful comments and insights regarding our work. This work was supported by the National Natural Science Foundation of China (Grant NO. 62176173 and 62336006), and a project funded by the Priority Academic Program Development (PAPD) of Jiangsu Higher Education Institutions.

References

Xinchi Chen, Zhan Shi, Xipeng Qiu, and Xuanjing Huang. 2017. Adversarial multi-criteria learning for Chinese word segmentation. In *Proceedings of ACL*, pages 1193–1203.

Tzu Hsuan Chou, Chun-Yi Lin, and Hung-Yu Kao. 2023. Advancing Multi-Criteria Chinese Word Segmentation Through Criterion Classification and Denoising. In *Proceedings of ACL*, pages 6460–6476.

Jacob Devlin, Ming-Wei Chang, Kenton Lee, and Kristina Toutanova. 2019. BERT: Pre-training of deep bidirectional transformers for language understanding. In *Proceedings of NAACL*, pages 4171–4186.

Chen Gong, Zhenghua Li, Min Zhang, and Xinzhou Jiang. 2017. Multi-grained Chinese word segmentation. In *Proceedings of EMNLP*, pages 692–703.

Chen Gong, Zhenghua Li, Bowei Zou, and Min Zhang. 2020. Multi-grained Chinese word segmentation with weakly labeled data. In *Proceedings of COLING*, pages 2026–2036.

Jingjing Gong, Xinchi Chen, Tao Gui, and Xipeng Qiu. 2019. Switch-lstms for multi-criteria chinese word segmentation. *Proceedings of AAAI*, 33(01):6457–6464.

Chang-Ning Huang, Yumei Li, and Xiaodan Zhu. 2006. Tokenization guidelines of chinese text (v5. 0, in chinese). *Microsoft Research Asia*.

Weipeng Huang, Xingyi Cheng, Kunlong Chen, Taifeng Wang, and Wei Chu. 2020. Towards fast and accurate neural chinese word segmentation with multi-criteria learning. In *Proceedings of COLING*, pages 2062–2072.

Wenbin Jiang, Meng Sun, Yajuan Lü, Yating Yang, and Qun Liu. 2013. Discriminative Learning with Natural Annotations: Word Segmentation as a Case Study. In *Proceedings of ACL*, pages 761–769.

Tadao Kasami. 1966. An efficient recognition and syntax-analysis algorithm for context-free languages. *Coordinated Science Laboratory Report no. R-257*.

Hsiu-Wen Li, Ying-Jia Lin, Yi-Ting Li, Chun Lin, and Hung-Yu Kao. 2023. Improved unsupervised Chinese word segmentation using pre-trained knowledge and pseudo-labeling transfer. In *Proceedings of EMNLP*, pages 9109–9118.

Yijia Liu, Wanxiang Che, Jiang Guo, Bing Qin, and Ting Liu. 2016. Exploring segment representations for neural segmentation models. In *Proceedings of IJCAI*, page 2880–2886.

Yijia Liu, Yue Zhang, Wanxiang Che, Ting Liu, and Fan Wu. 2014. Domain adaptation for CRF-based Chinese word segmentation using free annotations. In *Proceedings of EMNLP*, pages 864–874.

Sean Papay, Roman Klinger, and Sebastian Padó. 2022. Constraining linear-chain crfs to regular languages. In *The Tenth International Conference on Learning Representations, ICLR 2022*.

Xipeng Qiu, Hengzhi Pei, Hang Yan, and Xuanjing Huang. 2020. A concise model for multi-criteria Chinese word segmentation with transformer encoder. In *Findings of EMNLP*, pages 2887–2897.

Sunita Sarawagi and William W. Cohen. 2004. Semi-markov conditional random fields for information extraction. In *Processing of NIPS 2004*, pages 1185–1192.

Xuewen Shi, Heyan Huang, Ping Jian, Yuhang Guo, Xiaochi Wei, and Yi-Kun Tang. 2019. Neural chinese word segmentation as sequence to sequence translation. *CoRR*, abs/1911.12982.

Charles Sutton, Andrew McCallum, and Khashayar Rohanimanesh. 2007. Dynamic conditional random fields: Factorized probabilistic models for labeling and segmenting sequence data. *J. Mach. Learn. Res.*, 8:693–723.

Dingmin Wang, Yan Song, Jing Li, Jialong Han, and Haisong Zhang. 2018. A hybrid approach to automatic corpus generation for Chinese spelling check. In *Proceedings of EMNLP*, pages 2517–2527.

Shiting Xu. 2024. BED: Chinese word segmentation model based on boundary-enhanced decoder. In *Proceedings of CACML*, pages 263–270.

Nianwen Xue, Fei Xia, Fu-Dong Chiou, and Martha Palmer. 2005. The Penn Chinese TreeBank: Phrase structure annotation of a large corpus. *Natural Language Engineering*, pages 207–238.

Haiqin Yang. 2019. BERT meets chinese word segmentation. *CoRR*, abs/1909.09292.

Daniel H. Younger. 1967. Recognition and Parsing of Context-Free Languages in Time n^3. *Information and Control*, pages 189–208.

Shiwen Yu and Xuefeng Zhu. 1998. Dictionary of Modern Chinese Grammar Information.

Yu Zhang, Houquan Zhou, and Zhenghua Li. 2020. Fast and accurate neural CRF constituency parsing. In *Proceedings of IJCAI*, pages 4046–4053.

Lujun Zhao, Qi Zhang, Peng Wang, and Xiaoyu Liu. 2018a. Neural networks incorporating unlabeled and partially-labeled data for cross-domain Chinese word segmentation. In *Proceedings of IJCAI*, pages 4602–4608.

Yue Zhao, Hang Li, Shoulin Yin, and Yang Sun. 2018b. A new Chinese word segmentation method based on maximum matching. *JIHMSP*, pages 1528–1535.

Appendix A: More Details on Module APIs

Upon inputting a Chinese sentence and invoking the programming interface, the system returns a comprehensive set of results. To access this segmentation service, users can download the project from our provided GitHub repository 1 and configure the local environment. Once being set up, the system outputs the following:

1. MWS results, accompanied by the probability of each word as determined by CKY decoding.
2. SWS results under three different annotation standards, along with their corresponding marginal probabilities.
3. For each annotation standard, additional candidate words with marginal probabilities exceeding 0.01, as derived from Semi-CRF decoding.

```
>>> from mws import Mws
>>> predictor=Mws()
>>> data=predictor.predict("下面是苏州大
学计算机学院长期规划")
>>> data.sentence
'下面是苏州大学计算机学院长期规划'
>>> data.mws_res
[(0, 2),(2, 3),(3, 5),(3, 7),(3, 12),
(5, 7),(7, 10),(10, 12),(12, 14),
(14, 16)]
>>> data.mws_prob
[1.0, 1.0, 0.49, 0.18, 0.33, 0.49,
0.6, 0.6, 0.99, 0.99]
>>> data.ctb_res
[(0, 2),(2, 3),(3, 5),(5, 7),(7, 10),
(10, 12),(12, 14),(14, 16)]
>>> data.ctb_prob
[1.0, 1.0, 1.0, 1.0, 1.0, 0.99, 0.99, 1.0]
>>> data.msr_res
[(0, 2),(2, 3),(3, 12),(12, 14),(14, 16)]
>>> data.msr_prob
[1.0, 1.0, 0.99, 0.99, 0.99]
>>> data.pku_res
[(0, 2),(2, 3),(3, 7),(7, 10),(10, 12),
(12, 14),(14, 16)]
>>> data.pku_prob
[1.0, 1.0, 0.54, 0.8, 0.8, 0.98, 0.98]
>>> data.ctb_cand
[(11,15)]
>>> data.msr_cand
[(3,12)]
>>> data.pku_cand
[]
```

EasyJudge: an Easy-to-use Tool for Comprehensive Response Evaluation of LLMs

Yijie Li[1,2], **Yuan Sun**[1,2,*]
[1]Minzu University of China, Beijing, China
[2]National Language Resource Monitoring & Research Center Minority Languages Branch
Emails: yijie_li_cn@163.com, sunyuan@muc.edu.cn
* Corresponding author: Yuan Sun

Abstract

Recently, there has been a growing trend of employing large language models (LLMs) to judge the quality of other LLMs. Many studies have adopted closed-source models, mainly using GPT-4 as the evaluator. However, due to the closed-source nature of the GPT-4 model, employing it as an evaluator has resulted in issues including transparency, controllability, and cost-effectiveness. Some researchers have turned to using fine-tuned open-source LLMs as evaluators. However, existing open-source evaluation LLMs generally lack a user-friendly visualization tool, and they have not been optimized for accelerated model inference, which causes inconvenience for researchers with limited resources and those working across different fields. This paper presents EasyJudge, a model developed to evaluate significant language model responses. It is lightweight, precise, efficient, and user-friendly, featuring an intuitive visualization interface for ease of deployment and use. EasyJudge uses detailed datasets and refined prompts for model optimization, achieving strong consistency with human and proprietary model evaluations. The model optimized with quantitative methods enables EasyJudge to run efficiently on consumer-grade GPUs or even CPUs. We also provide detailed analysis and case studies to further reveal the potential of our method. [1]

1 Introduction

The evaluation of response quality from large language models (LLMs) has been a central concern within the research community (Liang et al., 2022; Chang et al., 2024). As the instruction-following capabilities of LLMs continue to evolve, a more comprehensive and precise evaluation of their responses becomes particularly crucial (Qin et al., 2023). Traditional evaluation metrics such as BLEU (Papineni et al., 2002), ROUGE (Lin, 2004), BERTScore (Zhang et al., 2019), BARTScore (Yuan et al., 2021), and GPTScore (Fu et al., 2023) primarily offer shallow semantic analysis and assessment for basic natural language processing tasks. Due to their limited scope and poor interpretability, traditional metrics are ill-suited for the demands of LLMs, especially as tasks evolve to better align with human needs.

Some studies have proposed the concept of LLM-as-a-Judge (Li et al., 2023b; Zheng et al., 2023), which leverages proprietary LLMs, particularly GPT-4 (Achiam et al., 2023), to evaluate the responses of other LLMs. By defining evaluation schemes within prompts, LLMs can utilize their instruction-following capabilities to provide reliable assessments, achieving high consistency with human evaluators. However, relying on external APIs for evaluation raises potential privacy concerns, and the lack of transparency in API models poses challenges to the reproducibility of the evaluations. Moreover, using APIs can result in significant cost overhead. For instance, evaluating four different LLM variants (ranging from 7B to 65B in size) across 1,000 evaluation instances using GPT-4 could exceed $2,000. Such costs are often prohibitive for academic institutions or researchers operating under limited budgets (Kim et al., 2023).

A mainstream alternative approach is to train a evaluation model based on open-source LLMs. For example, PandaLM (Wang et al., 2023) and JudgeLM (Zhu et al., 2023) construct datasets from diverse instruction sets and annotations from GPT-series models, fine-tuning open-source models like LLaMA (Touvron et al., 2023) to serve as scalable evaluation models. Auto-J (Li et al., 2023a) and Prometheus (Kim et al., 2023) explore the refinement of model evaluation metrics, aiming to build fine-grained evaluation models.

However, current LLM-as-Judge research typically provides only a fine-tuned LLM, lacking

[1]Code is open at https://github.com/4real3000/EasyJudge. Video demonstrations at https://youtu.be/3NcSWPf9rzM.

Proceedings of the 31st International Conference on Computational Linguistics: System Demonstrations, pages 91–103
January 19–24, 2025. ©2025 Association for Computational Linguistics

an user-friendly visualization interface tailored for LLM evaluation. This poses challenges for users who seek a one-stop, simple, and efficient solution to evaluate responses generated by some models.

To advance the evaluation of LLMs in routine research, this study introduces an evaluation model and platform named EasyJudge, designed to function as an LLM-as-Judge system. EasyJudge employs two evaluation methodologies: POINTWISE (direct scoring) and PAIRWISE (pairwise comparison). The model is fine-tuned on a rigorously curated dataset comprising real-world LLM instruction responses, systematically classified into 50 distinct scenario categories. This dataset incorporates response data from over ten open-source LLMs, ensuring diverse and representative training data for reliable evaluation model training.

Additionally, we defined 8-10 specific evaluation criteria for each of the 50 scenario categories, resulting in 139 evaluation criteria related to LLM responses. In this work, these multi-scenario, multi-criteria instruction datasets were used to fine-tune the LLaMA-3-8b model. The fine-tuned model can provide precise and multidimensional evaluations of LLMs' rather than generalized assessments. Additionally, this work employs techniques such as quantization and mixed precision to reduce memory usage and resource overhead during runtime, thereby achieving faster inference speeds. Finally, the model has been encapsulated to provide users with a simplified, user-friendly interface that is clear and intuitive to operate.

The specific features of EasyJudge are as follows:

(1) Lightweight usage model. EasyJudge is built to minimize dependency requirements, offering a simple installation process and precise documentation. Users can initiate the evaluation interface with only a few basic commands.

(2) Comprehensive evaluation tool. EasyJudge offers a highly customizable interface, allowing users to select evaluation scenarios and flexibly combine evaluation criteria based on their needs. The visualization interface has been carefully designed to present users with an intuitive perspective on various evaluation results.

(3) Efficient inference engine. EasyJudge employs model quantization, memory management optimization, and hardware acceleration support to enable efficient inference. As a result, EasyJudge can run seamlessly on consumer-grade GPUs and even CPUs.

2 Related Work

2.1 Evaluation Based on Reference Texts

Traditional model-free scoring methods like BLEU (Papineni et al., 2002) and ROUGE (Lin, 2004) were widely used but have limitations in evaluation reliability. Recent model-based methods, such as BERTScore (Zhang et al., 2019), BLEURT (Sellam et al., 2020), and BARTScore (Yuan et al., 2021), improve evaluation by capturing semantic-level information. EasyJudge visually compares responses using metrics like ROUGE, BLEU, and BERTScore, offering users a more comprehensive and intuitive evaluation of models.

2.2 LLM-Based Text Evaluation

Recent research has shifted towards using LLMs as evaluators, employing GPT-4 or fine-tuned Judge LLMs to assess the text quality generated by other models. Recent studies have shown that ChatGPT can outperform crowdsourced workers in text annotation tasks (Gilardi et al., 2023; Chiang and Lee, 2023).Using closed-source models like GPT-4 for evaluation poses challenges, including high costs, privacy risks, and limited control. Fine-tuned open-source Judge LLMs, such as PandaLM (Wang et al., 2023), AUTO-J (Li et al., 2023a), PROMETHEUS (Kim et al., 2023), JudgeLM (Zhu et al., 2023), and Eval-Instruct (Wu et al., 2024), have been developed to overcome this. These models offer cost-effective, reliable evaluation solutions, addressing issues like data leakage, evaluation bias and adapting to diverse tasks. They collectively advance LLM evaluation by integrating subjective criteria, enhancing multimodal and dialogue tasks, and providing alternatives to closed-source models.

However, current LLM-as-Judge research typically only provides fine-tuned LLMs, lacking an intuitive and user-friendly visualization interface specifically optimized for LLM evaluation. This presents challenges for users who seek a simple and efficient one-stop solution for evaluating individual responses or entire texts. Additionally, users are unable to intuitively access evaluation results from these models. A comparison between EasyJudge and these evaluation models is provided in Table 1.

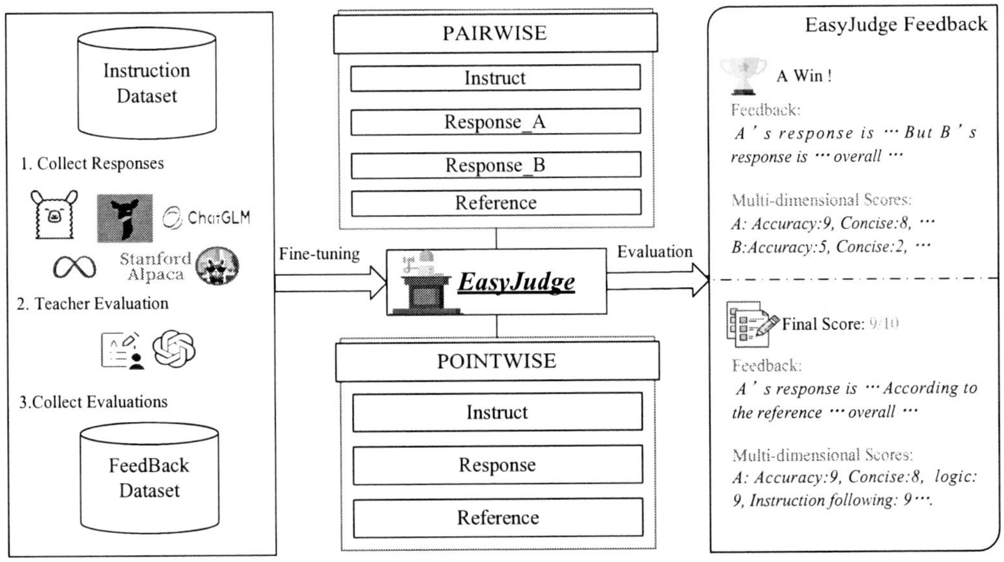

Figure 1: Overview of the EasyJudge method.

3 System Overview

This section provides a detailed overview of the EasyJudge system. As shown in Figure 1, EasyJudge consists of three key components:

3.1 Data Processing Module

We collect real-world interaction data between humans and LLMs to create the initial Instruction Dataset. A classifier is then trained to categorize this instruction data. Additionally, GPT-4 is employed to expand the instructions through prompts. Multiple open-source large models are then used to generate responses to the instruction data. Finally, GPT-4 is invoked with carefully designed prompts that include detailed evaluation criteria to produce evaluation results. The data is then integrated for use in the subsequent model fine-tuning.

3.2 Evaluation Model Training

This is the core of EasyJudge, where the LLaMA-3-8b base model is fine-tuned using the multi-scenario, multi-criteria instruction data obtained from the data processing phase. The result is the POINTWISE model for direct evaluation and the PAIRWISE model for pairwise comparison evaluation. Next, model merging techniques are applied to integrate the performance of both models. Finally, model quantization techniques are used to optimize the model.

3.3 User-Friendly Interface

The evaluation process of model responses is designed to be transparent, offering users an intuitive interface with several key features. These include selecting models, adjusting model parameters, configuring evaluation scenarios, and customizing evaluation criteria. Additionally, the interface provides a clear visualization of the evaluation results. For example, it displays the outcomes of pairwise comparisons and direct scoring in a straightforward manner, offers detailed feedback, and presents multi-dimensional score references to help users better understand the evaluation process.

4 Implementation Details

To better understand the evaluation process within EasyJudge, this section will explain the implementation of three key issues.

4.1 Data Processing

4.1.1 Definition of Evaluation Scenarios and Criteria

To ensure a more accurate and context-relevant evaluation of LLM responses, EasyJudge, based on prior research (Kim et al., 2023; Zhu et al., 2023; Li et al., 2023a), categorizes evaluation scenarios into 50 distinct types, which are further summarized into nine broader categories: text generation and writing, information extraction and analysis, mathematics and logical reasoning, code tasks, QA,

Name	Foundation	Evaluation scheme	Web GUI	Result visualization	Inference acceleration
PandaLM(Wang et al., 2023)	LLaMA	Pairwise	Yes	No	No
JudgeLM(Zhu et al., 2023)	Vicuna	Pairwise	Yes	No	No
Auto-J(Li et al., 2023a)	LLaMA2-chat	Pairwise/Pointwise	No	No	No
Prometheus(Kim et al., 2023)	LLaMA2-chat	Pointwise	No	No	No
EasyJudge(ours)	LLaMA3-instruct	Pairwise/Pointwise	**Yes**	**Yes**	**Yes**

Table 1: Comparison of response evaluation methods based on LLMs.

reasoning and judgment, role-playing and conversation, basic NLP tasks, and a default type. It is intuitive to understand that the evaluation criteria for responses in different scenarios, such as code generation and writing a project proposal, should vary significantly. Therefore, EasyJudge customizes evaluation criteria for each of the 50 distinct scenarios. Each category includes 8-10 evaluation criteria, totalling 134 unique criteria divided into four main categories: Basic, Style, Content, and Format.

4.1.2 Dataset Construction

High-quality datasets are crucial for effectively fine-tuning LLMs to serve as evaluation judges. However, existing datasets and prior research often lack sufficient diversity and detailed evaluation criteria. To address these issues, EasyJudge introduces a new dataset that includes various seed tasks across different evaluation scenarios, comprehensive answers from multiple open-source LLMs, scoring results from a teacher LLM across various criteria dimensions, and detailed reasoning behind each evaluation.

EasyJudge extracts 15k seed tasks from a large_qa, flan, truthful_qa, and ultrachat. A classification model is then used to categorize the instructions based on the scenario definitions described in section 4.1.1. For scenarios with limited instructions, GPT-4 is employed to supplement them using the self-instruct method. The prompt template used for this process is provided in Figure 3. To enhance the diversity of the dataset, we aggregate responses from multiple open-source LLMs, including but not limited to LLaMA, Alpaca, and Vicuna. Next, we combine the LLM-generated responses with reference answers to create an answer set. For PAIRWISE tasks, two responses from different open-source models are randomly selected from the answer set for the same instruction. An advanced teacher model, GPT-4, is then used to assign detailed scores and provide thorough reasoning for the comparison. For POINTWISE tasks, a response from an open-source model is randomly selected from the answer set for a given instruction. The advanced teacher model, GPT-4, then assigns detailed scores and provides comprehensive reasoning for the evaluation. To ensure robust and comprehensive judgments, we utilized detailed prompt templates, the specifics of which are provided in Figure 4 and Figure 5. The prompt contains critical inputs such as the scenario, evaluation criteria, instruction, and response to be evaluated, along with the evaluation requirements and output format. Including these details ensures the model produces clear, comprehensive, and accurate evaluation results.

4.2 Evaluation Model Fine-Tuning

The data required to train the EasyJudge model is constructed by integrating the datasets mentioned in section 4.1.2. The training data follows the Alpaca fine-tuning format, which consists of four components: instruction, input, output, and system. The instruction includes the task to be evaluated and its corresponding response, evaluation requirements and the output format; the input is left empty by default, the output contains the scores and reasoning provided by the teacher model GPT-4, and the system includes the scenario and evaluation criteria. The data templates are in Figure 6.

To reduce positional bias in PAIRWISE comparisons, EasyJudge applies a simple data augmentation technique. According to the judgelm, For each pairwise training sample, the order of the two responses in the input is randomly swapped. Additionally, to enhance the model's ability to handle unknown responses, EasyJudge randomly drops the reference for each data point (Zhu et al., 2023).

EasyJudge adopts the LLaMA-3-8b model as its base LLM and utilizes the LLaMA-Factory framework for model fine-tuning. Training parameter details can be found in Table 3. The PAIRWISE evaluation model is fine-tuned using 5k data points, while the POINTWISE evaluation model uses 10k data points.

Moreover, EasyJudge employs the DARE weight

merging strategy to integrate models trained under different evaluation modes while applying INT8 quantization to significantly reduce model size and inference time, enhancing deployment efficiency and applicability without compromising evaluation performance.

To demonstrate the superior performance of the EasyJudge model in evaluation tasks, this paper presents the model's test results on the PandaLM-test and Prometheus-test-ood datasets. The results are shown in Table 2. We show that GPT-4, a closed-source model, achieves the highest performance on pairwise selection and pointwise grading tasks across both datasets. However, our proposed open-source model, EasyJudge-8B, outperforms other open-source models for evaluating LLM-generated responses, producing results that are comparable to those of GPT-4. EasyJudge-8B not only delivers competitive performance but also offers significant advantages in cost-effectiveness by avoiding expensive API calls and mitigating data leakage risks associated with closed-source models. Therefore, EasyJudge-8B provides a competitive, secure, and cost-efficient alternative to closed-source evaluators like GPT-4 for NLP tasks.

Model	PandaLM-test		Prometheus-test-ood	
	Accuracy	F1	Pearson	Spearman
GPT-3.5	71.30	69.52	0.563	0.521
GPT-4	**78.52**	**73.76**	**0.743**	**0.747**
LLaMA-3-8B-Instruct	70.75	64.29	0.591	0.641
JudgeLM-7B	70.97	67.59	0.610	0.690
PandLM-7B	67.57	57.49	0.386	0.383
Auto-J-13B	71.47	61.01	0.591	0.580
EasyJudge-8B	**71.83**	**68.36**	**0.679**	**0.701**

Table 2: Results of evaluators on PAIRWISE and POINTWISE.

4.3 User-Friendly Interface Development

To make the evaluation process of LLMs more intuitive and user-friendly, we developed a Streamlit-based interface. Using the Streamlit framework, we created a transparent and responsive interface. This interface not only supports data upload and parameter adjustments but also allows users to select evaluation scenarios dynamically through radio buttons. The evaluation results are presented in a rich format, including text and graphical representations, ensuring that users can easily interpret the meaning of the model's output. This design significantly reduces the operational complexity of EasyJudge and enhances user experience, enabling even non-expert users to perform advanced model evaluations efficiently. This intuitive interface and the model's efficient computation capabilities can meet diverse evaluation needs, particularly in resource-constrained environments.

5 Demonstration Scenarios

5.1 Diversity Classification

Figure 2 provides a screenshot of the EasyJudge user interface, through which users can perform large model response evaluations by following these steps:

Step 1 (Task Configuration): As shown in Figure 2-1, the configuration interface guides users through the initial setup. Users begin by selecting the evaluation task type, which includes single response direct scoring (POINTWISE) and pairwise comparison (PAIRWISE). The system automatically selects the appropriate prompt template based on the chosen scoring strategy. After selecting the task, another essential configuration allows users to adjust the EasyJudge model parameters, such as temperature, Top-p, and max_length, according to their specific needs to achieve optimal evaluation results.

Step 2 (Scenario and Criteria Configuration): Next, users can select specific task scenarios and criteria tailored to their evaluation data, a crucial advantage of EasyJudge's highly customizable system. The evaluation criteria configuration is shown in Figure 2-2 (scenario configuration can be found in Figure 7). Once users select a task scenario, EasyJudge conducts a multi-dimensional evaluation based on the specific criteria. Alternatively, users can opt not to select a scenario where EasyJudge will evaluate the model response using the default scenario. The default scenario encompasses ten standard evaluation criteria suitable for most task evaluations. For more customized evaluation results, users can manually select the criteria. EasyJudge currently offers 40 evaluation criteria across four main categories for tailored evaluation. If custom criteria are selected, the system will automatically bypass scenario selection.

Step 3 (Data Upload): As shown in Figure 2-3, EasyJudge provides two methods for data upload. Suppose a user is evaluating a single data instance. In that case, they can sequentially copy the instruction, Model 1's response, Model 2's response, and the reference answer into the corresponding input fields, then click the submit button to initiate the

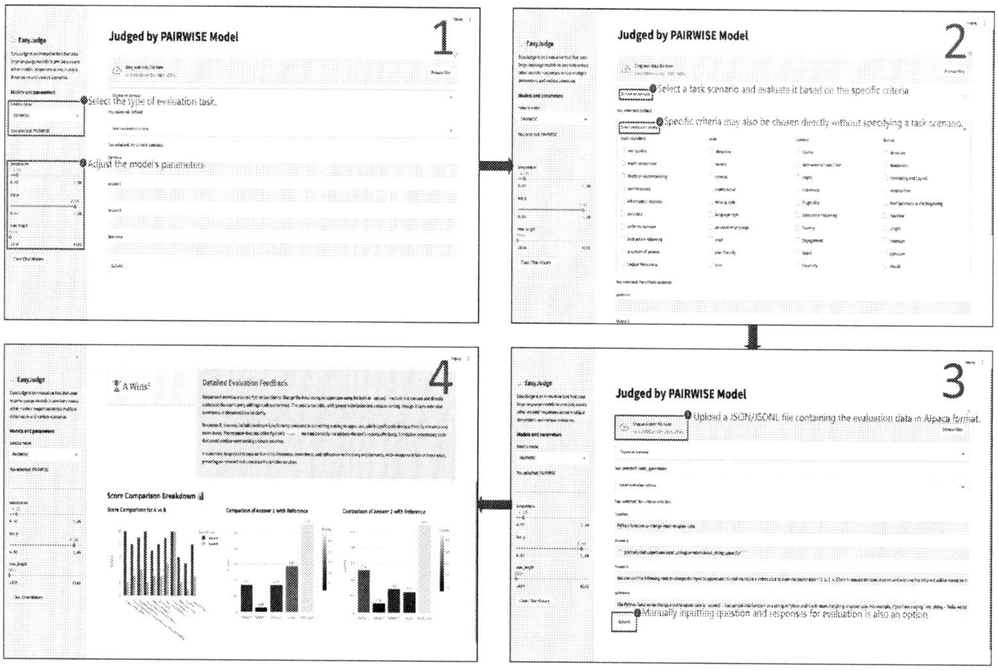

Figure 2: A screenshot of EasyJudge with an example evaluation task of PAIRWISE.

evaluation. To evaluate multiple data instances, users must upload a JSON/JSONL file containing the evaluation data in Alpaca format. After uploading the file, users can click the submit button to start the evaluation process. The interface for single data evaluation in the POINTWISE mode is shown in Figure 8.

Step 4 (Results Display): In this step, EasyJudge presents the final evaluation results, providing users with clear evaluation information that helps them intuitively understand the quality of the responses. Taking PAIRWISE evaluation as an example (Details on POINTWISE evaluation can be found in Appendix C.), as shown in Figure 2-4, the top of the page displays the final evaluation results. At the same time, the middle section presents the Detailed Evaluation Feedback from the EasyJudge model. At the bottom, three charts (labeled as Figures A, b, and c) are provided: Figure A shows the scores of Response A and Response B across different evaluation criteria dimensions and compares the two responses in each dimension. Figure b compares Response A with the reference text, displaying evaluation results based on traditional metrics, including ROUGE, BLEU, BERTScore, BLEURT, and BARTScore. Figure c compares Response B with the reference answer evaluated using traditional metrics. Finally, if users choose to upload a JSON/JSONL file, then they can finally download a JSON file containing the evaluation result data by clicking the "Download" button.

6 Conclusion

This paper introduces EasyJudge, an innovative tool for evaluating LLMs with advanced models, offering a customizable interface and precise, multi-dimensional assessments. It enhances efficiency through model quantization, enabling use on consumer-grade GPUs and CPUs. Future research plans include integrating new technologies to extend EasyJudge's capabilities to evaluate multimodal models, Retrieval-Augmented Generation (RAG), and intelligent agents, contributing to advancing Artificial General Intelligence (AGI) while improving evaluation accuracy and practicality across diverse scenarios.

Acknowledgements

This work is supported by the National Social Science Foundation (22&ZD035), the National Nature Science Foundation (61972436), and the Minzu University of China Foundation (GRSCP202316, 2023QNYL22, 2024GJYY43).

References

Josh Achiam, Steven Adler, Sandhini Agarwal, Lama Ahmad, Ilge Akkaya, Florencia Leoni Aleman, Diogo Almeida, Janko Altenschmidt, Sam Altman, Shyamal Anadkat, et al. 2023. Gpt-4 technical report. *arXiv preprint arXiv:2303.08774*.

Yupeng Chang, Xu Wang, Jindong Wang, Yuan Wu, Linyi Yang, Kaijie Zhu, Hao Chen, Xiaoyuan Yi, Cunxiang Wang, Yidong Wang, et al. 2024. A survey on evaluation of large language models. *ACM Transactions on Intelligent Systems and Technology*, 15(3):1–45.

Cheng-Han Chiang and Hung-yi Lee. 2023. Can large language models be an alternative to human evaluations? *arXiv preprint arXiv:2305.01937*.

Jinlan Fu, See-Kiong Ng, Zhengbao Jiang, and Pengfei Liu. 2023. Gptscore: Evaluate as you desire. *arXiv preprint arXiv:2302.04166*.

Fabrizio Gilardi, Meysam Alizadeh, and Maël Kubli. 2023. Chatgpt outperforms crowd workers for text-annotation tasks. *Proceedings of the National Academy of Sciences*, 120(30):e2305016120.

Seungone Kim, Jamin Shin, Yejin Cho, Joel Jang, Shayne Longpre, Hwaran Lee, Sangdoo Yun, Seongjin Shin, Sungdong Kim, James Thorne, et al. 2023. Prometheus: Inducing fine-grained evaluation capability in language models. In *The Twelfth International Conference on Learning Representations*.

Junlong Li, Shichao Sun, Weizhe Yuan, Run-Ze Fan, Hai Zhao, and Pengfei Liu. 2023a. Generative judge for evaluating alignment. *arXiv preprint arXiv:2310.05470*.

Xuechen Li, Tianyi Zhang, Yann Dubois, Rohan Taori, Ishaan Gulrajani, Carlos Guestrin, Percy Liang, and Tatsunori B Hashimoto. 2023b. Alpacaeval: An automatic evaluator of instruction-following models.

Percy Liang, Rishi Bommasani, Tony Lee, Dimitris Tsipras, Dilara Soylu, Michihiro Yasunaga, Yian Zhang, Deepak Narayanan, Yuhuai Wu, Ananya Kumar, et al. 2022. Holistic evaluation of language models. *arXiv preprint arXiv:2211.09110*.

Chin-Yew Lin. 2004. Rouge: A package for automatic evaluation of summaries. In *Text summarization branches out*, pages 74–81.

Kishore Papineni, Salim Roukos, Todd Ward, and Wei-Jing Zhu. 2002. Bleu: a method for automatic evaluation of machine translation. In *Proceedings of the 40th annual meeting of the Association for Computational Linguistics*, pages 311–318.

Chengwei Qin, Aston Zhang, Zhuosheng Zhang, Jiaao Chen, Michihiro Yasunaga, and Diyi Yang. 2023. Is chatgpt a general-purpose natural language processing task solver? *arXiv preprint arXiv:2302.06476*.

Thibault Sellam, Dipanjan Das, and Ankur P Parikh. 2020. Bleurt: Learning robust metrics for text generation. *arXiv preprint arXiv:2004.04696*.

Hugo Touvron, Thibaut Lavril, Gautier Izacard, Xavier Martinet, Marie-Anne Lachaux, Timothée Lacroix, Baptiste Rozière, Naman Goyal, Eric Hambro, Faisal Azhar, et al. 2023. Llama: Open and efficient foundation language models. *arXiv preprint arXiv:2302.13971*.

Yidong Wang, Zhuohao Yu, Zhengran Zeng, Linyi Yang, Cunxiang Wang, Hao Chen, Chaoya Jiang, Rui Xie, Jindong Wang, Xing Xie, et al. 2023. Pandalm: An automatic evaluation benchmark for llm instruction tuning optimization. *arXiv preprint arXiv:2306.05087*.

Wenhao Wu, Wei Li, Xinyan Xiao, Jiachen Liu, and Sujian Li. 2024. Instructeval: Instruction-tuned text evaluator from human preference. In *Findings of the Association for Computational Linguistics ACL 2024*, pages 13462–13474.

Weizhe Yuan, Graham Neubig, and Pengfei Liu. 2021. Bartscore: Evaluating generated text as text generation. *Advances in Neural Information Processing Systems*, 34:27263–27277.

Tianyi Zhang, Varsha Kishore, Felix Wu, Kilian Q Weinberger, and Yoav Artzi. 2019. Bertscore: Evaluating text generation with bert. *arXiv preprint arXiv:1904.09675*.

Lianmin Zheng, Wei-Lin Chiang, Ying Sheng, Siyuan Zhuang, Zhanghao Wu, Yonghao Zhuang, Zi Lin, Zhuohan Li, Dacheng Li, Eric Xing, et al. 2023. Judging llm-as-a-judge with mt-bench and chatbot arena. *Advances in Neural Information Processing Systems*, 36:46595–46623.

Lianghui Zhu, Xinggang Wang, and Xinlong Wang. 2023. Judgelm: Fine-tuned large language models are scalable judges. *arXiv preprint arXiv:2310.17631*.

A Prompt Templates

This section lists all the prompt templates that EasyJudge used. Figure 3 shows the prompt for invoking GPT-4 extended instructions. Figure 4 shows the prompt used for PAIRWISE instruction evaluation. Figure 5 details the prompt for POINTWISE instruction evaluation. Figure 6 displays the ALPACA fine-tuning data template.

B User Interface Display

This section shows more user interface. Figure 7 displays all the available scenarios for users, Figure 8 shows one input method for POINTWISE evaluation, Figure 9 presents an example of detailed

Invoke GPT-4 extended instructions

You are asked to provide 10 diverse prompts. These task prompts will be provided to a GPT model and we will evaluate the ability of the GPT model to reply to these prompts.
The type of the generated prompt needs to be {category_name}. Do not generate other types of prompts.
The following are some examples:
{examples}
Here are the requirements you need to follow to provide prompts:
1.The prompts need to be complete sentences, not phrases or fragments.
2.The prompts need to be varied, do not use similar prompts.
3.the prompts need to be meaningful, do not use meaningless prompts.
4.The prompts need to have a variety of tones, e.g., combining interrogative and imperative sentences.
5.The prompts need to be challenging, do not use simple directions.
6.The prompts need to be something that the Large Language Model can accomplish. For example, don't ask the assistant to create any visual or audio output. For example, don't ask the assistant to wake you up at 5pm or set a reminder because it can't perform any action. For example, prompts should not be related to audio, video, images, hyperlinks.
7.The prompts are in English, except for translation-related questions.
8.Some prompts can provide contextual information, should involve realistic data, and should not contain simple placeholders. Not all prompts require input. For example, when an prompts asks for general knowledge information, such as "What is the tallest mountain in the world?", it does not need to provide specific context.
After you have provided the prompts, please add the category of the prompts in a pair of && sign after the prompt and surround the prompt with in a pair of @@ sign.
For example, if the prompt is "@@Explain what `COUNT(Time[@[Start ]:[Finish]])=4` does in Excel. @@&& {category_name} &&", then the category is {category_name}.
Note that the category of prompt you provide must be {category_name}.
Here are some examples of prompts you provide:
@@example prompt1@@ &&category&&
@@example prompt2@@ &&category&&
...
@@example prompt9@@ &&category&&
@@example prompt10@@ &&category&&
The following is a list of 10 good task prompts with serial numbers and category

Figure 3: The prompt for invoking GPT-4 extended instructions.

feedback for a POINTWISE evaluation, and Figure 10 shows a detailed scoring breakdown for a POINTWISE evaluation.

C Training Details

This section shows the parameter settings for training EasyJudge, as shown in Table 3.

PAIRWISE instruction evaluation prompt

You are given the criteria to craft good responses for this type of query from users:
{scenario}
The criteria are as follows:
[Criteria start]
{criteria}
[Criteria end]

You are assessing two submitted responses on a given user's query and judging which response is better or they are tied. Here is the data:
[BEGIN DATA]
***
[Query]: {question_body}
***
[Response 1]: {answer1_body}
***
[Response 2]: {answer2_body}
***
[Reference]: {reference}
***
[END DATA]
Please follow the evaluation process outlined below:
1. First, using the given scoring criteria and reference answer, evaluate responses A and B from various dimensions, scoring each dimension from 1 to 10. In the answer section, return all your scoring results in the following dictionary format (including brackets), and ensure your scores are integers: {{'Dimension One': Score, 'Dimension Two': Score, ..., 'Overall Score': Score}}, e.g., {{'Factual Accuracy': 9, 'User Need Fulfillment': 6, ..., 'Overall Score': 7}}.
2. Calculate the final score for responses A and B separately. The final score is the average of the scores for each dimension. Specifically, add the scores of all dimensions and divide by the total number of dimensions, where Dimensions 1 and 2 have a weight of 2, and the rest have a weight of 1. Round the result to the nearest integer.
3. Compare the final scores of response A and response B, and conclude which is better, or if they are equally good.
4. Write detailed feedback explaining why A or B is better, focusing on aspects emphasized in the evaluation criteria. Additionally, brainstorm and provide a more detailed comparative feedback result. When writing feedback, compare responses A and B directly, mentioning their similarities and differences. Try to articulate a reasoning process that explores the commonalities and differences between the two responses, mentioning these reasons at the end.
5. In the detailed feedback, do not explicitly mention the reference answer. For example, avoid phrases like "compared to the reference answer." Assume you inherently know the reference answer, which can be used to identify details missing in the two evaluated responses. Also, do not explicitly mention the scoring results in the detailed feedback as these have already been provided.
6. Do not generate any additional introductions, conclusions, or explanations.
The output format should be as follows: "@@@{{response A: Scores per dimension: ['Dimension One': Score, 'Dimension Two': Score, ..., 'Overall Score': Score]}}@@@{{response B: Scores per dimension: ['Dimension One': Score, 'Dimension Two': Score, ..., 'Overall Score': Score]}}###Final Result: {{A or B or Tie}}&&&Detailed Evaluation Feedback: {{Evaluation Content}}***"

Figure 4: The prompt used for PAIRWISE instruction evaluation.

POINTWISE instruction evaluation prompt

You are assessing submitted response on a given user's query based on the criteria you have known and evaluating the quality of a response. Here is the data:
[BEGIN DATA]
***
[Query]: {question_body}
***
[Response]: {answer_body}
***
***
[Reference]: {reference}
***
[END DATA]
Please follow the evaluation process below:
1.Review the response and the given criteria. Using the reference answer as a guide, evaluate the AI assistant's response from different dimensions, assigning a score of 1 to 10 for each dimension. For the scoring, return all your results in the following dictionary format (including the brackets), and ensure that your scores are integers: {{'Dimension 1': score, 'Dimension 2': score, ..., 'Overall Score': score}}, for example: {{'Factual Accuracy': 9, 'Meeting User Needs': 6, ..., 'Overall Score': 7}}.
2.Calculate the final score for responses A and B separately. The final score is the average of the scores for each dimension. Specifically, add the scores of all dimensions and divide by the total number of dimensions, where Dimensions 1 and 2 have a weight of 2, and the rest have a weight of 1. Round the result to the nearest integer.
3.Please Write detailed feedback. Based on the provided scoring criteria and reference answer, write detailed evaluation feedback that strictly assesses the response quality rather than offering a general assessment. Ensure a comprehensive evaluation in line with the scoring criteria without breaking them down into points or making repetitive statements. Additionally, brainstorm to deliver thorough feedback that demonstrates the assessment thought process.
4.In the detailed feedback, do not explicitly mention the reference answer. For example, avoid phrases like "compared to the reference answer." Assume you inherently know the reference answer, which can be used to identify details missing in the two evaluated responses. Also, do not explicitly mention the scoring results in the detailed feedback as these have already been provided.
5. Please do not generate any additional openings, conclusions, or explanations.
The output format should be as follows:
@@@Dimension Scores: {{'Dimension 1': score, 'Dimension 2': score, ..., 'Overall Score': score}}###Overall Score: {{score}}&&&Detailed Evaluation Feedback: {{evaluation content}}***

Figure 5: The prompt used for POINTWISE instruction evaluation.

ALPACA fine-tuning data template

```
Training PAIRWISE Models:
"PAIRWISE": {
    "file_name": "your file path",
    "columns": {
        "prompt": "instruction",
        "query": "input",
        "response": "output",
        "system": "system"
    }
}

Training POINTWISE Models:
"POINTWISE": {
    "file_name": "your file path",
    "columns": {
        "prompt": "instruction",
        "query": "input",
        "response": "output",
        "system": "system"
    }
}
```

Figure 6: ALPACA fine-tuning data template.

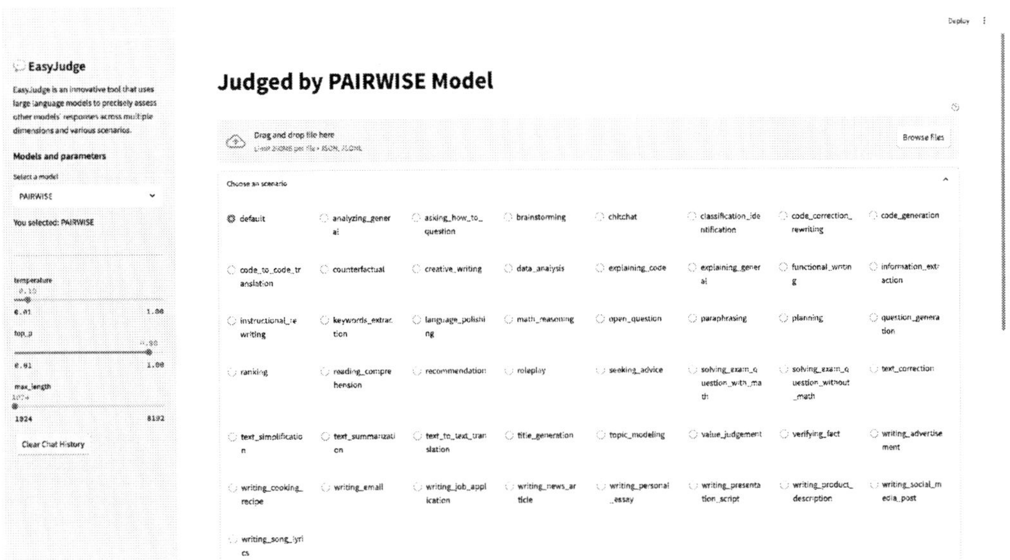

Figure 7: This interface displays all the available scenario for users.

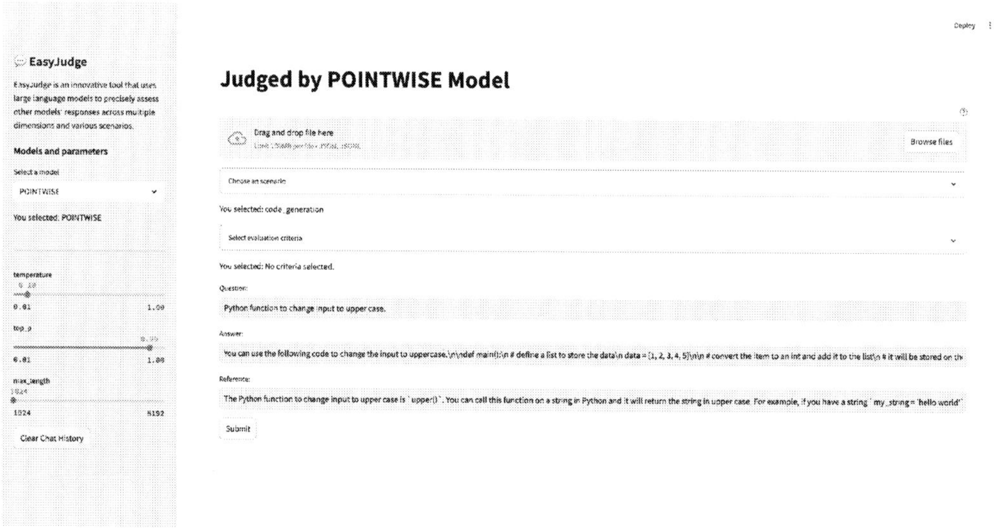

Figure 8: This interface displays one input method for POINTWISE evaluation.

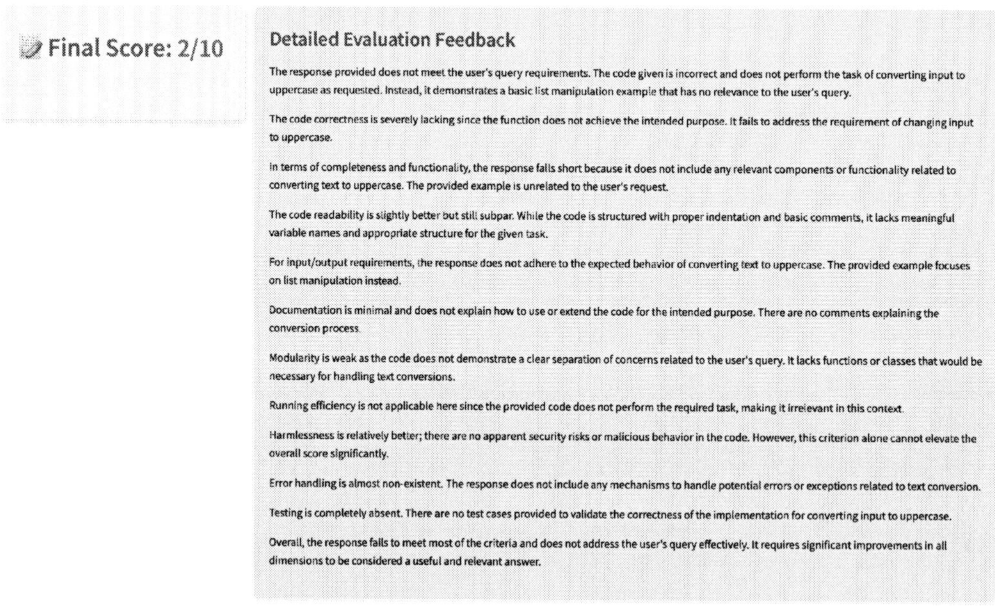

Figure 9: This interface shows an example of detailed feedback for a POINTWISE evaluation.

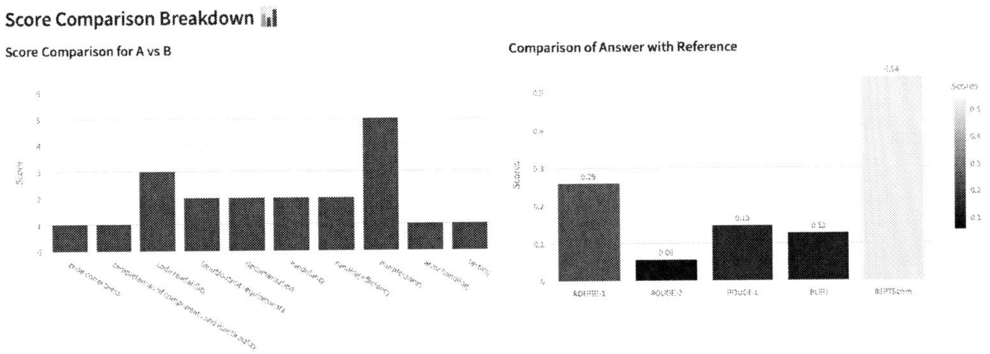

Figure 10: This interface displays a detailed scoring breakdown for a POINTWISE evaluation.

Parameters	Value
cutoff_len	2048
finetuning_type	lora
per_device_train_batch_size	4
lr_scheduler_type	cosine
lora_rank	8
lora_target	q_proj, v_proj
additional_target	embed_tokens, lm_head, norm
learning_rate	2×10^{-4}
num train epochs	1
gradient accumulation steps	2
max grad norm	1
lora dropout	0.05
warmup steps	0
fp16	TRUE

Table 3: The training parameters of the EasyJudge.

LUCE: A Dynamic Framework and Interactive Dashboard for Opinionated Text Analysis

Omnia Zayed, Gaurav Negi, Sampritha Manjunath, Devishree Pillai, and Paul Buitelaar
Insight SFI Research Centre for Data Analytics
Data Science Institute
University of Galway
IDA Business Park, Lower Dangan, Galway, Ireland
{firstname.lastname}@universityofgalway.ie

Abstract

We introduce *LUCE*, an advanced dynamic framework with an interactive dashboard for analysing opinionated text aiming to understand people-centred communication. The framework features computational modules of text classification and extraction explicitly designed for analysing different elements of opinions, e.g., sentiment/emotion, suggestion, figurative language, hate/toxic speech, and topics. We designed the framework using a modular architecture, allowing scalability and extensibility with the aim of supporting other NLP tasks in subsequent versions. *LUCE* comprises trained models, python-based APIs, and a user-friendly dashboard, ensuring an intuitive user experience. *LUCE* has been validated in a relevant environment, and its capabilities and performance have been demonstrated through initial prototypes and pilot studies.

1 Introduction

In an era where user-generated content on social media, forums, surveys, and review sites plays a pivotal role in shaping public opinion and influencing decision-making, understanding these opinionated discourse becomes essential. This sheer amount of opinionated content opened a wide range of possibilities for businesses, researchers, policymakers, and other stakeholders. At the same time, it creates a pressing need for automated language analysis to understand public discourse and visualise patterns through statistical analysis and results aggregation. However, analysing this data accurately and efficiently remains a challenge due to its sheer volume, diversity, and rapid pace of evolution. The preliminary research we conducted identified several critical gaps in existing opinion analysis applications: 1) tailored for commercial brand monitoring, making them difficult to adapt to other sectors (Nanda and Kumar, 2021); 2) limited to the analysis of particular tasks (e.g., sentiment analysis) instead of offering a holistic approach to opinion analysis; 3) high language-dependence (mostly English); 4) high domain-dependence (Purnat et al., 2021; White et al., 2023), requiring significant manual development for their adaptation to new domains.

We introduce *LUCE*, Italian for *light* and short for ***L**isten, **U**nderstand, **C**onnect, **E**ngage*, an advanced dynamic AI-powered framework for analysing opinionated text that aims to study people-centred public communication. The framework features an interactive dashboard to ensure a comfortable and intuitive user experience. This framework addresses the aforementioned gaps by leveraging state-of-the-art natural language processing (NLP) techniques to analyse public communication on multiple interconnected levels, including sentiment, emotion, suggestions, hate speech, sarcasm, figurative language, and topics. *LUCE* is designed to be domain, sector, and language-independent, which means that it is not limited to social media text or specific language. *LUCE*'s modular design ensures scalability and adaptability to various use cases and applications.

The initial version of *LUCE* focuses on text classification and extraction through three main modules to identify 1) opinion dimensions, 2) topics (aspect terms and categories), and 3) shorter text spans of suggestions. We employ dynamic transfer learning-based computational models for domain adaptation (Negi et al., 2024). Additionally, the introduced modules are designed to support domain and language independence through utilising language-agnostic embeddings (Feng et al., 2022) and cross-lingual transfer learning (Singla et al., 2018). One of the core objectives of *LUCE* is to allow end-users to analyse opinionated text automatically based on their needs through a user-friendly dashboard supporting data integration, results aggregation, and output visualisation. The visual analytics components offered by the dashboard allow

Proceedings of the 31st International Conference on Computational Linguistics: System Demonstrations, pages 104–116
January 19–24, 2025.

end-users to understand the discourse and visualise patterns/relationships.

In this paper, we present the first prototype of *LUCE*[1], which has been validated in a relevant environment, and its capabilities and performance have been demonstrated through various use cases and pilot studies. Examples include the EU-funded PANDEM-2 project[2], which included a social media analysis (SMA) component that was a forerunner of *LUCE* to support two-way communication during pandemics where reactions from the general public to government measures during the pandemic were successfully analysed. Similarly, the SFI-National Challenge-funded project Platform Urbanism[3], in collaboration with Galway City Council, employed the initial forerunner of LUCE to analyse public communication around urban development. Currently, the *LUCE* prototype is being used in the University of Galway Research Process Improvement project to analyse staff survey responses to university support of excellent and impactful research. The main contributions of this paper are summarised as follows:

1. We introduce the *LUCE* dynamic framework for opinionated text analysis developed with state-of-the-art performance.
2. We validated the proposed technology in relevant environments through pilot studies on various domains.
3. We designed the framework using a modular architecture, allowing scalability and extensibility to support other NLP tasks in subsequent versions.
4. We introduce a user-friendly web-based dashboard encompassing the framework's pre-trained models and Python-based APIs, ensuring an intuitive user experience.

2 *LUCE* Framework and Interactive Dashboard

2.1 Architecture

LUCE follows a modular architecture, as shown in Figure 1, to allow scalability and extensibility. The framework comprises three main modules, which currently enable 1) the classification of opinion dimensions in a given text (e.g., survey responses, social media posts, etc.); 2) the identification of core aspect terms and categories related to people's perceptions; 3) the extraction of shorter spans (e.g., of suggestions or hate speech) from a given text.

The development process of *LUCE* is based on a structured pipeline divided into four stages, as depicted in Figure 2. The data preparation step focuses on collecting, preparing, and preprocessing benchmark datasets for each task the framework supports. These datasets are used for training and evaluating the developed models. The development stage of each module is designed to allow the ease of modification and extensibility by utilising state-of-the-art approaches for text classification (e.g., sentiment classification, emotion classification, suggestion mining, etc.), aspect terms and categories extraction (e.g., term extraction, keyphrase extraction, and clustering), and span extraction. Quantitative and qualitative evaluation schemes were followed to assess the performance of each developed model. The quantitative analysis employed the traditional metrics of measuring the performance of each task. For example, the performance of the classification models is evaluated in terms of precision, recall, F1-score and accuracy (Rijsbergen, 1979) and the performance of the extraction models is evaluated in terms of BLEU (Papineni et al., 2002) and ROUGE (Lin, 2004) scores.

2.2 System Components

LUCE has a Python-based back-end and an interactive front-end dashboard. The architecture is designed to provide seamless interaction between data processing, opinion analysis, and output visualisation, with each component integrated through well-defined workflows.

Python-based Back-end. The back end is responsible for processing the input data, running opinion analysis models, and managing interactions with the front end. It utilises several components to ensure efficient and scalable operations. Communication between the back-end and front-end is facilitated through REST API endpoints. These endpoints handle requests, such as data submission, analysis initiation, and result retrieval. The opinion analysis modules encompass trained deep models served using TorchServe[4]. The entire back-end is encapsulated within a self-contained Docker image, ensuring consistency and ease of deployment

[1]This first prototype corresponds to *LUCE* Beta v0.1.

[2]https://pandem-2.eu

[3]https://www.sfi.ie/challenges/future-digital/cathair-shamhlu/

[4]https://pytorch.org/serve/

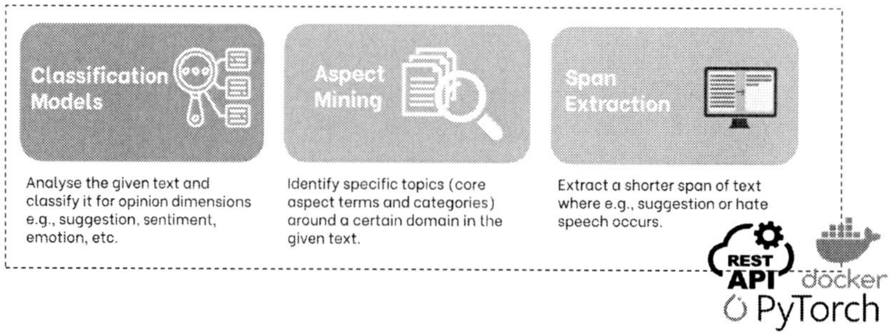

Figure 1: Main Modules in the current prototype of *LUCE*.

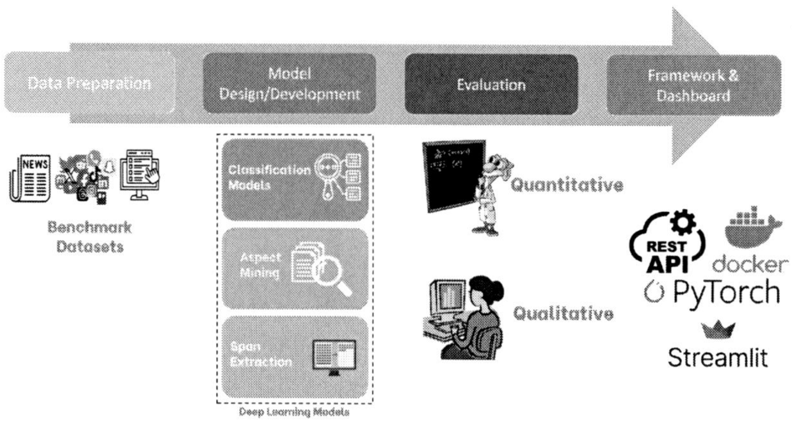

Figure 2: *LUCE*'s Structured Development Process.

across different environments. Docker enables the system to run with all necessary dependencies, facilitating portability and simplifying the installation process. The back-end is hosted locally on a Linux-based server.

Interactive Front-end Dashboard. The front end is implemented using Streamlit[5], an open-source Python library that simplifies the creation of interactive web-based dashboards. *LUCE*'s dashboard allows users to interact with the framework, view the results of the opinion analysis, and explore the data visually. Users can upload text data through the dashboard (in two formats, as discussed in Section 2.3), initiate the analysis process, and view outputs such as sentiment scores, emotion classes, top terms, and detailed visualisations. The front end is designed to be simple and easy to use, ensuring that both technical and non-technical users can easily navigate the interface.

Workflow. The following steps summarise the workflow between the back and front end.

- Data Input: The user uploads opinionated text data through the dashboard, which triggers a request to the back-end via a REST API.
- Model Processing: The back-end receives the data (as JSON objects), processes it, and passes it to the TorchServe model for inference.
- Opinion Analysis: The trained models analyse the text data, identifying opinion dimensions and aspect terms/categories. The results are then packaged (as JSON objects) and sent to the front end.
- Data Visualisation: The results are then displayed on the Streamlit-based dashboard, where users can interact with the various visual components and extract meaningful insights.
- Real-Time Feedback: The system ensures real-time feedback by updating the dashboard with results as soon as they are available, pro-

[5]`https://streamlit.io`

viding an intuitive and responsive user experience.

The following section demonstrates this workflow in detail, and Section 3 navigates through real-world use cases where *LUCE* has been deployed within various projects.

2.3 System Demonstration

LUCE's dashboard allows an interactive user experience through multiple visualisation components to facilitate the analysis of opinionated text. This section provides a guided tour of the interactive dashboard, highlighting *LUCE*'s main features.

Figure 7 shows a snapshot of the Home page showing the main modules on the left-hand menu. This page serves as the entry point to the framework. It briefly introduces users to *LUCE* and explains how to upload and analyse their data.

Each module page has its upload page, which allows users to submit their text data for analysis. The dashboard accepts two input formats, raw text and text file (comma-separated dataset), making it adaptable for different needs. Figure 3 shows both options side by side. Once the data is uploaded, the user can choose various options to proceed with the analysis through drop-down menus, such as the type of opinion classification, e.g., sentiment, emotion, suggestion, etc., the language[6], the trained model (e.g., Attention-based (Baziotis et al., 2017; Chronopoulou et al., 2018), Transformer-based (Devlin et al., 2019; Liu et al., 2019), LLM-based (Negi et al., 2024) models), the aspect term extraction techniques (e.g., term extraction (Frantzi et al., 2000; Zhang et al., 2016), keyphrase extraction (Boudin, 2018; Campos et al., 2020)), and aspect clustering mechanisms (e.g., centroid-based (MacQueen, 1967) or hierarchical density-based (McInnes et al., 2017)). Furthermore, when uploading a comma-separated file, the user can specify the file format in terms of text column, delimiter type, quotation type, etc.

Once the analysis is complete, the results will automatically appear through a number of interactive visual components in a dedicated section on each module's page. Generally, the result section comprises the following:

- Opinion Distribution: The distribution of each opinion dimension is represented by pie charts that break down the opinion categories within the dataset. Below these pie charts, users can find a bar chart highlighting the top 10 bigrams and a word cloud highlighting the most frequently used words. Figure 4 shows an example of the results section of opinion classification on a University Survey data.
- Text-level Analysis: A data frame view showing individual text entries with their corresponding identified opinion dimensions and probabilities (e.g., sentiment polarity, emotions categories, suggestion class, etc.) as shown in Figure 8.
- Interactive Filters: Users can filter the results based on specific criteria, such as opinion class or keyword.

2.4 Supported Functionality

The current prototype provides language analysis in terms of 1) opinion dimensions and 2) topics (aspect terms and categories)[7]. For opinion dimensions, the current version of *LUCE* supports sentiment analysis, emotion analysis, and suggestion classification. Sentiment analysis is concerned with identifying whether a sentence holds a positive, negative, or neutral sentiment (Liu and Zhang, 2012; Rosenthal et al., 2017). Emotion analysis further identifies emotional expressions conveyed in the text by utilising various psychological classification schemes. We employ an extension of the Plutchik (1980) model to identify 11 expressions (Mohammad et al., 2018): *anger, anticipation, disgust, fear, joy, love, optimism, pessimism, sadness, surprise,* and *trust*. The task of suggestion detection focuses on classifying a given post as to whether it contains a suggestion or not (Negi et al., 2019).

The uploaded data can revolve around a specific theme or topic. However, it is essential to analyse it on a fine-grained level to understand the subtopics (aspects) discussed. This analysis is referred to as aspect mining, where aspect terms and categories are extracted from opinionated text through a multi-stage process that involves the extraction of aspect terms (features) of an entity or object in a particular domain and figuring out opinions about those aspects. The process can also involve assigning

[6]The dashboard is currently hosting the English-based models, we will include the implemented multilingual models in subsequent versions.

[7]The framework already supports suggestion span extraction, but it was not included in the dashboard when this manuscript was submitted.

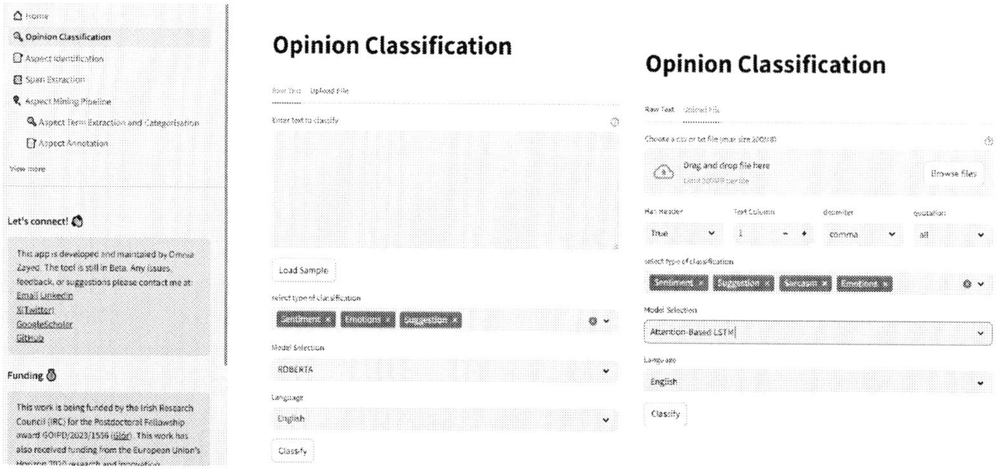

Figure 3: A snapshot of the input formats, raw text and text file, which *LUCE*'s dashboard offers.

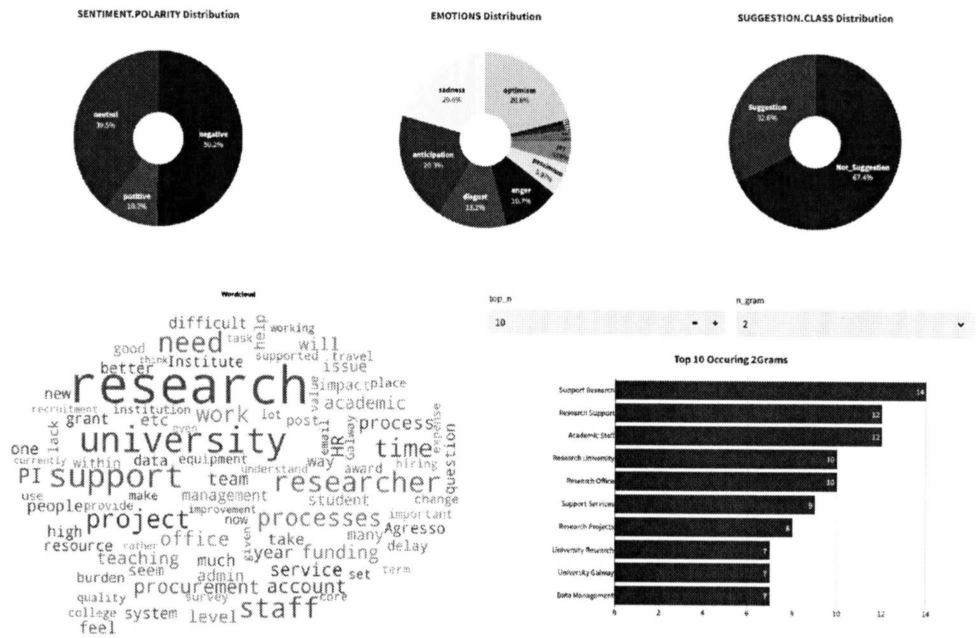

Figure 4: A snapshot of the pie charts in the opinion dimension analysis result.

the identified aspect terms to predefined higher-level categories (Pang and Lee, 2008; Liu, 2020). Aspect term identification is hosted on a separate page on the dashboard where the user can upload text dataset as shown in Figure 5. Once the analysis is done, aspect terms and their corresponding categories will be visualised in a tabular format. Additionally, the end-user can inspect a visualisation of the clustered aspects, as shown in Figure 6. Furthermore, the aspect categories identified for a given dataset can be reused to annotate new unseen text from the same domain (see Figure 9 in Appendix A).

3 Use Cases

An initial prototype of *LUCE* has been deployed within multiple projects to address a wide range of use cases across various domains and types of text.

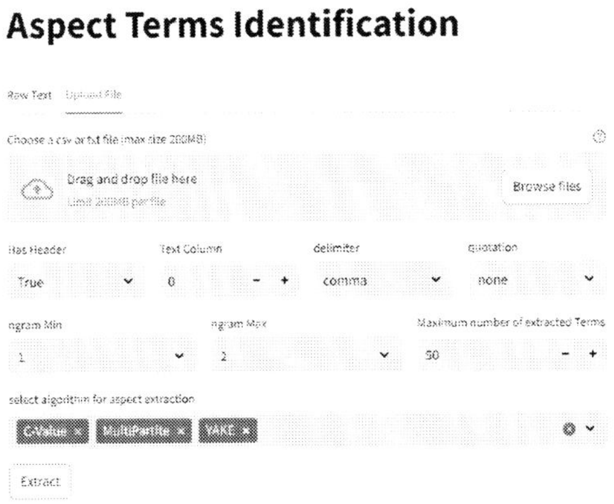

Figure 5: A snapshot of the data loading option on the Aspect Identification page. The user can upload raw text or a text file.

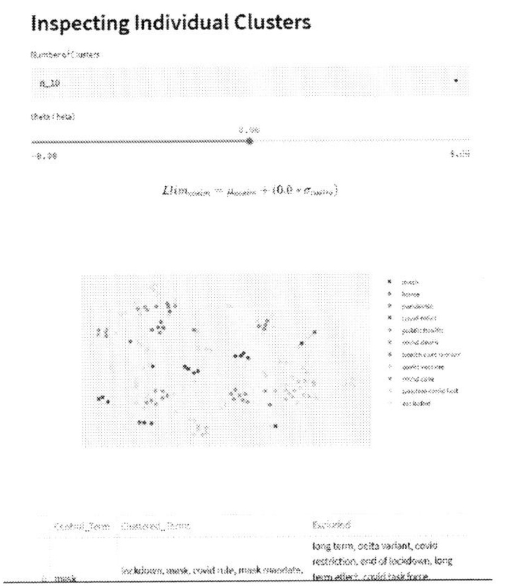

Figure 6: A screenshot of the aspect clustering result of the COVID dataset.

Public Health. The forerunner prototype of *LUCE* has been deployed in the EU-funded PANDEM-2 project. The project focused on pandemic preparedness and response and included an initial prototype of the language analysis framework to support two-way communication[8] on social media during pandemics. Public health agencies within the project's consortium have extensively used the proposed solution and validated the need for insight extraction from social media with the framework's demonstrated capabilities. In this project, tweets (rebranded as X posts) related to COVID-19 were analysed in real-time. The live streaming of tweets was done using the ECDC-developed tool Epitweetr (Espinosa et al., 2022) before discontinuing the free API access. Figure 10[9] shows a snapshot of the social media analysis page on the PANDEM-2 dashboard showing trending topics at a specific period during the COVID-19 pandemic, along with sentiment/emotion analysis. The interactive dashboard permitted the comparison of opinion dimensions across countries based on the end-user choice (Figure 11). Moreover, the conducted suggestion analysis gave public health managers the ability to sift through the communicated suggestions on social media by the general public based on dynamically identified categories (as shown in Figure 12). The implemented filtering mechanisms in the user interface facilitated analysing public communication in a particular country, in a particular language, or time period according to the needs of end-users. In addition to analysing real-time tweets, the system was used to analyse a stratified hydrated random sample of around 500K tweets of a publicly available large-scale COVID dataset of tweets (Lamsal, 2021).

Urban Development. Following the successful implementation of the advanced opinion analysis technology in the PANDEM-2 project, the SFI-National Challenge-funded Platform Urbanism project, in collaboration with Galway City Council, was encouraged to use it to analyse public communication. The project specifically concentrated on analysing Reddit posts around Galway City[10] to identify various opinion dimensions and aspects of concern to the Irish citizens regarding the city's urban development.

University Research Process Improvement. Currently, the *LUCE* prototype is being used in the University of Galway Research Process Improvement project to analyse staff survey responses to university support of excellent and impactful research. The language analysis is conducted on the textual responses to open-ended questions from the survey. The management and consultants use the outcome to understand the barriers within the current processes and operating models to enable

[8]Two-way communication ensures the mutual flow of information between multiple parties, e.g., the public and public health agencies.

[9]Some figures are moved to Appendix A due to space limitations.

[10]https://www.reddit.com/r/galway/

research and innovation.

4 Conclusion and Future Work

We introduced *LUCE*, an advanced dynamic framework for opinionated text analysis to study public communication. The current beta prototype of *LUCE* features computational state-of-the-art neural-based modules of text classification and extraction explicitly designed for analysing different elements of opinions, e.g., sentiment/emotion, suggestion, and topics. The framework is designed with a modular architecture to ensure scalability and extensibility for future versions, supporting a wide range of NLP tasks. *LUCE* comprises pre-trained models, python-based APIs, and a user-friendly dashboard, ensuring an intuitive user experience. We have validated the technology in relevant environments and demonstrated its capabilities and performance across diverse use cases in different domains and applications. Currently, we are expanding the opinion dimensions module to encompass additional identification tasks such as sarcasm and hate speech and enhancing the dashboard design to include an extraction module developed for analysing suggestion text.

5 Broader Impact

The *LUCE* framework and the proposed technology will have substantial societal, political, and academic impacts due to the universal need of organisations, such as public service agencies, government entities, and corporations, to understand opinionated data produced in massive volumes daily. Such understanding permits 1) the adjustment of communication approaches, 2) the support of decision-making and policies, and 3) the building of public trust, ultimately improving public/private service delivery. The deployment of this prototype in various projects, such as the EU-funded PANDEM-2, proved its timeliness and necessity. We have engaged with potential stakeholders in the public health sectors and beyond, gathering valuable feedback to refine the proposed technology. Prospective national and international stakeholders showed interest in the prototype and are seeking to beta-test future versions of *LUCE*. Other prospective stakeholders include national public agencies, research institutions, and companies. In all cases, the stakeholders have emphasised the need for insight extraction from user-generated content with the capabilities demonstrated using the *LUCE* prototype.

6 Ethical Considerations

Privacy/Copyright. One of the ethical considerations we are tackling is the privacy and copyright of the uploaded datasets by end-users. Since the framework relies on collecting and analysing text data, it is crucial to ensure that 1) the framework is secure enough to handle and protect private data and 2) the uploaded data is collected without infringing copyright or redistribution policies.

Bias. The computational models implemented in the *LUCE* framework are trained on benchmark datasets that may reflect inherent bias, which, in turn, can affect the fairness and accuracy of the analysis. To mitigate this, we conduct regular qualitative analysis[11] on the data to understand the framework's performance to improve fairness and reduce bias.

Acknowledgments

This publication has emanated from research conducted with the financial support of Taighde Éireann – Research Ireland for the Postdoctoral Fellowship award GOIPD/2023/1556 (Glór). This work has also received funding from the European Union's Horizon 2020 research and innovation programme under grant agreement No 883285 (PANDEM-2). Additionally, this work has been partially funded by the Science Foundation Ireland (SFI) under Grant Number SFI/12/RC/2289_P2 (Insight_2).

References

Christos Baziotis, Nikos Pelekis, and Christos Doulkeridis. 2017. DataStories at SemEval-2017 task 4: Deep LSTM with attention for message-level and topic-based sentiment analysis. In *Proceedings of the 11th International Workshop on Semantic Evaluation (SemEval-2017)*, pages 747–754, Vancouver, Canada. Association for Computational Linguistics.

Florian Boudin. 2018. Unsupervised keyphrase extraction with multipartite graphs. In *Proceedings of the 2018 Conference of the North American Chapter of the Association for Computational Linguistics: Human Language Technologies, Volume 2 (Short Papers)*, pages 667–672, New Orleans, Louisiana. Association for Computational Linguistics.

[11]The results of this qualitative analysis are out of the scope of this demo paper.

Ricardo Campos, Vítor Mangaravite, Arian Pasquali, Alípio Jorge, Célia Nunes, and Adam Jatowt. 2020. Yake! keyword extraction from single documents using multiple local features. *Information Sciences*, 509:257–289.

Alexandra Chronopoulou, Aikaterini Margatina, Christos Baziotis, and Alexandros Potamianos. 2018. NTUA-SLP at IEST 2018: Ensemble of neural transfer methods for implicit emotion classification. In *Proceedings of the 9th Workshop on Computational Approaches to Subjectivity, Sentiment and Social Media Analysis*, pages 57–64, Brussels, Belgium. Association for Computational Linguistics.

Jacob Devlin, Ming-Wei Chang, Kenton Lee, and Kristina Toutanova. 2019. BERT: Pre-training of deep bidirectional transformers for language understanding. In *Proceedings of the 2019 Conference of the North American Chapter of the Association for Computational Linguistics: Human Language Technologies, Volume 1 (Long and Short Papers)*, pages 4171–4186, Minneapolis, Minnesota. Association for Computational Linguistics.

Laura Espinosa, Ariana Wijermans, Francisco Orchard, Michael Höhle, Thomas Czernichow, Pietro Coletti, Lisa Hermans, Christel Faes, Esther Kissling, and Thomas Mollet. 2022. Epitweetr: Early warning of public health threats using Twitter data. *Eurosurveillance*, 27(39).

Fangxiaoyu Feng, Yinfei Yang, Daniel Cer, Naveen Arivazhagan, and Wei Wang. 2022. Language-agnostic BERT sentence embedding. In *Proceedings of the 60th Annual Meeting of the Association for Computational Linguistics (Volume 1: Long Papers)*, pages 878–891, Dublin, Ireland. Association for Computational Linguistics.

Katerina Frantzi, Sophia Ananiadou, and Hideki Mima. 2000. Automatic recognition of multi-word terms: The c-value/nc-value method. *International Journal on Digital Libraries*, 3(2):115–130.

Rabindra Lamsal. 2021. Design and analysis of a large-scale covid-19 tweets dataset. *applied intelligence*, 51:2790–2804.

Chin-Yew Lin. 2004. ROUGE: A package for automatic evaluation of summaries. In *Text Summarization Branches Out*, pages 74–81, Barcelona, Spain. Association for Computational Linguistics.

Bing Liu. 2020. *Aspect and Entity Extraction*, page 168–226. Studies in Natural Language Processing. Cambridge University Press.

Bing Liu and Lei Zhang. 2012. *A Survey of Opinion Mining and Sentiment Analysis*, pages 415–463. Springer US, Boston, MA.

Yinhan Liu, Myle Ott, Naman Goyal, Jingfei Du, Mandar Joshi, Danqi Chen, Omer Levy, Mike Lewis, Luke Zettlemoyer, and Veselin Stoyanov. 2019. Roberta: A robustly optimized BERT pretraining approach. *ArXiv*, abs/1907.11692.

J. B. MacQueen. 1967. Some methods for classification and analysis of multivariate observations. In *Proceedings of the fifth Berkeley Symposium on Mathematical Statistics and Probability*, volume 1, pages 281–297. University of California Press.

Leland McInnes, John Healy, and Steve Astels. 2017. hdbscan: Hierarchical density based clustering. *Journal of Open Source Software*, 2(11):205.

Saif Mohammad, Felipe Bravo-Marquez, Mohammad Salameh, and Svetlana Kiritchenko. 2018. SemEval-2018 Task 1: Affect in tweets. In *Proceedings of the 12th International Workshop on Semantic Evaluation*, SemEval '18, pages 1–17, New Orleans, LA, USA.

Pooja Nanda and Vikas Kumar. 2021. Social media analytics: tools, techniques and present day practices. *International Journal of Services Operations and Informatics*, 11(4):422.

Gaurav Negi, Rajdeep Sarkar, Omnia Zayed, and Paul Buitelaar. 2024. A hybrid approach to aspect based sentiment analysis using transfer learning. In *Proceedings of the 2024 Joint International Conference on Computational Linguistics, Language Resources and Evaluation (LREC-COLING 2024)*, pages 647–658, Torino, Italia. ELRA and ICCL.

Sapna Negi, Tobias Daudert, and Paul Buitelaar. 2019. SemEval-2019 task 9: Suggestion mining from online reviews and forums. In *Proceedings of the 13th International Workshop on Semantic Evaluation*, pages 877–887, Minneapolis, Minnesota, USA. Association for Computational Linguistics.

Bo Pang and Lillian Lee. 2008. Opinion mining and sentiment analysis. *Found. Trends Inf. Retr.*, 2(1–2):1–135.

Kishore Papineni, Salim Roukos, Todd Ward, and Wei-Jing Zhu. 2002. Bleu: a method for automatic evaluation of machine translation. In *Proceedings of the 40th Annual Meeting of the Association for Computational Linguistics*, ACL '02, pages 311–318, Philadelphia, Pennsylvania, USA. Association for Computational Linguistics.

Robert Plutchik. 1980. Chapter 1 - a general psychoevolutionary theory of emotion. In Robert Plutchik and Henry Kellerman, editors, *Theories of Emotion*, pages 3–33. Academic Press.

Tina D. Purnat, Paolo Vacca, Stefano Burzo, Tim Zecchin, Amy Wright, Sylvie Briand, and Tim Nguyen. 2021. WHO Digital Intelligence Analysis for Tracking Narratives and Information Voids in the COVID-19 Infodemic. In John Mantas, Lăcrămioara Stoicu-Tivadar, Catherine Chronaki, Arie Hasman, Patrick Weber, Parisis Gallos, Mihaela Crişan-Vida, Emmanouil Zoulias, and Oana Sorina Chirila, editors, *Studies in Health Technology and Informatics*. IOS Press.

C. J. Van Rijsbergen. 1979. *Information Retrieval*, 2nd edition. Butterworth-Heinemann.

Sara Rosenthal, Noura Farra, and Preslav Nakov. 2017. SemEval-2017 task 4: Sentiment analysis in Twitter. In *Proceedings of the 11th International Workshop on Semantic Evaluation (SemEval-2017)*, pages 502–518, Vancouver, Canada. Association for Computational Linguistics.

Karan Singla, Dogan Can, and Shrikanth Narayanan. 2018. A multi-task approach to learning multilingual representations. In *Proceedings of the 56th Annual Meeting of the Association for Computational Linguistics (Volume 2: Short Papers)*, pages 214–220, Melbourne, Australia. Association for Computational Linguistics.

Becky K White, Arnault Gombert, Tim Nguyen, Brian Yau, Atsuyoshi Ishizumi, Laura Kirchner, Alicia León, Harry Wilson, Giovanna Jaramillo-Gutierrez, Jesus Cerquides, Marcelo D'Agostino, Cristiana Salvi, Ravi Shankar Sreenath, Kimberly Rambaud, Dalia Samhouri, Sylvie Briand, and Tina D Purnat. 2023. Using Machine Learning Technology (Early Artificial Intelligence–Supported Response With Social Listening Platform) to Enhance Digital Social Understanding for the COVID-19 Infodemic: Development and Implementation Study. *JMIR Infodemiology*, 3:e47317.

Ziqi Zhang, Jie Gao, and Fabio Ciravegna. 2016. JATE 2.0: Java automatic term extraction with Apache Solr. In *Proceedings of the Tenth International Conference on Language Resources and Evaluation (LREC'16)*, pages 2262–2269, Portorož, Slovenia. European Language Resources Association (ELRA).

A Appendix

This Appendix includes additional figures showing snapshots from the *LUCE* dashboard and snapshots from the social media analysis component that was a forerunner of *LUCE* deployed as part of the PANDEM-2 project.

Figure 7: *LUCE*'s Structured Development Process.

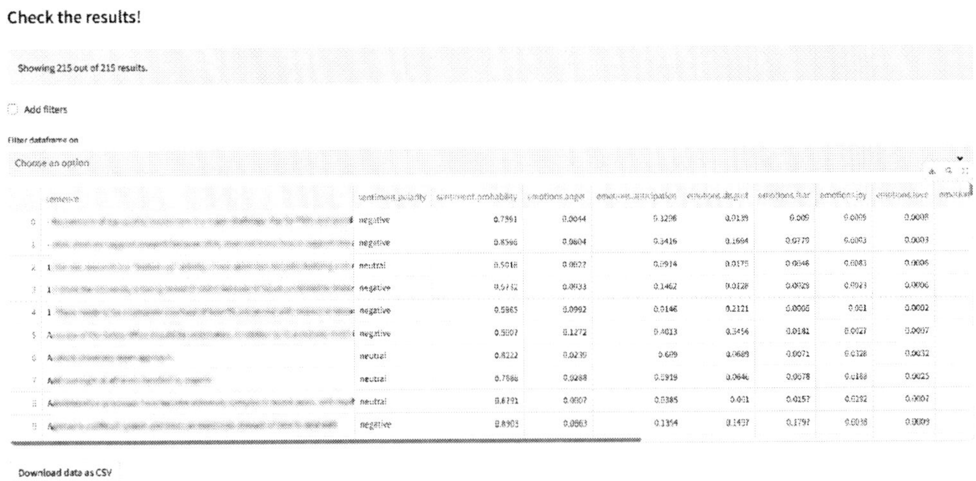

Figure 8: A snapshot of the tabular output of the opinion dimension analysis on the University Survey Data. The text is blurred due to copyright restrictions.

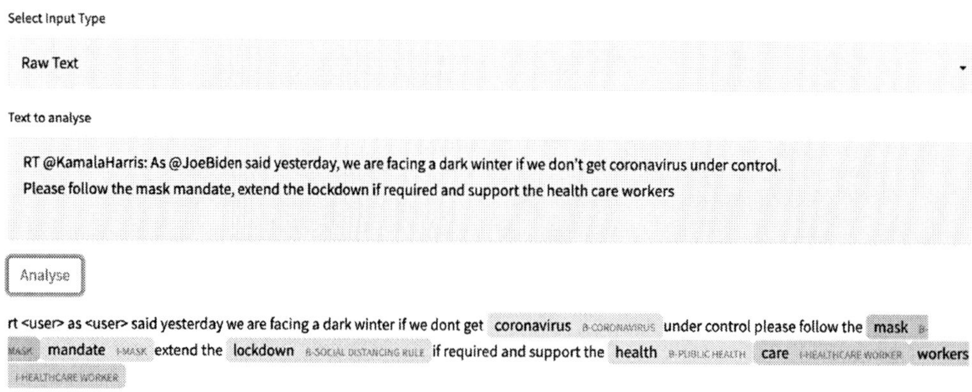

Figure 9: A snapshot of aspect annotation of a new given text.

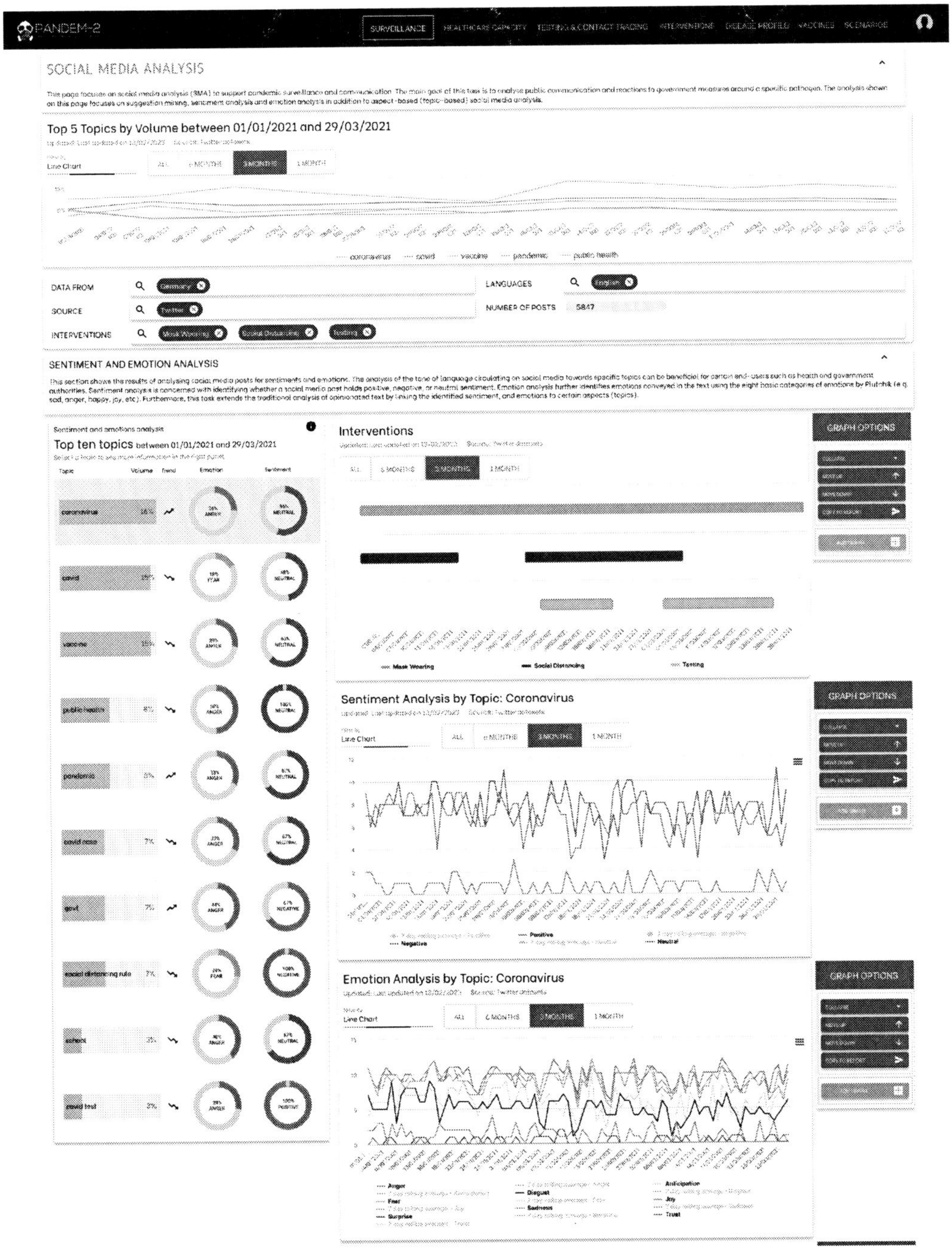

Figure 10: A snapshot of the social media analysis page of the forerunner prototype of *LUCE* deployed within the PANDEM-2 project.

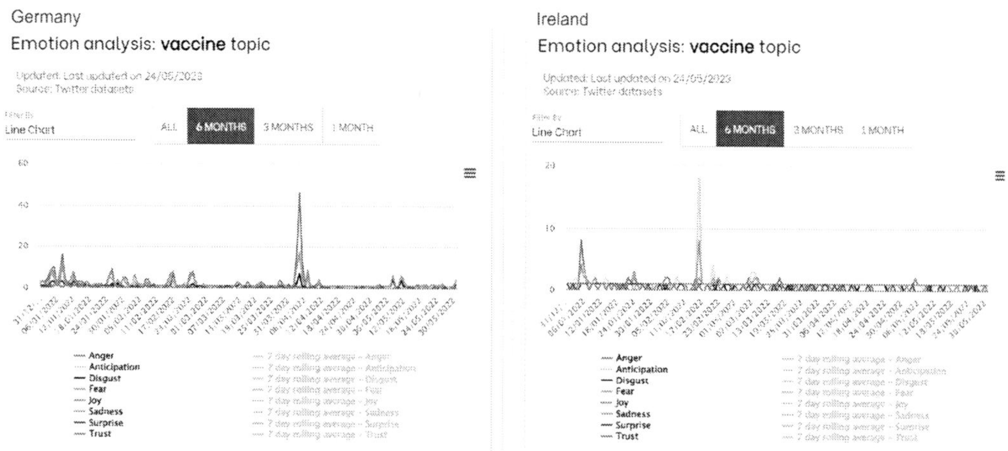

Figure 11: A snapshot comparing the emotions extracted around vaccine topic in Germany versus Ireland using the forerunner prototype of *LUCE* deployed within the PANDEM-2 project.

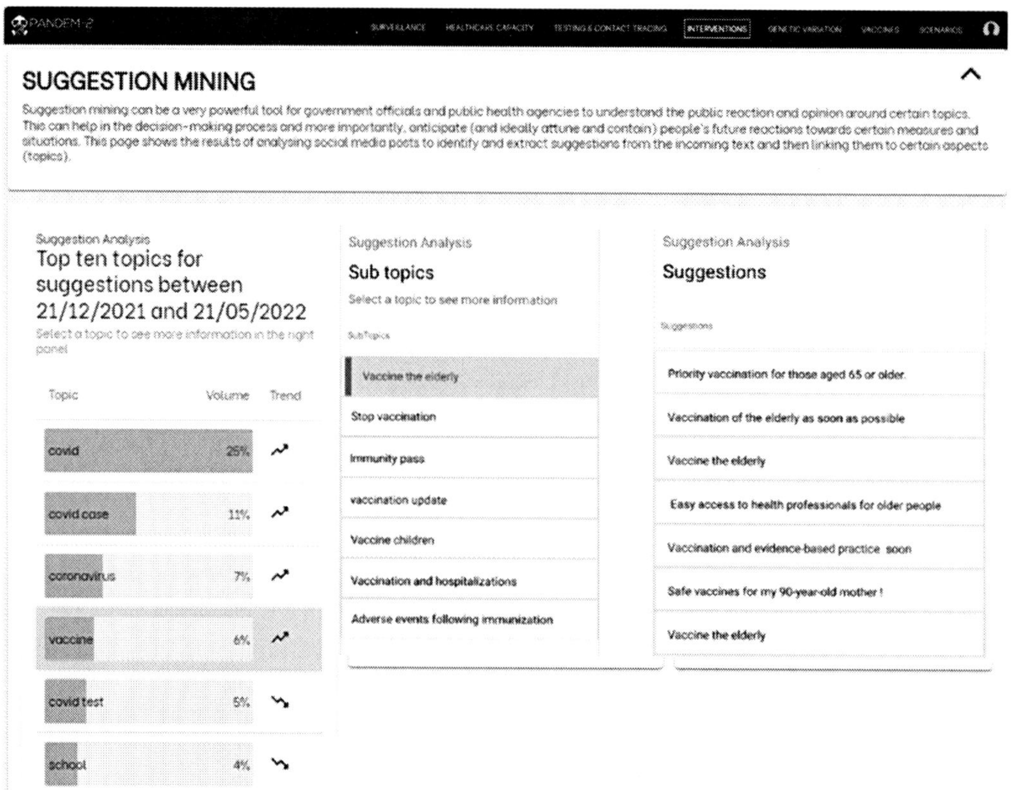

Figure 12: A snapshot of the results of the suggestion analysis module in the forerunner prototype of *LUCE* deployed within the PANDEM-2 project.

RAGthoven: A Configurable Toolkit for RAG-enabled LLM Experimentation

Gregor Karetka[1,2] **Demetris Skottis**[2] **Lucia Dutková**[2,3]
Peter Hraška[2] **Marek Šuppa**[2,4]
[1]Brno University of Technology [2]Cisco Systems
[3]Linnaeus University [4]Comenius University in Bratislava
Correspondence: marek@suppa.sk

Abstract

Large Language Models (LLMs) have significantly altered the landscape of Natural Language Processing (NLP), having topped the benchmarks of many standard tasks and problems, particularly when used in combination with Retrieval Augmented Generation (RAG). Despite their impressive performance and relative simplicity, its use as a baseline method has not been extensive. One of the reasons might be that adapting and optimizing RAG-based pipelines for specific NLP tasks generally requires custom development which is difficult to scale. In this work we introduce RAGthoven, a tool for automatic evaluation of RAG-based pipelines. It provides a simple yet powerful abstraction, which allows the user to start the evaluation process with nothing more than a single configuration file. To demonstrate its usefulness we conduct three case studies spanning text classification, question answering and code generation usecases. We release the code, as well as the documentation and tutorials, at `https://github.com/ragthoven-dev/ragthoven` [1]

1 Introduction

Large Language Models (LLMs), when combined with Retrieval Augmented Generation (RAG) (Lewis et al., 2020), have consistently demonstrated state-of-the-art performance across numerous NLP tasks, including question answering (Siriwardhana et al., 2023), text classification (Loukas et al., 2023), and code generation (Bassamzadeh and Methani, 2024). However, despite their proven success, as demonstrated by various surveys such as (Gao et al., 2023), RAG in combination with LLMs remains significantly underutilized, particularly in research settings where establishing strong baselines is crucial. Standardized use cases such as benchmarking new datasets or competing in shared tasks often overlook RAG's potential due to the complexities involved in its implementation. Researchers and practitioners frequently default to simpler models, leaving the full power of retrieval-augmented systems untapped.

One reason for this underutilization might be the significant custom development required to tailor RAG pipelines to specific tasks. Most RAG frameworks require users to write custom code, adjust for task-specific nuances, and optimize the pipeline stages. These barriers deter many from using RAG as a baseline method, despite its potential to improve performance in shared tasks, where strong, consistent baselines are essential. That in turn limits broader experimentation with RAG in academia and industry, especially for those working with new datasets or aiming to quickly establish competitive baselines for NLP tasks.

The contributions of this paper address these challenges through the introduction of RAGthoven, a toolkit designed to automate the evaluation of RAG-based pipelines. First, RAGthoven provides an easy-to-use configuration-driven interface that abstracts away the complexity of RAG implementation, making it accessible even to users with limited programming expertise. Second, it supports a broad range of NLP tasks out of the box, allowing researchers to quickly set up robust baselines for new datasets or shared tasks. Third, RAGthoven includes modules for indexing, retrieval, re-ranking, and generation, all of which can be configured independently, ensuring flexibility and adaptability for task-specific optimization. Through the tool's case studies in text classification, question answering, and code generation, we demonstrate its ability to simplify RAG based evaluations while maintaining competitive performance, thereby promoting wider adoption of retrieval-augmented models in research and practical applications.

[1]A walkthrough video can be found at `https://ragthoven-dev.github.io/walkthrough.mp4`

Proceedings of the 31st International Conference on Computational Linguistics: System Demonstrations, pages 117–125
January 19–24, 2025.

2 Related Work

Since its introduction, Retrieval Augmented Generation (Lee et al., 2019; Lewis et al., 2020; Guu et al., 2020) has been found useful for varied set of tasks, such as language modeling (Ram et al., 2023), machine translation (Cheng et al., 2024; Wang et al., 2022), text summarization (Li et al., 2023), question answering (Huang et al., 2023), information extraction (Wang et al., 2021; Glass et al., 2023), dialogue systems (King and Flanigan, 2023), as well as text classification (Abdullahi et al., 2024).

To support the diverse needs of the various tasks that could benefit from Retrieval Augmented Generation, a large number of frameworks and platforms have been introduced. These include extensive mature platforms such as for instance `haystack` (Pietsch et al., 2019), `Verba` [2] or `RAGFlow` [3] which are tailored towards production-oriented and/or document understanding use cases, as well as `cognita`[4], `canopy` [5], `fastRAG` (Izsak et al., 2023) and `FlashRAG` (Jin et al., 2024) which are oriented more towards experimentation. Virtually all of these frameworks and platforms require the end user to interact with them by producing custom Python code tailored to a specific task. This, however, makes them inaccessible to a significant number of users who might benefit from being able to experiment with Retrieval Augmented Generation without being proficient in Python. To the best of our knowledge RAGthoven is the only toolkit that, while also usable as a Python library, has been built with the "no code" ethos in mind and as such can be utilized by larger target audience of non-programmers as well.

3 System Description

RAGthoven is composed of four key modules: indexing, retrieval, re-ranking, and generation. Each module can be configured independently, allowing users to adapt the pipeline to specific NLP tasks. The following sections describe the function and configuration of each module in the RAGthoven pipeline.

3.1 Indexing

The indexing module is responsible for creating a searchable representation of the dataset, which is generally loaded using the `datasets` library (Lhoest et al., 2021). This module supports both vector-based indexing, which utilizes dense embeddings, and traditional text-based indexing, which leverages tokenized text data. Users can configure the indexing module to use different models for vectorization or tokenization, depending on the nature of the data and the retrieval requirements. The indexing module is powered by the ChromaDB[6] and can be configured to make use of any of the embedding models available on HuggingFace Hub. Importantly, the same model configuration is shared between the indexing and retrieval modules to ensure consistency in data representation.

3.2 Retrieval

The retrieval module fetches relevant documents or pieces of information from the indexed data. It supports vector-based retrieval, utilizing similarity search on dense embeddings. Users can configure the retrieval module with the same model used in indexing, ensuring alignment between how the data is indexed and retrieved. By default, the `sentence-transformers/all-MiniLM-L6-v2` model is utilized for embedding generation. The module can also be configured to output a specific number of retrieved items from the index based on the input using the `k` option in the `embed` section, making it a hyperparameter for end-users to optimize.

3.3 Re-ranking

After the retrieval step, the re-ranking module prioritizes the retrieved documents, ensuring that the most relevant items are forwarded to the generation module. Re-ranking is particularly useful when a large volume of data is retrieved, and further refinement is required to improve the relevance of the final output. In such a case, the Retrieval module is generally instructed to retrieve a larger number of samples whereas the re-ranking module is then tasked with reordering them based on how relevant they are to the input query. By default, the `ms-marco-MiniLM-L-12-v2` model is utilized to re-rank the samples obtained in the previous step. The number of items to finally return can again be configured using the `k` option in the `rerank` section.

This module can be configured to use different re-ranking models supported by the `flashrank` li-

[2] https://github.com/weaviate/Verba

[3] https://github.com/infiniflow/ragflow

[4] https://github.com/truefoundry/cognita

[5] https://github.com/pinecone-io/canopy

[6] https://www.trychroma.com/

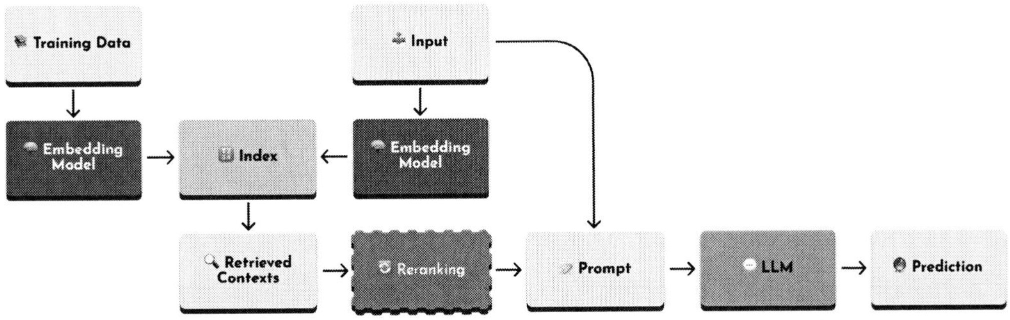

Figure 1: A diagram of a standard RAG system. Note that the Index and Re-ranking steps are optional in principle, but have been included in the diagram for clarity.

brary (Damodaran, 2023), allowing users to adjust ranking mechanisms based on task-specific needs or preferences.

3.4 Generation

The generation module uses a pre-trained LLM to generate final outputs based on the re-ranked documents. As it is built on top of the `litellm` library[7], it can be configured to make use of various LLM API providers, such as OpenAI, Anthropic, Google Vertex or Cohere. The specific model parameters, such as number of tokens to geenrate, or the temperature to use for generation, as well as the system (`sprompt`) and user (`uprompt`) prompt to be used can be specified as well in the `llm` section of the configuration file. In the interest of reproducibility, the temperature defaults to 0.

3.5 Configuration

The central part of the RAGthoven toolkit is the configuration file, a sample of which can be found in Figure 2. The configuration file aims to be a "one-stop shop" for defining the experiment RAGthoven will execute, describing both the input dataset as well as the hyperparameters to be used.

The configuration file can also be used to describe multiple hyperparameter options RAGthoven ought to iterate over during its execution. A sample configuration that makes use of this approach can be seen in Figure 3. As we can see, compared to Figure 2 the values for `k` and `model` have become of the `list` type instead of being `int` or `str`, respectively. The RAGthoven identifies these as configuration parameters that are to be iterated over, and proceeds with running the respective experiments, using a specific combination of the parameters in each of them. Thanks to this succint format, the configuration definition outlined in Figure 3 can be viewed as representing 24 fully interpolated configurations as described in Figure 2.

4 Case Studies

We present three case studies demonstrating RAGthoven's effectiveness and ease of use. These case studies, drawn from well-defined Shared Tasks, showcase how RAGthoven simplifies the implementation of competitive baselines.

4.1 Climate Activism Hate Speech Detection

The Hate Speech Detection subtask from the CASE 2024 Shared Task on Climate Activism Stance and Hate Event Detection required participants to classify tweets related to climate activism into two categories: `Hate` and `Non-Hate`. The dataset consisted of labeled tweets, with 6,385 examples of `Non-Hate` and 899 examples of `Hate` in the training set. The tweets were drawn from discussions related to climate activism, with a notable proportion of messages centered around prominent figures such as Greta Thunberg. A more detailed overview of the task can be found at (Thapa et al., 2024) and an extensive description of the approached explored in the case study can be found in (Suppa et al., 2024).

4.1.1 Baseline and Task Approaches

In this case study, GPT-4 was evaluated on its ability to perform hate speech detection using a zero-shot setup, few-shot prompting, and retrieval-augmented generation (RAG). The baseline established for the subtask was the majority class and the baseline model was GPT-4 in a zero-shot setting, where no specific examples were provided in the prompt. The RAGthoven toolkit

[7] https://github.com/BerriAI/litellm

```
training_data:
  dataset: "Jinyan1/COLING_2025_MGT_en"
  input_feature: "text"
  label_feature: "label"
  split_name: "train"
validation_data:
  input_feature: "text"
  split_name: "valid"
  dataset: "data/data.jsonl"
embed:
  k: 10
rerank:
  k: 3
llm:
  sprompt: |
    You are a helpful assistant that classifies
    text as Human or Machine generated.

    Here are some of very similar texts and
    their respective labels:
    {{ examples }}
  uprompt: |
    Please determine the category of the text
    use "0" for Human and "1" for Machine Generated:

    {{ text }}
    ANSWER ONLY WITH SINGLE NUMBER!
```

Figure 2: A sample RAGthoven configuration file. Note that the configuration describes a real use-case – a Shared Task on "Binary Multilingual Machine-Generated Text Detection" introduced as part of the COLING 2025 Workshop on Detecting AI Generated Content. More details can be found at `https://genai-content-detection.gitlab.io/sharedtasks`

was configured to index the dataset using the `sentence-transformers/all-MiniLM-L6-v2` model and retrieve relevant examples from the dataset to augment the input prompts. Re-ranking was performed using the `ms-marco-MiniLM-L-12-v2` model to prioritize the most relevant retrieved examples for hate speech classification.

4.1.2 Results and Analysis

The results, as shown in Table 1, demonstrate the effectiveness of retrieval-augmented generation in improving hate speech classification performance. The baseline zero-shot GPT-4 model achieved an accuracy of 93.5% and an F1 score of 85.6. When augmented with retrieval, the performance improved, with the best RAG configuration (RAG all, $k = 6$) achieving an F1 score of 88.1, outperforming the few-shot model. Notably, re-ranking did not enhance performance over basic retrieval, suggesting that the retrieval mechanism alone contributed the most significant gains.

```
training_data:
  dataset: "Jinyan1/COLING_2025_MGT_en"
  input_feature: "text"
  label_feature: "label"
  split_name: "train"
validation_data:
  input_feature: "text"
  split_name: "valid"
  dataset: "data/data.jsonl"
embed:
  k: [10, 20, 30]
  model: [
    "sentence-transformers/all-MiniLM-L6-v2",
    "sentence-transformers/all-mpnet-base-v1"
  ]
rerank:
  k: [3, 5]
  model: [
    "ms-marco-MiniLM-L-12-v2",
    "ms-marco-MultiBERT-L-12"
  ]
llm:
  sprompt: |
    You are a helpful assistant that classifies
    text as Human or Machine generated.

    Here are some of very similar texts and
    their respective labels:
    {{ examples }}
  uprompt: |
    Determine the text category and respond
    "0" for Human and "1" for Machine Generated:

    {{ text }}
    ANSWER WITH SINGLE NUMBER ONLY!
```

Figure 3: A sample RAGthoven configuration file denoting different hyperparameters to run experiments over. Note in particular the `k` and `model` keys in the `embed` and `rerank` sections.

The results indicate that retrieval augmentation, particularly with `all-mpnet-base-v2` embeddings, substantially improves performance in hate speech detection, confirming that task-specific information retrieval helps GPT-4 adapt to the nuances of the dataset. However, re-ranking did not yield additional benefits in this task, likely due to the already high relevance of the top-retrieved examples. The full RAGthoven configuration can be found in Appendix A and Figure 4.

4.2 Multilingual Text Detoxification 2024 Case Study

The Multilingual Text Detoxification (TextDetox) 2024 task aimed to address the problem of toxicity in text by rewriting toxic content to maintain its original meaning while removing offensive language. Participants were provided with multilingual datasets containing toxic texts from various languages such as German, Chinese, Russian, and

Model	Acc	P	R	F1
`baseline`	0.901	-	-	0.708
`GPT-4 Zero-Shot`	0.935	0.835	0.880	0.856
`+ Few-Shot (k=6)`	0.932	0.826	0.895	0.855
`+ RAG (k=6)`	0.941	0.851	0.889	0.868
`+ RAG all (k=6)`	**0.948**	**0.866**	**0.899**	**0.881**
`+ RAG + Re-Rank (k=6)`	0.941	0.853	0.877	0.864

Table 1: Results for the Hate Speech Detection Task in terms of Accuracy (Acc), Precision (P), Recall (R) and F1 score. The best performance is bolded.

more. The objective was to generate neutralized outputs that were both non-toxic and contextually accurate. Automatic and manual evaluations were performed by the task organizers to assess the quality of the submissions. A more detailed overview of the task itself can be found in (Dementieva et al., 2024) and an extensive description of the approach our case study is based on can be found in (Řehulka and Šuppa, 2024).

4.2.1 Baseline and Task Approaches

The baseline approach chosen by the organizers was the "duplicate" baseline, which simply responded with the original text, without making any changes.

Our baseline approach utilized a zero-shot setup of the Llama3 model (Dubey et al., 2024). This configuration simply provided instructions for detoxification without any specific contextual examples. However, this method proved suboptimal, as the model tended to rewrite the entire sentence, altering the meaning significantly. To address this, we employed few-shot prompting with relevant examples in English and other languages.

The system was then enhanced using Retrieval Augmented Generation (RAG), which integrated toxic-neutral text pairs from external datasets, including `textdetox/multilingual_paradetox` (TextDetox, 2023). For each input, dynamically generated prompts included relevant detoxified examples and instructions to maintain the original context. This approach significantly improved detoxification results across all languages.

To further refine the outputs, we also introduced a *reverse* approach. In this method, retrieved examples were presented in reverse order in the prompt, placing the most relevant examples at the end. This subtle change helped the model prioritize closer matches in detoxification, particularly for challenging languages like Russian.

4.2.2 Results and Analysis

In the final evaluation, we assessed the performance using three metrics: (1) the absence of toxic content, measured via an `xlm-roberta-large` classifier, (2) semantic preservation, quantified by cosine similarity using LaBSE embeddings, and (3) grammatical correctness, measured using the ChrF metric. The composite score was the product of these three metrics. Table 2 summarizes the performance across different languages for the various configurations.

The reverse approach, where we reordered examples in the prompt, improved the model's performance across several languages, particularly German and Russian. The only language in which our system did not manage to beat the original, organizer-provided baseline was Amharic. We attribute this to the specific script of the langauge as well as its low-resource nature.

4.2.3 Manual Evaluation

In addition to automatic evaluation, a manual evaluation of 100 detoxified samples per language was conducted. In this evaluation, our system ranked 5th overall, with notable performance in German, where it surpassed the human reference. The reverse approach further contributed to gains in this manual evaluation.

In conclusion, the combination of RAG with dynamic prompt generation and the reverse approach allowed us to effectively tackle the Multilingual Text Detoxification 2024 task. Our system demonstrated strong cross-lingual detoxification performance, especially for German and Chinese, showing the flexibility and power of the RAGthoven system in handling diverse NLP tasks. The full RAGthoven configuration can be found in Appendix A and Figure 5.

4.3 Code Generation for Optimization Problems

In this case study, we apply RAGthoven to the task of automating code generation for solving optimization problems. This task was inspired by the ICML 2024 Automated Math Reasoning Challenge, specifically Track 3, which involves generating Python code that solves optimization problems using the PuLP library[8]. The challenge requires models to understand problem descriptions presented in natural language and produce executable

[8]https://www.codabench.org/competitions/2438/

Model	avg	en	es	de	zh	ar	hi	uk	ru	am
baseline	0.126	0.061	0.090	0.287	0.069	0.294	0.035	0.032	0.048	**0.217**
Llama 3	0.380	0.525	0.448	0.530	0.161	0.488	0.185	0.507	0.461	0.112
+ RAG	0.403	**0.527**	0.483	**0.576**	0.152	0.483	0.176	0.534	0.504	0.193
+ reverse	**0.420**	**0.527**	**0.499**	0.563	**0.169**	**0.538**	**0.193**	**0.602**	**0.523**	0.167

Table 2: Performance across different languages for various models and configurations (average scores of automatic evaluation) in the Text Detoxification 2024 Shared Task. The highest performance per language is boldfaced.

Python code that computes optimal solutions using specific solvers. For example, the input description might include details such as the objective function and constraints, with the expected output being Python code that computes the solution and prints specific variables.

4.3.1 Baseline and Task Approaches

This Shared Task did not feature a baseline established by its organizers.

Our baseline for this task involved directly prompting models like GPT-4 and GPT-4o using a system prompt that instructed the LLM to generate Python code for optimization problems. The model used retrieval to augment its output by pulling relevant examples from a dataset indexed using the `all-MiniLM-L6-v2` model. If the initial code generation failed—due to syntax errors or failure to produce expected outputs—a second pipeline was introduced, wherein the generated code, along with a Python traceback, was sent to GPT-4 for correction. We experimented with two LLMs: GPT-4 and GPT-4o. In addition, an ensemble approach was tested, where the final output was determined by combining the outputs from multiple models and selecting the most frequent one.

4.3.2 Results and Discussion

The performance of each model on the public and private leaderboards of the ICML challenge is summarized in Table 3. The performance is measured based on the accuracy of the generated code in solving the optimization problems.

The results demonstrate that the RAGthoven-augmented pipeline, especially when paired with GPT-4o, performs robustly on both the public and private leaderboards. Interestingly, increasing the number of examples in the prompt (k) did not consistently lead to performance improvements, and the ensemble approach did not significantly outperform the individual models. This suggests that retrieval-based augmentation, combined with prompt-tuning, can provide strong baselines for code generation tasks. However, there may be diminishing returns when adding more examples or using model ensembles.

Model	Public	Private
GPT-4 (k=2)	0.840	**0.8171**
GPT-4 (k=3)	0.815	0.7862
GPT-4 (k=4)	0.835	0.7933
GPT-4o (k=3)	**0.850**	0.8147
GPT-4o (k=4)	0.820	0.8052
GPT-4o (k=5)	0.845	0.8147
Ensemble	**0.850**	**0.8171**

Table 3: Results for code generation models on the public and private leaderboards of the ICML 2024 Automated Math Reasoning Challenge. k denotes the number of examples in the prompt. Bold values represent the highest performance for each leaderboard.

The full RAGthoven configuration for the outlined experiments can be found in Appendix A and seen in Figure 6.

5 Conclusion

In this paper, we introduce RAGthoven, a toolkit designed to simplify the evaluation of RAG-based pipelines. By offering a configuration-driven interface, RAGthoven makes retrieval-augmented models accessible to both technical users and non-programmers. Its modular nature allows for easy extension, ensuring future adaptability across diverse NLP tasks. Through case studies in text classification, question answering, and code generation, we demonstrate that RAGthoven maintains competitive performance while streamlining setup. Our results highlight its potential to lower the barriers for wider adoption of RAG across academia and industry. To this end we release RAGthoven under the terms of the MIT license, hoping it will contribute increased RAG usage in the future.

References

Tassallah Abdullahi, Ritambhara Singh, and Carsten Eickhoff. 2024. Retrieval augmented zero-shot text classification. In *Proceedings of the 2024 ACM SIGIR International Conference on Theory of Information Retrieval*, pages 195–203.

Nastaran Bassamzadeh and Chhaya Methani. 2024. A comparative study of dsl code generation: Fine-tuning vs. optimized retrieval augmentation. *arXiv preprint arXiv:2407.02742*.

Xin Cheng, Di Luo, Xiuying Chen, Lemao Liu, Dongyan Zhao, and Rui Yan. 2024. Lift yourself up: Retrieval-augmented text generation with self-memory. *Advances in Neural Information Processing Systems*, 36.

Prithiviraj Damodaran. 2023. FlashRank, Lightest and Fastest 2nd Stage Reranker for search pipelines.

Daryna Dementieva, Daniil Moskovskiy, Nikolay Babakov, Abinew Ali Ayele, Naquee Rizwan, Frolian Schneider, Xintog Wang, Seid Muhie Yimam, Dmitry Ustalov, Elisei Stakovskii, Alisa Smirnova, Ashraf Elnagar, Animesh Mukherjee, and Alexander Panchenko. 2024. Overview of the multilingual text detoxification task at pan 2024. In *Working Notes of CLEF 2024 - Conference and Labs of the Evaluation Forum*. CEUR-WS.org.

Abhimanyu Dubey, Abhinav Jauhri, Abhinav Pandey, Abhishek Kadian, Ahmad Al-Dahle, Aiesha Letman, Akhil Mathur, Alan Schelten, Amy Yang, Angela Fan, et al. 2024. The llama 3 herd of models. *arXiv preprint arXiv:2407.21783*.

Yunfan Gao, Yun Xiong, Xinyu Gao, Kangxiang Jia, Jinliu Pan, Yuxi Bi, Yi Dai, Jiawei Sun, and Haofen Wang. 2023. Retrieval-augmented generation for large language models: A survey. *arXiv preprint arXiv:2312.10997*.

Michael Glass, Xueqing Wu, Ankita Rajaram Naik, Gaetano Rossiello, and Alfio Gliozzo. 2023. Retrieval-based transformer for table augmentation. *arXiv preprint arXiv:2306.11843*.

Kelvin Guu, Kenton Lee, Zora Tung, Panupong Pasupat, and Mingwei Chang. 2020. Retrieval augmented language model pre-training. In *International conference on machine learning*, pages 3929–3938. PMLR.

Jie Huang, Wei Ping, Peng Xu, Mohammad Shoeybi, Kevin Chen-Chuan Chang, and Bryan Catanzaro. 2023. Raven: In-context learning with retrieval augmented encoder-decoder language models. *arXiv preprint arXiv:2308.07922*.

Peter Izsak, Moshe Berchansky, Daniel Fleischer, and Ronen Laperdon. 2023. fastRAG: Efficient Retrieval Augmentation and Generation Framework.

Jiajie Jin, Yutao Zhu, Xinyu Yang, Chenghao Zhang, and Zhicheng Dou. 2024. Flashrag: A modular toolkit for efficient retrieval-augmented generation research. *Preprint*, arXiv:2405.13576.

Brendan King and Jeffrey Flanigan. 2023. Diverse retrieval-augmented in-context learning for dialogue state tracking. *arXiv preprint arXiv:2307.01453*.

Kenton Lee, Ming-Wei Chang, and Kristina Toutanova. 2019. Latent retrieval for weakly supervised open domain question answering. *arXiv preprint arXiv:1906.00300*.

Patrick Lewis, Ethan Perez, Aleksandra Piktus, Fabio Petroni, Vladimir Karpukhin, Naman Goyal, Heinrich Küttler, Mike Lewis, Wen-tau Yih, Tim Rocktäschel, et al. 2020. Retrieval-augmented generation for knowledge-intensive nlp tasks. *Advances in Neural Information Processing Systems*, 33:9459–9474.

Quentin Lhoest, Albert Villanova Del Moral, Yacine Jernite, Abhishek Thakur, Patrick Von Platen, Suraj Patil, Julien Chaumond, Mariama Drame, Julien Plu, Lewis Tunstall, et al. 2021. Datasets: A community library for natural language processing. *arXiv preprint arXiv:2109.02846*.

Xiaonan Li, Kai Lv, Hang Yan, Tianyang Lin, Wei Zhu, Yuan Ni, Guotong Xie, Xiaoling Wang, and Xipeng Qiu. 2023. Unified demonstration retriever for in-context learning. *arXiv preprint arXiv:2305.04320*.

Lefteris Loukas, Ilias Stogiannidis, Odysseas Diamantopoulos, Prodromos Malakasiotis, and Stavros Vassos. 2023. Making llms worth every penny: Resource-limited text classification in banking. In *Proceedings of the Fourth ACM International Conference on AI in Finance*, pages 392–400.

Malte Pietsch, Timo Möller, Bogdan Kostic, Julian Risch, Massimiliano Pippi, Mayank Jobanputra, Sara Zanzottera, Silvano Cerza, Vladimir Blagojevic, Thomas Stadelmann, Tanay Soni, and Sebastian Lee. 2019. Haystack: the end-to-end NLP framework for pragmatic builders.

Ori Ram, Yoav Levine, Itay Dalmedigos, Dor Muhlgay, Amnon Shashua, Kevin Leyton-Brown, and Yoav Shoham. 2023. In-context retrieval-augmented language models. *Transactions of the Association for Computational Linguistics*, 11:1316–1331.

Erik Řehulka and Marek Šuppa. 2024. Rag meets detox: Enhancing text detoxification using open large language models with retrieval augmented generation.

Shamane Siriwardhana, Rivindu Weerasekera, Elliott Wen, Tharindu Kaluarachchi, Rajib Rana, and Suranga Nanayakkara. 2023. Improving the domain adaptation of retrieval augmented generation (rag) models for open domain question answering. *Transactions of the Association for Computational Linguistics*, 11:1–17.

Marek Suppa, Daniel Skala, Daniela Jass, Samuel Sucik, Andrej Svec, and Peter Hraska. 2024. Bryndza at climateactivism 2024: Stance, target and hate event detection via retrieval-augmented gpt-4 and llama. *ArXiv*, abs/2402.06549.

TextDetox. 2023. Multilingual paradetox. https://huggingface.co/datasets/textdetox/multilingual_paradetox. Accessed: 2024-05-30.

Surendrabikram Thapa, Kritesh Rauniyar, Farhan Ahmad Jafri, Shuvam Shiwakoti, Hariram Veeramani, Raghav Jain, Guneet Singh Kohli, Ali Hürriyetoğlu, and Usman Naseem. 2024. Stance and hate event detection in tweets related to climate activism-shared task at case 2024. In *7th Workshop on Challenges and Applications of Automated Extraction of Socio-Political Events from Text, CASE 2024*, pages 234–247. Association for Computational Linguistics.

Shuohang Wang, Yichong Xu, Yuwei Fang, Yang Liu, Siqi Sun, Ruochen Xu, Chenguang Zhu, and Michael Zeng. 2022. Training data is more valuable than you think: A simple and effective method by retrieving from training data. *arXiv preprint arXiv:2203.08773*.

Xinyu Wang, Yong Jiang, Nguyen Bach, Tao Wang, Zhongqiang Huang, Fei Huang, and Kewei Tu. 2021. Improving named entity recognition by external context retrieving and cooperative learning. *arXiv preprint arXiv:2105.03654*.

A RAGthoven Configurations


```
training_data:
  dataset: SubTaskA-train.csv
  input_feature: "text"
  output_feature: "prediction"
validation_data:
  dataset: SubTaskA-test.csv
  input_feature: "text"
embed:
  k: [6, 12]
  model: [
    "sentence-transformers/all-MiniLM-L6-v2",
    "sentence-transformers/all-mpnet-base-v1"
  ]
rerank:
  k: 6
llm:
  model: "gpt4"
  sprompt: |
    Analyze the input tweet to determine if it
    is hate speech or not, based on the
    following criteria:

    ## Hate Speech Patterns

    ...

    ## Non-Hate Speech Patterns

    ...

    ## Evaluation

    - If the tweet aligns more with the
    Hate Speech Patterns, output:
    'Prediction: 1' (indicating it is
    hate speech).

    - If the tweet aligns more with the
    Non-Hate Speech Patterns, output:
    'Prediction: 0' (indicating it is
    not hate speech).

    ## Examples
    {{ examples }}
  uprompt: |
    {{ text }}
```


Figure 4: The RAGthoven configuration file associated with the The Hate Speech Detection subtask from the CASE 2024 Shared Task on Climate Activism Stance and Hate Event Detection. The ellipsis (...) in both Hate and Non-Hate Speech patterns denotes parts of the prompt that has been omitted for brevity.

```
training_data:
  dataset: "textdetox/multilingual_paradetox"
  input_feature: "toxic_sentence"
  output_feature: "neutral_sentence"
validation_data:
  dataset: "textdetox/multilingual_paradetox_test"
  input_feature: "toxic_sentence"
embed:
  k: 10
llm:
  model: "ollama/llama3"
  sprompt: |
    ## Task

    You are a text detoxifier. On input you receive
    a text which may be toxic or harmful. Your task
    is to rewrite this text in a way that does not
    contain any toxicity or harmful words, while
    preserving the original content and context.

    The Output contains only the detoxified text
    and nothing else like notes or additional
    information. You do not add any more context
    to the resulting text, which is not in the
    original text.
    Do not rewrite the original text too much,
    just either remove the toxic part completely,
    or replace it with some non-toxic words while
    preserving the meaning and context.

    The language of the input is {{ language }}
    and the language of the response must be the
    same.

    ## Examples
    {{ examples }}
  uprompt: |
    {{ text }}
```

Figure 5: The RAGthoven configuration file associated with the Text Detoxification 2024 Shared Task.

```
training_data:
  dataset: optim-with-code-train.json
  input_feature: "task_definition"
  output_feature: "code"
validation_data:
  dataset: optim-with-code-val.json
  input_feature: "task_definition"
embed:
  k: [2, 3, 4, 5]
llm:
  model: ["gpt-4", "gpt-4o"]
  sprompt: |
    You are an Optimization Problem-Solving
    expert that solves optimization tasks using
    the PuLP library in Python.

    # Task
    You will be given a description of an
    optimization problem on the input and will be
    asked to output a Python script that uses the
    PuLP library that solves the task.

    The Python code should compute ALL of the
    expected variables and print their output out.
    Use the EXACT SAME variable names in the
    output VERBATIM as the ones provided in the
    input.

    Do not add any additional formatting to the
    output (e.g. no '$' signs, no commas, etc.).

    Format the output as float values.

    Output ONLY the resulting Python code and
    nothing else.

    Follow the format in the examples below.
    Do not attempt to compute anything yourself,
    only output Python code that does the
    computation.

    # Examples
    {{examples}}
  uprompt: |
    {{ text }}
```

Figure 6: The RAGthoven configuration file associated with the ICML 2024 Automated Math Reasoning Challenge.

MuRAR: A Simple and Effective Multimodal Retrieval and Answer Refinement Framework for Multimodal Question Answering

Zhengyuan Zhu[1], **Daniel Lee**[2], **Hong Zhang**[2],
Sai Sree Harsha[2], **Loic Feujio**[2], **Akash Maharaj**[2], **Yunyao Li**[2]
[1]University of Texas at Arlington, [2]Adobe
zhengyuan.zhu@mavs.uta.edu, dlee1@adobe.com, yunyaol@adobe.com

Abstract

Recent advancements in retrieval-augmented generation have demonstrated impressive performance on the question-answering task. However, most previous work predominantly focuses on text-based answers. Although some studies have explored multimodal data, they still fall short in generating comprehensive multimodal answers, especially step-by-step tutorials for accomplishing specific goals. This capability is especially valuable in application scenarios such as enterprise chatbots, customer service systems, and educational platforms. In this paper, we propose a simple and effective framework, MuRAR (**Mu**ltimodal **R**etrieval and **A**nswer **R**efinement). MuRAR starts by generating an initial text answer based on the user's question. It then retrieves multimodal data relevant to the snippets of the initial text answer. By leveraging the retrieved multimodal data and contextual features, MuRAR refines the initial text answer to create a more comprehensive and informative response. This highly adaptable framework can be easily integrated into an enterprise chatbot to produce multimodal answers with minimal modifications. Human evaluations demonstrate that the multimodal answers generated by MuRAR are significantly more useful and readable than plain text responses. A video demo of MuRAR is available at https://youtu.be/ykGRtyVVQpU.

1 Introduction

The emergence of retrieval-augmented generation (RAG) techniques (Lewis et al., 2020; Gao et al., 2023) and large language models (LLMs), such as GPT models (Brown et al., 2020; OpenAI, 2023), Gemini (Anil et al., 2023), and Llama (Touvron et al., 2023), has significantly transformed the field of question answering (QA) and improved the quality of responses generated by AI assistants. However, the current generation of AI assistants has limitations in delivering comprehensive multimodal answers to user questions, especially step-by-step tutorials on accomplishing specific goals. This capability is particularly valuable in enterprise scenarios, where critical information can often be extracted from product documentation that includes multimodal data. In such cases, images, tables, and videos are often *crucial* for understanding complex, domain-specific topics. Enhancing AI assistants with the ability to incorporate multimodal information can, therefore, significantly improve user comprehension and engagement (Zhang et al., 2024; Singh et al., 2021). This improvement offers several benefits, including increased productivity, reduced barriers to entry, higher product adoption rates, enhanced creativity, and improved user experiences.

Previous work (Talmor et al., 2021; Kumar et al., 2020; Joshi et al., 2024) has primarily focused on leveraging various techniques to better understand multimodal data as input and generate plain text answers to a given query. In another scenario (Singh et al., 2021; Wu et al., 2023), the output may consist of either a text answer or a text answer accompanied by a retrieved image or video appended at the end. However, the existing solutions fail to adequately address the challenges posed by complex questions that require illustrating multiple steps to achieve a goal and integrating various multimodal content within the answer.

In summary, the main challenges are: **a)** How to retrieve the relevant multimodal data that are related and helpful to answer the user questions, and **b)** How to generate a coherent multimodal answer that integrates the retrieved multimodal data. To address these challenges, we present MuRAR (**Mu**ltimodal **R**etrieval and **A**nswer **R**efinement). This simple and effective framework generates coherent multimodal answers containing retrieved multimodal data, such as images, videos, and tables. Our framework comprises three main components: text answer generation, source-based multimodal retrieval, and multimodal answer refinement.

Proceedings of the 31st International Conference on Computational Linguistics: System Demonstrations, pages 126–135
January 19–24, 2025.

The text answer generation component retrieves relevant text documents based on the user's query and generates an initial text answer using an LLM. The source-based multimodal retrieval component retrieves multimodal data that are relevant to the text answer snippets in the initial text answer. Finally, the multimodal answer refinement component prompts an LLM to generate the final answer by integrating the retrieved multimodal data with the initial text answer.

We implemented and applied this framework on an enterprise-level AI assistant. To verify the framework's effectiveness, we evaluated the quality of the multimodal answers on a human-annotated dataset of 300 questions and answers. The human evaluation results show that the MuRAR framework effectively retrieves useful and relevant multimodal data while maintaining answer readability. Furthermore, the multimodal answers were consistently preferred over plain text answers. Our framework can be adapted to other enterprise-level AI assistants by collecting topic-specific multimodal data and fine-tuning a topic-specific text retrieval model. This work is, to our knowledge, the first to address the problem of generating coherent multimodal answers to user questions.

2 Design of MuRAR

Formally, given a user question q as input and a set of multimodal data $\mathcal{D} = \{D_S, D_I, D_T, D_V\}$, where $\{D_S, D_I, D_T, D_V\}$ denote collections of text document snippets, images, tables, and videos, respectively, the objective is to generate a multimodal answer $A_{mm} = F(S, I, T, V)$. Here, F denotes a function that organizes a set of retrieved multimodal data $(S, I, T, V) \in D$, relevant to the user's question, into a coherent and informative answer.

To achieve a high quality A_{mm}, we propose MuRAR, as illustrated in Figure 1. The text answer generation component uses a RAG-style approach (Lewis et al., 2020; Gao et al., 2023), first retrieving relevant text document snippets $S = \{s_1, s_2, ..., s_n\} \in D_S$ based on user query q and then generating an initial text answer A_t by prompting an LLM. Next, we retrieve multimodal data, namely, $I = \{i_1, i_2, ..., i_m\} \in D_I$, $T = \{t_1, t_2, ..., t_k\} \in D_T$, and $V = \{v_1, v_2, ..., v_l\} \in D_V$ that are relevant to the text answer. Finally, the multimodal answer refinement component generates a final multimodal answer A_{mm} by incorporating the retrieved multimodal data into the initial text answer.

Notably, directly prompting or using techniques such as chain-of-thought (Wei et al., 2022) with LLMs for tasks involving both text and multimodal data is ineffective for two reasons. First, the complexity of the task overwhelms the LLM as it needs to determine which data to reference, decide whether to display multimodal data and figure out where to place it within the answer. Additionally, this complexity results in low-quality multimodal answers.

2.1 Text Answer Generation

Our text answer generation component follows the RAG-style approach. Specifically, we fine-tuned a pre-trained text embedding model (Reimers and Gurevych, 2019) on an in-house annotated dataset, which includes labels indicating whether a text document snippet s_i is relevant to a user query q. The fine-tuned embedding model is then applied to the text document snippets D_S to create vector indexes using FAISS (Johnson et al., 2019). These vector indexes serve as a database for retrieving relevant text document snippets by calculating the cosine similarity between the user query q and each text document snippet s_i. For each user query q, the top five relevant text snippets are selected. An LLM is then prompted with the user query q and the retrieved top five text snippets to generate initial text answer A_t. The detailed prompt is provided in Appendix A.4.

2.2 Source-Based Multimodal Retrieval

The source-based multimodal retrieval component involves two steps: source attribution and section-level multimodal data retrieval.

Source Attribution. The initial text answer A_t is segmented into multiple sentences, with each sentence representing a continuous text answer snippet $a_{[i,j]}$ spanning from the i-th token to the j-th token in A_t. Each text answer snippet $a_{[i,j]}$ is then compared to every text document snippet in D_S by calculating the cosine similarity between their embeddings. The text document snippet s_i with the highest cosine similarity score is identified as the source for $a_{[i,j]}$. Notably, if the highest similarity score is below 0.6, no source is assigned to $a_{[i,j]}$. These text answer snippets and their sources are the foundation for retrieving multimodal data.

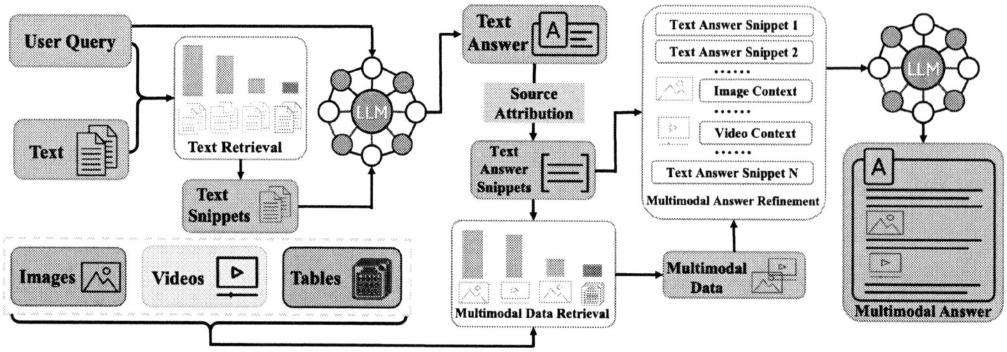

Figure 1: The architecture of the MuRAR framework.

Section-Level Multimodal Data Retrieval. For each text answer snippet $a_{[i,j]}$ and its corresponding source s_i, we first locate the original web document containing s_i. We then identify the section where s_i resides and collect all multimodal data within that section. This approach significantly reduces the search space for multimodal data and improves the precision of the retrieval results. The multimodal data may include images, tables, and videos. Multimodal data are represented using contextual and LLM-generated text features. The contextual text features are derived from the paragraphs before and after the multimodal data. For the LLM-generated text features, we utilize the image captions generated by GPT-4 and the "alt" text attribute extracted from the raw document HTML for images. For tables and videos, we use summarized table content and summarized video transcripts generated by the LLM, respectively.

To efficiently encode these text features, text embeddings are computed using the same fine-tuned embedding model employed for text document retrieval. The multimodal data included in the multimodal answer are retrieved based on the cosine similarity between the text answer snippet $a_{[i,j]}$ and the text embeddings of multimodal data. Only the highest-ranked multimodal data are selected for a text answer snippet. However, the same multimodal data may occasionally be selected for multiple text answer snippets, resulting in duplication within the multimodal answer. To address this, we only keep the multimodal data with the highest similarity score from the retrieval results.

2.3 Multimodal Answer Refinement

After retrieving the multimodal data, an LLM is prompted to refine the initial text answer into a multimodal answer. The prompt includes the user question q, initial text answer A_t, and retrieved multimodal data accompanied by their contextual text features.

To guide the LLM to generate multimodal answers, placeholders are inserted into A_t after the textual answer snippets corresponding to retrieved multimodal data. Each placeholder includes the URL of the multimodal data and its contextual text features, ensuring the LLM incorporates relevant information while minimizing the risk of generating irrelevant details and hallucinations. Additionally, the prompt includes several illustrative question-answering examples to demostrate how multimodal data should be integrated into the final answer. An example prompt is provided in Appendix A.4. The LLM is instructed to replace the placeholders with appropriate descriptions and modify the text answer snippets to produce a coherent and readable multimodal response. Finally, for display in the user interface, the URLs for multimodal data are converted into HTML elements, enabling users to interact with the multimodal content directly.

3 User Interface

We implemented the MuRAR framework and integrated it into a prototype version of the AI assistant within Adobe Experience Platform.[1] As illustrated in Figure 2, when a user queries the AI assistant (A), for example by asking, "What is a good tutorial for creating a schema?", MuRAR retrieves relevant text snippets (B) from documents on Adobe Experience League[2] and generates an initial text answer.

[1] https://experienceleague.adobe.com/en/docs/experience-platform/ai-assistant/home

[2] https://experienceleague.adobe.com/en/docs

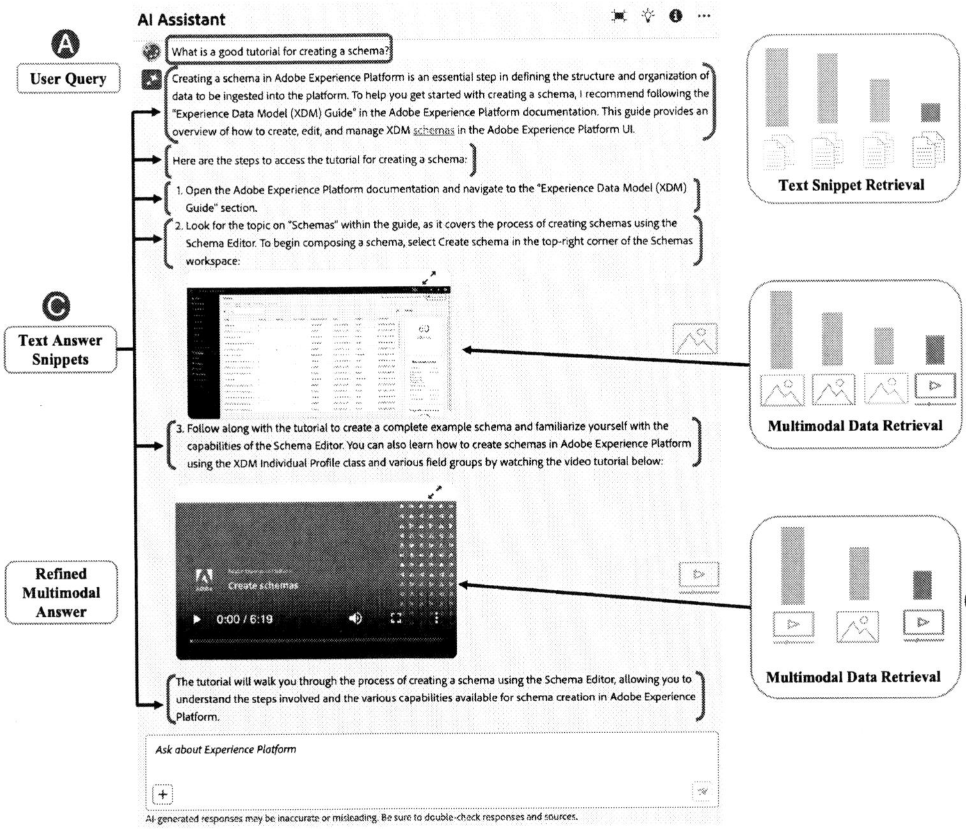

Figure 2: The interface of AI Assistant demonstrating multimodal answers is constructed by combining multimodal data retrieval and answer refinement.

Subsequently, source attribution is applied to each text answer snippet (C) to identify potential multimodal data candidates. Next, MuRAR retrieves the most relevant multimodal data (D1 and D2), which, in this case, include a screenshot of the Schemas Workspace and a video tutorial explaining the schema creation process. Finally, MuRAR integrates the relevant multimodal data into the initial text answer through multimodal answer refinement. Notably, the multimodal elements are interactive: when a user clicks on an element, a pop-up window appears, displaying the multimodal data in full size for detailed viewing.

4 Data Collection

We curated two datasets to support the development of the MuRAR framework and facilitate human evaluation. A multimodal document dataset was created to serve as $\mathcal{D}$ for developing the MuRAR framework. Additionally, a multimodal question-answering dataset was collected and annotated for use in human evaluation.

4.1 Multimodal Document Dataset

The multimodal document dataset was collected from 2,173 web documents from Adobe Experience League [3]. As summarized in Table 1, the dataset contains four modalities: text, image, table, and video. The textual data includes both plain text and tabular content, while the visual data comprises images and videos. Additional details about the data collection process can be found in Appendix A.1.

The text content was scraped from web documents and tokenized using the GPT-2 tokenizer (Radford et al., 2019). Each document was segmented into smaller snippets ranging from 11 to 1,500 tokens, resulting in a total of 18,071 text snippets. For image data, we extracted image URLs along with their surrounding textual context, which includes the text preceding the image (pre-image

[3]https://experienceleague.adobe.com/en/docs

Modality	Metric	Value
Text	Count	18,071
	Avg content tokens	192
Image	Count	6,320
	Avg context tokens	238
	Avg caption tokens	94
Video	Count	253
	Avg context tokens	91
	Avg summary tokens	33
Table	Count	2,644
	Avg context tokens	160
	Avg table tokens	223

Table 1: Multimodal dataset statistics.

context) and the text following it (post-image context). To enrich the dataset with more text features for multimodal retrieval, GPT-4 was used to generate captions for the images, resulting in 6,320 annotated image entries. Tables were extracted in JSON format, along with their associated contextual text. As with the image data, the contextual text for tables includes the text preceding and following the table. This process yielded 2,646 table entries. For video content, we collected video URLs, contextual text, and transcripts. In cases where transcripts were unavailable, videos were downloaded, and Whisper (Radford et al., 2023) was used to generate transcripts from the audio. GPT-4 was then employed to summarize these transcripts, resulting in 253 video entries. For all modalities, additional metadata were gathered, including the titles of the web document and the headings of the sections where the multimodal data were located.

4.2 Multimodal Question Answering Dataset

To construct a multimodal question-answer dataset, we collected 764 real customer questions and applied MuRAR to generate answers. Among these, 306 questions were answered with multimodal data. For human evaluation, we randomly sampled 150 questions from this subset of 306 to assess the quality of the generated answers. To analyze the impact of different backbone LLMs on the quality of multimodal answers, we conducted a comparative study using GPT-3.5 and GPT-4. For each model, we generated 150 text-based and multimodal answers, resulting in a total of 300 question-answer pairs. This evaluation enabled us to compare the effectiveness and coherence of multimodal responses across the two models, providing insights into how the choice of LLM influences performance.

5 Human Evaluation

To assess the effectiveness of our multimodal question-answering system, we conducted a human evaluation study in two phases: (1) single-model evaluation and (2) pairwise comparison. The single-model psychometric evaluation was designed to measure three key metrics: usefulness, readability, and relevance of the multimodal answer. For the pairwise comparison, we used a preference-based ranking to determine the overall user preference between text-only and multimodal responses. Notably, we did not assess the quality of the text content itself but rather the added value of integrating multimodal data into the text answers.

5.1 Study Setup

We compiled a dataset of 300 question-answer pairs, evenly distributed between outputs from GPT-3.5 and GPT-4 models. For each question, both text-only and multimodal answers were generated. To evaluate the quality of these outputs, we recruited eight expert annotators, all holding advanced degrees in computer science with substantial experience in natural language processing (NLP). The annotation process was conducted on LabelStudio (Tkachenko et al., 2020-2022), with each question-answer pair evaluated by at least three experts.

5.2 Evaluation Schema

The annotators were asked to rate each multimodal answer on a 5-point Likert scale (1 being lowest, 5 being highest) for the following metrics, which were adapted from (Pradeep et al., 2024):

- **Usefulness:** This metric measures the extent to which multimodal elements contribute to the user's comprehension of the text content. High scores indicate that the multimodal output provides valuable additional information, clarifies complex concepts, or illustrates key points in ways that significantly aid understanding.
- **Readability:** This assesses how well the multimodal elements are integrated with the text, considering factors such as placement, size, and formatting. High scores indicate seamless integration that enhances the overall reading experience.
- **Relevance:** This measures how closely the multimodal elements relate to the content of the

text. High scores indicate that the multimodal output directly supports or illustrates the textual content.

Metric	Model GPT-3.5	GPT-4	Average
Usefulness	3.34	**3.60**	3.47
Readability	3.49	**3.76**	3.63
Relevance	3.66	**3.90**	3.78
Preference Rate	0.82	**0.90**	0.86

Table 2: Evaluation results for multimodal answers generated by GPT-3.5 and GPT-4.

After rating the multimodal answers, annotators were asked to indicate their overall preference between the text-only version, the multimodal version, or if they found them equally effective ("Same").

5.3 Results

Psychometric Evaluation Results. The psychometric evaluation focused on three key aspects: usefulness, readability, and relevance. As shown in Table 2, when examining the answers generated by both GPT-3.5 and GPT-4, the usefulness metric achieved an average score of 3.47, while readability and relevance scored 3.63 and 3.78, respectively. These scores, all above the midpoint of the scale as reflected in Figure 3, suggest that our approach performs well in producing useful, readable, and relevant output. Qualitative feedback from annotators further supports this conclusion, indicating that the multimodal answer provides informative additions to the text, is understandable through its placement, and remains relevant to the associated content. In addition, the average preference rating of 0.86 demonstrates a strong overall preference for our method compared to the text-only alternative. When comparing GPT-3.5 with GPT-4, we found that using GPT-4 as the backbone LLM increased all the metrics, showcasing its superior performance in generating high-quality, multimodal content within our framework.

Inter-Annotator Agreement. To assess annotation reliability, we calculated two inter-annotator agreement (IAA) measures (Table 3). Krippendorff's alpha (Krippendorff, 2011) was 0.4179 overall, indicating moderate agreement across all annotators. However, Cohen's kappa (Cohen, 1960)

Metric&Model	Agreement Metric $K\text{-}\alpha_{normal}$	$K\text{-}\alpha_{combined}$	$C\text{-}\kappa$
Overall	0.4179	0.3437	0.7100
$Usefulness_{GPT\text{-}3.5}$	0.4150	0.3468	0.6879
$Usefulness_{GPT\text{-}4}$	0.5424	0.4993	0.7900
$Usefulness_{all}$	0.4758	0.4164	0.7383
$Readability_{GPT\text{-}3.5}$	0.3418	0.2147	0.6852
$Readability_{GPT\text{-}4}$	0.3187	0.2502	0.7048
$Readability_{all}$	0.3424	0.2374	0.6968
$Relevance_{GPT\text{-}3.5}$	0.3369	0.2958	0.6459
$Relevance_{GPT\text{-}4}$	0.4465	0.3664	0.7291
$Relevance_{all}$	0.3925	0.3323	0.6872

Table 3: The inter-annotator agreement among the eight annotators.

Metric	Model GPT-3.5	GPT-4	GPT-3.5 & GPT-4
Usefulness	0.9741	0.9059	0.9496
Readability	0.7686	0.7059	0.7500
Relevance	0.8576	0.8301	0.8519

Table 4: Standard deviation of evaluation metrics for multimodal answers generated by GPT-3.5 and GPT-4.

between the top two annotators was 0.71, suggesting substantial agreement when excluding outlier data points. To investigate this discrepancy, we conducted further analyses. The standard deviation ranged from 0.8519 to 0.9496, indicating a relatively tight distribution of scores (Table 4). An annotator-specific analysis (Table 5) revealed that Annotators 2 and 4, accounting for 26% and 5.8% of annotations, respectively, had lower average scores compared to others. Annotator 2 averaged 3.0619 (SD = 0.5648), while Annotator 4 averaged 3.3836 (SD = 0.253). These findings suggest that the lower Krippendorff's alpha may be attributed to systematic differences in scoring patterns among a subset of annotators rather than widespread disagreement. It is worth noting that while annotators were provided with in-depth instructions, they did not undergo formal training.

In conclusion, despite some variability in IAA results, the high Cohen's kappa for the top annotators, combined with strong psychometric evaluation scores and preference ratings, supports the overall reliability and effectiveness of our approach. The MuRAR framwork demonstrates clear benefits over text-only alternatives, providing valuable enhancements to textual content.

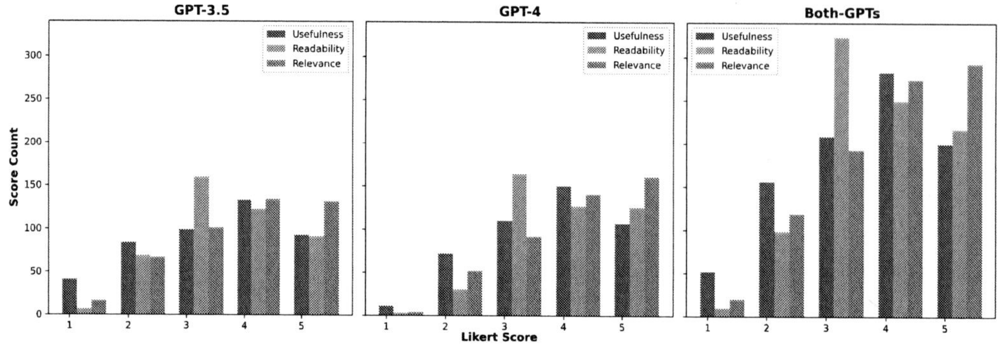

Figure 3: Distribution of score counts for GPT-3.5, GPT-4, and the combined results of GPT-3.5 and GPT-4.

5.4 Limitations

We analyzed the errors and mistakes made by the MuRAR framework during our human evaluation. We identified some issues in the multimodal retrieval component. Although source attribution ensures precision, it can result in low recall, *i.e.*, relevant multimodal data for a text answer snippet may not be in the same section or even the same web document. Additionally, readability can be affected by the multimodal answer refinement component. For instance, multimodal data may contain duplicated information already explained in plain text. This repetition can negatively impact the readability and clarity of the multimodal answer, making it less effective for users.

6 Conclusion and Future Work

We introduced MuRAR, a framework designed to enhance text-based responses by incorporating images, tables, and videos. Human evaluations showed that MuRAR's multimodal answers are more useful, readable, and relevant than text-only responses. The system integrates text answer generation, source-based multimodal retrieval, and answer refinement to produce coherent multimodal answers. Future work will focus on two key areas: improving the quality of multimodal answers and enhancing the user experience. To improve the quality of multimodal answers, we plan to incorporate a broader range of multimodal documents to expand the dataset, train a custom LLM to replace reliance on proprietary models such as GPT-3.5, and address the relatively low recall performance in multimodal data retrieval. To enhance the user experience, future developments could include features such as enabling videos to jump directly to time segments relevant to the user's question and providing a more intuitive and seamless interaction for users.

7 Ethical Considerations

Content Appropriateness. The MuRAR framework integrates diverse data modalities, such as images and videos, into answers. The multimodal data used in this work is sourced from the Adobe Experience Platform, a business-focused document repository considered free from harmful content. However, our framework is designed for flexibility and can be applied to a wide range of multimodal question-answering systems and data sources. This flexibility introduces the risk of retrieving inappropriate, offensive, or irrelevant material from poorly regulated or curated sources. Such content could harm users or erode trust and safety. To address this risk, it is essential to implement robust mechanisms for filtering, validating, and contextualizing multimodal content.

Privacy Concerns. Multimodal data retrieval could inadvertently expose sensitive information. Although the data source used in this work consists of enterprise-level documents devoid of sensitive content, the flexible nature of the MuRAR framework allows integration with diverse data sources, where privacy concerns may arise. Privacy-preserving techniques are essential to protect sensitive user and organizational data during retrieval and integration, ensuring compliance with regulations and maintaining trust.

References

Rohan Anil, Sebastian Borgeaud, Yonghui Wu, Jean-Baptiste Alayrac, Jiahui Yu, Radu Soricut, Johan Schalkwyk, Andrew M. Dai, Anja Hauth, Katie Millican, David Silver, Slav Petrov, Melvin Johnson, Ioannis Antonoglou, Julian Schrittwieser, Amelia Glaese, Jilin Chen, Emily Pitler, Timothy P. Lillicrap, Angeliki Lazaridou, Orhan Firat, James Molloy, Michael Isard, Paul Ronald Barham, Tom Hennigan, Benjamin Lee, Fabio Viola, Malcolm Reynolds, Yuanzhong Xu, Ryan Doherty, Eli Collins, Clemens Meyer, Eliza Rutherford, Erica Moreira, Kareem Ayoub, Megha Goel, George Tucker, Enrique Piqueras, Maxim Krikun, Iain Barr, Nikolay Savinov, Ivo Danihelka, Becca Roelofs, Anaïs White, Anders Andreassen, Tamara von Glehn, Lakshman Yagati, Mehran Kazemi, Lucas Gonzalez, Misha Khalman, Jakub Sygnowski, and et al. 2023. Gemini: A family of highly capable multimodal models. *CoRR*, abs/2312.11805.

Tom B. Brown, Benjamin Mann, Nick Ryder, Melanie Subbiah, Jared Kaplan, Prafulla Dhariwal, Arvind Neelakantan, Pranav Shyam, Girish Sastry, Amanda Askell, Sandhini Agarwal, Ariel Herbert-Voss, Gretchen Krueger, Tom Henighan, Rewon Child, Aditya Ramesh, Daniel M. Ziegler, Jeffrey Wu, Clemens Winter, Christopher Hesse, Mark Chen, Eric Sigler, Mateusz Litwin, Scott Gray, Benjamin Chess, Jack Clark, Christopher Berner, Sam McCandlish, Alec Radford, Ilya Sutskever, and Dario Amodei. 2020. Language models are few-shot learners. In *Advances in Neural Information Processing Systems 33: Annual Conference on Neural Information Processing Systems 2020, NeurIPS 2020, December 6-12, 2020, virtual.*

Jacob Cohen. 1960. A coefficient of agreement for nominal scales. *Educational and psychological measurement*, 20(1):37–46.

Yunfan Gao, Yun Xiong, Xinyu Gao, Kangxiang Jia, Jinliu Pan, Yuxi Bi, Yi Dai, Jiawei Sun, Qianyu Guo, Meng Wang, and Haofen Wang. 2023. Retrieval-augmented generation for large language models: A survey. *CoRR*, abs/2312.10997.

Jeff Johnson, Matthijs Douze, and Hervé Jégou. 2019. Billion-scale similarity search with GPUs. *IEEE Transactions on Big Data*, 7(3):535–547.

Pankaj Joshi, Aditya Gupta, Pankaj Kumar, and Manas Sisodia. 2024. Robust multi model rag pipeline for documents containing text, table & images. In *2024 3rd International Conference on Applied Artificial Intelligence and Computing (ICAAIC)*, pages 993–999. IEEE.

Klaus Krippendorff. 2011. Computing krippendorff's alpha-reliability.

Abhishek Kumar, Trisha Mittal, and Dinesh Manocha. 2020. MCQA: multimodal co-attention based network for question answering. *CoRR*, abs/2004.12238.

Patrick S. H. Lewis, Ethan Perez, Aleksandra Piktus, Fabio Petroni, Vladimir Karpukhin, Naman Goyal, Heinrich Küttler, Mike Lewis, Wen-tau Yih, Tim Rocktäschel, Sebastian Riedel, and Douwe Kiela. 2020. Retrieval-augmented generation for knowledge-intensive NLP tasks. In *Advances in Neural Information Processing Systems 33: Annual Conference on Neural Information Processing Systems 2020, NeurIPS 2020, December 6-12, 2020, virtual.*

OpenAI. 2023. GPT-4 technical report. *CoRR*, abs/2303.08774.

Ronak Pradeep, Daniel Lee, Ali Mousavi, Jeff Pound, Yisi Sang, Jimmy Lin, Ihab Ilyas, Saloni Potdar, Mostafa Arefiyan, and Yunyao Li. 2024. Convkgyarn: Spinning configurable and scalable conversational knowledge graph qa datasets with large language models.

Alec Radford, Jong Wook Kim, Tao Xu, Greg Brockman, Christine McLeavey, and Ilya Sutskever. 2023. Robust speech recognition via large-scale weak supervision. In *International Conference on Machine Learning, ICML 2023, 23-29 July 2023, Honolulu, Hawaii, USA*, volume 202 of *Proceedings of Machine Learning Research*, pages 28492–28518. PMLR.

Alec Radford, Jeffrey Wu, Rewon Child, David Luan, Dario Amodei, Ilya Sutskever, et al. 2019. Language models are unsupervised multitask learners. *OpenAI blog*, 1(8):9.

Nils Reimers and Iryna Gurevych. 2019. Sentence-bert: Sentence embeddings using siamese bert-networks. In *Proceedings of the 2019 Conference on Empirical Methods in Natural Language Processing*. Association for Computational Linguistics.

Hrituraj Singh, Anshul Nasery, Denil Mehta, Aishwarya Agarwal, Jatin Lamba, and Balaji Vasan Srinivasan. 2021. MIMOQA: multimodal input multimodal output question answering. In *Proceedings of the 2021 Conference of the North American Chapter of the Association for Computational Linguistics: Human Language Technologies, NAACL-HLT 2021, Online, June 6-11, 2021*, pages 5317–5332. Association for Computational Linguistics.

Alon Talmor, Ori Yoran, Amnon Catav, Dan Lahav, Yizhong Wang, Akari Asai, Gabriel Ilharco, Hannaneh Hajishirzi, and Jonathan Berant. 2021. Multimodalqa: complex question answering over text, tables and images. In *9th International Conference on Learning Representations, ICLR 2021, Virtual Event, Austria, May 3-7, 2021*. OpenReview.net.

Maxim Tkachenko, Mikhail Malyuk, Andrey Holmanyuk, and Nikolai Liubimov. 2020-2022. Label Studio: Data labeling software. Open source software available from https://github.com/heartexlabs/label-studio.

Hugo Touvron, Thibaut Lavril, Gautier Izacard, Xavier Martinet, Marie-Anne Lachaux, Timothée Lacroix,

Baptiste Rozière, Naman Goyal, Eric Hambro, Faisal Azhar, Aurélien Rodriguez, Armand Joulin, Edouard Grave, and Guillaume Lample. 2023. Llama: Open and efficient foundation language models. *CoRR*, abs/2302.13971.

Jason Wei, Xuezhi Wang, Dale Schuurmans, Maarten Bosma, Brian Ichter, Fei Xia, Ed H. Chi, Quoc V. Le, and Denny Zhou. 2022. Chain-of-thought prompting elicits reasoning in large language models. In *Advances in Neural Information Processing Systems 35: Annual Conference on Neural Information Processing Systems 2022, NeurIPS 2022, New Orleans, LA, USA, November 28 - December 9, 2022*.

Shengqiong Wu, Hao Fei, Leigang Qu, Wei Ji, and Tat-Seng Chua. 2023. Next-gpt: Any-to-any multimodal LLM. *CoRR*, abs/2309.05519.

Lichao Zhang, Jia Yu, Shuai Zhang, Long Li, Yangyang Zhong, Guanbao Liang, Yuming Yan, Qing Ma, Fangsheng Weng, Fayu Pan, Jing Li, Renjun Xu, and Zhenzhong Lan. 2024. Unveiling the impact of multimodal interactions on user engagement: A comprehensive evaluation in ai-driven conversations. *CoRR*, abs/2406.15000.

A Appendix

A.1 Multimodal Scraper Design

Our multimodal scraper design collects various fields and metadata from Adobe Experience League for images, videos, and tables. For images, we gather the link to the image and the surrounding context, specifically the text between the previous and current image and between the current and next image. The metadata collected includes the title of the document, the header of each section containing the image, and the URL of the document. For videos, the fields collected include the URL of the video, the context text before the video, and the video transcript. The metadata gathered is similar, including the document title, section headers, and document URL. For tables, we collect the table content in the form of a JSON string, the context text before the table, and the document URL. Additional metadata includes the document title and the header of each section containing the table.

A.2 Human Evaluation Metrics

Usefulness Usefulness measures how much the multimodal elements contribute to the user's comprehension of the text content.

- 1 - Not at all useful: Multimodal elements provide no additional understanding or actively confuse the user.
- 2 - Slightly useful: Multimodal elements offer minimal enhancement to understanding.
- 3 - Moderately useful: Multimodal elements provide some additional clarity or information.
- 4 - Very useful: Multimodal elements significantly enhance understanding of the text.
- 5 - Extremely useful: Multimodal elements are crucial for full comprehension of the text.

Readability Readability assesses how well the multimodal elements are integrated with the text.

- 1 - Severely impairs readability: Multimodal elements are poorly placed, causing significant disruption to reading flow.
- 2 - Somewhat impairs readability: Multimodal elements are not well-integrated, causing minor disruptions.
- 3 - Neutral impact on readability: Multimodal elements neither enhance nor impair the reading experience.
- 4 - Enhances readability: Multimodal elements are well-placed, supporting smooth reading flow.

Annotator	Answers	Usefulness	Readability	Relevance	Preference (Multi-Modal / Text Only / Same)
No.1	294	3.6463	3.8367	4.0170	207 (70.41%) / 41 (13.95%) / 46 (15.65%)
No.2	237	2.8861	3.0295	3.2700	115 (48.52%) / 81 (34.18%) / 41 (17.30%)
No.3	259	3.7452	3.8340	3.8764	205 (79.15%) / 28 (10.81%) / 26 (10.04%)
No.4	53	3.0566	3.5094	3.5849	30 (56.60%) / 16 (30.19%) / 7 (13.21%)
No.5	9	4.1111	4.4444	4.4444	9 (100.0%) / 0 (0.0%) / 0 (0.0%)
No.6	22	4.0000	4.0909	4.1818	19 (86.36%) / 2 (9.09%) / 1 (4.55%)
No.7	24	4.2500	4.2083	4.6250	23 (95.83%) / 0 (0.0%) / 0 (0.0%)
No.8	2	4.0000	4.5000	4.5000	2 (100.0%) / 0 (0.0%) / 0 (0.0%)

Table 5: Per-annotator average scores and preference.

- 5 - Significantly enhances readability: Multimodal elements are perfectly integrated, greatly improving the reading experience.

Relevance Relevance measures how closely the multimodal elements relate to the text content.

- 1 - Completely irrelevant: Multimodal elements have no apparent connection to the text.
- 2 - Mostly irrelevant: Multimodal elements have only a tenuous connection to the text.
- 3 - Somewhat relevant: Multimodal elements relate to the text but not be entirely on-point.
- 4 - Highly relevant: Multimodal elements clearly support and illustrate the text content.
- 5 - Perfectly relevant: Multimodal elements are essential to the text, providing crucial illustrations or data.

Preference Grading Annotators also indicate their overall preference between the text answer and the multimodal answer:

- **Text Only**: Choose this if you believe the text alone would be more effective without the multimodal elements.
- **Multi-Modal**: Select this if you think the combination of text and multimodal elements provides the best experience.
- **Same**: Choose this if you feel text-only and multimodal versions are equally effective.

A.3 Additional Human Evaluation Results

Due to space constraints, we include additional human evaluation results in the Appendix. The average score and preference per annotator are presented in Table 5.

A.4 Prompts

Please note that the actual prompts used in the system development differ from the prompts shown below. These are simplified versions that capture the essence of the prompt design.

Prompt for Text Answer Generation The prompt for text answer generation can be found in Figure 4.

```
Your task is to answer the user question using the provided documents. Your goal is to provide comprehensive, coherent, and actionable responses that answer the user question. You have access to some documents that may help you in generating your response. The documents may be incomplete or irrelevant.: {{documents}}. This is the current user question that you will need to answer: {{query}}
Present yourself as "AI Assistant" and generate your response considering the following guidelines:
- Ignore all irrelevant details in the provided documents.
- Adopt a tone that is friendly, positive, and informative.
- Your response must have good transitions between section s and be logically structured and formatted.
- Your response must be actionable and provide clear guidance to the user.
- Provide all relevant details and present a well-rounded and insightful perspective on the user question.
- Rephrase the details into a sequence of numbered sections, but do not create nested lists.
- Break your response into multiple paragraphs. The paragraphs must be ordered by importance and relevance to the user question.
- Do NOT repeat details in your response.
- Do NOT summarize your response. Instead, conclude with extra insights useful to the reader.
- Do NOT ask the user if they have any other questions.
- Do not ask the user to refer to external resources, documentation, tutorials, guides, etc.

###EXAMPLE USER QUESTIONS AND RESPONSES###
### START EXAMPLES
Example 1: {{Example 1}}
Example 2: {{Example 2}}
Example 3: {{Example 3}}
### END EXAMPLES
AI Assistant:
```

Figure 4: Prompt for text answer generation.

Prompt for Multimodal Answer Refinement The prompt for multimodal answer refinement can be found in Figure 5.

```
You are an expert at interleaving original answers with extra data represented in text format. Below are a user query, the original answer and extra data in the placeholders.
<<User Query>> {{query}} <</User Query>>
<<ORIGINAL ANSWER>> {{response_with_placeholder}} <</ORIGINAL ANSWER>>
Here are the potential extra data and some surrounding context that can be revised and integrated into the ORIGINAL ANSWER.
  {{multimodal_data}}
To create a cohesive and informative response, please follow these guidelines:
- Based on the context in the extra data, REPHRASE the details of the ORIGINAL ANSWER to ensure a smooth flow of final response.
- Do NOT repeat information that is already mentioned in your final response.
- To maintain coherence, use introductory phrases, such as "as shown in the image/video/table below", "see the image/video/table below", "refer to the following image/video/table", or "as illustrated in the image/video/table below". Vary the phrases to ensure a natural flow and avoid repetition.
- Feel free to reposition the extra data if there's a more suitable location based on the context in the ORIGINAL ANSWER.
- Preserve the original format of content in HTML tags or markdown style.
- Avoid including hallucinated content, such as <<PLACEHOLDER>>.
- Your response must be nicely formatted, easily readable, and understandable by a human.
### EXAMPLE USER QUESTIONS, ORIGINAL ANSWERS, POTENTIAL PLACEHOLDERS, AND GROUD-TRUTH RESPONSES
### START EXAMPLES
Example 1: {{Example 1}}
Example 2: {{Example 2}}
Example 3: {{Example 3}}
### END EXAMPLES
AI Assistant:
```

Figure 5: Prompt for multimodal answer refinement.

Human-Like Embodied AI Interviewer: Employing Android ERICA in Real International Conference

Zi Haur Pang, Yahui Fu, Divesh Lala, Mikey Elmers, Koji Inoue, and Tatsuya Kawahara
Graduate School of Informatics, Kyoto University, Japan
{pang, fu, lala, elmers, inoue, kawahara}@sap.ist.i.kyoto-u-ac.jp

Abstract

This paper introduces the human-like embodied AI interviewer which integrates android robots equipped with advanced conversational capabilities, including attentive listening, conversational repairs, and user fluency adaptation. Moreover, it can analyze and present results post-interview. We conducted a real-world case study at SIGDIAL 2024 with 42 participants, of whom 69% reported positive experiences. This study demonstrated the system's effectiveness in conducting interviews just like a human and marked the first employment of such a system at an international conference. The demonstration video is available at https://youtu.be/jCuw9g99KuE.

1 Introduction

Qualitative interviews are foundational to social science research, offering deep insights through open-ended conversations. However, these interviews require considerable time and human effort. Earlier efforts to alleviate these demands involved using virtual agents (Nunamaker et al., 2011; Anderson et al., 2013; SB et al., 2021). Yet, these systems often failed to provide the sophisticated human-like interaction needed for quality research, limited to simple behaviors like head nodding and assuming participants' full understanding and fluent speech. This basic approach does not account for the complexities of real-world interactions, such as varied understanding and communication skills among participants, resulting in data quality and engagement shortfalls.

To address these limitations, this paper introduces a novel, **human-like interview system** that employs android and humanoid robots. This system is equipped with functionalities like advanced listening behaviors, conversational repair strategies, and user-fluency adaptation, which significantly enhance interaction quality. Beyond mere data gathering, our approach includes an end-to-end **post-interview processing workflow** where chained large language models (LLMs) handle data processing, analysis and presentation creation. We conducted a **real-world case study** at an international academic conference, where it facilitated numerous interactions, demonstrating its practical utility and efficiency. Notably, this marks the first instance of such a system being used at an international conference, showcasing our pioneering approach in the field. The comparative effectiveness of our system relative to traditional interview methodologies is detailed in Table 1.

2 Human-like Interview System

In this section, we describe the architecture of our human-like interview system, as depicted in Figure 1. The system initiates with a speech processing module that serves as the primary input mechanism. The core component, the dialogue manager, orchestrates tasks from language comprehension to response generation, including a Voice-Activity-Projection (VAP) based Multilingual Turn-Taking Module for effective turn management (Inoue et al., 2024a,b). Additional features of the system, such as speech synthesis and gesture generation, are outlined in subsequent subsections. Following the discussion of these components, the interview dialogue flow and the post-interview processing workflow are detailed. The system has been implemented across two distinct embodied conversational agents (ECAs): ERICA (Glas et al., 2016; Inoue et al., 2016; Kawahara, 2019), a human-like android robot, and TELECO (Horikawa et al., 2023), a less anthropomorphic, teleoperated humanoid robot.

2.1 Speech Processing

For automatic speech recognition (ASR) and the extraction of prosodic features, we utilize a hand

Proceedings of the 31st International Conference on Computational Linguistics: System Demonstrations, pages 136–150
January 19–24, 2025.

System	Agent	Agent Behavior	Dialogue Features	Post-Interview Processing Workflow
SPECIES (Nunamaker et al., 2011)	Virtual	Eye Blink, Head Nodding	Follow-up Question	No
Maya (SB et al., 2021)	Virtual	Gestures, Head Nodding	Follow-up Question	No
ERICA (Inoue et al., 2021)	Robotic	Eye Blink, Lip Sync, Head Nodding	Follow-up Question	No
ERICA & TELECO (Ours)	Robotic	Eye Blink, Lip Sync, Gestures, Head Nodding, **Verbal Backchannel**	Follow-up Question, **Conversational Repair**, **User Fluency Adaptation**	**Yes**

Table 1: Comparison of embodied AI interview systems. Bold highlights features unique to our proposed system.

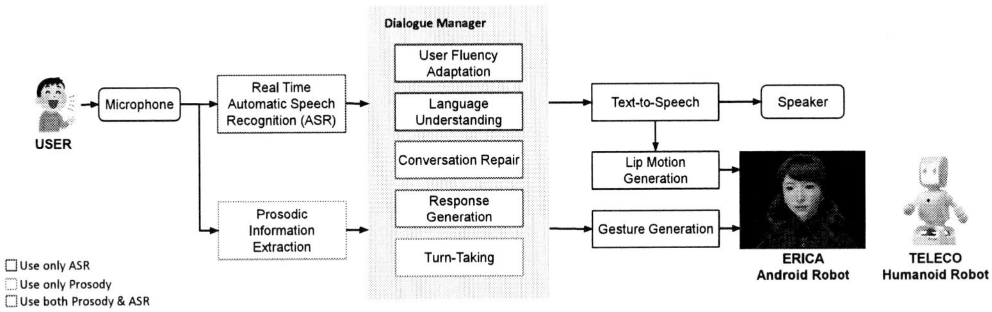

Figure 1: Overall architecture of human-like interview system

microphone. The ASR system is implemented via a real-time ASR module[1], which is based on the faster-whisper model[2]. This setup facilitates the extraction of critical prosodic information, including fundamental frequency (F0) and power, from the spoken input.

2.2 Dialogue Manager

The dialogue manager, a key component in our interview system, manages response selection based on user input. It comprises several sub-modules that improve interaction quality: a language understanding module that interprets user context to generate follow-up questions or smooth transitions; a backchannel module that predicts and delivers verbal and non-verbal cues, adding naturalness to the conversation; and a conversation repair module that detects and corrects communication breakdowns. Figure 2 depicts the architecture of the dialogue manager, highlighting the interplay among these components in response generation.

2.2.1 Language Understanding

The language understanding module uses ASR outputs for sentiment analysis, identifying keywords

[1]https://github.com/KoljaB/RealtimeSTT

[2]https://github.com/SYSTRAN/faster-whisper

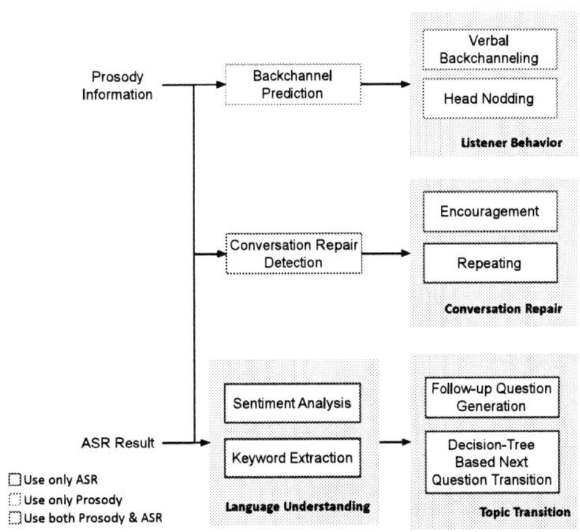

Figure 2: Overall architecture of interview system response generation

indicative of positive, neutral, and negative sentiments from a predefined polarity word list. For generating follow-up questions, the system considers context length and keyword presence—significant keywords include "because" and "as." A follow-up question is generated if the context is under five words or lacks these keywords, using our predefined list of questions. Utilizing a decision-tree method, responses indicating agreement or disagreement guide the direction of subsequent questions. An example of dialogue processing and response generation by our system is detailed in the Appendix A.

2.2.2 Backchannel

Backchanneling, where listeners indicate attentiveness through verbal, non-verbal, or combined responses, is crucial in conversations. Previous research has documented its use across languages (Cutrone, 2005; Ike, 2010) and settings (Widiyati, 2016; Maynard, 1986), including interviews (Wulandari, 2017; Nurjaleka, 2019; Laforest, 1994). Effective backchanneling and active listening enhance the interviewer's appeal and improve response quality (Louw et al., 2011; Rogers and Farson, 1957; Nurjaleka, 2023). Despite advancements in LLMs, generating appropriate backchannels remains challenging, underscoring their importance in achieving human-like conversations. Previous human-robot interactions have primarily used non-verbal cues like head nodding without verbal responses (Inoue et al., 2021).

To address this, our system separates backchannel prediction and generation. We utilize a Multilingual-VAP based model (Inoue et al., 2024a), fine-tuned with attentive listening data, to predict appropriate moments for backchanneling based on prosodic cues. For generation, we developed a repertoire of verbal backchannels—such as "hmm," "erm," and "mhmm"—and diverse head-nodding patterns that vary in frequency and speed for use in conversations. This approach supports simultaneous verbal and non-verbal backchannels to enhance the realism and effectiveness of the robot.

2.2.3 Conversation Repair

Conversation breakdowns frequently disrupt dialogues, particularly in spoken interviews, and can stem from issues from either the user or the system. For users, misunderstandings or difficulty in expressing thoughts can cause interruptions, whereas, for the system, challenges such as unrecognized speech or delays in processing can impede conversational flow.

To mitigate these disruptions, our system incorporates a conversation repair module that employs strategies of repeating and encouraging based on keyword detection. Utilizing prosodic cues and ASR results, the module identifies phrases indicating confusion, like "pardon?" or "could you say that again?" to repeat questions for clarity. Similarly, if expressions such as "I have no idea" or "I don't know" are detected, the system offers supportive responses, encouraging users to continue sharing their thoughts.

In cases where speech recognition fails despite clear voice activity, the system may use simple backchannels like "mhmm" to encourage continuation. Furthermore, to address processing delays that might lead to pauses, the system deploys interim responses like "That's interesting!" or "That's a good point!" from a predefined list, maintaining the conversational momentum while preparing the next question.

2.2.4 User Fluency Adaptation

User fluency significantly affects the smoothness of conversational flow during interviews. Fluent users usually engage without issues, but those less proficient may need additional time to articulate their thoughts, often resulting in longer silences and potential misunderstandings if the conversational pace is too rapid. This is particularly the case with non-native speakers. Our system includes a user fluency adaptation module that adjusts speaking speeds and extends turn-taking intervals according to user proficiency.

This module utilizes a Words-Per-Minute (WPM) based strategy, specifically designed to accommodate users with a WPM of 75 or below—indicative of beginner levels A1 to A2 according to the Common European Framework of References for Languages (CEFR)[3]. For these users, the system slows down its speech and allows longer response times. This adaptation helps non-fluent speakers engage effectively with our system, as standard conversational speeds in English, typically between 150-190 WPM and reaching up to 197 WPM in formal interviews (Marslen-Wilson, 1973; Richards, 1983; Wang, 2021), far exceed what beginners can handle. Even academic presentations, which generally maintain a slower pace of 100–125 WPM for clarity (Wong, 2009), surpass optimal speeds for these users. Utilizing user fluency adaptation, our system ensures the interview process accommodates speakers of varying proficiency, which is crucial in international conferences with diverse linguistic backgrounds.

[3] https://magoosh.com/english-speaking/english-proficiency-levels-a-guide-to-determining-your-level/

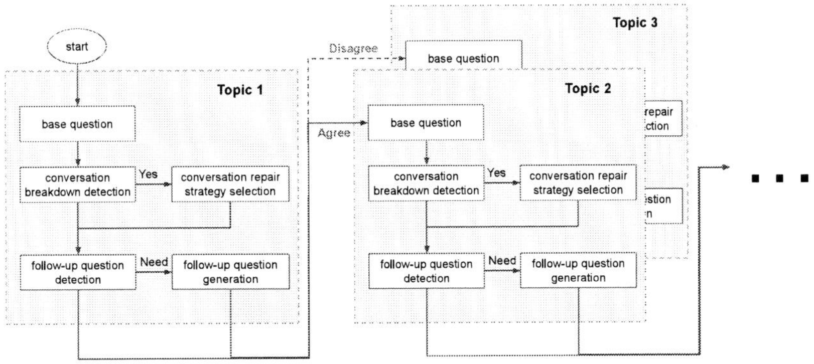

Figure 3: Overall architecture of interview dialogue flow

2.3 Speech Synthesis

For speech synthesis, our system uses the Julie voice provided by the VoiceText engine from Hoya Corporation[4]. Although this engine capably synthesizes standard speech, it struggles with the nuanced pronunciation of verbal backchannels such as "mhmm" or "hmm". These elements are crucial for natural conversational flow but are not adequately represented when generated directly by typical text-to-speech (TTS) systems due to their unique phonetic characteristics.

To overcome this limitation, we manually adjusted and refined the pronunciation of each backchannel, subsequently creating the corresponding .wav files. This approach allows our system to incorporate a diverse array of backchannels, varying in form and speed, to enhance the realism and dynamic nature of interactions.

2.4 Gesture Generation

To enhance the human-like quality of our interview system, we developed a range of gestures that extend beyond mere head nodding. Among these, an open palm gesture, which signifies openness and accessibility, fostering an environment conducive to free expression and interaction[5]. Additionally, we have implemented gestures such as leaning back to indicate surprise during interactions, and a bowing gesture to signify respect and formality after completing an interview. These gestures are strategically designed to mimic human non-verbal cues, thereby enhancing the naturalness and effectiveness of the robot's interactions with users.

[4]https://readspeaker.jp/

[5]https://www.globallisteningcentre.org/body-language-of-listeners/

2.5 Interview Dialogue Flow

The interview dialogue flow in our human-like interview system is managed via finite state transitions, as depicted in Figure 3. The process initiates with a base question. Based on the user's response, the system evaluates whether a conversational breakdown has occurred and if interventions, such as repeating or encouraging, are necessary. If such responses are required, the system generates them and maintains the current question state. Otherwise, the system assesses whether the user has provided sufficient information. If the information is inadequate, a follow-up question is posed. Subsequently, the system determines the next set of questions to be addressed based on the user's latest response. This cycle continues throughout the interview. Concurrently, to enhance human likeness and express interest in the user's responses, the system delivers both verbal and non-verbal backchanneling while receiving user input.

2.6 Interview Question Strategy

For the interview question strategy, we adopted a hybrid approach that integrates both template-based and generative question sets. On one hand, we employed LLMs (i.e., GPT-4o-mini API[6]) to dynamically produce follow-up inquiries, thereby adapting naturally to user responses and maintaining a human-like conversational flow. On the other hand, we use a fixed set of template-based questions for the primary prompts central to our data collection, ensuring that these core questions remain consistent across all interviews. This balance not only supports reliable downstream analysis but also

[6]https://openai.com/index/gpt-4o-mini-advancing-cost-efficient-intelligence/

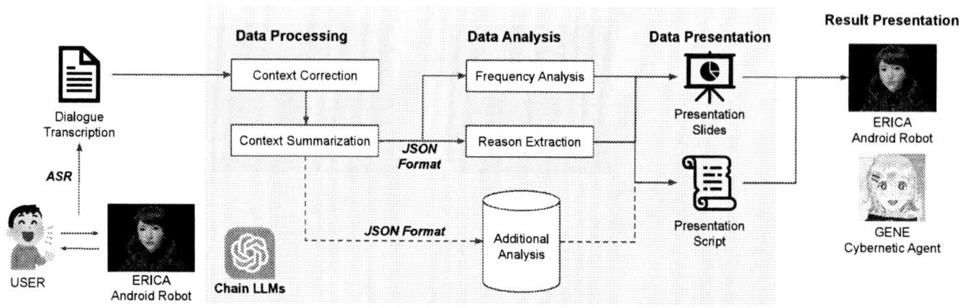

Figure 4: Overall architecture of post-interview processing workflow

enables adaptability through the generative component. Additionally, the system's modular design allows for flexible expansion for both the template-based and generative prompts, reducing the need for extensive manual rule-crafting. However, to ensure the highest level of analytic rigor in a research setting, the real-world case study presented in Section 3 relied solely on the template-based approach, maintaining question stability, which is necessary for accurate evaluation.

2.7 Post-Interview Processing Workflow

The post-interview processing workflow in our system facilitates data processing, analysis, and presentation. Utilizing a series of chained LLMs, specifically GPT-4o-mini[7], our system segments tasks into distinct subtasks with targeted prompts. This modular approach enhances task specificity and enables precise control over the process, allowing for modifications at any stage to suit specific research needs. The workflow's structure is detailed in Figure 4.

The pipeline consists of three main phases: data processing, analysis, and presentation. Initial data processing corrects ASR errors, ensuring data integrity, and prepares data in JSON format for subsequent analysis. The analysis involves evaluating opinion distributions and motivations, with flexibility for additional inquiries. Presentation materials, such as scripts and slides, are generated from the analysis results, using tools like the python-pptx library[8]. This automated system concludes with presentations delivered by conversational agents such as robots or virtual agents. Each subtask's detailed prompts are provided in the Appendix B.

3 Real-World Case Study

To evaluate our human-like embodied AI interviewer's effectiveness in a real-world setting, we conducted a case study at SIGDIAL 2024, attended by over 160 participants[9]. This study assessed perceptions of conversational AI's human-likeness, exploring themes such as essential interaction qualities, the importance of human-like traits, the inclusion of negative traits, and strategies against misuse.

Participants engaged in brief interviews lasting 2-3 minutes with one of two robots at the conference: ERICA, an android resembling a female adult, and TELECO, a humanoid robot with an OLED display face and simplified joint structures. Both robots exhibited identical dialogue behaviors, gestures, and facial expressions. Figure 5 illustrates a user interacting with ERICA during the conference[10]. Another user interacting with TELECO during the conference is illustrated in Figure 6. The example dialogues are provided in Appendix C, and the setup details and interview results are documented in Appendix D.

Interviews occurred over the first two days of the conference, with findings presented on the final day. To ensure a natural interaction environment, no formal questionnaire feedback was solicited. Instead, experiences were gathered directly during the interviews and through spontaneous post-interview discussions with participants. Insights from these interactions are elaborated in the subsequent subsection.

Consent was obtained by informing attendees at the conference's opening session and through clearly displayed notices in the interview room, advising that only transcripted dialogues from ASR

[7] https://openai.com/index/gpt-4o-mini-advancing-cost-efficient-intelligence/

[8] https://python-pptx.readthedocs.io/en/

[9] https://2024.sigdial.org/

[10] Demo video is available at https://youtu.be/v1vfRJu_UJ4

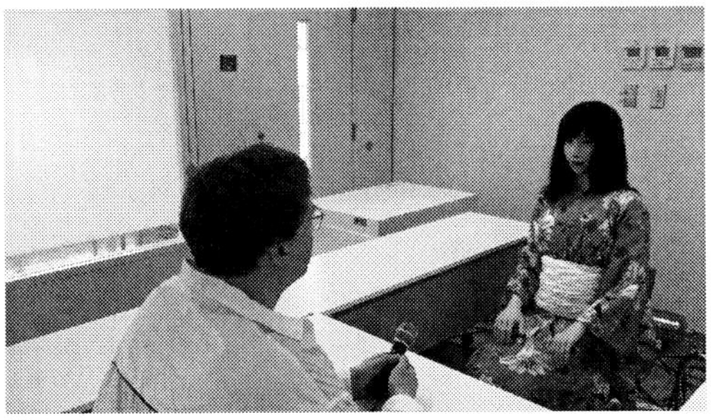

Figure 5: Photo of interview dialogue with ERICA by SIGDIAL participant

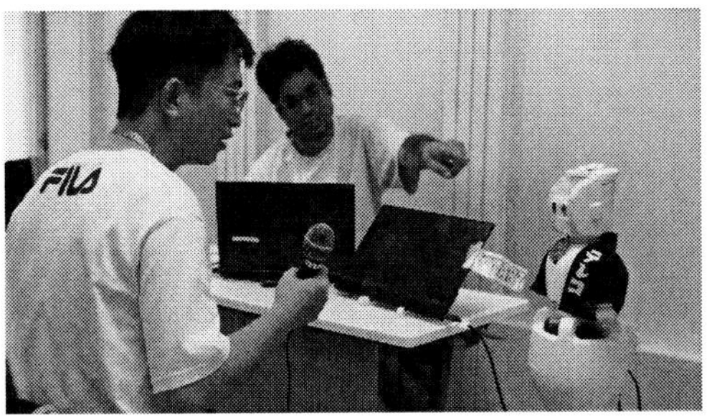

Figure 6: Photo of interview dialogue with TELECO by SIGDIAL participant

would be recorded.

3.1 Reporting on Panel Discussion

In academia, panel discussions usually involve a group of experts and a moderator to foster an informative exchanges of viewpoints. Such settings are advantageous for gathering expert opinions across various fields, providing a deep understanding of specific topics (Rasmussen, 2008; Tempero et al., 2011; Filbeck et al., 2017). However, these discussions often face time constraints and typically limit participation to high-level experts like professors, restricting the diversity of perspectives.

Our system extends beyond this limitation by collecting opinions from conference participants at all levels, not just from high-level experts, ensuring that all participants had the opportunity to express their opinions. During the panel discussion session on the last day, our system presented the analyzed results. Due to logistical challenges, instead of presenting with ERICA on stage, we utilized a computer-generated (CG) agent, Gene (Lee, 2023), who presented the results[11]. The presentation by Gene is illustrated in Figure 7.

[11]Demo video is available at `https://youtu.be/pSgaouAUkZk`.

Figure 7: Photo of Gene's presentation during the panel discussion session at SIGDIAL

3.2 Result and Discussion

The feedback from participants was predominantly positive, affirming the system's effectiveness in facilitating engaging and memorable interactions. Of 42 participants, 29 described the interaction as "enjoyable and engaging" and felt it encouraged them to share more thoughts. These comments reflect the system's success in engaging users effectively, with the overall results illustrated in Table 2.

However, not all feedback was positive. From two participants, critical insights emerged, highlighting the repetitive nature of the interview, with remarks like "The interview felt repetitive as the robot asked fixed questions." This feedback underscores the need for more adaptive and personalized follow-up questions, potentially through enhanced use of LLMs to enable dynamic conversation flows. Additionally, some participants expressed discomfort with the robots' human-like appearance, indicating a need for careful calibration to balance human-likeness and user comfort.

Further feedback from spontaneous post-interview conversations revealed mixed reactions to the system's backchanneling capabilities. While many appreciated the verbal and non-verbal backchannels for enhancing the perception of attentiveness and human-likeness, there were criticisms about the naturalness of synthesized backchannels like "mhmm," suggesting that the current speech synthesis engine may not effectively capture the casual tone required for everyday conversational backchannels. This opens avenues for future research into developing more human-like and context-appropriate backchannel generation.

Discussions also revealed diverse preferences concerning the appearances of our robots, particularly between the highly human-like android ERICA and the less human-like humanoid TELECO.

Some participants found ERICA's resemblance unsettling, while others valued the genuine sense of co-presence she provided. In contrast, TELECO's less human-like features did not evoke the same level of co-presence. These varied responses highlight cultural or personal differences in acceptance and preference of robot aesthetics, suggesting a rich area for further investigation into how culture and personality influence human reactions to the human-likeness of robots.

Experience	Common Reasons
Positive	1. Interaction is engaging
(69.05)	2. Interesting human-like robot
Neutral	1. Interesting but experienced an error
(26.19)	2. Interesting but wanted more support
Negative	1. Questions felt repetitive
(4.76)	2. Robot appearance caused discomfort

Table 2: Overall Interview Experience Result [%]

4 Conclusion

In this paper, we introduced the human-like embodied AI interviewer, integrating android and humanoid robots with chained LLMs to support researchers in data collection, analysis, and presentation. Our system improved interview quality by incorporating advanced conversational behaviors such as attentive listening, conversational repairs, and user fluency adaptation, and automated the analysis and presentation processes post-interview.

A two-day case study at an international academic conference validated our system's effectiveness, with 69% of participants reporting positive experiences. The system also streamlined data analysis and presentation. Notably, this was the first use of such a system at an international conference, demonstrating its applicability in real-world research settings.

Looking forward, we aim to enhance the human-like features of our system, focusing on improving backchannel generation and exploring cultural and personal preferences for robot appearances to optimize user interactions. We hope that these enhancements will bring us closer to achieving human-level interaction capabilities in android robots, further bridging the gap between technology and natural human communication.

5 Limitations

While our preliminary two-day case study at an international academic conference offered initial validation, the relatively small sample size (42 participants) limits the generalizability of our findings. To improve the generalizability of our findings, we plan to conduct larger-scale studies with more diverse participant groups.

Another limitation lies in the repetitive nature of the template-based questioning utilized in the real-world case study. While these fixed templates ensured stability for analysis, they reduced conversational variability. In future work, we aim to incorporate LLMs to generate questions more dynamically, exploring methods to maintain question stability without compromising adaptability and user engagement.

Lastly, the current system relies solely on speech input, which constrains its capacity to fully interpret users' states and behaviors. Moving forward, we will integrate richer multimodal inputs—including facial expressions, body language, and environmental context—to achieve more responsive, context-aware interactions and enhance the overall user experience.

Acknowledgments

The authors thank the participants of SIGDIAL 2024 for their contributions, which were crucial for the analysis and conclusions of this study. This research was supported by the JST Moonshot R&D Goal 1 Avatar Symbiotic Society Project (JPMJMS2011).

References

Keith Anderson, Elisabeth André, Tobias Baur, Sara Bernardini, Mathieu Chollet, Evi Chryssafidou, Ionut Damian, Cathy Ennis, Arjan Egges, Patrick Gebhard, et al. 2013. The tardis framework: intelligent virtual agents for social coaching in job interviews. In *International conference on advances in computer entertainment technology*, pages 476–491. Springer.

Pino Cutrone. 2005. A case study examining backchannels in conversations between japanese–british dyads. *Multilingua*, 24(3):237–274.

Greg Filbeck, Victor Ricciardi, Harold R Evensky, Steve Z Fan, Hunter M Holzhauer, and Andrew Spieler. 2017. Behavioral finance: A panel discussion. *Journal of Behavioral and Experimental Finance*, 15:52–58.

Dylan F Glas, Takashi Minato, Carlos T Ishi, Tatsuya Kawahara, and Hiroshi Ishiguro. 2016. Erica: The erato intelligent conversational android. In *2016 25th IEEE International symposium on robot and human interactive communication (RO-MAN)*, pages 22–29. IEEE.

Yukiko Horikawa, Takahiro Miyashita, Akira Utsumi, Shogo Nishimura, and Satoshi Koizumi. 2023. Cybernetic avatar platform for supporting social activities of all people. In *2023 IEEE/SICE International Symposium on System Integration (SII)*, pages 1–4. IEEE.

Saya Ike. 2010. Backchannel: a feature of japanese english. In *JALT 2009 Conference Proceedings*, volume 205, page 215. JALT Tokyo.

Koji Inoue, Kohei Hara, Divesh Lala, Shizuka Nakamura, Katsuya Takanashi, and Tatsuya Kawahara. 2021. A job interview dialogue system with autonomous android erica. In *Increasing Naturalness and Flexibility in Spoken Dialogue Interaction: 10th International Workshop on Spoken Dialogue Systems*, pages 291–297. Springer.

Koji Inoue, Bing'er Jiang, Erik Ekstedt, Tatsuya Kawahara, and Gabriel Skantze. 2024a. Multilingual turn-taking prediction using voice activity projection. *arXiv preprint arXiv:2403.06487*.

Koji Inoue, Bing'er Jiang, Erik Ekstedt, Tatsuya Kawahara, and Gabriel Skantze. 2024b. Real-time and continuous turn-taking prediction using voice activity projection. *arXiv preprint arXiv:2401.04868*.

Koji Inoue, Pierrick Milhorat, Divesh Lala, Tianyu Zhao, and Tatsuya Kawahara. 2016. Talking with erica, an autonomous android. In *Proceedings of the 17th Annual Meeting of the Special Interest Group on Discourse and Dialogue*, pages 212–215.

Tatsuya Kawahara. 2019. Spoken dialogue system for a human-like conversational robot erica. In *9th International Workshop on Spoken Dialogue System Technology*, pages 65–75. Springer.

Marty Laforest. 1994. Listening strategies in sociolinguistic interviews. convergence and divergence. *Culture*, 14(2):51–61.

Akinobu Lee. 2023. MMDAgent-EX.

Stephen Louw, R Watson Todd, and Pattamawan Jimarkon. 2011. Active listening in qualitative research interviews. In *Proceedings of the International Conference: Research in Applied Linguistics, April*, pages 71–82.

William Marslen-Wilson. 1973. Linguistic structure and speech shadowing at very short latencies. *Nature*, 244(5417):522–523.

Senko K Maynard. 1986. On back-channel behavior in japanese and english casual conversation. *Linguistics*, 24(6):1079–1108.

Jay F Nunamaker, Douglas C Derrick, Aaron C Elkins, Judee K Burgoon, and Mark W Patton. 2011. Embodied conversational agent-based kiosk for automated interviewing. *Journal of Management Information Systems*, 28(1):17–48.

Lisda Nurjaleka. 2019. Backchannel behavior in interview discourse: A contrastive study between japanese and indonesian. In *Eleventh Conference on Applied Linguistics (CONAPLIN 2018)*, pages 451–457. Atlantis Press.

Lisda Nurjaleka. 2023. Backchannels responses as conversational strategies in the interaction of indonesian speakers in interview setting. *REiLA: Journal of Research and Innovation in Language*, 5(2):99–114.

Terje Rasmussen. 2008. Panel discussion ii: Culture and media technology. the internet and differentiation in the political public sphere. *nordicom Review*, 29(2):73–83.

Jack C Richards. 1983. Listening comprehension: Approach, design, procedure. *TESOL quarterly*, 17(2):219–240.

Carl Ransom Rogers and Richard Evans Farson. 1957. *Active listening*. Industrial Relations Center of the University of Chicago Chicago, IL.

Pooja Rao SB, Manish Agnihotri, and Dinesh Babu Jayagopi. 2021. Improving asynchronous interview interaction with follow-up question generation. *IJIMAI*, 6(5):79–89.

MA Tempero, J Berlin, M Ducreux, D Haller, P Harper, D Khayat, H-J Schmoll, A Sobrero, and E Van Cutsem. 2011. Pancreatic cancer treatment and research: an international expert panel discussion. *Annals of oncology*, 22(7):1500–1506.

Li Wang. 2021. British english-speaking speed 2020. *Acad. J. Humanit. Soc. Sci*, 4:93–100.

Elok Widiyati. 2016. The features of interrupting, collaborating, and backchannelling used by broadcaster and caller in telephone conversation. *EduLite: Journal of English Education, Literature and Culture*, 1(1):1–16.

Linda Wong. 2009. *Essential study skills*. Houghton Mifflin.

Nur Wulandari. 2017. A conversation analysis of verbal backchannel response in radio program valentine in the morning interview with michael bublé. *Sastra Inggris-Quill*, 6(6):585–596.

Appendix

A Language Understanding Dialogue Example

Below is a dialogue example demonstrating our language understanding system. **R** indicates an utterance by the system, while **U** indicates an utterance by the user. Dialogue 1 demonstrates a scenario where the system generates a follow-up question due to the absence of keywords like "because" or "as". In contrast, Dialogue 2 shows a scenario where the system does not generate a follow-up question because the user spoke extensively.

Dialogue 1
R1 What do you think is the most important thing when interacting with a conversational AI?
U1 Uh, well, I would say the response time maybe.
R2 Interesting! Can you tell me more about why you think that's so important? (Generated a follow-up question as no keywords were detected)

Dialogue 2
R1 What do you think is the most important thing when interacting with a conversational AI?
U1 I think it should be that I am properly understood and my questions are addressed accurately. I think that if I'm talking with somebody, I really would like to be understood, so I think that's very important.
R2 That's a good point! So, let's move on. (Moved to the next question since the user spoke a lot)

The example dialogues below showcase how responses guide the flow of the interview, especially when determining the next question. In the *importance of human-like traits* question, when keywords like "agree", "yes", "yeah" are detected indicating agreement, the next question shifts to *the inclusion of negative traits*, as shown in Dialogue 3. Conversely, if the user disagrees, the next questions will be about *strategies against misuse*, as shown in Dialogue 4.

Dialogue 3
R1 Do you think conversational AI should aim to be human-like?
U1 Yeah, not only human-like but also considering the user's preferences.
R2 Okay, that's interesting! And what about negative human traits? Should conversational AI include these as well? (Moved to the *inclusion of negative traits* topic since the user agreed)

Dialogue 4
R1 Do you think conversational AI should aim to be human-like?
U1 Um, not really. I think that conversational AI can be useful even if it's not human-like.
R2 Makes sense! So, what would you do to prevent misuse of conversational AI? (Moved to the *strategies against misuse* topic as the user disagreed)

Sentiment analysis was implemented in our proposed system to determine the appropriate response. For instance, when querying user experiences about being interviewed by a robot, the robot's response will change based on the sentiment of the user's utterance. This adaptation is illustrated below in Dialogue 5 and Dialogue 6.

Dialogue 5
R1 How did you feel about being interviewed by me, a human-like robot?
U1 Yeah, it was a really interesting experience because this is my first time.
R2 I'm glad that you enjoyed this conversation. I appreciate your time! Have a wonderful day! (Concludes positively in response to the user's enjoyment)

Dialogue 6
R1 How did you feel about being interviewed by me, a human-like robot?
U1 It's a little creepy.
R2 I'm sorry to hear that, but I appreciate your honesty. Thank you for your time. (Responds courteously to the user's negative feedback)

B Prompts

Below are the prompts provided to the LLMs to facilitate response generation. In the post-interview processing workflow, our system used a series of chained LLMs to handle data through context correction, summarization, data analysis, and the generation of presentation slides and scripts. The pipeline involves a cascading approach where the input from each subtask is passed to the next task. This approach comprehensively manages processing, analysis, and presentation generation. Detailed prompts for each subtask are depicted in Figures 8 to 12.

C Case Study Dialogue Example

See Figure 13 for a dialogue example[12] that explores participant perceptions of the *human-likeness of conversational AI*. This example addresses four primary topics: essential interaction qualities, the importance of human-like traits, the inclusion of negative traits, and strategies to prevent misuse. In the dialogue, **ROBOT** denotes system utterances, while **HUMAN** represents user responses. As detailed in Section 2.3, verbal backchannels cannot be directly synthesized by our speech engine; therefore, we manually created these sounds and played the corresponding .wav files as needed. In the dialogue example, any system utterance ending with .wav indicates a generated verbal backchannel. Due to the simultaneous occurrence of verbal backchannels and user utterances, the log file records system backchannels before user responses.

D Case Study Details

As discussed in Section 3, we conducted a real-world case study at the SIGDIAL international conference. During the initial two days, participants were interviewed by our embodied conversational agents, ERICA and TELECO, for data collection purposes. Figure 5 and 6 illustrate a user interacting with ERICA and TELECO, respectively, during one of these sessions. On the final day of the conference, our system analyzed and presented the results of these interactions during a panel discussion session. Figure 7 displays Gene, our CG agent, presenting these results. Figure 14 showcases the script, while Figure 15 displays the slides used during the presentation.

[12]Demo video is available at `https://youtu.be/v1vfRJu_UJ4`

```
Given a raw transcript of a dialogue between a human and a robot, please correct any
obvious errors in the human's responses that seem misrecognized by the automatic
speech recognition (ASR) system. When correcting the user responses, you should
correct them based on the question asked by the robot.

You should:
-Retain all natural elements of spoken dialogue such as fillers, hesitations, and
repetitions, as they reflect the natural speaking style.
-Only correct parts that are clear misinterpretations or irrelevant to the context
provided by the robot's questions.
-Ensure the corrections align logically with the questions asked by the robot.
-Correct the conversation and maintain the format and context.

For example:
"Yeah like I have to wait for quite a while yeah because um yeah my research
interest is still about that Yeah so I have to deal with the conversation and quite
a lot actually"

You should correct it to something like

"Yeah like I have interacted quite a lot actually yeah because um yeah my research
interest is still about that Yeah so I have to deal with the conversation and quite
a lot actually"

Remember, it must remain in the original context except those that seem irrelevant,
which the ASR system misrecognized.

The conversation is as follows:
```

Figure 8: Prompt for correcting dialogue context due to ASR error

```
Given the transcript of a conversation between a robot and a human during an interview
about conversational AI, summarize the human's opinions into a structured JSON object
using specified categories. Each category should be clearly structured with
subcategories as follows:

- 'Interact_with_AI_Before': Answer as 'yes' or 'no'.
- 'Important_Aspect': Provide 'aspect' which part of conversational AI is considered
important, and 'reason' explaining why.
- 'Should_Human_Like': Provide 'agreement' as agree/disagree, and 'reason' for the
view.
- 'Include_Negative_Traits': Provide 'agreement' as agree/disagree, and 'reason' for
the view.
- 'Precautions': Mention the 'aspect' of necessary precautions for conversational AI,
and the 'reason' for them.
- 'Interview_Experience': Describe the experience as 'opinion' being positive,
neutral, or negative, and provide a 'reason'.

Ensure accuracy and clarity in the responses, and maintain the context of the
conversation. The conversation is as follows:
```

Figure 9: Prompt for summarizing dialogue context into JSON format

```
You are a PowerPoint presentation specialist. You are asked to create the content for an academic
presentation for the academic conference SIGIDAL on the analysis result report regarding human-like
conversational AI interview research. This study employs two conversational robots to conduct interviews
during the conference, gathering attendees' perspectives on the realism and effectiveness of AI-driven
communication. The data collected from these interviews will be analyzed and presented by a virtual agent
named Gene. Your role is to generate the slides and script automatically, with the final script to be
manually inputted into Gene, who will execute the presentation.

The first slide should be the presentation title and the Presenter's name only. The subsequent slides will
present the analysis of the interview data.

Structure the information for a PowerPoint presentation aimed at a researcher audience. Each slide should
have a title, content summarized in bullet points, and, when applicable, chart data to visually represent
the analysis result, remember to include the "others" category if cannot fix all the results. The charts
should include percentages and category names.

Output Format:
Return the structured information as a JSON object, where each slide specifies the content in bullet
points and the type of chart with its corresponding data. Your answer should only contain the JSON - no
markdown formatting or explanatory text.

Example:
{
  "slides": [
    {"title": "Title Slide", "content": "Presentation Title: Analysis of Participant Opinions"},
    {
      "title": "Understanding Participant Demographics",
      "content": [
        "Summary of participant age groups",
        "Insights into demographic distribution"
      ],
      "chart": {
        "type": "bar_chart",
        "data": {
          "categories": ["Under 25", "25-40", "Over 40"],
          "values": [10, 15, 5],
          "labels": ["10%", "15%", "5%"]
        }
      }
    },
      {"title": "Conclusion Slide", "content": "Main conclusions and future research directions"}
  ]
}

The information is as follows:
```

Figure 10: Prompt for generating presentation slide context

```
You are a PowerPoint presentation specialist tasked with creating Python code to generate a professional
academic presentation for the SIGIDAL conference on human-like conversational AI research. You will use
the python-pptx package and a previously generated JSON script detailing slide contents, including text
and chart data.

Design Guidelines:
Fonts: Use Arial for titles (size 32, bold) and Tahoma for content (size 24). Justify all content text.
Color and Emphasis: Bold and use red font color for important keywords in the content.
Bullet Points: Format content with multiple pieces of information as bullet points. Determine whether
content should be bullet points or sub-bullets based on context.
Title Slide: Use the title slide layout, including the conference and the presenter's name as the
subtitle.

Python Code Instructions:
Generate slides based on the JSON input. If a slide specifies a chart, integrate the chart using the data
provided. Your response should contain only the Python code, no explanatory text.
Example JSON Input:

{
  "slides": [
    {"title": "Introduction", "content": "Overview of the project objectives and key results"},
    {
      "title": "Data Analysis",
      "content": "Graphical representation of data trends, statistical summaries",
      "chart": {
        "type": "bar_chart",
        "data": {
          "categories": ["Category 1", "Category 2", "Category 3"],
          "values": [20, 30, 50],
          "labels": ["20%", "30%", "50%"]
        }
      }
    },
    {"title": "Conclusion", "content": "Summary of findings, future research directions"}
  ]
}

The information is as follows:
```

Figure 11: Prompt for generating presentation slide python script from the presentation slide context

```
Generate an academic presentation script based on the provided data analysis summary of
interview experiences with conversational AI. The script should be spoken in English, last
approximately 5 minutes, and adhere to the following guidelines:

1. The presentation is to be delivered by a virtual agent named Gene at SIGDIAL 2024.
2. Begin with an opening that includes:
   - Introduction of the virtual presenter, Gene.
   - A greeting that mentions enjoyment of SIGDIAL 2024 so far.
   - A special thanks to ERICA and TELECO for the data collection.
3. Proceed to detail the data analysis summary which includes:
   - Number of participants and their previous experience with AI.
   - Important aspects of AI interaction highlighted by participants.
   - Opinions on AI exhibiting human-like traits and the inclusion of human-like flaws.
   - Precautions and ethical considerations suggested by participants.
   - General sentiment and specific feedback from participants about their interaction
experiences.
4. Conclude the presentation by:
   - Summarizing the insights on how human-like qualities in AI impact user experience.
   - Emphasizing the need for a balanced approach in AI development that incorporates
human-like interaction dynamics without compromising ethical standards.
   - A closing statement that does not invite questions, thanking the audience for their
attention.

Please use clear, professional, and engaging language suitable for an academic audience.
Ensure the script is structured for smooth delivery by the virtual agent.
Only use the periods, commas, and exclamation marks for punctuation. Please put the commas
at the places where you would naturally pause while speaking. Your script should use I'm
instead of I am, for a more conversational tone. Only output the script content, excluding
any system prompts or any sectional headers.

The script is as follows:
```

Figure 12: Prompt for generation presentation script

```
ROBOT: Hi! I'm ERICA, nice to meet you!
ROBOT: emm_speed150.wav
HUMAN: Hi Erica, nice to meet you!
ROBOT: I'm doing a survey on conversational AI. And I wonder if I can ask you a few questions?
ROBOT: mhm_question.wav
HUMAN: Yes, please go ahead.
ROBOT: Great, thank you! To start off, Have you interacted with a conversational AI before?
HUMAN: Yes, I interact with them quite a lot.
ROBOT: That's great! So what do you think is the most important thing when interacting with a
conversational AI?
ROBOT: erm_speed225.wav
ROBOT: erm_speed225.wav
HUMAN: That's a very good question. Personally, I think the most important aspect would be
making sure the conversational AI matches the scenario or situation.
ROBOT: That's a good point! So do you think conversational AI should aim to be human-like?
ROBOT: erm_speed225.wav
ROBOT: mhm_question.wav
ROBOT: m.wav
HUMAN: Yeah, to follow up on my last response, I think it depends on the situation. So for
example, if it's more of a situation where you would expect some kind of human-level service,
I think it makes a lot of sense to act human-like.
ROBOT: Okay, That's interesting! And what about negative human traits? Should conversational
AI include these as well?
ROBOT: emm_speed150.wav
ROBOT: emm_speed150.wav
HUMAN: Yeah, that's a very good point. I think in some situations, it's very good to have some
negative traits so that the conversational AI will appear even more human. But if you're
trying to come off as professional, maybe it'd be better to omit some of those.
ROBOT: Ok, interesting! So what would you do to prevent misuse with conversational AI?
ROBOT: emm_speed150.wav
ROBOT: m.wav
ROBOT: erm_speed150.wav
HUMAN: Yeah, there are a lot of different steps I think that can be taken, and it's an area
where I believe there'll need to be continual improvement. But I think one area that's very
easy to address right now is making sure that the AI is not hallucinating and saying things
that are not true.
ROBOT: Ok, That's a good point! Before we wrap up, how did you feel about being interviewed
by, me, a human-like robot?
HUMAN: This was actually very enjoyable. Thank you very much for the experience.
ROBOT: I'm glad that you enjoyed this conversation. I appreciate your time! Have a wonderful
day!
ROBOT: erm_speed225.wav
HUMAN: I appreciate your time as well. Have a great day, Erica!
ROBOT: see you next time!
```

Figure 13: Dialogue example collected during the case studies

Good afternoon, everyone. My name is Gene, and I'm a virtual agent glad to be presenting to you today at SIGDIAL 2024. I hope you are enjoying this conference as much as I am.

Today, I'm presenting a detailed analysis of interview experiences with conversational AI, which sheds light on user interactions and perspectives. We conducted interviews with a total of 42 participants, with 34 having prior experiences with AI and 8 having none. This diverse group allowed us to capture a broad range of insights.

Several important aspects of AI interaction were highlighted by participants. The most frequently mentioned factors including response time, clarity, accuracy, and human-like communication. Participants emphasized that smooth and coherent conversations are essential for enhancing user experience. They expect conversational AI to understand their inputs without requiring adjustments or corrections on their part. The accuracy and efficiency of responses were deemed crucial; slow response times were particularly noted as a barrier to creating a natural flow in conversation.

When discussing whether conversational AI should exhibit human-like traits, 28 of the participants agreed it should, while 10 disagreed. Many expressed that human-like qualities can improve the overall interaction. However, some experienced users preferred a more functional and efficient AI that doesn't necessarily mimic human behavior. The varying opinions underscore the complexity of user preferences and expectations.

A fascinating aspect of our findings was the mixed sentiments regarding the inclusion of negative traits in AI. Just 13 participants agreed that AI should reflect negative human traits, indicating a strong preference for positivity in user interactions. Many felt that such traits could diminish trust and satisfaction, suggesting that while some might find realism in flaws, a focus on positive characteristics is more beneficial in fostering a good user experience.

Further, participants raised pertinent precautions and ethical considerations for the development of conversational AI. Key takeaways included the necessity for data testing, preventing misuse, and establishing trust with users. Many emphasized that clear guidelines should be enacted to ensure ethical interactions and safety, while also educating users about the capabilities and limitations of conversational AI.

Overall, the sentiment towards interview experiences with conversational AI was quite positive, with 29 participants rating their experience favorably. The engaging nature of the interaction was frequently noted, although there were instances of confusion and discomfort, especially related to communication dynamics."

In conclusion, our analysis underscores that human-like qualities in AI play a significant role in shaping user experiences. However, there exists a delicate balance that needs to be maintained. While aiming for human-like interactions can enhance engagement, it is equally important to uphold ethical standards and avoid negative traits that can undermine trust.

Thank you for your kind attention! and let's continue to explore the fascinating possibilities of conversational AI together!

Figure 14: Presentation script created by our system for Gene's presentation at the SIGDIAL conference

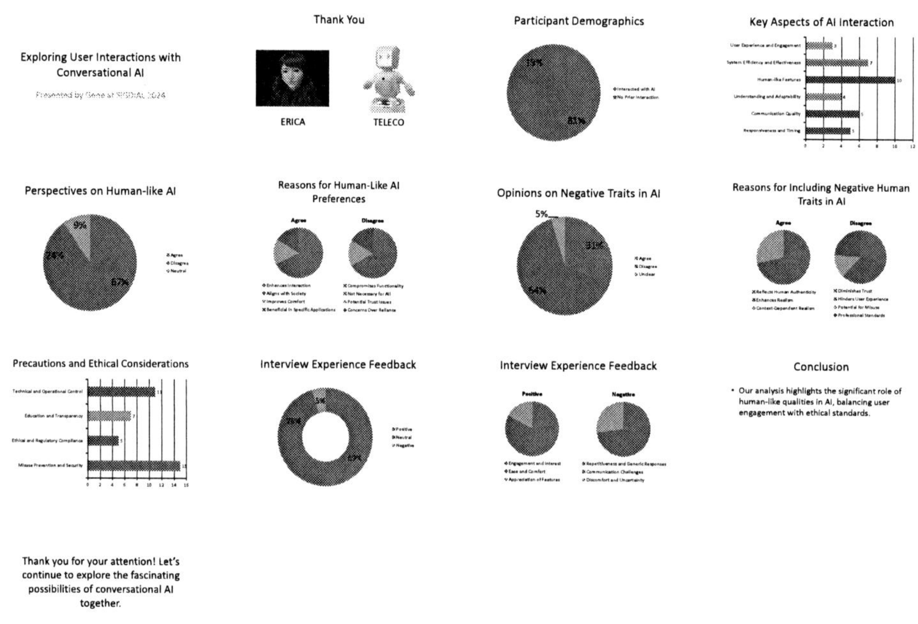

Figure 15: Presentation slides created by our system for Gene's presentation at the SIGDIAL conference.

CASE: Large Scale Topic Exploitation for Decision Support Systems

Lorena Calvo-Bartolomé
Universidad Carlos III
lcalvo@pa.uc3m.es

Jerónimo Arenas-García
Universidad Carlos III
jarenas@ing.uc3m.es

David Pérez-Fernández
Universidad Autónoma de Madrid
david.perez@inv.uam.es

Abstract

In recent years, there has been growing interest in using NLP tools for decision support systems, particularly in Science, Technology, and Innovation (STI). Among these, topic modeling has been widely used for analyzing large document collections, such as scientific articles, research projects, or patents, yet its integration into decision-making systems remains limited. This paper introduces CASE, a tool for exploiting topic information for semantic analysis of large corpora. The core of CASE is a Solr engine with a customized indexing strategy to represent information from Bayesian and Neural topic models that allow efficient topic-enriched searches. Through *ad-hoc* plug-ins, CASE enables topic inference on new texts and semantic search. We demonstrate the versatility and scalability of CASE through two use cases: the calculation of aggregated STI indicators and the implementation of a web service to help evaluate research projects.

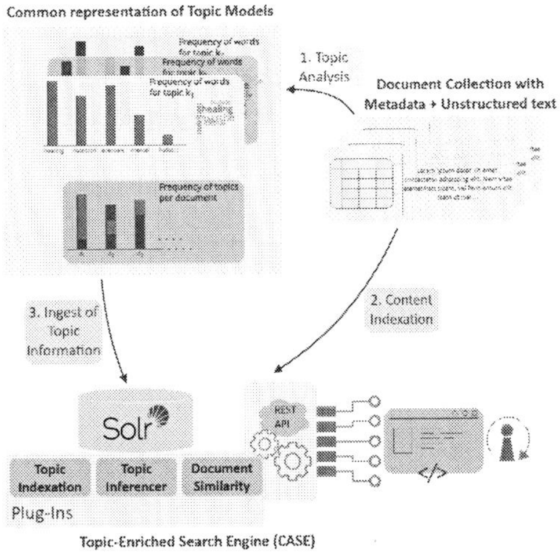

Figure 1: System Overview: A Solr-powered search engine enhanced with custom plug-ins for indexing topic model, and providing real-time topic inference capabilities. A REST API provides access for web services or direct user interaction.

1 Introduction

How can public administration officials efficiently manage thousands of grant proposals? How to find the most appropriate researchers for specific funding calls? Topic models, beyond their traditional uses in information retrieval and summarization (Boyd-Graber et al., 2017), can play a major role in these tasks tailored to Science, Technology, and Innovation (STI) (Zhang et al., 2016).

Despite the recent dominance of large language models (LLMs) in topic modeling research (Lam et al., 2024; Pham et al., 2024; Reuter et al., 2024), Bayesian and Neural topic models (Blei et al., 2003; Bianchi et al., 2021a; Dieng et al., 2020) remain pertinent, particularly in their interpretability and ability to preserve document-topic and word-topic distributions –which most of these new algorithms disregard. This approach tailors applications such as thematic trend analysis, topic-based document retrieval, or similarity search.

Though LLM-based ranking models (Khattab and Zaharia, 2020; Santhanam et al., 2022) excel in information retrieval (IR) tasks requiring deep contextual understanding, they rely on dense vectors (*embeddings*) that behave as black-box models, offering high-dimensional representations that lack interpretability for answering specific STI-related questions. Furthermore, the growing use of dedicated vector stores (e.g., FAISS, Pinecone) for efficient retrieval introduces new approaches to IR architectures, but their capabilities largely overlap with those of established systems like Lucene (Yang et al., 2018; Xian et al., 2024).

Several studies have underscored the potential of integrating topic information with Lucene (Hassan et al., 2011; George et al., 2014; Chen and Xu, 2016; Rajapaksha and Silva, 2019). There is also considerable work on developing topic modeling tools focused on training and visualization (Ter-

Proceedings of the 31st International Conference on Computational Linguistics: System Demonstrations, pages 151–162
January 19–24, 2025.

ragni et al., 2021; Babb et al., 2021). However, these efforts do not directly address the exploitation of topic models, particularly their integration into more complex IR systems. This gap highlights the necessity for tools that enhance the practical application of topic models within broader information systems, leveraging their interpretability and thematic analysis capabilities.

To address this, we propose CASE, a tool designed for leveraging topic models and semantic analysis in large-scale, thematically diverse datasets. CASE's core is a Solr search engine optimized for search and retrieval tasks involving large datasets. Using a novel approach for indexing topic information and integrating several plugins for topic-based similarity searches, CASE enables:

- **Searching and filtering** by document metadata and topic information;
- **Efficient aggregation** of search results with partial document-topic assignments; and
- **Semantic similarity searches** based on topic-based representations.

CASE aims to support STI managers and public administration officials by simplifying tasks such as expert identification, project proposals classification, similarity checks against previously funded projects, and alignment of researchers with relevant funding opportunities. The tool includes a RESTful API for seamless indexing and retrieval, compatible with standalone usage or a user-friendly frontend, packaged in Docker for easy deployment.

CASE is available on GitHub under an MIT license,[1] with a demo showcasing its functionalities.[2]

2 CASE

This section describes CASE's solution for indexing corpus and topic model information. It also covers its architectural and functional descriptions.

2.1 Common representation of topic models

CASE employs a Solr engine to jointly index document metadata and topic model information (see Fig. 1). It supports any topic model adhering to the common representation described in this section, ensuring compatibility with various algorithms. Let c_d $(d = 1, \ldots, D)$ denote each document in corpus C with a vocabulary size V, with w_v, $v = 1, \ldots V$ being each of the words in the vocabulary. We assume that any topic model trained on C with K topics provides:

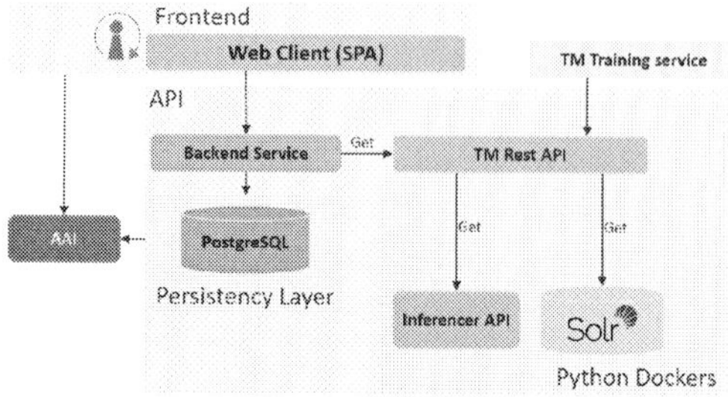

Figure 2: CASE architecture: A Python-based REST API interacts with the Solr engine, the user or frontend, and the Inferencer service. In this setup, CASE is integrated into a complete exploitation system.

Word-to-topic assignments. Each topic t_k $(k = 1, \ldots, K)$ is characterized by an over-the-words distribution, where $\beta_{k,v}$ is the probability of observing word w_v given topic t_k:

$$\boldsymbol{\beta}_k = [\beta_{k,v}, v = 1, \ldots, V], \tag{1}$$

$$\beta_{k,v} = P(w_v \mid t_k), \tag{2}$$

Document-to-topic assignments. Each document is represented as a mixture of topics:

$$\boldsymbol{\theta}_d = [\theta_{d,k}, k = 1, \ldots, K], \tag{3}$$

$$\theta_{d,k} = P(t_k \mid c_d), \tag{4}$$

where $\boldsymbol{\theta}_d$ and $\theta_{d,k}$ are the topic-based vector and probability of topic t_k for document c_d.

For training, we use TARS,[3] a software that supports interactive, user-in-the-loop topic modeling within CASE's common representation. TARS includes algorithms such as LDA-MALLET (McCallum, 2002) (Bayesian-based), CTM (Bianchi et al., 2021c,b), and BERTopic (Grootendorst, 2022) (neural-based). Models can also be trained using other implementations and subsequently mapped to CASE's structure. We exclude newer LLM-based implementations (LLMs) (Lam et al., 2024; Pham et al., 2024; Reuter et al., 2024) because they either disregard or poorly approximate word-topic and document-topic distributions, which are essential for CASE's indexed information.

2.2 Selection of most relevant documents

Selecting the most representative documents for a given topic is crucial for the correct interpretation

[1] https://github.com/Nemesis1303/CASE
[2] https://youtu.be/Iv366i9lEXc
[3] https://github.com/IntelCompH2020/topicmodeler

of the topics. This is usually done based on the documents with the highest θ values for the topic. However, CASE implements a newly proposed criterion:

$$S3_{d,k} = \frac{1}{n_d} \sum_{i=1}^{n_d} \beta_{k,w_{d,i}}, w_{d,i} \in \{w_v\}_{v=1}^{V}. \quad (5)$$

Here, $S3_{d,k}$ represents the average of the topic-word distribution values for all words in document d for topic k, normalized to account for document length. $S3_{d,k}$ is thus large for documents containing many words that fit well with topic k. We expect the proposed method to provide more representative documents than the θ criterion, as the latter may select documents containing words that are not very representative of the target topic (small $\beta_{k,v}$), as long as no other topic fits better these words, whereas $S3_{d,k}$ is robust to this situation.

2.3 Architecture

CASE is a multi-container application (see Fig. 2, *"Python Dockers"*) that builds on an Apache Solr search engine in *SolrCloud*[4] mode for data storage and retrieval. A Python-based RESTful API serves as intermediate between the Solr engine and the user (or frontend service) to provide a series of endpoints for indexation and exploitation of both collections and topic models. The Inferencer API computes topic representations for new texts.

2.4 Corpus and topic information indexation

SolrCloud mode utilizes *collections* of shards/cores to create logical indexes. A *Document* (the basic unit stored and indexed within a collection) contains one or more *Fields*, akin to rows and columns in a traditional database. For CASE, we define three collection types (see Fig. 3):

Corpus. Each dataset of text documents is associated with one *Corpus* collection, and contains corpus-related metadata, as well as topical document representations, and pair-to-pair similarities for each model associated to the corpus.

Model. Each topic model is stored in a different *Model* collection, representing its topics as Solr documents. Each model is associated with a *Corpus* collection (its training datasct).

[4]SolrCloud is chosen over User-Managed mode to automate shard creation for large document corpora, removing the need for manual configuration by the end user.

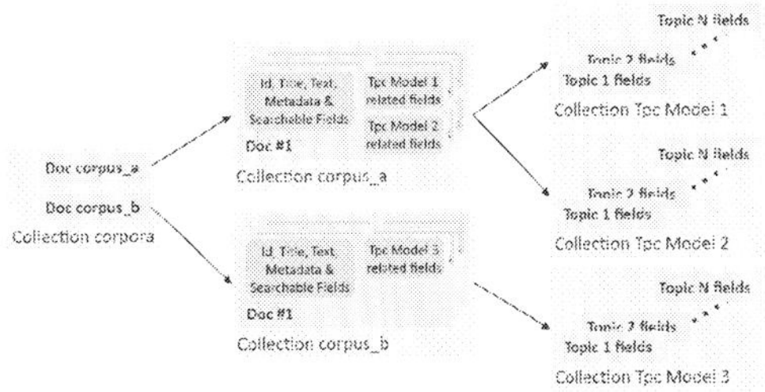

Figure 3: Organization of Solr Collections: *Corpora* contains one document per ingested corpus; each *Corpus* collection stores information on the documents text and metadata, as well as document-related topic information; each topic model requires also its own collection and is associated to just one *Corpus* collection.

Endpoint	Description
getModelInfo	Retrieve statistics for all topics in a model
getBetasTopicById	Retrieve the β_k for the indicated model and topic
getMostCorrelatedTopics	Retrieve the list of most similar topics (and their similarity) to a given topic
getThetasDocById	Retrieve the topic representation for a particular document
inferDoc	Infer the topic representation for a provided text fragment
getDocsWithHighSim	Get the most similar documents to the one provided based on topic representation
getTopicsLabels	Retrieve the labels for all topics in a model
getTopicTopDocs	Retrieve the ids of the most representative documents for a given topic

Table 1: Selection of endpoints available at the system RESTful APIs. The endpoints included in the table are associated to queries related to topic model exploitation.

Corpora. Each element of the collection represents a distinct *corpus*, including its associated models and metadata. Only one *Corpora* collection can exist per CASE deployment.

To store document-topic representations, we add a new field to each document in the corpus collection for every trained model. This field utilizes Lucene's payloads –custom binary data associated with token positions and encoded in base64– to store the representations, for which inverted indexes are automatically created. Using this document representation, along with Solr's built-in plugins for payload-based operations, enables efficient storage, filtering, and retrieval of topic scores associated with documents.

2.5 Functional description

To support information management and exploitation from Solr and connected web services, CASE includes two RESTful APIs. The first API handles basic Solr operations, including collection management (creation, indexing, deletion) and topic-based operations, such as filtering documents relevant for a topic, or aggregating results, which can be efficiently carried out benefiting from Solr inverted indexes and caching implementations.

In addition to this, there are scenarios where deriving the document-topic distribution for a user-provided document not included in the dataset is necessary. For this purpose, the second API (Inferencer API) provides endpoints using a wrapper that supports topic inference using LDA-MALLET and can be easily extended to other technologies, such as CTM or BERTopic. While this endpoint can function independently, it is primarily used as an internal server within the TM API ecosystem.

Finally, we have developed two Java plug-ins for Solr to enable semantic search based on the representation of documents in the topic space. The first plug-in allows to calculate the documents most similar to a given text, while the second plug-in exploits the pairwise distances among all indexed documents, allowing to identify pairs of documents very similar to each other. This process involves calculating the complete similarity matrix during the indexing phase, which scales quadratically with the number of documents in the collection. To address this, an approximation has been implemented to improve scalability and efficiency.

Table 1 lists selected endpoints for queries using topic model information. Appendix §A shows the complete lists of available endpoints at CASE's backend.

3 Case Studies

We demonstrate how CASE supports decision support systems in the STI domain through two real-world use cases.

3.1 Topic-enriched aggregated indicators

Analyzing STI data is crucial for policy-making, especially during the agenda-setting phase. Key data sources include scientific abstracts, research project summaries, and patents. This subsection presents the analysis of scientific production in Artificial Intelligence (Gago and Barroso, 2024) and Cancer (Levi, 2024), two living labs (LLs) from the H2020 IntelComp project.[5]

These living labs (LLs) validated IntelComp's tools, including CASE, by co-creating STI policies within their domains. Identifying policy questions is the first step toward determining STI policy needs (Markianidou et al., 2021). Using CASE, the LLs addressed analysis of the research-related datasets, providing relevant indicators for agenda setting. For example, Fig. 4 represents the evolution of the number of papers per year and topic in the Cancer domain. Based on this graph, stakeholders can identify prevailing research trends (e.g., "Transcription and Molecular Mutations"), emerging or declining topics (e.g., the decline in publications from 2009 to 2010 and after 2019, probably due to the financial crisis and the COVID-19 irruption, respectively), and potential research gaps or areas of oversaturation to make decisions about future funding or policy priorities.

Each living lab employed various datasets, including one derived from OpenAIRE,[6] which includes metadata such as publication date, authors, affiliations, and funding entities. The AI and Cancer datasets comprise $574,346$ and $2,329,760$ publications, respectively, with AI publications identified using expert-validated keywords and Cancer publications selected by domain experts.

Topic models were trained on these datasets using LDA-MALLET via TARS[3]. The number of topics (K) was set to 25 after two domain experts evaluated models with $K \in [10, 40]$ for AI and $K \in [25, 50]$ for Cancer (see §3.2). LDA was chosen over other TARS models for its superior topic quality, as judged by project experts. The final models were indexed in CASE's Solr engine, along with document metadata and topic information, enabling retrieval of aggregated indicators, such as:

I1. Number of publications per topic and year, assigning each publication to all active topics.

I2. Same as I1, but with fractional counting, i.e., each publication's contribution to its topics is weighted by $\beta_{d,k}$.

I3. Number of publications per topic containing terms *deep learning* (AI) / *metastasis* (cancer).

I4. Similar to I3, but using fractional counting.

Table 2 presents the calculation times and resource consumption (CPU and memory) for indicators I1-I4 across the AI and Cancer collections. We compare Pandas filtering as a baseline for direct computation with Solr queries to measure the advantage of Solr's built-in functionalities over

[5] https://intelcomp.eu/

[6] https://graph.openaire.eu/

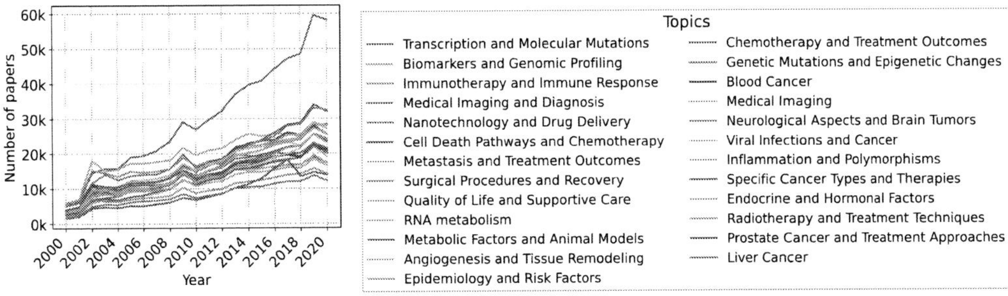

Figure 4: Evolution of publication shares across topics from 2000 to 2020 in the Cancer domain. The topic model was calculated with TARS, using LDA-MALLET for training. Labels were provided by ChatGPT and validated by Cancer LL users.

Query	**AI - Pandas**			**AI - Solr**		
	Time (s)	**CPU (%)**	**Memory (MB)**	**Time (s)**	**CPU (%)**	**Memory (MB)**
I1	0.82 ± 0.09	81.87 ± 7.25	$4\,773.7 \pm 93.1$	0.08 ± 0.015	118.95 ± 66.39	$1\,149.3 \pm 4.9$
I2	1.95 ± 0.10	97.48 ± 13.27	$5\,548.9 \pm 146.5$	0.49 ± 0.009	102.99 ± 13.94	$1\,208.4 \pm 4.7$
I3	0.75 ± 0.05	65.32 ± 5.29	$4\,404 \pm 0.00$	0.009 ± 0.001	82.04 ± 40.8	$1\,271.9 \pm 42.9$
I4	0.79 ± 0.07	79.94 ± 6.54	$4\,404 \pm 0.00$	0.013 ± 0.001	68.94 ± 13.76	$1\,308.1 \pm 3.2$
Query	**Cancer - Pandas**			**Cancer - Solr**		
	Time (s)	**CPU (%)**	**Memory (MB)**	**Time (s)**	**CPU (%)**	**Memory (MB)**
I1	2.18 ± 0.16	55.73 ± 48.11	$19\,444.8 \pm 168.6$	0.20 ± 0.013	102.4 ± 25.08	$1\,319.6 \pm 1$
I2	7.06 ± 0.22	96.29 ± 10.14	$20\,866.2 \pm 494.2$	1.35 ± 0.19	104.12 ± 7.05	$1\,324.3 \pm 2.2$
I3	1.95 ± 0.16	97.69 ± 15.32	$18\,473.66 \pm 0.00$	0.008 ± 0.001	60.22 ± 21.64	$1\,332.8 \pm 0.2$
I4	2.74 ± 0.33	99.91 ± 4.24	$18\,627 \pm 27.5$	0.02 ± 0.001	82.53 ± 14.74	$1\,337.8 \pm 4.2$

Table 2: Computation Time (s), CPU usage (%), and memory usage (MB) for indicators I1-I4 using Pandas vs. Solr-based Service across AI and Cancer datasets. Pandas statistics are derived by averaging the execution times across 1000 runs of each query, with resource consumption measured at 1-second intervals. For Solr, the calculations are based on 10 000 executions, aggregating the resource usage of all Docker containers involved in the CASE process and monitoring also computational resource consumption every second.

Python data structures. To obtain comparable measurements, all calculations were carried out on a server with 96 Intel Xeon @ 2.10GHz CPUs. For Pandas, the execution times are reported as the mean and standard deviation over 1000 runs, with CPU usage and RAM consumption monitored at 1-second intervals throughout the process. Similarly, for Solr, the same monitoring approach is used; however, the number of runs is increased to 10 000 to obtain a reliable estimate of resource consumption, considering the shorter execution times.

In all cases, Lucene's inverted indexes allow for a much faster filtering operation than Python. The results show particularly significant gains for CASE in the calculation of indicators I3 and I4, thanks to Solr's efficient term filtering capabilities. Notably, CASE demonstrates excellent scalability for these indicators, with execution times remaining virtually constant as the dataset size increases. Indeed, scalability stands out as one of the key advantages of the Solr-based service, as CPU and memory consumption remain almost unchanged when querying the AI and Cancer datasets.

When comparing Solr to the Pandas implementation in terms of resource usage, Solr exhibits slightly higher CPU consumption but significantly lower memory requirements, which appear to be mostly independent of the dataset size. Additionally, fractional counting (I2, I4) introduces a noticeable CPU overhead in Pandas, whereas Solr handles these calculations with minimal impact on CPU or memory usage. This confirms the efficiency of Solr's payload-based approach for indexing document topics.

3.2 *Ex-ante* evaluation of research projects

This use case demonstrates the integration of CASE within a complete system exploiting topic models for the *ex-ante* evaluation of research projects, the Evaluation Workbench (EWB). The service was co-designed with Hcéres[7] in the context of IntelComp[5]. While this study focuses on a dataset of projects funded by Hcéres, the service can be easily extended for semantic exploration and search of other text collections.

With the corpus and model information indexed in the Solr database, deploying dashboards meeting specific user requirements is straightforward (see Figs. 6-12, and also the EWB demo video[11] in Appendix §B). The general view showcases an interactive dashboard displaying various topics within the model. Top keywords and a label are displayed for each topic. Clicking on a topic provides detailed information, including top defining words, word weights within the topic, topic statistics (size, active document count, relevance, and coherence), and a list with the most representative documents for the topic. Similar actions are available in the temporal view, which is the direct result of indicator I2 described in §3.1. All these operations rely on CASE's functionalities, in particular they activate the endpoints `getModelInfo`, `getBetasTopicById`, `getTopicsLabels`.

Using the plugins discussed in §2.4, we can also create similarity-based services. For example, users can input a text fragment, and the service displays the most similar projects. This service uses the `InferDoc` endpoint to calculate the topic representation of the text and the `getDocsWithHighSim` plugin for searching similar documents.

We conclude this subsection with an analysis of the performance of the document selection criterion S3 (see §2.2). Fig. 5 illustrates the performance comparison between the θ and $S3$ criteria for selecting documents relevant to the identified topics. For each topic, we selected 10 documents based on each criterion and calculated the average number of unique terms (left column) and total terms (right column) from the topics' top-10 relevant words that appear in the selected documents.

It can be seen that the documents retrieved using $S3$ consistently contain a similar number of unique terms as those retrieved using θ, but a significantly higher number of topic-relevant terms (as indicated by the majority of topics lying above the diagonal).

[7]https://www.hceres.fr/en

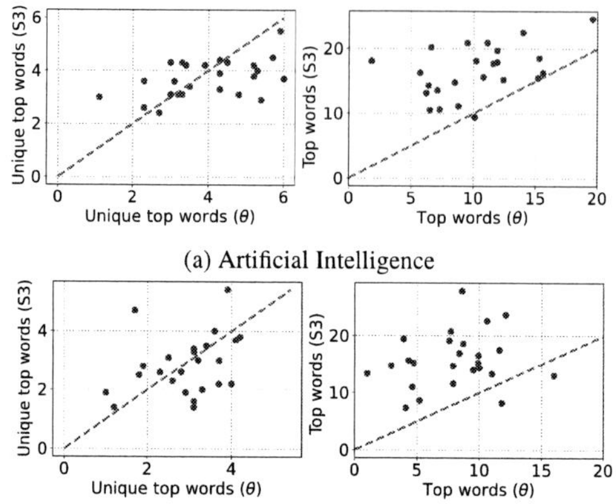

(a) Artificial Intelligence

(b) Cancer

Figure 5: Average occurrences of the top 10 terms in topics for the 10 most representative documents selected according to larger $\theta_{d,k}$ vs $S3_{d,k}$. Each dot represents a different topic. Left: average number of unique terms. Right: average top-word occurrences.

In summary, $S3$ enables the identification of documents that align more closely with the top words of each topic.

4 Future work

We plan to extend CASE functionality to support additional features, such as:

Model updates. Currently, the system supports updates to collections by either adding new documents using a pre-trained model or introducing new topic models for an existing document collection. However, enabling functionality to update an already indexed topic model when adding new documents could be valuable. This would require implementing queries that facilitate the training or updating of the existing model and re-indexing the document representations accordingly. When deploying such functionality, the availability of GPUs must be considered, as training or updating neural models may become impractical without adequate computational resources.

Contextual embeddings-based similarity. Recent advances in language models and contextual embeddings provide potentially more accurate methods for calculating semantic similarity compared to the current approach in the service, which relies on the presence of topics in documents. Preliminary implementations of this functionality are already in place.

Personalized dashboards. Solr can be used as a backend to implement dashboards for navigating and filtering topic-related information and other metadata in its indexed datasets. While Solr provides efficient metadata filtering out-of-the-box, filtering by topic information requires fractional counting and specific plugins.

Natural language request processing with LLMs. With the rise of conversational systems based on LLMs, a natural extension would be to allow user queries in natural language. This approach offers a more intuitive and flexible information retrieval mechanism, ensuring the system's responses are based on controlled data and methodologies.

5 Related Work

Several tools focus on visualizing topic models. *pyLDAvis*[8] is widely used for representing topics in 2D space, allowing analysis of inter-topic distances, topic content, and relevance. The *Topic Model Visualization Engine (TMVE)*[9] facilitates document navigation and provides a corpus summary with links to individual documents. *stmBrowser* enables web-based exploration of Structural Topic Models (STM) (Roberts et al., 2019), and David Mimno's *jsLDA* offers a similar platform for LDA models. *tsLDA* builds upon *jsLDA* introducing new features like hyperparameter optimization, intuitive visualizations, and streamlined workflows. *dfr-browser*[10] integrates topics, documents, words, and metadata into a comprehensive visual field.

Despite their user-friendly designs, these tools are not easy to deploy for users without programming skills, and, apart frompyLDAvis, they are tied to specific topic modeling libraries, limiting their flexibility compared to an API-driven solution.

There is also some work on integrating topic models with search engines to enhance information retrieval. Hassan et al. 2011 applied LDA with Lucene for indexing OCR-extracted documents, representing topics as numeric fields in Solr documents, and using numeric range queries for topic vectors. George et al. 2014 used LDA and latent semantic indexing (LSI) to represent documents in a topic space, improving retrieval by finding document similarities in this space with various ranking methods, but did not integrate topic-based similarity within Lucene. Chen and Xu 2016 developed the Educational Resource Retrieval Mechanism (ERRM) using Lucene and LDA-based topic indexing, demonstrating improved retrieval performance. Rajapaksha and Silva 2019 proposed a hybrid semantic retrieval approach combining LDA, community preferences, and collaborative filtering, leveraging Lucene's payloads for topic indexing and re-ranking results based on topic content after initial Lucene retrieval.

6 Conclusion

In this paper we have presented CASE, a Solr-based system based for the joint indexing of metadata and information from topic models. CASE allows efficient implementation of functions such as search or filtering by metadata and/or topics. Available plugins provide semantic search based on text or topic representations, including the possibility of performing inference for texts provided by the user.

Two use cases in the field of STI demonstrated the system's versatility in supporting various services, providing good scalability to work with large document collections.

Acknowledgements

This project has received funding from the European Union's Horizon 2020 research and innovation program under grant agreement No 101004870 (IntelComp project) and from Grant TED2021-132366B-I00 funded by MICIU/AEI/10.13039/501100011033 and by the "European Union NextGenerationEU/PRTICIU.

References

Simon Babb, Mia Celeste, Dana Harris, Ingrid Wu, Theo Bayard de Volo, Alfredo Gomez, Tatsuki Kuze, Taeyun Lee, David Mimno, and Alexandra Schofield. 2021. Introducing tslda: A workflow-oriented topic modeling tool. *WeCNLP (West Coast NLP) Summit.*

Federico Bianchi, Silvia Terragni, and Dirk Hovy. 2021a. Pre-training is a hot topic: Contextualized document embeddings improve topic coherence. In *Proc. 59th Annual Meeting of the ACL and 11th Intl. Joint conf. on NLP (Volume 2: Short Papers)*, pages 759–766.

Federico Bianchi, Silvia Terragni, and Dirk Hovy. 2021b. Pre-training is a hot topic: Contextualized document embeddings improve topic coherence. In *Proc. 59th Annual Meeting of the Association for Computational Linguistics and the 11th Intl. Joint*

[8]https://github.com/bmabey/pyLDAvis

[9]https://github.com/ajbc/tmv

[10]https://github.com/agoldst/dfr-browser?tab=readme-ov-file

Conf. Natural Language Processing (Volume 2: Short Papers)*, pages 759–766.

Federico Bianchi, Silvia Terragni, Dirk Hovy, Debora Nozza, and Elisabetta Fersini. 2021c. Cross-lingual contextualized topic models with zero-shot learning. In *Proc. 16th Conf. European Chapter Association for Computational Linguistics: Main Volume*, pages 1676–1683.

David M Blei, Andrew Y Ng, and Michael I Jordan. 2003. Latent dirichlet allocation. *Journal of Machine Learning Research*, 3(Jan):993–1022.

Jordan Boyd-Graber, Yuening Hu, David Mimno, et al. 2017. Applications of topic models. *Foundations and Trends® in Information Retrieval*, 11(2-3):143–296.

Xiaomei Chen and Lizhen Xu. 2016. An educational resource retrieval mechanism based on lucene and topic index. In *2016 13th Web Information Systems and Applications Conf. (WISA)*, pages 125–128. IEEE.

Adji B. Dieng, Francisco J. R. Ruiz, and David M. Blei. 2020. Topic modeling in embedding spaces. *Trans. ACL*, 8:439–453.

D. Gago and M. J. Barroso. 2024. Report on the artificial intelligence living lab. Zenodo.

Clint Pazhayidam George, Sahil Puri, Daisy Zhe Wang, Joseph N Wilson, and William F Hamilton. 2014. Smart electronic legal discovery via topic modeling. In *Proc. 27th Intl. Flairs Conf.*

Maarten Grootendorst. 2022. Bertopic: Neural topic modeling with a class-based TF-IDF procedure. *arXiv preprint arXiv:2203.05794*.

Ehtesham Hassan, Vikram Garg, SK Mirajul Haque, Santanu Chaudhury, and Madan Gopal. 2011. Searching OCR'ed text: An LDA based approach. In *2011 Intl. Conf. on Document Analysis and Recognition*, pages 1210–1214. IEEE.

Omar Khattab and Matei Zaharia. 2020. Colbert: Efficient and effective passage search via contextualized late interaction over bert. In *Proc. the 43rd Intl. ACM SIGIR Conf. on research and development in Information Retrieval*, pages 39–48.

Michelle S Lam, Janice Teoh, James Landay, Jeffrey Heer, and Michael S Bernstein. 2024. Concept induction: Analyzing unstructured text with high-level concepts using lloom. *arXiv preprint arXiv:2404.12259*.

T. Enock Levi. 2024. Report on the health living lab. Zenodo.

P. Markianidou, L. Tsipouri, A. Kossack, and J. Sanmartin. 2021. Report on the needs of science, technology and innovation policy in artificial intelligence, blue economy and cancer (1.1). https://doi.org/10.5281/zenodo.5704976.

Andrew Kachites McCallum. 2002. Mallet: A machine learning for language toolkit. *http://mallet. cs. umass. edu*.

Chau Minh Pham, Alexander Hoyle, Simeng Sun, Philip Resnik, and Mohit Iyyer. 2024. Topicgpt: A prompt-based topic modeling framework. *Preprint*, arXiv:2311.01449.

Minuri Rajapaksha and Thushari Silva. 2019. Semantic information retrieval based on topic modeling and community interests mining. In *2019 Moratuwa Eng. Research Conf. (MERCon)*, pages 60–65. IEEE.

Arik Reuter, Anton Thielmann, Christoph Weisser, Sebastian Fischer, and Benjamin Säfken. 2024. Gptopic: Dynamic and interactive topic representations. *Preprint*, arXiv:2403.03628.

Margaret E Roberts, Brandon M Stewart, and Dustin Tingley. 2019. Stm: An r package for structural topic models. *Journal of statistical software*, 91:1–40.

Keshav Santhanam, Omar Khattab, Jon Saad-Falcon, Christopher Potts, and Matei Zaharia. 2022. Colbertv2: Effective and efficient retrieval via lightweight late interaction. In *Proceedings of the 2022 Conference of the North American Chapter of the Association for Computational Linguistics: Human Language Technologies*, pages 3715–3734.

Silvia Terragni, Elisabetta Fersini, Bruno Giovanni Galuzzi, Pietro Tropeano, and Antonio Candelieri. 2021. OCTIS: Comparing and optimizing topic models is simple! In *Proc. 16th Conf. EACL: System Demonstrations*, pages 263–270.

Jasper Xian, Tommaso Teofili, Ronak Pradeep, and Jimmy Lin. 2024. Vector search with openai embeddings: Lucene is all you need. In *Proc. 17th ACM Intl. Conf. on Web Search and Data Mining*, pages 1090–1093.

Peilin Yang, Hui Fang, and Jimmy Lin. 2018. Anserini: Reproducible ranking baselines using lucene. *Journal of Data and Information Quality (JDIQ)*, 10(4):1–20.

Yi Zhang, Guangquan Zhang, Hongshu Chen, Alan L Porter, Donghua Zhu, and Jie Lu. 2016. Topic analysis and forecasting for science, technology and innovation: Methodology with a case study focusing on big data research. *Technological forecasting and social change*, 105:179–191.

Appendix

A Complete list of available endpoints in TM RESTful API

The TM REST API is equipped with the following functionalities, as shown in Figs. 7 and 8.

Generic Solr operations. Create/delete collection, list available collections, and generic queries.

Corpora operations. Actions at the corpus level, including creating and indexing corpora, deleting and listing corpora, and managing fields for textual searches. This encompasses tasks such as searching for documents with specific strings in their titles, listing document collections (i.e., collections storing corpus information for a specific data collection), displaying metadata in a frontend (if developed) for that corpus, and listing models associated with a corpus.

Models operations. Actions at the model level, including creating and indexing models, deleting, and listing.

Queries to retrieve information from Solr.

The Inferencer API provides endpoints for inference, as well as for managing the inference models created during the process (see Fig. 9).

B More on the *ex-ante* evaluation of research projects

Figs. 10a and 10b display the interactive dashboard illustrating the general and temporal evolution of the topics identified by the selected model. By clicking on any topic within these views, users can access detailed information, including top defining words, word weights within the topic, topic statistics (size, active document count, relevance, and coherence), and a list of the most representative documents for the topic.

User studies revealed that users value the ability to perform an initial evaluation of topics and mark those deemed valuable for a more thorough evaluation later, as this saves time. To address this, we incorporated user-specific information into the Solr collections. Each user is assigned a unique identifier, allowing us to index relevant topics for individual users through the *Model* collection. Based on their selections, users can choose to visualize either all topics or only those they have marked as relevant (see Fig. 6), as showcased in Fig. 11 for the General View.

A video showcasing CASE's full integration with a frontend for the *ex-ante* evaluation of STI funding proposals in the H2020 IntelComp project[5] (§3.2) through the Evaluation Workbench (EWB) is also available from the project's YouTube channel.[11]

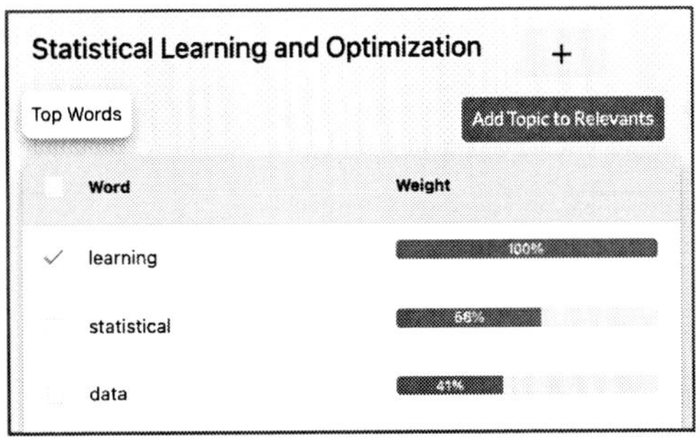

(a) Add to relevant topics

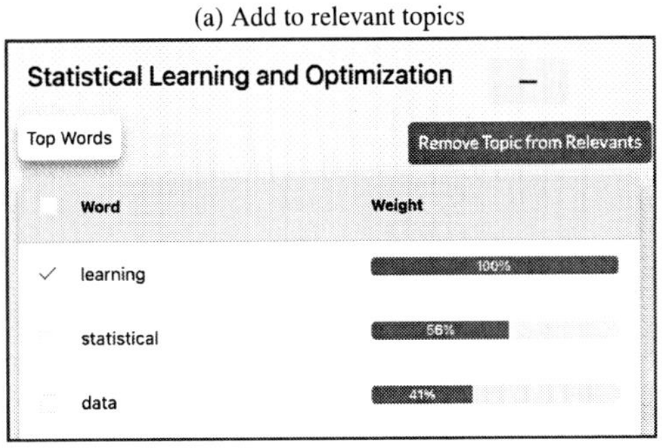

(b) Remove from relevant topics

Figure 6: Users can manage the relevance of topics from the detailed topic information view.

[11]https://www.youtube.com/watch?v=wIjwIsrJmFo&ab_channel=FECYTciencia

Figure 7: Complete list of endpoints used for managing generic Solr collections, along with specific endpoints for handling our *Corpus* and *Model* collections, as displayed on the Swagger interface.

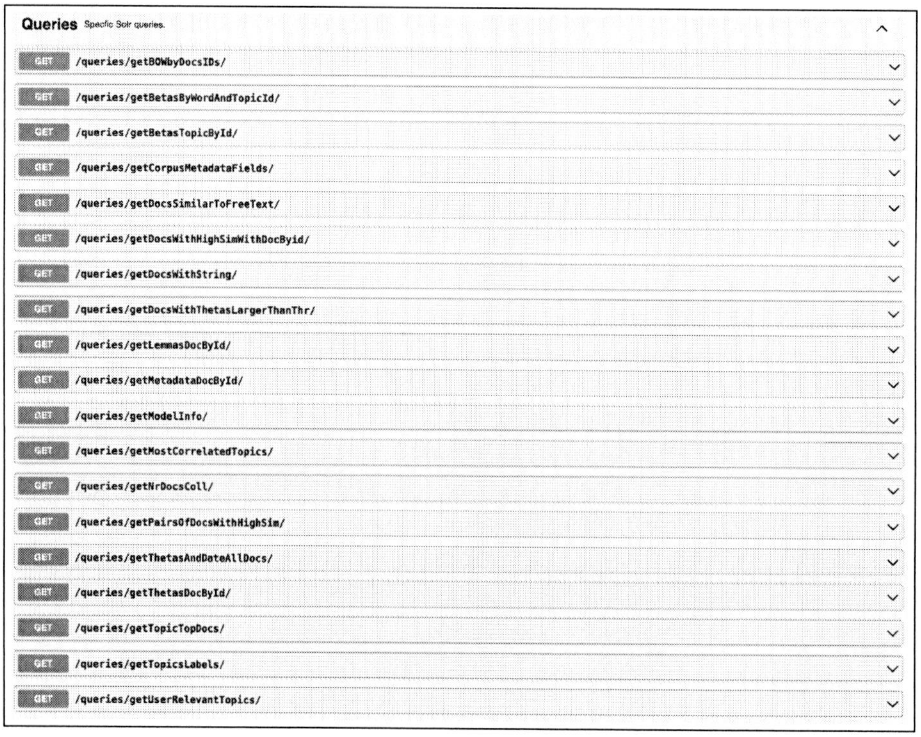

Figure 8: List of query endpoints for retrieving information from the Solr collections (Swagger interface).

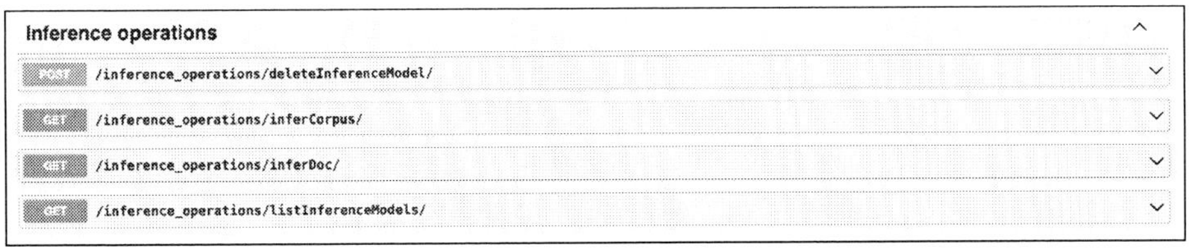

Figure 9: List of endpoints available in the Inference API, as displayed on the Swagger interface.

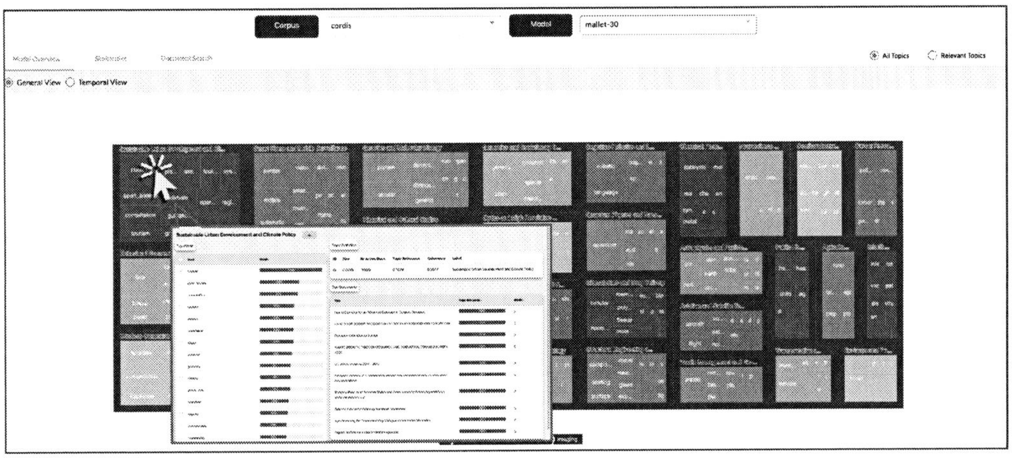

(a) General View

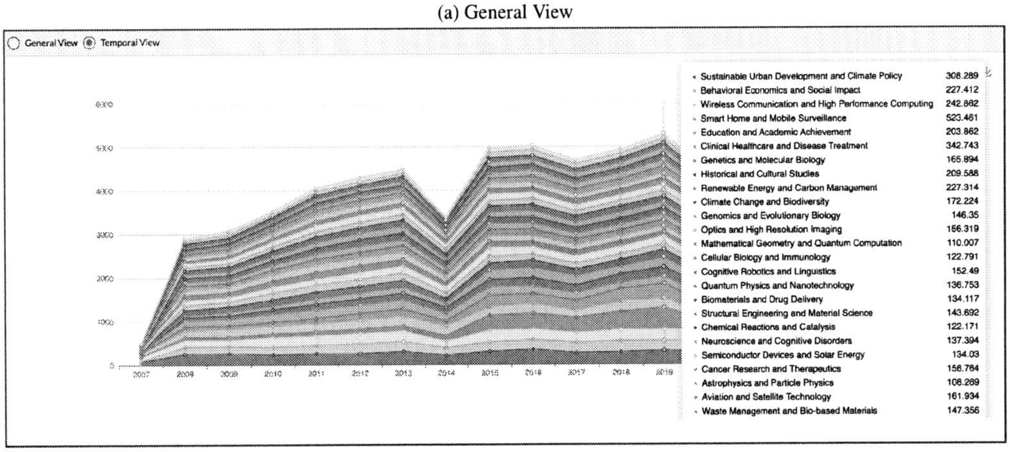

(b) Temporal View

Figure 10: Dashboards offering an overview of the topics in the HFRI collection. Each topic is depicted by a differently colored square, with detailed information accessible by clicking on it. (a) General overview. Detailed topic information can be accessed by clicking on it. The pop-up window shows topic statistics, the top defining words, and its most representative projects. (b) Temporal evolution of the topics in the collection.

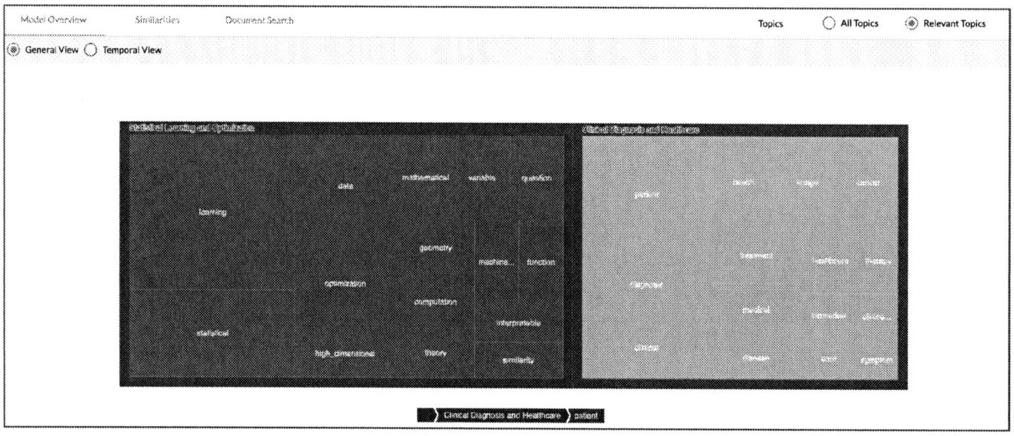

Figure 11: Dashboard providing an overview of user-relevant topics within a specified collection. All functionalities from the "All Topics" view (see Fig. 10a) are available.

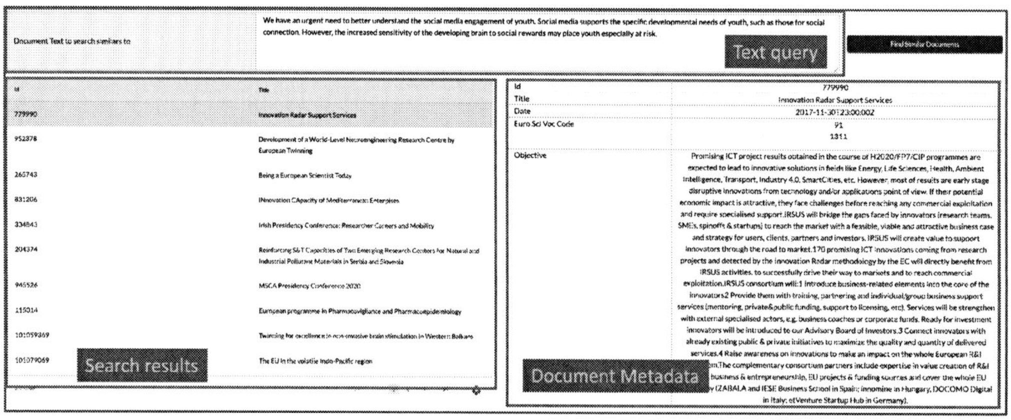

Figure 12: Service to retrieve documents indexed in Solr similar to a user-inputted document based on a trained topic model. Users can then inspect the specific metadata of the retrieved documents.

GECTurk WEB: An Explainable Online Platform for Turkish Grammatical Error Detection and Correction

Ali Gebeşçe[1,2], **Gözde Gül Şahin**[1,2]
[1]Computer Engineering Department, Koç University, Istanbul, Turkey
[2] KUIS AI Lab, Istanbul, Turkey
`https://gglab-ku.github.io/`

Abstract

Sophisticated grammatical error detection/correction tools are available for a small set of languages such as English and Chinese. However, it is not straightforward—if not impossible—to adapt them to morphologically rich languages with complex writing rules like Turkish which has more than 80 million speakers. Even though several tools exist for Turkish, they primarily focus on spelling errors rather than grammatical errors and lack features such as web interfaces, error explanations and feedback mechanisms. To fill this gap, we introduce GECTURK WEB, a light, open-source, and flexible web-based system that can detect and correct the most common forms of Turkish writing errors, such as the misuse of diacritics, compound and foreign words, pronouns, light verbs along with spelling mistakes. Our system provides native speakers and second language learners an easily accessible tool to detect/correct such mistakes and *also to learn from their mistakes* by showing the explanation for the violated rule(s). The proposed system achieves 88,3 system usability score, and is shown to help learn/remember a grammatical rule (confirmed by 80% of the participants). The GECTURK WEB is available both as an offline tool [1] or at `www.gecturk.net`.

1 Introduction

Grammatical Error Correction/Detection (GEC/D) (Bryant et al., 2023) is a well-established NLP task, that aims to detect and correct various errors in text, including grammatical issues like missing prepositions, mismatched subject-verb agreement, as well as orthographic and semantic errors such as misspellings and inappropriate word choices. Tools that can perform GEC/D have recently gained attention due to the rise in digital communication, remote work, and global interactions, which demand clear and professional writing. With the inclusion of the detection module, GEC/D formulation facilitates the *teaching of grammar rules*, empowering users not only to produce error-free writing but also to enhance their language skills and comprehension gradually.

Therefore, developing open-source GEC/D tools is particularly crucial, yet challenging for languages with complex writing rules, such as Turkish. The writing rules for such languages generally involve multiple linguistic layers—phonetic, syntactic, and semantic—which makes them difficult to follow and remember even for native speakers. While several tools exist for high-resource languages such as GECko+ (Calò et al., 2021) and ALLECS (Qorib et al., 2023), they often suffer from discontinuation of support or lack adaptability for languages such as Turkish. Moreover, while advanced commercial tools such as LanguageTool[2] offer support for 31 languages, yet Turkish is notably absent from their list. Furthermore, as highlighted in § 2, numerous offline tools are accessible for Turkish spelling correction, whereas only two models (not tools) (Uz and Eryiğit, 2023; Kara et al., 2023) are dedicated to Turkish GEC/D.

To bridge this gap, we leverage the state-of-the-art pretrained GEC/D (Kara et al., 2023)[3] and spelling correction models; and, for the first time, provide a user-friendly web-interface to them. Our system does not only correct errors but also display them in different colors, while providing explanations for each correction through interactive elements in the interface. Additionally, the system includes a feedback mechanism to foster continuous improvement and enhance user engagement. Our system is lightweight and flexible, allowing easy adaptation to other languages through pretrained sequence tagging models. The results of

[1] `https://github.com/GGLAB-KU/gecturkweb`

[2] `https://languagetool.org/`

[3] We use the pretrained sequence tagging model that has been trained on 130,000 high-quality sentences covering more than 20 expert-curated grammar rules (a.k.a., writing rules) implemented through complex transformation functions.

Proceedings of the 31st International Conference on Computational Linguistics: System Demonstrations, pages 163–173
January 19–24, 2025.

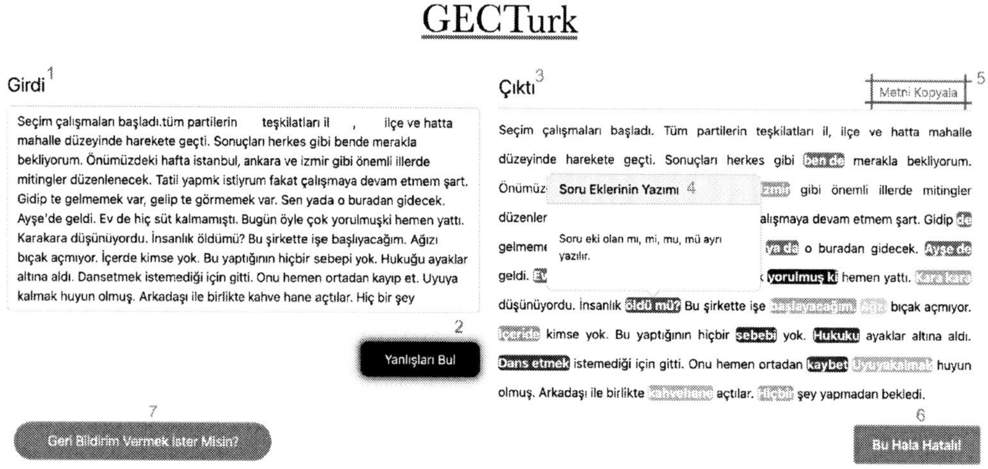

Figure 1: The screenshot of UI after user entering an input. **1-** Girdi (Input): The input area for the user. **2-** Yanlışları Bul (Find Errors): A button which is pressed after entering an input. **3-** Çıktı (Output): The output area for the tagged and corrected text. Note that each error is categorized (colored) according to Table 2. **4-** Pop-up: Each corrected word is represented as button. When clicked the violated rule, i.e., error type, is shown. **5-** Metni Kopyala (Copy Text): A button for copying corrected text. **6-** Bu Hala Hatalı (Still Erroneous): A button for giving feedback in case the user thinks the output still contains errors. When clicked, a pop-up is shown and user is expected to write the corrected version. **7-** Geri Bildirim Vermek İster Misin? (Give Feedback): A button for collecting general suggestions.

the user study (see §4) demonstrate excellent usability and a significant impact on learning and retention of grammar rules. GECTURK WEB, shown in Fig. 1, is accessible both as an offline tool and online at `www.gecturk.net` and source code licensed with CC BY-SA 4.0 is available at `https://github.com/GGLAB-KU/gecturkweb`.

2 Previous Systems

High-Resource Languages: Numerous GEC/D models exist for high-resource languages such as English (Lai et al., 2022; Tarnavskyi et al., 2022; Sorokin, 2022; Qorib et al., 2022a) and Chinese (Ren et al., 2018; Qiu and Qu, 2019; Wu and Wu, 2022; Xu et al., 2022). However, these models lack user interfaces, which are crucial for accessibility to non-specialists. Although fewer in number compared to models, several GEC/D tools are available. For instance, GECko+ (Calò et al., 2021) integrates the GECToR XLNet model for sentence-level grammatical correction with a sentence ordering model (Prabhumoye et al., 2020). It processes texts by segmenting them into sentences, applying corrections, and then reordering them. Initially, GECko+ offered a web interface, but it is currently inactive. Now, the only access is through downloading the source code and running it locally, which is inconvenient for general users. Similarly, MiSS (Li et al., 2021), a Multi-Style Simultaneous Translation system that includes a GEC/D feature using GECToR XLNet, initially had a web interface which is now inactive.

The most recent non-commercial GEC/D tool is ALLECS (Qorib et al., 2023), which uses GECToR-RoBERTa, GECToR-XLNet, and T5-Large models, alongside two combination methods: ESC (Qorib et al., 2022b) and MEMT (Heafield and Lavie, 2010). ALLECS takes input and displays corrected errors with clickable buttons, and has an easy-to-use web interface. Despite its advantages, ALLECS lacks a feedback mechanism and an enhanced interface that uses color coding to distinguish between different types of errors. Moreover, its implementation is not flexible enough to be extended to other languages, i.e., one cannot simply upload a Turkish GEC/D model and expect the application to function without significant modifications to the source code.

Morphologically Rich Languages: In the case of morphologically rich languages, there are fewer GEC/D models available. Examples include Arabic (Solyman et al., 2022), Bengali (Hossain et al.,

	Spelling	Offline	Open Source	Grammatical	Explanation	Feedback	Web Interface
Google Docs	✓						✓
Microsoft Word	✓	✓					✓
Zemberek (Akın, 2017)	✓	✓	✓				
Hunspell (Zafer, 2017)	✓	✓	✓				
TurkishNLP(Çetinkaya, 2018)	✓	✓	✓				
TrNLP (Bayol, 2018)	✓	✓	✓				
Starlang Yıldız (2019)	✓	✓	✓				
VNLP (Turker, 2021)	✓	✓	✓				✓
Mukayese (Safaya et al., 2022)	✓	✓	✓				
Rule-based (Uz and Eryiğit, 2023)	✓	✓	✓	✓	✓		
GECTurk (Kara et al., 2023)		✓	✓	✓	✓		
GECTurk WEB (Ours)	✓	✓	✓	✓	✓	✓	✓

Table 1: Comparison of features in previous grammatical and spelling error correction tools for Turkish, contrasted with ours. Spelling: Correction of spelling errors. Grammatical: Detection of grammatical errors. Explanation: Explanations for error types. Feedback: User feedback mechanism for model and interface improvement. Web Interface: Availability of a web-based interface.

2024), Czech (Náplava and Straka, 2019; Náplava et al., 2022), and Russian (Rozovskaya and Roth, 2019). However, again these systems lack user interfaces, making them merely as models rather than practical tools, thus limiting their usability for general users. One exception exists in Arabic; however, this tool just underlines mistakes (Alkhatib et al., 2020) and not explain the errors. Also it lacks a web support, making it less suitable for general users.

Commercial Tools: Grammarly[4] offers advanced features for improving writing tone on several aspects like clarity, engagement, and delivery. However, it is not open-source and supports only English. Also, full access to its features requires a paid subscription [5]. LanguageTool, being open-source, supports multiple languages and addresses some of Grammarly's limitations. However, it imposes a 10,000-character limit on inputs, expandable only through a paid subscription [6]. More importantly, despite supporting 31 languages [7], Turkish is not among them.

Turkish: Since aforementioned systems are either commercial or not directly applicable to Turkish GEC/D, we have surveyed commonly available tools and resources that offer support for Turkish, given in Table 1. Google Docs [8] and Microsoft Word [9], widely accessible for their user-friendly interfaces, provide basic spelling error detection.

However, they fall short in addressing the specific grammatical nuances of the Turkish language. For instance, these tools fail to correctly apply essential rules, such as the proper separation of the conjunction "-de/-da." In Turkish grammar, the conjunction "-de/-da," meaning "too" or "also," should always be written separately from the preceding word when used in this context. However, neither tool detects or corrects this mistake. For example, in the sentence "Bende okula gideceğim." (English: "I am going to the school too"), the correct form is "Ben de okula gideceğim," with "de" separated. Unfortunately, both tools overlook this error, leaving the grammatical mistake uncorrected and potentially perpetuating improper language use. Additionally, these tools are not open-source, lack explanations for corrections, and do not offer a mechanism for user feedback.

There are also open-source tools, such as Zemberek (Akın, 2017), Hunspell (Zafer, 2017), TurkishNLP (Çetinkaya, 2018), TrNLP (Bayol, 2018), StarlangSoftware (Yıldız, 2019), VNLP (Turker, 2021) and MukayeseSpellChecker (Safaya et al., 2022), however they only provide an offline spelling. To the best of our knowledge, there are only two resources for Turkish GEC/D (Uz and Eryiğit, 2023; Kara et al., 2023). Uz and Eryiğit (2023) propose a rule-based, offline GED system that employs common, universal error types (Bryant et al., 2017), while Kara et al. (2023) provide several pre-trained GEC and GED models that can detect expert-curated language specific writing rules and show significant improvements on existing and proposed benchmarks. In this work, we combine the state-of-the-art GEC/D (Kara et al., 2023) and spelling correction models; and, for the first time, provide a user-friendly web-interface to them. Additionally, we provide colorful explanations for a wide range of error types to train the

[4] https://www.grammarly.com/

[5] https://www.grammarly.com/plans

[6] https://languagetool.org/premium_new

[7] https://dev.languagetool.org/languages

[8] https://docs.google.com

[9] https://www.microsoft.com/word

Category	Rule ID	Description	Example Correction	Color
-DE/-DA	1. CONJ_DE_SEP	Conjunction "-de/-da" is written separately.	Durumu [oğlunada → oğluna da] bildirdi.	Red
-KI	7. CONJ_KI_SEP	Conjunction "-ki" is written separately.	Bugün öyle çok [yorulmuşki → yorulmuş ki] hemen yattı.	Navy
FOREIGN	9. FOREIGN_R1	Words that start with double consonants of foreign origin are written without adding an "-i" between the letters.	[gıram → gram]	Purple
BISYL	13. BI-SYLL_HAPL_VOW	Some bisyllabic words undergo haplology when they get a suffix starting with a vowel.	[ağızı → ağzı]	Pink
LIGHT VERB	17. LIGHT_VERB_SEP	Light verbs such as "etmek, edilmek, eylemek, olmak, olunmak" are written separately in case of no phonological assimilation	[arzetmek → arz etmek]	Blue
COMPOUND	20. COMP_VERB_ADJ	Compound words formed by knowing, giving, staying, stopping, coming, and writing are written adjacent if they have a suffix starting with -a, -e, -ı, -i, -u, -ü.	[uyuya kalmak → uyuyakalma], [gide durmak → gidedurmak]	Turquoise
SINGLE	22. PRONOUN_EXC	Traditionally, some pronouns are written adjacent.	[hiç bir → hiçbir], [her hangi → herhangi]	Orange

Table 2: A selection of grammatical error types covered in the system from Kara et al. (2023).

users, and incorporate a feedback mechanism for continuous training of pre-trained models.

3 GECTurk WEB

Our system has four main components: i) frontend, ii) backend, iii) grammatical error correction/detection (GEC/D), and iv) spelling correction modules. GECTurk WEB is based on the Python Django framework,[10] which manages everything related to performance, security, scalability, and database handling. The architecture of our system, incorporating these components along with the data flow, is shown in Figure 2.

3.1 Frontend

For the user interface, we use the Bootstrap framework [11] that provides us with modern, responsive, and mobile compatible HTML and CSS. Initially, empty "Input" and "Output" fields are shown. After identifying and correcting grammatical and spelling errors in the input, the output is enriched with error types (see Figure 1). For each correction, HTML snippets are created to wrap the corrected words and transforms them to actionable buttons. These snippets use Bootstrap's pop-over functionality to provide an interactive way to display the error type, an explanation, and the correction. Each correction is highlighted with a specified background color and font size for visibility. Additional information about each error type is retrieved from a predefined set of rules given in Table 2[12]. This information includes a textual explanation and a title for the error, which are both used in the content of the pop-over. For instance, if there is a misspelling of "-de/da", this is displayed as *Conjunction "-de/da" is always written separately.* The tokens within the input text are replaced with the generated HTML snippets, respecting the original positions of errors. This involves calculating the offsets to accurately place the HTML snippets within the text, considering the length of the corrected phrases. The corrected tokens are joined back together into strings for each line, and then all lines are combined into a single HTML paragraph (<p> tags).

3.2 Backend

Our system uses Django, a high-level Python web framework, to create a strong backend infrastructure. The architecture of Django, known as Model-View-Template (MVT), supports a clear separation of responsibilities. Here, the Model is responsible for data storage and retrieval. The View handles user requests and provides responses, and the Template dynamically generates HTML pages for user interaction.

View The `send_data` function is used for accommodating various actions including text submission for correction, feedback submission, and API interactions. Upon receiving a POST request given the input text, the function invokes a text correction process through `get_text_corrector`. Text correction process starts with sentence tokenization using NLTK's `sent_tokenize` function (Bird et al., 2009) and continues with the grammatical error correction process, which is described in detail in §3.3. The corrected text, alongside original input and HTML-formatted output for interactive display, is then encapsulated within a Text model instance for persistence. Feedback submission, whether specific to text corrections or general website feedback, is similarly processed and stored.

Model Our data model chas two main entities: Text and GeneralFeedback. The Text model

[10] https://www.djangoproject.com
[11] https://getbootstrap.com

[12] We refer the readers to Kara et al. (2023) for details on each writing rule and how they are handled by the model.

captures the essence of each correction session, storing original and corrected texts, HTML-tagged corrected text for frontend display, and any user feedback. This allows for a comprehensive audit trail of user interactions and system outputs. The GENERALFEEDBACK model, on the other hand, aggregates general user impressions and feedback about the website, enabling continuous improvement based on user insights.

Database and Server Thanks to Django's ORM capabilities, we easily integrate these models with our MySQL[13] database, as the database management system. We use AWS Elastic Beanstalk[14] for deployment.

3.3 Grammatical Correction

We employ the state-of-the-art GEC/D model, SequenceTagger, previously described in Kara et al. (2023). Briefly, SequenceTagger finetunes a strong encoder model (e.g., BERTurk (Schweter, 2020)) to classify tokens into grammatical error classes, enabling efficient error detection rather than merely correction. For illustrative purposes, we provide one sample error type from each category in Table 2. Then, corrections are performed with reverse transformations. The model weights and associated files, such as the tokenizer and vocabulary, are securely stored on Amazon S3[15]. Deployment is simplified through the use of AWS Elastic Beanstalk, requiring only the compression of the project (including the model itself) and uploading it to the AWS Elastic Beanstalk application. We have adapted the original code from (Kara et al., 2023) into a class named TEXTCORRECTOR and an API function `process_text` for performing correction operations with this model. For further details, we encourage consulting the source code of Kara et al. [16] and our implementation [17].

3.4 Spelling Correction

It should be noted that users not only make grammatical mistakes but also commonly commit spelling errors. Since the GEC/D model is not designed for spelling error correction, we employ external tools to extend our system. For mistakes in proper nouns and common typos, we survey external Turkish spelling correction tools. After evaluating different options, we find VNLP (Turker, 2021), StarlangSoftware (Yıldız, 2019), and TurkishNLP (Çetinkaya, 2018) unsatisfactory by means of efficiency and accuracy. As a result, we integrated TrNlp (Bayol, 2018) and ZemberekNLP (Akın and Akın, 2007; Akın, 2017; Uz, 2020) to our system. We apply corrections using TrNlp for proper noun capitalization (e.g., "ankara" $\rightarrow$ "Ankara")—e.g., any proper noun violating it is capitalized by the tool. Following the proper noun corrections, we leverage ZemberekNLP's TURKISHSENTENCENORMALIZER for the common typos. Sentences are processed to ensure that the words are not corrupted (e.g., "yapmk" $\rightarrow$ "yapmak") and that consistency is maintained across the text. With the combination of TrNlp and ZemberekNLP, our system now not only fixes grammatical errors but also performs spelling correction in Turkish.

4 Evaluation

To evaluate GECTURK WEB, we conduct an in-depth user study. This study aims to assess the usability and effectiveness of the tool in facilitating learning and retention. The voluntary user study is announced on communication platforms involving 10 undergraduate students. The recruited participants are native Turkish speakers, aged between 20 and 22. Two of the undergraduates are medical students, while the rest are engineering students.

The user study is structured into two parts. First, participants are asked to follow a user scenario, where they input 10 short sentences into GECTURK WEB. These sentences are selected to cover all four possible outcomes: True Positives (TP), where the system accurately identifies and corrects an error; True Negatives (TN), where no error exists and the system appropriately refrains from making changes; False Positives (FP), where the system erroneously alters a correct sentence; and False Negatives (FN), where the system overlooks an error. Reflecting on the performance of GECTURK (Kara et al., 2023), which demonstrated a detection precision of 0.89 and a correction F1-score of 0.84, we have designed a representative sample to mirror these results. Therefore, the set of 10 sentences includes 7 True Positives (TPs) and 1 of each other outcome types. It is important to note that the participants are unaware of this distribution. To guide the participants on each potential outcome, we create four videos and present them to participants before they begin

[13] https://www.mysql.com/
[14] https://docs.aws.amazon.com/elasticbeanstalk/latest/dg
[15] https://aws.amazon.com/s3
[16] https://github.com/GGLAB-KU/gecturk
[17] https://github.com/GGLAB-KU/gecturkweb

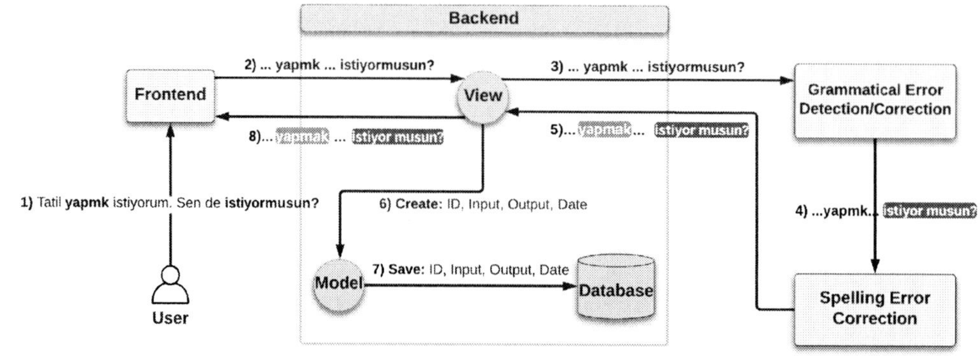

Figure 2: The GECTURK WEB Architecture. **1)** User inputs text containing two errors: a spelling error, "**yapmk**" (shown in red) and a grammatical error, "**istiyormusun**" (shown in green). **2-3)** The view receives the input from the frontend and forwards it to the GEC/D model. **4)** The GEC/D model corrects the grammatical error and adds tags for the frontend to display, as shown in 1. **5)** The SEC module corrects the spelling error, tags it, and sends it back to the View. **6-7)** The model compiles relevant information such as ID, Input, Output, and Date, and records these in the database. **8)** The View sends the prepared output back to the frontend for display.

experimenting with GECTURK WEB, which is described in detail in §A.1. After viewing these videos, participants are instructed to input each sentence and classify it according to one of the possible outcomes. The complete list of 10 sentences can be found in §A.1. We restrict the average duration of this part to be 45 minutes to align with findings from studies (Lavrakas, 2008; Kost and da Rosa, 2018; Sharma, 2022) on the optimal length for questionnaires.After completing this part, participants are asked several questions to assess the system based on the evaluation metrics. We employ two established metrics to test usability and user satisfaction: the System Usability Scale (SUS) (Brooke, 1995) and the Standardized User Experience Percentile Rank Questionnaire (SUPR-Q) (Sauro, 2015). These metrics are widely recognized for their reliability in assessing user satisfaction and system usability. To understand the effectiveness of GECTURK WEB, we also ask a yes/no question about whether participants learned or remembered a grammatical rule. The SUS questionnaire contains ten five-level Likert scale questions. The SUPR-Q includes seven five-level and one ten-level Likert scale questions. Including our yes/no question, we ask a total of 19 questions. All of these questions are in §A.2.

The evaluation results from 10 users are noteworthy, particularly in terms of usability and user satisfaction. The average SUS score is 88.3 (out of a possible 100; the average benchmark is 69 (Bangor et al., 2009)), indicating an excellent level of usability. Similarly, the average score for the SUPR-Q was 4.34 (out of a possible 5; the average benchmark is 3.93 (Sauro, 2015)), suggesting high user satisfaction with the web interface and functionality. These scores are significantly above the average benchmarks, highlighting the effectiveness of GECTURK WEB in providing a user-friendly and satisfying experience. Notably, 80% of participants report that they learned or remembered a grammatical rule, underscoring the tool's impact on learning and retention. Additionally, we measure the time-efficiency of the system and provide the results in Appendix §B.

5 Extension to Other Languages

As depicted in Figure 2, our system exhibits flexibility and seamless adaptability for multilingual support. Expanding our system to support other languages merely requires the replacement of the GED/C model and the spelling error correction module. Specifically, the sequence tagger model must be trained to identify the distinct grammatical error patterns of the target language. Similarly, the spelling error correction module can be replaced with an existing spelling corrector for the target language. Both modules can be adjusted by modifying the "text_corrector.py" script and the associated model weights files, facilitating straightforward integration.

6 Conclusion

In this work, we present GECTURK WEB, a practical online platform for Turkish grammatical error detection and correction (GED/C) along with spelling error correction (SEC). Our system aims to not only correct mistakes but also to facilitate learning of complex writing rules via user-friendly rule explanations. Furthermore, the user feedback mechanism allows for continual support and training of the tool. The high SUS and SUPR-Q scores, significantly above average benchmarks, alongside the positive feedback on learning outcomes, validate the platform's design philosophy and its focus on user-centric development. Furthermore, GECTURK WEB is built with a flexible architecture, suggesting that adaptation to additional languages is within reach. Source code and the web-based tool is publicly and freely available.

Limitations

Major limitation of our system is the number of concurrent user interactions it can process. Currently, the system operates on a single AWS i4i.large instance, which can efficiently manage up to ten simultaneous users. Beyond this threshold, performance begins to degrade, necessitating additional instances to preserve service quality. However, it's essential to highlight that this limitation can easily be overcome by enhancing our infrastructure given the budget. Should the GECTURK WEB platform experience a surge in popularity, we are prepared to scale our resources horizontally by incorporating more instances.

Ethics Statement

The development and deployment of GECTURK WEB adhere to ethical considerations crucial for language processing tools. We ensure that user data is handled with the utmost confidentiality and integrity, in accordance with data protection regulations. The feedback system is designed to be non-intrusive and respectful of user privacy.

Acknowledgements

We thank Asu Tutku Gökçek, Gökçe Sevimli, and Yakup Enes Güven for their cnotributions to the project. This work has been supported by the Scientific and Technological Research Council of Türkiye (TÜBİTAK) as part of the project "Automatic Learning of Procedural Language from Natural Language Instructions for Intelligent Assistance" with the number 121C132. The authors also gratefully acknowledge KUIS AI Lab for providing computational support.

References

Ahmet Afsin Akın and Mehmet Dündar Akın. 2007. Zemberek, an open source nlp framework for turkic languages. *Structure*, 10(2007):1–5.

Ahmet Akın. 2017. Zembereknlp - natural language processing tools for turkish.

Manar Alkhatib, Azza Abdel Monem, and Khaled Shaalan. 2020. Deep learning for arabic error detection and correction. *ACM Trans. Asian Low Resour. Lang. Inf. Process.*, 19(5):71:1–71:13.

Aaron Bangor, Philip Kortum, and James Miller. 2009. Determining what individual sus scores mean: adding an adjective rating scale. *J. Usability Studies*, 4(3):114–123.

Esat Mahmut Bayol. 2018. Trnlp - tr natural language processing.

Steven Bird, Ewan Klein, and Edward Loper. 2009. *Natural language processing with Python: analyzing text with the natural language toolkit.* " O'Reilly Media, Inc.".

John Brooke. 1995. Sus: A quick and dirty usability scale. *Usability Eval. Ind.*, 189.

Christopher Bryant, Mariano Felice, and Ted Briscoe. 2017. Automatic annotation and evaluation of error types for grammatical error correction. In *Proceedings of the 55th Annual Meeting of the Association for Computational Linguistics (Volume 1: Long Papers)*, pages 793–805, Vancouver, Canada. Association for Computational Linguistics.

Christopher Bryant, Zheng Yuan, Muhammad Reza Qorib, Hannan Cao, Hwee Tou Ng, and Ted Briscoe. 2023. Grammatical error correction: A survey of the state of the art. *Comput. Linguistics*, 49(3):643–701.

Eduardo Calò, Léo Jacqmin, Thibo Rosemplatt, Maxime Amblard, Miguel Couceiro, and Ajinkya Kulkarni. 2021. GECko+: a grammatical and discourse error correction tool. In *Actes de la 28e Conférence sur le Traitement Automatique des Langues Naturelles. Volume 3 : Démonstrations*, pages 8–11, Lille, France. ATALA.

Kenneth Heafield and Alon Lavie. 2010. CMU multi-engine machine translation for WMT 2010. In *Proceedings of the Joint Fifth Workshop on Statistical Machine Translation and MetricsMATR, WMT@ACL 2010, Uppsala, Sweden, July 15-16, 2010*, pages 301–306. Association for Computational Linguistics.

Nahid Hossain, Mehedi Hasan Bijoy, Salekul Islam, and Swakkhar Shatabda. 2024. Panini: a transformer-based grammatical error correction method for bangla. *Neural Comput. Appl.*, 36(7):3463–3477.

Atakan Kara, Farrin Marouf Sofian, Andrew Bond, and Gözde Şahin. 2023. GECTurk: Grammatical error correction and detection dataset for Turkish. In *Findings of the Association for Computational Linguistics: IJCNLP-AACL 2023 (Findings)*, pages 278–290, Nusa Dua, Bali. Association for Computational Linguistics.

Rhonda G. Kost and Joel Correa da Rosa. 2018. Impact of survey length and compensation on validity, reliability, and sample characteristics for ultrashort-, short-, and long-research participant perception surveys. *Journal of Clinical and Translational Science*, 2:31 – 37.

Shaopeng Lai, Qingyu Zhou, Jiali Zeng, Zhongli Li, Chao Li, Yunbo Cao, and Jinsong Su. 2022. Type-driven multi-turn corrections for grammatical error correction. In *Findings of the Association for Computational Linguistics: ACL 2022, Dublin, Ireland, May 22-27, 2022*, pages 3225–3236. Association for Computational Linguistics.

Paul J Lavrakas. 2008. *Encyclopedia of survey research methods*. Sage publications.

Zuchao Li, Kevin Parnow, Masao Utiyama, Eiichiro Sumita, and Hai Zhao. 2021. Miss: An assistant for multi-style simultaneous translation. In *Proceedings of the 2021 Conference on Empirical Methods in Natural Language Processing: System Demonstrations, EMNLP 2021, Online and Punta Cana, Dominican Republic, 7-11 November, 2021*, pages 1–10. Association for Computational Linguistics.

Jakub Náplava and Milan Straka. 2019. Grammatical error correction in low-resource scenarios. In *Proceedings of the 5th Workshop on Noisy User-generated Text, W-NUT@EMNLP 2019, Hong Kong, China, November 4, 2019*, pages 346–356. Association for Computational Linguistics.

Jakub Náplava, Milan Straka, Jana Straková, and Alexandr Rosen. 2022. Czech grammar error correction with a large and diverse corpus. *Trans. Assoc. Comput. Linguistics*, 10:452–467.

Shrimai Prabhumoye, Ruslan Salakhutdinov, and Alan W. Black. 2020. Topological sort for sentence ordering. In *Proceedings of the 58th Annual Meeting of the Association for Computational Linguistics, ACL 2020, Online, July 5-10, 2020*, pages 2783–2792. Association for Computational Linguistics.

Zhaoquan Qiu and Youli Qu. 2019. A two-stage model for chinese grammatical error correction. *IEEE Access*, 7:146772–146777.

Muhammad Reza Qorib, Geonsik Moon, and Hwee Tou Ng. 2023. ALLECS: A lightweight language error correction system. In *Proceedings of the 17th Conference of the European Chapter of the Association for Computational Linguistics. EACL 2023 - System Demonstrations, Dubrovnik, Croatia, May 2-4, 2023*, pages 298–306. Association for Computational Linguistics.

Muhammad Reza Qorib, Seung-Hoon Na, and Hwee Tou Ng. 2022a. Frustratingly easy system combination for grammatical error correction. In *Proceedings of the 2022 Conference of the North American Chapter of the Association for Computational Linguistics: Human Language Technologies, NAACL 2022, Seattle, WA, United States, July 10-15, 2022*, pages 1964–1974. Association for Computational Linguistics.

Muhammad Reza Qorib, Seung-Hoon Na, and Hwee Tou Ng. 2022b. Frustratingly easy system combination for grammatical error correction. In *Proceedings of the 2022 Conference of the North American Chapter of the Association for Computational Linguistics: Human Language Technologies, NAACL 2022, Seattle, WA, United States, July 10-15, 2022*, pages 1964–1974. Association for Computational Linguistics.

Hongkai Ren, Liner Yang, and Endong Xun. 2018. A sequence to sequence learning for chinese grammatical error correction. In *Natural Language Processing and Chinese Computing - 7th CCF International Conference, NLPCC 2018, Hohhot, China, August 26-30, 2018, Proceedings, Part II*, volume 11109 of *Lecture Notes in Computer Science*, pages 401–410. Springer.

Alla Rozovskaya and Dan Roth. 2019. Grammar error correction in morphologically-rich languages: The case of russian. *Trans. Assoc. Comput. Linguistics*, 7:1–17.

Ali Safaya, Emirhan Kurtulus, Arda Göktogan, and Deniz Yüret. 2022. Mukayese: Turkish NLP strikes back. In *Findings of the Association for Computational Linguistics: ACL 2022, Dublin, Ireland, May 22-27, 2022*, pages 846–863. Association for Computational Linguistics.

Jeff Sauro. 2015. Supr-q: A comprehensive measure of the quality of the website user experience. *J. Usability Studies*, 10(2):68–86.

Stefan Schweter. 2020. Berturk - bert models for turkish.

Hunny Sharma. 2022. How short or long should be a questionnaire for any research? researchers dilemma in deciding the appropriate questionnaire length. *Saudi journal of anaesthesia*, 16(1):65–68.

Aiman Solyman, Zhenyu Wang, Qian Tao, Arafat Abdulgader Mohammed Elhag, Rui Zhang, and Zeinab Mahmoud. 2022. Automatic arabic grammatical error correction based on expectation-maximization routing and target-bidirectional agreement. *Knowl. Based Syst.*, 241:108180.

Alexey Sorokin. 2022. Improved grammatical error correction by ranking elementary edits. In *Proceedings of the 2022 Conference on Empirical Methods in Natural Language Processing, EMNLP 2022, Abu Dhabi, United Arab Emirates, December 7-11, 2022*, pages 11416–11429. Association for Computational Linguistics.

Maksym Tarnavskyi, Artem N. Chernodub, and Kostiantyn Omelianchuk. 2022. Ensembling and knowledge distilling of large sequence taggers for grammatical error correction. In *Proceedings of the 60th Annual Meeting of the Association for Computational Linguistics (Volume 1: Long Papers), ACL 2022, Dublin, Ireland, May 22-27, 2022*, pages 3842–3852. Association for Computational Linguistics.

Meliksah Turker. 2021. Vnlp - nlp library for turkish language.

Harun Uz. 2020. Zemberek-python - python implementation of zembereknlp.

Harun Uz and Gülşen Eryiğit. 2023. Towards automatic grammatical error type classification for Turkish. In *Proceedings of the 17th Conference of the European Chapter of the Association for Computational Linguistics: Student Research Workshop*, pages 134–142, Dubrovnik, Croatia. Association for Computational Linguistics.

Xiuyu Wu and Yunfang Wu. 2022. From spelling to grammar: A new framework for chinese grammatical error correction. In *Findings of the Association for Computational Linguistics: EMNLP 2022, Abu Dhabi, United Arab Emirates, December 7-11, 2022*, pages 889–902. Association for Computational Linguistics.

Lvxiaowei Xu, Jianwang Wu, Jiawei Peng, Jiayu Fu, and Ming Cai. 2022. FCGEC: fine-grained corpus for chinese grammatical error correction. In *Findings of the Association for Computational Linguistics: EMNLP 2022, Abu Dhabi, United Arab Emirates, December 7-11, 2022*, pages 1900–1918. Association for Computational Linguistics.

Olcay Taner Yıldız. 2019. Turkish spell checker - starlangsoftware.

Harun Reşit Zafer. 2017. hunspell-tr.

Metehan Çetinkaya. 2018. Turkishnlp - turkish nlp with python.

Appendix

A User Study

A.1 The user scenario

Participants are given 10 short sentences and are requested to input them into GECTurk WEB. To help participants understand the potential outcomes, we produced four instructional videos and showed them to the participants before they started using GECTurk WEB. Figures 3 through 6 display screenshots of each scenario along with its English transcription. Following the video demonstration, participants are directed to input each sentence and categorize it based on the possible outcomes. The full list of the 10 sentences is provided in Table 3.

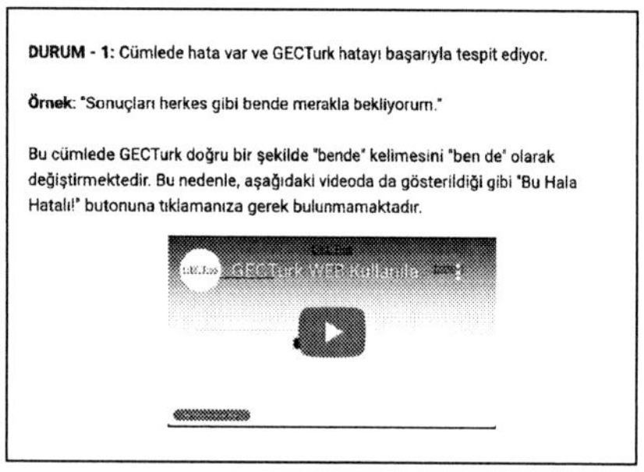

Figure 3: **CASE - 1:** The sentence contains an error and GECTurk successfully detects the error. **Example:** "Sonuçları herkes gibi bende merakla bekliyorum." In this sentence, GECTurk correctly changes "bende" to "ben de". Therefore, there is no need to click on the "This is still incorrect!" button, as shown in the video below.

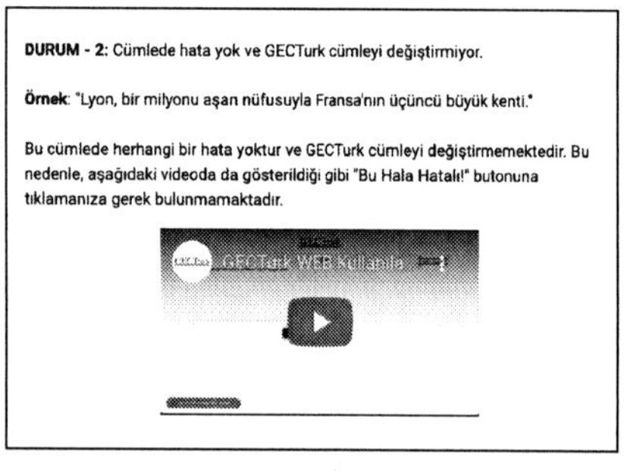

Figure 4: **CASE - 2:** There is no error in the sentence and GECTurk does not change the sentence. **Example:** "Lyon, bir milyonu aşan nüfusuyla Fransa'nın üçüncü büyük kenti." There are no errors in this sentence and GECTurk does not change the sentence. Therefore, there is no need to click on the "This is still incorrect!" button, as shown in the video below.

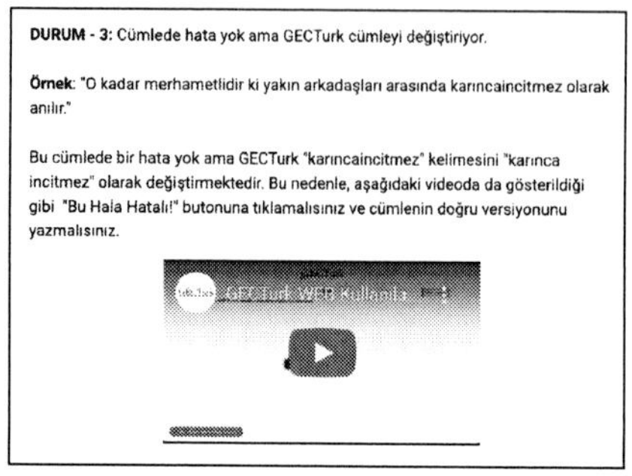

Figure 5: **CASE - 3:** There is no error in the sentence but GECTurk changes the sentence. **Example:** "O kadar merhametlidir ki yakın arkadaşları arasında karıncaincitmez olarak anılır." There is no mistake in this sentence, but GECTurk changes the word "karıncaincitmez" to "karınca incitmez". Therefore, you should click on the "This is still incorrect!" button and type the correct version of the sentence, as shown in the video below.

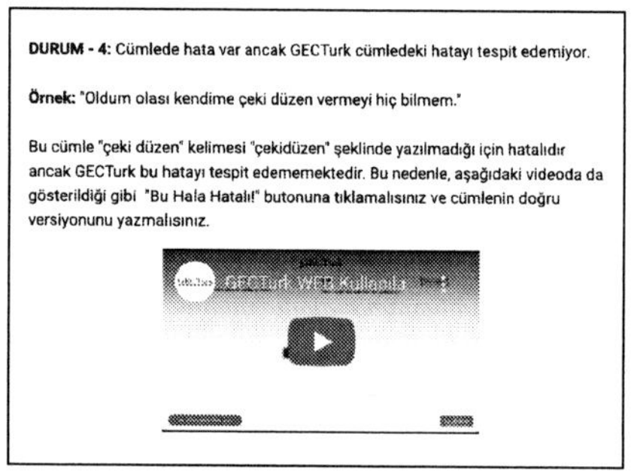

Figure 6: **CASE - 4:** There is an error in the sentence but GECTurk cannot detect it. **Example:** "Oldum olası kendime çeki düzen vermeyi hiç bilmem." This sentence is incorrect because the word "çekidüzen" is incorrectly spelled as "çeki düzen", but GECTurk is unable to detect this error. Therefore, you should click on the "This is still incorrect!" button and type the correct version of the sentence, as shown in the video below.

Input No	Input	GECTurk WEB Output	Ground Truth	Case No
1	Dilin birey ve toplum hayatında taşıdığı önem, **anadili** öğretimini de önemli kılmaktadır.	UNCHANGED	... [anadili → ana dili] ...	4
2	Onu baban görmeden hemen ortadan **kayıp et**.	... [kayıp et → kaybet] ...	... [kayıp et → kaybet] ...	1
3	Tatil yapmak **istiyrum** fakat çalışmaya devam etmem şart.	... [istiyrum → istiyorum] ...	... [istiyrum → istiyorum] ...	1
4	Bugün hep beraber gittiğimiz geziye **Ayşe'de** geldi.	... [Ayşe'de → Ayşe de] ...	... [Ayşe'de → Ayşe de] ...	1
5	**Bir takım** ansiklopediye dünyanın parasını ödedim.	[Bir takım → Birtakım] ...	UNCHANGED	3
6	Düştüğü bu durumdan kurtulmak için **karakara** düşünüyordu.	... [karakara → kara kara] ...	... [karakara → kara kara] ...	1
7	Bugün öyle çok **yorulmuşki** hemen yattı.	... [yorulmuşki → yorulmuş ki] ...	... [yorulmuşki → yorulmuş ki] ...	1
8	Bu yaptığının elle tutulur **sebepi** yok.	... [sebepi → sebebi] ...	... [sebepi → sebebi] ...	1
9	Sanki uyurgezer biri gibi çarşıyı baştan başa adımladı.	UNCHANGED	UNCHANGED	2
10	**İçerde** kimsenin olmadığını gördü ve bağırmaya başladı.	[İçerde → İçeride] ...	[İçerde → İçeride] ...	1

Table 3: The complete list of 10 sentences is given to the participants. For each sentence, participants are required to enter the **Input** and observe the **GECTurk WEB Output**. Based on this output, they decide the **Case No**. Note that participants have no access to the **Ground Truth**.

A.2 User Evaluation

In the second part of the user study, participants are asked to complete the SUS and SUPR-Q questionnaires based on their experience in the first half of the study. Additionally, participants are asked a yes/no question regarding whether they learned or remembered a grammatical rule. The SUS questionnaire comprises ten five-level Likert scale questions, while the SUPR-Q consists of seven five-level Likert scale questions and one ten-level Likert scale question, making a total of 19 questions including the yes/no question.

B Time Efficiency

This section highlights the model's performance in terms of time efficiency, demonstrating a linear relationship between the volume of words processed and the response time. The data suggests that the system can process up to 14,000 words in under 90 seconds, affirming its ability to scale effectively while retaining user engagement. This performance is supported by robust hardware specifications of an AWS i4i.large instance, including 2 vCPUs, 16.0 GiB of memory, and a 3.5 GHz Intel Xeon 8375C processor, which collectively ensure minimal latency even under significant text processing loads. For visual representation, see Figure 7.

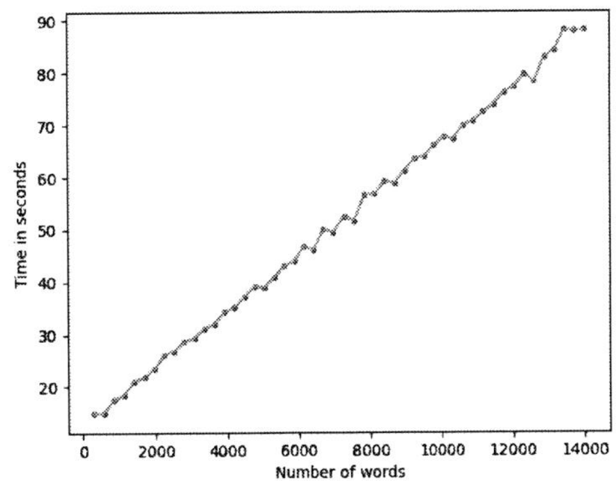

Figure 7: The relationship between the number of words processed by the GECTURK model and the response time, demonstrating the model's time efficiency.

GR-NLP-TOOLKIT: An Open-Source NLP Toolkit for Modern Greek

Lefteris Loukas[1,3], Nikolaos Smyrnioudis[1], Chrysa Dikonomaki[1], Spyros Barbakos[1], Anastasios Toumazatos[1], John Koutsikakis[1], Manolis Kyriakakis[1], Mary Georgiou[1], Stavros Vassos[3], John Pavlopoulos[1,2], Ion Androutsopoulos[1,2]
[1]Department of Informatics, Athens University of Economics and Business, Greece
[2]Archimedes/Athena RC, Greece
[3]helvia.ai

Abstract

We present GR-NLP-TOOLKIT, an open-source natural language processing (NLP) toolkit developed specifically for modern Greek. The toolkit provides state-of-the-art performance in five core NLP tasks, namely part-of-speech tagging, morphological tagging, dependency parsing, named entity recognition, and Greeklish-to-Greek transliteration. The toolkit is based on pre-trained Transformers, it is freely available, and can be easily installed in Python (`pip install gr-nlp-toolkit`). It is also accessible through a demonstration platform on HuggingFace, along with a publicly available API for non-commercial use. We discuss the functionality provided for each task, the underlying methods, experiments against comparable open-source toolkits, and future possible enhancements. The toolkit is available at: https://github.com/nlpaueb/gr-nlp-toolkit

1 Introduction

Modern Greek is the official language of Greece, one of the two official languages of Cyprus, and the native language of approximately 13 million people.[1] Despite continuous efforts (Papantoniou and Tzitzikas, 2020; Bakagianni et al., 2024), there are still very few natural language processing (NLP) toolkits that support modern Greek (§2).

We present GR-NLP-TOOLKIT, an open-source NLP toolkit developed specifically for modern Greek. The toolkit supports five core NLP tasks, namely part-of-speech (POS) tagging, morphological tagging (tagging for tense, voice, person, gender, case, number etc.), dependency parsing, named entity recognition (NER), and Greeklish-to-Greek transliteration (converting Greek written using Latin-keyboard characters to the Greek alphabet). We demonstrate the functionality that the toolkit provides per task (§3). We also discuss the underlying methods and experimentally compare GR-NLP-TOOLKIT to STANZA (Qi et al., 2020) and SPACY (Honnibal et al., 2020), two multilingual toolkits that support modern Greek, demonstrating that GR-NLP-TOOLKIT achieves state-of-the-art performance in POS tagging, morphological tagging, dependency parsing, and NER (§4). Previous work (Toumazatos et al., 2024) shows that the Greeklish-to-Greek converter included in GR-NLP-TOOLKIT is also state-of-the-art.

The toolkit can be easily installed in Python via PYPI (`pip install gr-nlp-toolkit`) and its code is publicly available on Github.[2] We showcase its functionality in an open-access demonstration space, hosted on HuggingFace.[3] We also release GREEK-NLP-API, a fully-documented and publicly available HTTP API, which allows using the toolkit in (non-commercial) applications developed in any programming language.[4]

2 Background and related work

Greek has evolved over three millennia.[5] Apart from its historical interest, Greek is also challenging from an NLP point of view. For example, it has its own alphabet (α,β,γ,..), and nowadays a much smaller number of speakers, compared to other widely used languages of the modern world. Although words of Greek origin can be found in many other languages (e.g., medical terms), they are written in different alphabets in other languages. Hence, Greek words written in the Greek alphabet are severely under-represented in modern multilingual corpora and, consequently, in the word and sub-word vocabularies of most multilingual Transformer models, e.g., XLM-R (Conneau et al., 2020).

[1]https://en.wikipedia.org/wiki/Greek_language

[2]https://github.com/nlpaueb/gr-nlp-toolkit/

[3]https://huggingface.co/spaces/AUEB-NLP/greek-nlp-toolkit-demo

[4]https://huggingface.co/spaces/AUEB-NLP/The-Greek-NLP-API/

[5]www.britannica.com/topic/Greek-language

Proceedings of the 31st International Conference on Computational Linguistics: System Demonstrations, pages 174–182
January 19–24, 2025. ©2025 Association for Computational Linguistics

This causes the tokenizers of these models to over-fragment Greek words, very often to characters (Koutsikakis et al., 2020), which increases processing time and cost, and makes it more difficult for models to reassemble tokens to more meaningful units. Greek is also highly inflected (e.g., different verb forms for different tenses, voices, moods, persons, numbers; similarly for nouns, adjectives, pronouns etc.), which makes POS tagging more difficult and morphological tagging (tagging also for tense, voice, gender, case etc.) desirable. Greek is also flexible in word order (e.g., subject-verb-object, object-verb-subject, verb-subject-object etc. are all possible with different emphasis), which makes parsing more challenging.

Modern Greek is normally written in the Greek alphabet. In online messages, however, especially informal email and chat, it is often written using characters available on Latin-character keyboards, a form known as Greeklish (Koutsogiannis and Mitsikopoulou, 2017). For example, 'ω' (omega) may be written as 'w' based on visual similarity, as 'o' based on phonetic similarity, or as 'v' based on the fact that 'ω' and 'v' use the same key on Greek-Latin keyboards, to mention just some possibilities. Greeklish was originally used in older computers that did not support the Greek alphabet, but continues to be used to avoid switching languages on multilingual keyboards, hide spelling mistakes (esp. when used by non-native speakers), or as a form of slang (mostly by younger people). There is no consensus mapping between Greek and Latin-keyboard characters.[6] Consequently, the same Greek word can be written in numerous different ways in Greeklish (Fig. 1). Even native Greek speakers may struggle to understand, and are often annoyed by Greeklish, which requires paying careful attention to context to decipher. Moreover, most Greek NLP datasets contain text written in the Greek alphabet, hence models trained on those datasets may be unable to handle Greeklish.

Phenomena of this kind motivated the development of GREEK-BERT (Koutsikakis et al., 2020), and more recently the MELTEMI large language model (LLM) for modern Greek (Voukoutis et al., 2024); the latter is based on MISTRAL-7b (Jiang et al., 2023). In this work, we leverage GREEK-BERT for most tasks, and BYT5 (Xue et al., 2022) for Greeklish-to-Greek, which can both be used even with CPU only, unlike larger LLMs (Luccioni et al., 2024). Nevertheless, in future versions of the toolkit, we plan to investigate how we can integrate 'small' Greek LLMs for on-device use.[7]

Figure 1: An example of a Greek sentence written in Greeklish. There is no consensus mapping. Greek characters may be replaced by Latin-keyboard characters based on visual similarity, phonetic similarity, shared keys etc. Figure from Toumazatos et al. (2024).

In previous modern Greek experiments, GREEK-BERT, when fine-tuned, was reported to outperform the multilingual XLM-R, again fine-tuned, in NER and natural language inference, while it performed on par with XLM-R in POS tagging (Koutsikakis et al., 2020). In subsequent work of two undergraduate theses (Dikonimaki, 2021; Smyrnioudis, 2021), we showed, again using modern Greek data, that GREEK-BERT largely outperformed XLM-R in dependency parsing, but found no substantial difference between the two models in morphological tagging and (another dataset of) NER. Greeklish was not considered in any of these previous studies. The two theses also created a first version of GR-NLP-TOOLKIT, which was largely experimental, did not include Greeklish-to-Greek, and was not published (apart from the two theses). The version of the toolkit that we introduce here has been completely refactored, it uses more recent libraries, has been tested more thoroughly, includes Greeklish-to-Greek, can be used via both PYPI and GREEK-NLP-API, and can also be explored via a HuggingFace demo (§1).

SPACY (Honnibal et al., 2020) and STANZA (Qi et al., 2020) are widely used multilingual NLP toolkits that support modern Greek. They both have limitations, however, discussed below (Table 1).

SPACY (Honnibal et al., 2020) is an open-source

[6]The ISO 843:1997 standard (`https://www.iso.org/standard/5215.html`) is almost never used.

[7]For example, see Meta's recently released 1B and 3B models in their blogpost.

Toolkit	POS Tagging	Morphological Tagging	Lemma-tization	Named Entity Recognition	Dependency Parsing	Greeklish-to-Greek Transliteration
SPACY	✓	✓	✓	✓	✓	✗
STANZA	✓	✓	✓	✗	✓	✗
NLTK	✗	✗	✗	✗	✗	✗
GR-NLP-TOOLKIT	✓✓	✓✓	✗	✓✓	✓✓	✓✓

Table 1: Comparison of NLP toolkits that support modern Greek. NLTK provides only a tokenizer and stop-word removal (not shown) for modern Greek. SPACY and STANZA both include a Greek lemmatizer. GR-NLP-TOOLKIT is the only one that includes Greeklish-to-Greek transliteration. Its other functions (POS tagging, morphological tagging, NER, dependency parsing) are based on GREEK-BERT, whereas SPACY and STANZA are based on Greek FASTTEXT embeddings and do not use Transformers. ✓✓ denotes using pretrained Transformers.

NLP library for efficient processing of text in many languages. In modern Greek, it supports POS tagging, morphological tagging, lemmatization (mapping all inflected forms of verbs, nouns etc. to their base forms), NER, and dependency parsing. However, it relies on static Greek FASTTEXT word embeddings (Prokopidis and Papageorgiou, 2017; Bojanowski et al., 2017), without utilizing pretrained Transformers for modern Greek, which restricts its performance. Also, SPACY does not support Greeklish-to-Greek transliteration.

Stanford's STANZA (Qi et al., 2020) is a Python-based NLP library with multilingual support. For modern Greek, it provides POS tagging, morphological tagging, dependency parsing, lemmatization, but not NER or Greeklish-to-Greek. Its modern Greek components are trained on two Greek Universal Dependencies treebanks, the default 'GDT' (Prokopidis and Papageorgiou, 2017, 2014; Prokopidis et al., 2005; Papageorgiou et al., 2006; Ghotsoulia et al., 2007) and 'GUD' (Markantonatou et al.). Under the hood, STANZA and SPACY use the same Greek FASTTEXT embeddings (Bojanowski et al., 2017) and no pretrained Transformers.

Another widely used NLP toolkit, NLTK (Bird et al., 2009), does not provide any functionality for modern Greek, other than a tokenizer and stop-word removal. In other related work, Prokopidis and Piperidis (2020) introduced models for Greek POS tagging, lemmatization, dependency parsing, and text classification, requiring manual integration with FASTTEXT and an outdated STANZA version. They also developed a closed-source API based on them. By contrast, we focus on ready-to-use open-source NLP toolkits.

3 Using GR-NLP-TOOLKIT

Using our toolkit in Python is straightforward. To install it, use `pip install gr-nlp-toolkit`. Subsequently, you can initialize, e.g., a pipeline for POS tagging (incl. morphological tagging), NER, dependency parsing (DP) by executing `nlp = Pipeline("pos, ner, dp")`. Applying the pipeline to a sentence, e.g., `doc = nlp("Η Ιταλία κέρδισε την Αγγλία στον τελικό το 2020.")`, tokenizes the text and provides linguistic annotations, including POS and morphological tags, NER labels, and dependency relations. In our example, the token 'Ιταλία' (English: 'Italy') gets the annotations `NER = S-ORG` (start token of organization name), `UPOS = PROPN` (proper name), and a dependency relation `nsubj` (nominal subject) linking it to the verb (see also Fig. 2).

Transliterating Greeklish to Greek (G2G) is equally simple. The G2G converter can be loaded by typing `nlp = Pipeline("g2g")`. Running `doc = nlp("h athina kai h thessaloniki einai poleis")` will convert the text to "η αθηνα και η θεσσαλονικη ειναι πολεις" (English: "athens and thessaloniki are cities"). This makes it easy to process Greeklish text before performing further Greek language processing. For example, you can also combine the G2G converter with POS, NER, DP in the same pipeline, using `nlp = Pipeline("g2g, pos, ner, dp")`.

4 Under the hood and experiments

The POS tagging, morphological tagging, NER, and dependency parsing tools of GR-NLP-TOOLKIT are powered by GREEK-BERT (Koutsikakis et al., 2020), with task-specific heads.[8] For Greeklish-to-Greek, we reproduced the BYT5-based converter of Toumazatos et al. (2024), which was the best among several methods considered, apart from GPT-4, which we excluded for efficiency reasons.[9]

[8] GREEK-BERT works as our backbone model in most tasks. While it is powerful, one limitation is that it automatically converts all text to lowercase and removes Greek accents.

[9] LLMs like GPT-4 or the Greek MELTEMI require a significant resources (cost, time, lots of VRAM), which typical end users do not have.

4.1 Named entity recognition

For the NER tool of GR-NLP-TOOLKIT, we fine-tuned GREEK-BERT (Koutsikakis et al., 2020) with a task-specific token classification head. We used the training subset of a modern Greek NER dataset published by Bartziokas et al. (2020). The dataset contains approx. 38,000 tagged entities and 18 entity types.[10] We tuned hyper-parameters to maximize the macro-F1 score on the development subset. We used cross-entropy loss, AdamW (Loshchilov et al., 2017), and grid search for hyper-parameter tuning (Table 6).

In Table 2, we compare SPACY against GR-NLP-TOOLKIT on the test subset of the NER dataset of Bartziokas et al. (2020), for the six entity types that SPACY supports.[11] We do not compare against STANZA here, since it does not support NER (Table 1). As seen in Table 2, GR-NLP-TOOLKIT outperforms SPACY in all entity types.[12] SPACY's score in the LOC (location) entity type is particularly low, because it classified most (truly) LOC entities as GPE (geo-political entity).

Entity type	SPACY	GR-NLP-TOOLKIT
EVENT	0.31	**0.64**
GPE	0.77	**0.93**
PERSON	0.82	**0.96**
LOC	0.01	**0.80**
ORG	0.65	**0.88**
PRODUCT	0.27	**0.75**

Table 2: F1 test scores of SPACY and GR-NLP-TOOLKIT in modern Greek NER, showed for the six entity types that SPACY supports.

4.2 POS tagging and morphological tagging

For POS tagging and morphological tagging, we used the modern Greek part of the Universal Dependencies (UD) treebank (Prokopidis and Papageorgiou, 2017). Every word occurrence is annotated with its gold universal POS tag (UPOS), morphological features (FEATS), as well as its syntactic head and the type of syntactic dependency. We refer the reader to the UD website, where complete lists of UPOS tags, morphological features, and dependency types are available.[13]

We fine-tuned a single GREEK-BERT instance for both POS tagging and morphological tagging, adding 17 token classification heads (linear layers), 16 for the morphological categories, and 1 additional token classification head for UPOS prediction. Each classification head takes as input the corresponding output (top-level) token embedding of GREEK-BERT. For every head, the class with the highest logit is chosen, as in multi-task learning. The model hyperparameters were tuned on the validation subset of the dataset optimizing the macro-F1 score, using grid search and AdamW (Loshchilov et al., 2017) (Table 6).

In Table 3, we compare SPACY and STANZA to the GR-NLP-TOOLKIT on the UPOS and morphological tagging test data of the modern Greek UD treebank. STANZA and GR-NLP-TOOLKIT perform on par, with SPACY ranking third.

Metric	SPACY	STANZA	GR-NLP-TOOLKIT
Micro-F1	0.95	**0.98**	**0.98**
Macro-F1	0.87	0.96	**0.97**

Table 3: Micro-F1 and macro-F1 test scores for UPOS tagging. The complete list of UPOS tags can be found in `https://universaldependencies.org/u/pos/`.

In the more complex morphological tagging task (Table 4), the differences between the systems are move visible, with GR-NLP-TOOLKIT performing slightly better in most categories than STANZA, while SPACY, again, ranks third. The largest differences are observed in 'Mood' and 'Foreign' (foreign word), where GR-NLP-TOOLKIT performs substantially better, and 'Degree' (degrees of adjectives), where STANZA is clearly better. Dikonimaki (2021) attributes some of these differences to very few training occurrences of the corresponding tags.

Morphological tag	SPACY	STANZA	GR-NLP-TOOLKIT
Case	0.68	**0.97**	**0.97**
Definite	0.89	**1.00**	**1.00**
Gender	0.68	0.97	**0.98**
Number	0.69	**0.99**	**0.99**
PronType	0.71	0.94	**0.97**
Foreign	0.65	0.79	**0.88**
Aspect	0.65	0.98	**0.99**
Mood	0.74	0.59	**0.83**
Person	0.68	0.98	**1.00**
Tense	0.76	0.98	**1.00**
VerbForm	0.65	**0.97**	0.93
Voice	0.65	**0.99**	0.96
NumType	0.67	0.93	**0.96**
Poss	0.59	0.96	**0.98**
Degree	0.48	**0.89**	0.50
Abbr	0.89	**0.96**	0.94

Table 4: F1 test scores for all of the morphological tags.

[10] The 18 entity types of GR-NLP-TOOLKIT are: ORG, PERSON, CARDINAL, GPE, DATE, PERCENT, ORDINAL, LOC, NORP, TIME, MONEY, EVENT, PRODUCT, WORK_OF_ART, FAC, QUANTITY, LAW, LANGUAGE.

[11] We provide the results only about the six shared NER entity types between SPACY and GR-NLP-TOOLKIT.

[12] Table 2 shows results of SPACY's large model (spaCy-lg). The smaller models (spacy-sm, spacy-md) performed worse.

[13] `https://universaldependencies.org/`

4.3 Dependency parsing

For dependency parsing, we use the model of Dozat et al. (2017), with the exception that we obtain contextualized word embeddings using GREEK-BERT instead of the BILSTM encoder of the original model.[14] Specifically, for each word of the sentence being parsed, we obtain its output (top-level) contextualized embedding e_i from GREEK-BERT. We then compute the following four variants of e_i. The $W^{(\cdots)}$ matrices are learnt during fine-tuning.

$$h_i^{(\text{arc-head})} = W^{(\text{arc-head})} e_i,\ h_i^{(\text{arc-dep})} = W^{(\text{arc-dep})} e_i$$

$$h_i^{(\text{rel-head})} = W^{(\text{rel-head})} e_i,\ h_i^{(\text{rel-dep})} = W^{(\text{rel-dep})} e_i$$

$h_i^{(\text{arc-head})}$, $h_i^{(\text{arc-dep})}$ represent the i-th word of the sentence when considered as the head or dependent (child) of a dependency relation, respectively. $h_i^{(\text{rel-head})}$, $h_i^{(\text{rel-dep})}$ are similar, but they are used when predicting the type of a relation (see below).

Each candidate arc from head word j to dependent word i is scored using the following formula, where $W^{(\text{arc})}$ is a learnt biaffine attention layer, and $b^{(\text{arc})}$ is a learnt bias capturing the fact that some words tend to be used more (or less) often as heads.

$$s_{ij}^{(\text{arc})} = (h_j^{(\text{arc-head})})^T W^{(\text{arc})} h_i^{(\text{arc-dep})} + (h_j^{(\text{arc-head})})^T b^{(\text{arc})}$$

At inference time, for each word i, we greedily select its (unique) most probable head $y_i^{(\text{arc})}$.[15]

$$y_i^{(\text{arc})} = \arg\max_j s_{ij}^{(\text{arc})}$$

During training, we minimize the categorical cross entropy loss of $y_i^{(\text{arc})}$, where the possible values of $y_i^{(\text{arc})}$ correspond to the other words of the sentence.

For a given arc from head word j to dependent word i, its candidate labels k are scored as follows, where $\oplus$ denotes vector concatenation.

$$s_{ijk}^{(\text{rel})} = (h_j^{(\text{rel-head})})^T U_k^{(\text{rel})} h_i^{(\text{rel-dep})} + w_k^T (h_i^{(\text{rel-head})} \oplus h_i^{(\text{rel-dep})}) + b_k^{(\text{rel})}$$

Here $U_k^{(\text{rel})}$ is a learnt biaffine layer, different per label k, whereas w_k^T is a learnt vector that in effect scores separately the head and the dependent word, and $b_k^{(rel)}$ is the bias of label k. At inference time, having first greedily selected the head $y_i^{(\text{arc})}$ of each dependent word i, we then greedily select the label of the arc as follows.

$$y_i^{(\text{rel})} = \arg\max_k s_{iy_i^{(\text{arc})}k}^{(\text{rel})}$$

During training, we minimize the categorical cross-entropy loss of $y_i^{(\text{rel})}$. The arc prediction and label prediction components are trained jointly, adding the two cross entropy losses.

The parser was trained and evaluated on the same modern Greek part of the Universal Dependencies dataset of Section 4.2, now using the dependency relation annotations. Consult Dikonimaki (2021) and Kyriakakis (2018) for more details.

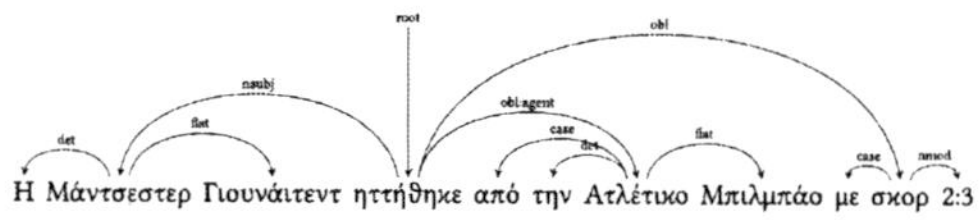

Figure 2: A dependency tree generated by GR-NLP-TOOLKIT for a Greek sentence whose English translation is "Manchester United was defeated by Atletico Bilbao with a 2:3 score." Figure from Smyrnioudis (2021). Tree drawn using SPACY's visualizer.

Table 5 evaluates the dependency parser of GR-NLP-TOOLKIT against those of SPACY and STANZA, using Unlabeled Attachment Score (UAS) and Labeled Attachment Score (LAS) on the test subset. UAS is the percentage of the sentence's words that get the correct head, while LAS is the percentage of words that get both the correct head and label. GR-NLP-TOOLKIT clearly provides state-of-the-art performance for this task too.

Score	SPACY	STANZA	GR-NLP-TOOLKIT
UAS	0.66	0.91	**0.94**
LAS	0.64	0.88	**0.92**

Table 5: Test UAS and LAS scores (dependency parsing).

4.4 Greeklish-to-Greek transliteration

For Greeklish-to-Greek, we reproduced the BYT5 model of Toumazatos et al. (2024), which was the best one, excluding GPT-4. BYT5 (Xue et al., 2022) operates directly on bytes, making it particularly well-suited for tasks involving text written in multiple alphabets (Greek and Latin in our case). Toumazatos et al. (2024) fine-tuned BYT5 especially for Greeklish-to-Greek, using synthetic data. The model was then evaluated on both synthetic and real-life Greeklish. Consult Toumazatos et al. (2024) for more details and evaluation results. Recall that no other modern Greek toolkit currently supports Greeklish-to-Greek (Table 1).

[14]When a word is broken into multiple sub-word tokens by GREEK-BERT's tokenizer, we take the embedding of the first token to represent the entire word.

[15]We leave for future work the possibility of adding a non-greedy decoder, e.g., based on the work of Chu and Liu (1965) and Edmonds (1967), which would also guarantee that the output is always a tree.

A limitation of the Greeklish-to-Greek model included in GR-NLP-TOOLKIT is that it has not been trained on Greeklish that also includes English (code switching), which is a common phenomenon in online modern Greek. This is a limitation inherited from the work of Toumazatos et al. (2024). We are currently working on an improved Greeklish-to-Greek model that will also handle code switching. We are also considering including in GR-NLP-TOOLKIT an older statistical Greeklish-to-Greek model (Chalamandaris et al., 2006), which still performed well in the experiments of Toumazatos et al. (2024) and can already handle code-switching.

5 The GR-NLP-TOOLKIT demo space

For users wishing to explore GR-NLP-TOOLKIT instantly, in a no-code fashion, we also developed a demonstration space, which is open access and hosted at https://huggingface.co/spaces/AUEB-NLP/greek-nlp-toolkit-demo. Users can select tasks (POS and morphological tagging, NER, dependency parsing, Greeklish-to-Greek), submit their input and see the results in the user interface. Figure 3 shows an example of Greeklish-to-Greek.

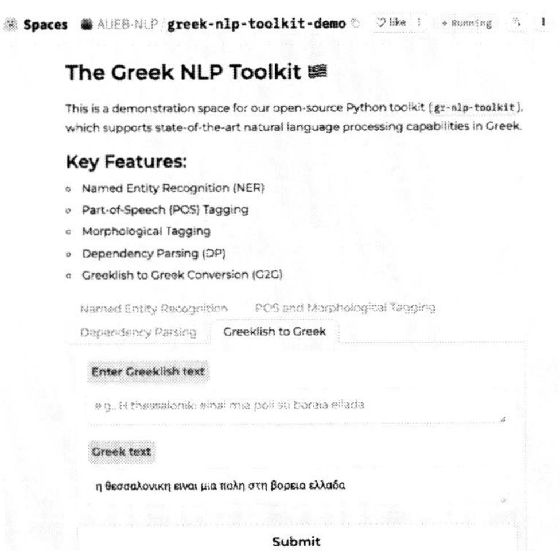

Figure 3: Example of GR-NLP-TOOLKIT's demonstration space at https://huggingface.co/spaces/AUEB-NLP/greek-nlp-toolkit-demo. The example shows Greeklish-to-Greek transliteration, but the demo provides access to the other functionalities too (POS and morphological tagging, dependency parsing, NER).

6 The GREEK-NLP-API

Based on GR-NLP-TOOLKIT, we also developed a publicly available API (with the same non-commercial license). The API is hosted at https://huggingface.co/spaces/AUEB-NLP/The-Greek-NLP-API. It is intended to be used in research and educational applications, even applications not developed in Python, via HTTP API calls and exchange of JSON objects. GREEK-NLP-API conforms to the OPENAPI standards.[16]

7 Conclusions

We introduced GR-NLP-TOOLKIT, an open-source NLP toolkit with state-of-the-art performance for modern Greek. It can be easily installed in Python (`pip install gr-nlp-toolkit`), and its code is available on Github (https://github.com/nlpaueb/gr-nlp-toolkit/).

The toolkit currently supports POS and morphological tagging, dependency parsing, named entity recognition, and Greeklish-to-Greek transliteration. We also presented an interactive no-code demonstration space that provides the full functionality of the toolkit (https://huggingface.co/spaces/AUEB-NLP/greek-nlp-toolkit-demo), as well as a publicly available API at https://huggingface.co/spaces/AUEB-NLP/The-Greek-NLP-API, which allows using the toolkit even in applications not developed in Python. We discussed the methods that power the toolkit under the hood, and reported experimental results against SPACY and STANZA.

In future work, we plan to add more tools, e.g., for toxicity detection and sentiment analysis. We welcome open-source collaboration.

Acknowledgments

This work has been partially supported by project MIS 5154714 of the National Recovery and Resilience Plan Greece 2.0 funded by the European Union under the NextGenerationEU Program. Also, a significant portion of this work was also conducted as part of the Google Summer of Code (2024) program with the Open Technologies Alliance (GFOSS) (https://eellak.ellak.gr/). Lastly, we would like to sincerely thank the Hellenic Artificial Intelligence Society (EETN) (https://www.eetn.gr/en/) for their sponsorship.

[16]https://www.openapis.org/

References

Juli Bakagianni, Kanella Pouli, Maria Gavriilidou, and John Pavlopoulos. 2024. Towards Systematic Monolingual NLP surveys: GenA of Greek NLP. *arXiv preprint arXiv:2407.09861*.

Nikos Bartziokas, Thanassis Mavropoulos, and Constantine Kotropoulos. 2020. Datasets and Performance Metrics for Greek Named Entity Recognition. In *11th Hellenic Conference on Artificial Intelligence (SETN 2020)*, SETN 2020, pages 160–167, New York, NY, USA. Association for Computing Machinery.

Steven Bird, Ewan Klein, and Edward Loper. 2009. *Natural Language Processing with Python: Analyzing Text with the Natural Language Toolkit*. " O'Reilly Media, Inc.".

Piotr Bojanowski, Edouard Grave, Armand Joulin, and Tomas Mikolov. 2017. Enriching Word Vectors with Subword Information. *Transactions of the Association for Computational Linguistics*, 5:135–146.

Aimilios Chalamandaris, Athanassios Protopapas, Pirros Tsiakoulis, and Spyros Raptis. 2006. All Greek to me! an automatic Greeklish to Greek transliteration system. In *Proceedings of the Fifth International Conference on Language Resources and Evaluation (LREC'06)*, Genoa, Italy. European Language Resources Association (ELRA).

Y.-J. Chu and T.-H Liu. 1965. On the shortest arborescence of a directed graph. *Science Sinica*, 14:1396–1400.

Alexis Conneau, Kartikay Khandelwal, Naman Goyal, Vishrav Chaudhary, Guillaume Wenzek, Francisco Guzmán, Edouard Grave, Myle Ott, Luke Zettlemoyer, and Veselin Stoyanov. 2020. Unsupervised Cross-lingual Representation Learning at Scale. In *Proceedings of the 58th Annual Meeting of the Association for Computational Linguistics*, pages 8440–8451, Online. Association for Computational Linguistics.

C. Dikonimaki. 2021. A Transformer-based natural language processing toolkit for Greek – Part of speech tagging and dependency parsing. Technical report, BSc thesis, Department of Informatics, Athens University of Economics and Business. `http://nlp.cs.aueb.gr/theses/dikonimaki_bsc_thesis.pdf`.

Timothy Dozat, Peng Qi, and Christopher D. Manning. 2017. Stanford's Graph-based Neural Dependency Parser at the CoNLL 2017 shared task. In *Proceedings of the CoNLL 2017 Shared Task: Multilingual Parsing from Raw Text to Universal Dependencies*, pages 20–30, Vancouver, Canada. Association for Computational Linguistics.

J. Edmonds. 1967. Optimum branchings. *Journal of Research of the National Bureau of Standards B*, 71(4):233–240.

Voula Ghotsoulia, Elina Desypri, Maria Koutsombogera, Prokopis Prokopidis, and Haris Papageorgiou. 2007. Towards a Frame Semantics Resource for Greek. In *Proceedings of The Sixth Workshop on Treebanks and Linguistic Theories (TLT 2007)*, Bergen, Norway. University of Bergen.

Matthew Honnibal, Ines Montani, Sofie Van Landeghem, and Adriane Boyd. 2020. spaCy: Industrial-strength Natural Language Processing in Python.

Albert Q. Jiang, Alexandre Sablayrolles, Arthur Mensch, Chris Bamford, Devendra Singh Chaplot, Diego de las Casas, Florian Bressand, Gianna Lengyel, Guillaume Lample, Lucile Saulnier, Lélio Renard Lavaud, Marie-Anne Lachaux, Pierre Stock, Teven Le Scao, Thibaut Lavril, Thomas Wang, Timothée Lacroix, and William El Sayed. 2023. Mistral 7B. *Preprint*, arXiv:2310.06825.

John Koutsikakis, Ilias Chalkidis, Prodromos Malakasiotis, and Ion Androutsopoulos. 2020. GREEK-BERT: The Greeks Visiting Sesame Street. In *11th Hellenic Conference on Artificial Intelligence*, SETN 2020, pages 110–117, New York, NY, USA. Association for Computing Machinery.

Dimitris Koutsogiannis and Bessie Mitsikopoulou. 2017. Greeklish and Greekness: Trends and Discourses of "Glocalness". *Journal of Computer-Mediated Communication*, 9(1):JCMC918.

M. Kyriakakis. 2018. Exploring deep neural network models of syntax with a focus on Greek. Technical report, MSc thesis, Department of Informatics, Athens University of Economics and Business. `http://nlp.cs.aueb.gr/theses/kiriakakis_msc_thesis.pdf`.

Ilya Loshchilov, Frank Hutter, et al. 2017. Fixing Weight Decay Regularization in Adam. *arXiv preprint arXiv:1711.05101*, 5.

Sasha Luccioni, Yacine Jernite, and Emma Strubell. 2024. Power Hungry Processing: Watts Driving the Cost of AI Deployment? In *Proceedings of the 2024 ACM Conference on Fairness, Accountability, and Transparency*, FAccT '24, page 85–99, New York, NY, USA. Association for Computing Machinery.

Stella Markantonatou, Vivian Stamou, and Socrates Vak. Gud Greek-GUD: Greek Universal Dependencies Treebank. `https://github.com/UniversalDependencies/UD_Greek-GUD`.

Harris Papageorgiou, Elina Desipri, Maria Koutsombogera, Kanella Pouli, and Prokopis Prokopidis. 2006. Adding Multi-layer Semantics to the Greek Dependency Treebank. In *Proceedings of The Fifth International Conference on Language and Evaluation (LREC-2006)*, Genoa, Italy. ELRA.

Katerina Papantoniou and Yannis Tzitzikas. 2020. NLP for the Greek language: A brief survey. In *11th Hellenic Conference on Artificial Intelligence*, SETN 2020, page 101–109, Athens, Greece.

Prokopis Prokopidis, Elina Desypri, Maria Koutsombogera, Haris Papageorgiou, and Stelios Piperidis. 2005. Theoretical and Practical Issues in the Construction of a Greek Dependency Treebank. In *Proceedings of The Fourth Workshop on Treebanks and Linguistic Theories (TLT 2005)*, pages 149–160, Barcelona, Spain. Universitat de Barcelona.

Prokopis Prokopidis and Haris Papageorgiou. 2017. Universal Dependencies for Greek. In *Proceedings of the NoDaLiDa 2017 Workshop on Universal Dependencies (UDW 2017)*, pages 102–106, Gothenburg, Sweden. Association for Computational Linguistics.

Prokopis Prokopidis and Harris Papageorgiou. 2014. Experiments for Dependency Parsing of Greek. In *Proceedings of the First Joint Workshop on Statistical Parsing of Morphologically Rich Languages and Syntactic Analysis of Non-Canonical Languages*, pages 89–96, Dublin, Ireland.

Prokopis Prokopidis and Stelios Piperidis. 2020. A neural nlp toolkit for greek. In *11th Hellenic Conference on Artificial Intelligence*, SETN 2020, page 125–128, New York, NY, USA. Association for Computing Machinery.

Peng Qi, Yuhao Zhang, Yuhui Zhang, Jason Bolton, and Christopher D. Manning. 2020. Stanza: A Python Natural Language Processing Toolkit for Many Human Languages. In *Proceedings of the 58th Annual Meeting of the Association for Computational Linguistics: System Demonstrations*, pages 101–108, Online. Association for Computational Linguistics.

N. Smyrnioudis. 2021. A Transformer-based natural language processing toolkit for Greek – Named entity recognition and multi-task learning. Technical report, BSc thesis, Department of Informatics, Athens University of Economics and Business. http://nlp.cs.aueb.gr/theses/smyrnioudis_bsc_thesis.pdf.

Anastasios Toumazatos, John Pavlopoulos, Ion Androutsopoulos, and Stavros Vassos. 2024. Still All Greeklish to Me: Greeklish to Greek transliteration. In *Proceedings of the 2024 Joint International Conference on Computational Linguistics, Language Resources and Evaluation (LREC-COLING 2024)*, pages 15309–15319, Torino, Italia. ELRA and ICCL.

Leon Voukoutis, Dimitris Roussis, Georgios Paraskevopoulos, Sokratis Sofianopoulos, Prokopis Prokopidis, Vassilis Papavasileiou, Athanasios Katsamanis, Stelios Piperidis, and Vassilis Katsouros. 2024. Meltemi: The first open Large Language Model for Greek. *Preprint*, arXiv:2407.20743.

Linting Xue, Aditya Barua, Noah Constant, Rami Al-Rfou, Sharan Narang, Mihir Kale, Adam Roberts, and Colin Raffel. 2022. ByT5: Towards a Token-Free Future with Pre-trained Byte-to-Byte Models. *Transactions of the Association for Computational Linguistics*, 10:291–306.

A Appendix

A.1 Hyperparameter tuning

Table 6 provides information on the hyperparameters of the models we use for NER, POS tagging, morphological tagging, and dependency parsing.

Hyperparameter	Range
Learning rate	[5e-5, 3e-5, 2e-5]
Dropout	[0, 0.1, 0.2]
Grad accumulation steps	[4, 8]
Weight decay (λ)	[0.2, 0.5, 0.8]

Table 6: Hyperparameter space of the NER, POS tagging, morphological tagging, and dependency parsing models.

A.2 List of Contributions[17]

Lefteris Loukas: Conceptualization, Software, Project administration, Funding acquisition, Writing. Lefteris led the software's refactoring to the current version, after identifying limitations in the first early one. He secured funding, supervised the development of the revamped toolkit, and created the demonstration space as well as the API. He also co-authored this publication.

Nikolaos Smyrnioudis: Methodology, Formal Analysis, Software, Writing. Nikolaos researched and created the NER methodology, and co-developed the first version of the toolkit. Consult Smyrnioudis (2021) for more information on his work, which is also summarized in §4.1.

Chrysa Dikonimaki: Methodology, Formal Analysis, Software, Writing. Chrysa researched and created the DP, POS, and morphological tagging methodologies, and co-developed the first version of the toolkit. Consult Dikonimaki (2021) for more information on her work, which is also summarized in §4.2 and §4.3.

Spyros Barbakos: Software, Resources, Methodology. Spyros refactored the previous version of the toolkit as a participant in Google's Summer of Code 2024, and enhanced it with the Greeklish-to-Greek transliteration component.

Anastasios Toumazatos: Software, Resources, Methodology. Anastasios provided guidance on how to integrate their Greeklish-to-Greek transliteration algorithm (Toumazatos et al., 2024) in the revamped introduced toolkit.

John Koutsikakis: Supervision, Software, Resources. John co-supervised the BSc theses of

[17]We follow the Contributor Role Taxonomy (CRediT). Consult http://www.credit.niso.org.

Dikonimaki (2021) and Smyrnioudis (2021), and assisted in their software and resources.

Manolis Kyriakakis: Software, Resources, Methodology. Manolis assisted in the development of the dependency parsing functionality, which was based on his MSc thesis (Kyriakakis, 2018).

Mary Georgiou: Software, Resources. Mary assisted in debugging and making pip-installable the first (older) version of the toolkit.

Stavros Vassos: Resources, Supervision. Stavros identified current limitations in Greek NLP and provided resources for the work on Greeklish-to-Greek of Toumazatos et al. (2024), as well as for this work.

John Pavlopoulos: Supervision, Writing, Methodology. John co-supervised the work on Greeklish-to-Greek of Toumazatos et al. (2024), and this work. He co-authored this publication.

Ion Androutsopoulos: Supervision, Writing, Methodology. Ion co-supervised the BSc theses of Dikonimaki (2021) and Smyrnioudis (2021), the Greeklish-to-Greek work of Toumazatos et al. (2024), this work, and co-authored this publication.

ViSoLex: An Open-Source Repository for Vietnamese Social Media Lexical Normalization

Anh Thi-Hoang Nguyen[1,2], **Dung Ha Nguyen**[1,2], **Kiet Van Nguyen**[1,2,*]
[1]University of Information Technology, Ho Chi Minh City, Vietnam
[2]Vietnam National University, Ho Chi Minh City, Vietnam
***Correspondence:** kietnv@uit.edu.vn
Contributing authors: 20520134@gm.uit.edu.vn, dungngh@uit.edu.vn

Abstract

ViSoLex is an open-source system designed to address the unique challenges of lexical normalization for Vietnamese social media text. The platform provides two core services: Non-Standard Word (NSW) Lookup and Lexical Normalization, enabling users to retrieve standard forms of informal language and standardize text containing NSWs. ViSoLex's architecture integrates pre-trained language models and weakly supervised learning techniques to ensure accurate and efficient normalization, overcoming the scarcity of labeled data in Vietnamese. This paper details the system's design, functionality, and its applications for researchers and non-technical users. Additionally, ViSoLex offers a flexible, customizable framework that can be adapted to various datasets and research requirements. By publishing the source code, ViSoLex aims to contribute to the development of more robust Vietnamese natural language processing tools and encourage further research in lexical normalization. Future directions include expanding the system's capabilities for additional languages and improving the handling of more complex non-standard linguistic patterns.

1 Introduction

The increasing presence of Non-Standard Words (NSWs) in social media has introduced significant challenges for natural language processing (NLP) systems. In Vietnamese, these challenges are particularly pronounced due to the informal, abbreviated, and non-canonical nature of social media language. Lexical normalization, which transforms NSWs into their standard forms, is essential for improving the performance of downstream tasks such as sentiment analysis, hate speech detection, and machine translation. While research on lexical normalization has made significant advancements globally, Vietnamese has lagged behind due to a lack of resources and standardized datasets.

To address these challenges, we introduce ViSoLex[1], an open-source repository for Vietnamese lexical normalization. ViSoLex provides a comprehensive solution by integrating multitask learning capabilities to simultaneously detect and normalize NSWs. This is achieved by leveraging pre-trained language models and weak supervision techniques, reducing the dependency on extensive manual labeling. Furthermore, ViSoLex incorporates a growing dictionary of NSWs for dictionary lookup, enabling efficient identification and normalization of non-standard words.

The repository is designed to address the unique linguistic challenges of Vietnamese social media text and fosters customization, allowing researchers to adapt the system for various datasets and languages. By offering a scalable and open-source solution, ViSoLex supports broader research and practical applications, advancing the field of Vietnamese NLP. This paper presents the system architecture, multitask training framework, and the extensive efforts made to improve the quality of Vietnamese NLP tasks through lexical normalization.

2 Related Works

The study of lexical normalization has seen significant advancements worldwide, especially in addressing the challenges of non-standard text. Early approaches like the Abbreviation Expander by Ciosici and Assent (2018) tackled abbreviation expansion in technical documents, providing a web-based solution for easy understanding of domain-specific terms. In 2019, MoNoise by van der Goot (2019) was introduced for vocabulary normalization, using spelling correction and word embeddings with a Feature-Based Random Forest Classifier. Initially for English, it later expanded to support multiple languages, becoming a widely used

[1]`https://github.com/HaDung2002/visolex`

Proceedings of the 31st International Conference on Computational Linguistics: System Demonstrations, pages 183–188
January 19–24, 2025.

multilingual tool. Furthermore, Muller et al. (2019) marked a shift toward using pre-trained language models for handling noisy text in user-generated content, framing normalization as a token prediction task. Nguyen et al. (2021) introduced the idea of capturing not just lexical meaning but also social context, a key aspect in understanding informal and non-canonical language. These developments paved the way for more robust normalization systems across various languages, demonstrating the potential of combining linguistic insights with modern NLP techniques.

In the Vietnamese context, Tran et al. (2021) employed deep learning models like Bidirectional-GRU to solve the problem of missing diacritics. Do et al. (2021) further advanced the field by using VSEC model, a Transformer-based approach, to correct Vietnamese spelling errors, significantly improving upon prior methods. Nguyen et al. (2024c) introduced the first corpus, called ViLexNorm, for Vietnamese lexical normalization, a critical resource for normalizing social media text and improving downstream tasks. Additionally, Nguyen et al. (2024a) introduced a Seq2Seq approach for normalizing NSWs, with a publicly available dataset for further research. Building upon this foundation, Nguyen et al. (2024b) proposed a novel framework that integrates semi-supervised learning with weak supervision techniques, leveraging pre-trained language models to enhance dataset quality, reduce manual labeling efforts, and normalize NSWs.

In this paper, we further advance our previous work proposed in Nguyen et al. (2024b), now named ViSoLex, by incorporating multitask learning capabilities to simultaneously detect and normalize NSWs. Additionally, we have integrated a dictionary lookup feature for non-standard word detection. The ViSoLex repository is designed as an open-source solution for Vietnamese lexical normalization, specifically addressing the unique linguistic challenges presented by social media text, and is made publicly available for broader use and development.

3 ViSoLex: Vietnamese Social Media Lexical Normalization

3.1 System Architecture

ViSoLex is designed to provide two key services: NSW Lookup and Lexical Normalization. Users can input a NSW for interpretation or enter a sentence containing NSWs for normalization. The architecture of ViSoLex, as illustrated in Figure 1, follows a modular design that integrates various components to streamline Vietnamese social media text normalization. At the core, user inputs flow through distinct paths depending on the requested service. Communication between the components ensures dynamic interaction and updates. This architecture enables independent updates to different system components while maintaining overall functionality.

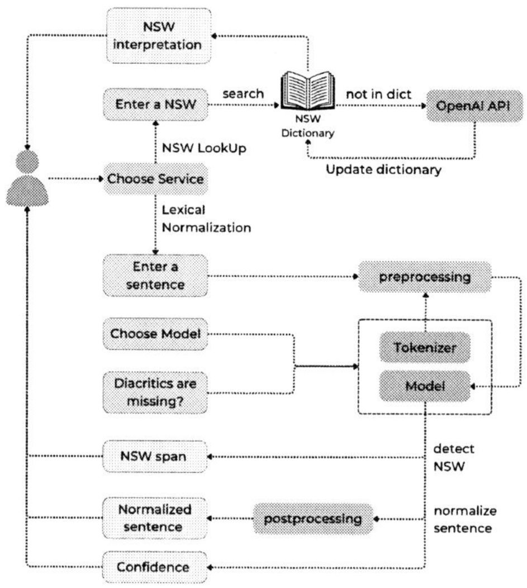

Figure 1: The Architecture of ViSoLex. The diagram illustrates the modular components enabling NSW Lookup and Lexical Normalization services, including their interactions and flow of user inputs.

3.1.1 NSW LookUp Service

The NSW LookUp service enables users to retrieve potential standard forms and interpretations of NSWs from an established dictionary. Upon choosing this service, users are asked to input an NSW, which is then checked against the existing dictionary. If found, the system returns the standard forms and definitions, along with relevant examples. If the word is not in the dictionary, the system consults the OpenAI GPT-4o API to suggest a possible normalization, which is then added to the dictionary for future use. This approach allows NSWs to be resolved either by utilizing existing data or dynamically learning from external models.

The NSW dictionary was built by leveraging the OpenAI GPT-4o API to generate definitions and examples for each entry in the Vietnamese Non-Standard Words Dictionary[2].

3.1.2 Lexical Normalization Service

The lexical normalization service transforms NSWs in a sentence into their standard forms. When users select this service, they input a sentence that may contain NSWs. The system tokenizes and preprocesses the input before applying a multitask-trained model (discussed in detail in Section 3.2) to identify non-standard tokens and predict their corresponding standard forms, each accompanied by confidence scores. The predicted output undergoes post-processing, where redundant spaces before punctuation are removed, and proper sentence capitalization and punctuation are applied. The final result provides a fully normalized sentence, along with a breakdown of each NSW, its standard equivalent, and the confidence score, ensuring precise normalization for Vietnamese social media text.

3.2 Lexical Normalizer Training

The updated lexical normalizer builds on the framework presented in our previous work Nguyen et al. (2024b), introducing multitask learning to enhance its capabilities. As illustrated in Figure 2, this weakly supervised framework leverages both labeled and unlabeled data to identify and standardize NSWs in Vietnamese social media text. Inspired by the ASTRA framework Karamanolakis et al. (2021), it incorporates two key components: the Lexical Normalizer, now enhanced with multitask learning as a student model, and a Rule Attention Network, acting as a teacher by embedding weak supervision rules. This integration of data-driven and rule-based approaches enables the model to generalize more effectively, handling the diverse and evolving NSW patterns in social media discourse.

3.2.1 Lexical Normalizer

The Lexical Normalizer is trained using a multitask framework to predict the standard forms of NSWs in Vietnamese social media text. It leverages pre-trained models, such as BARTpho Tran et al. (2022) and ViSoBERT Nguyen et al. (2023), fine-tuned for text normalization. The input consists of sentences with NSWs, and the model outputs both NSW detection and their normalized forms,

[2]https://github.com/AnhHoang0529/vn-nsw-dictionary

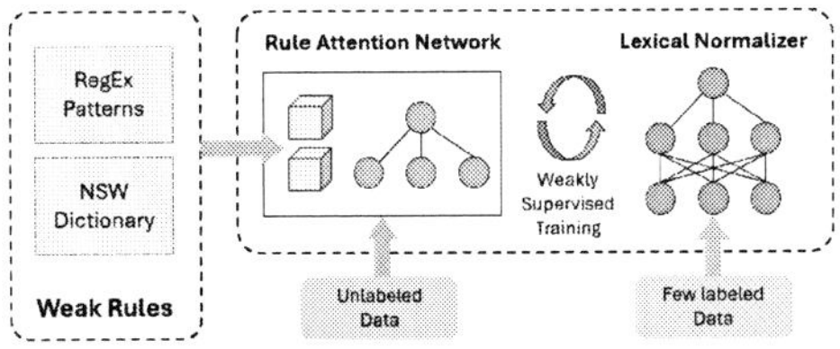

Figure 2: Weak Supervision Training. This figure illustrates the training process of the lexical normalizer, which integrates multitask learning and a Rule Attention Network guided by weak supervision rules to effectively standardize NSWs in Vietnamese social media text.

combining token classification with sequence generation for effective normalization.

ViSoLex introduces multitask learning to simultaneously handle NSW detection and lexical normalization. A shared encoder extracts input features, followed by task-specific heads that generate predictions. The model minimizes the binary cross-entropy loss $\mathcal{L}_{NSW}$ for NSW detection and cross-entropy loss $\mathcal{L}_{Norm}$ for normalization, with the total loss:

$$\mathcal{L}_{Total} = \alpha\mathcal{L}_{Norm} + \beta\mathcal{L}_{NSW} \quad (1)$$

where α and β balance the contributions of each task. This multitask approach enhances efficiency and performance in normalizing noisy social media text.

3.2.2 Rule Attention Network with Weak Rules

To further enhance the model's performance, a Rule Attention Network (RAN) is integrated, guided by weak supervision rules. These weak rules are derived from NSW dictionary and regular expression rules, capturing common patterns of NSWs in Vietnamese social media text. As shown in Figure 2, the RAN learns to assign different levels of attention to these rules during the training process. This network dynamically weighs the influence of each rule based on the context and reliability of the prediction, allowing the model to flexibly adapt to both well-defined and ambiguous cases of NSWs. The combination of weak supervision with the rule attention mechanism allows the model to effectively learn from limited labeled data, improving both NSW detection and normalization accuracy.

4 Evaluation

In this section, we evaluate the performance of multitask learning in comparison to the lexical normalization approach presented by Nguyen et al. (2024b). The evaluation employs three key metrics: the F1-score, which specifically measures the accuracy of normalizing NSWs; the Integrity Score, which assesses the preservation of words that do not require normalization; and Accuracy, which evaluates the overall correctness of the predicted sentences. These metrics are defined and explained in detail by Nguyen et al. (2024b).

Table 1 demonstrate the impact of multitask learning on model performance across different metrics, with p representing the diacritics removal ratio. The results show that multitask learning consistently enhances model performance. For BARTpho, improvements in F1-score are modest, with increases of 0.34% and 0.25% for different diacritics removal ratios ($p = 0$ and $p = 1$). ViSoBERT, however, benefits from multitask learning, particularly when all diacritics are removed ($p = 1$), with a notable 3.74% increase in F1-score.

In terms of Accuracy, both models see slight improvements, but again, ViSoBERT shows stronger gains, reinforcing its ability to normalize sentence with diacritics removal in traning and development dataset. Despite a small decrease in the Integrity Score for BARTpho, ViSoBERT improves, particularly in high diacritics removal scenarios.

Overall, multitask learning proves especially effective for ViSoBERT, leading to performance improvements in handling noisy text data with diacritic variations.

5 System Demonstration

In this section, we outline the system demonstration of ViSoLex, tailored to meet the needs of various user groups within the NLP community. We offer two distinct entry points to accommodate both technical and non-technical users.

5.1 For Researchers and Developers

We have published the source code on GitHub to allow researchers and developers to leverage the system's capabilities through the following features:

- **Model Training and Evaluation**: Users can utilize the top-level script `main.py` to retrain models, reproduce results, and evaluate performance. This offers comprehensive insight into the system's underlying methodologies and processes.
- **Demo Functionality**: For a quick overview, users can run an interactive terminal session using `demo.py`, which demonstrates the core functionalities of the system with minimal setup.

The framework is also designed for flexibility, allowing users to customize the model and its components for specific datasets and model selection, enhancing its adaptability to various research applications. Key customization options include:

- `data/`: Users can replace the default data with their own, ensuring they provide three labeled data files (`train.csv`, `dev.csv`, `test.csv`) and an unlabeled data file (`unlabeled.csv`).
- `dict/`: Users can integrate a custom NSW dictionary to further align the framework with their specific language or domain requirements.
- `aligned_tokenizer.py`: The token-level alignment tokenizer can be modified to suit the characteristics of different datasets and languages.
- `normalizer/model_construction/`: New models for lexical normalization, tailored to different languages or datasets, can be added here.
- `project_variables.py`: Global constants such as data directories or language-specific tokens can be modified to fit custom requirements.
- `arguments.py`: Users can configure additional settings for their projects and reset the default argument values.

This modular and customizable design allows researchers to tailor the system to meet their unique needs in lexical normalization tasks.

5.2 For Non-Experts

To accommodate non-technical users, we developed a user-friendly front-end interface using a Flask web application. The interface provides two main services, accessible through distinct endpoints:

Metric	Task	BARTpho		ViSoBERT	
		$p = 0.0$	$p = 1.0$	$p = 0.0$	$p = 1.0$
F1-score (%)	Single task	84.94	85.64	75.79	72.19
	Multitask	85.28	85.89	77.22	75.93
	Improvement	↑0.34	↑0.25	↑1.43	↑3.74
Integrity Score (%)	Single task	98.88	98.62	98.26	96.92
	Multitask	98.83	98.50	98.64	98.27
	Improvement	↓0.05	↓0.12	↑0.38	↑1.35
Accuracy (%)	Single task	96.06	96.16	95.42	94.42
	Multitask	96.14	96.26	95.08	94.76
	Improvement	↑0.08	↑0.10	↑0.34	↑0.34

Table 1: Comparison of Single Task and Multitask Learning Performance on BARTpho and ViSoBERT models with different diacritics removal ratios ($p = 0\%$ and $p = 100\%$

- **Interactive Dictionary Service**: This service, available via the `/dict_lookup` endpoint, allows users to search for non-standard words and retrieve their standard equivalents and definitions from our extensive dictionary. The interface for this service is illustrated in Figure 3.
- **Sentence Normalization**: Through the `/normalize_text` endpoint, users can input sentences containing non-standard words and receive real-time normalized outputs. The UI for this service is shown in Figure 4.

The Flask application enables seamless interaction between the front-end and back-end components, ensuring efficient and responsive user experiences. A self-hosting tutorial for deploying the UI is available in the project's GitHub repository, along with a demonstration video on how to use the interface, accessible via this Youtube URL[3].

6 Discussion and Future Directions

ViSoLex represents a significant advancement in the lexical normalization of Vietnamese social media text, offering researchers and developers a powerful and flexible tool to address the challenges posed by non-standard language. The system exhibits robust performance in both NSW detection and normalization, leveraging its integration of pretrained models and weakly supervised learning. Notably, ViSoLex achieves consistent improvements in F1-score and accuracy across multitask

[3]https://youtu.be/XBIAogDpF3o?si=PUXiMCuu9qDTfM3B

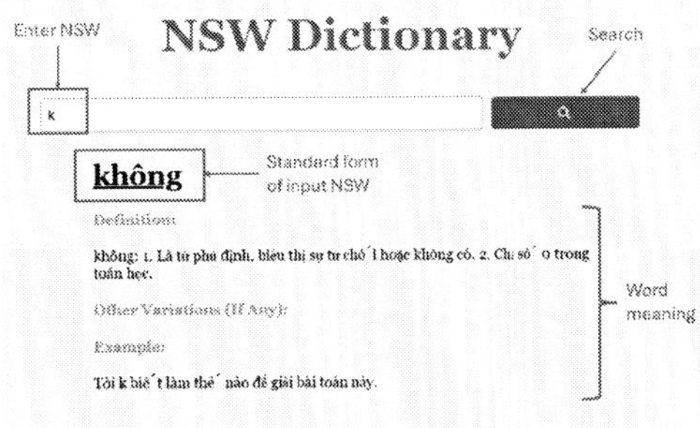

Figure 3: User Interface of NSW LookUp Service. This interface allows users to search for non-standard words and retrieve their standard equivalents, definitions, and examples from the dictionary.

settings when compared to the original framework Nguyen et al. (2024b), which was exclusively designed for lexical normalization without NSW detection. Through its open-source availability, ViSoLex encourages further research and application in Vietnamese NLP.

Looking ahead, future work on ViSoLex will focus on expanding its capabilities to support more complex non-standard patterns and handling additional languages. Efforts will also be made to enhance the model's adaptability, allowing it to better manage evolving trends in social media language. Furthermore, expanding the NSW dictionary and refining the system's ability to predict social-contextual meanings are promising directions. Lastly, improving user experience through more intuitive front-end interfaces and incorporating additional downstream NLP tasks will enhance ViSoLex's practical applications in real-world sce-

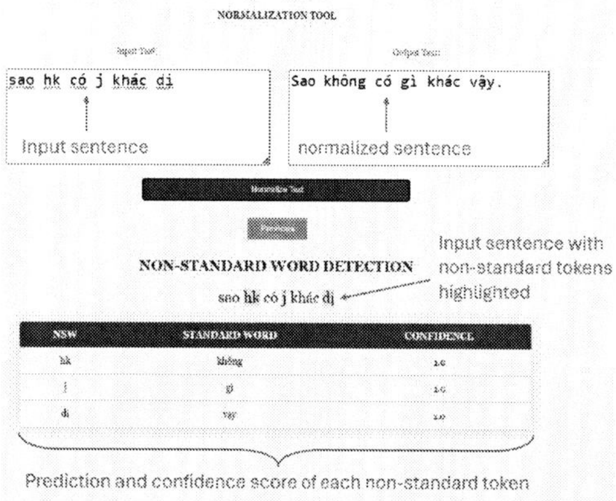

Figure 4: User Interface of Lexical Normalization Service. This interface enables users to input sentences with non-standard words and receive fully normalized outputs in real-time.

narios.

Acknowledgement

This research is funded by University of Information Technology-Vietnam National University Ho Chi Minh City under grant number D1-2024-75.

References

Manuel R. Ciosici and Ira Assent. 2018. Abbreviation expander - a web-based system for easy reading of technical documents. In *Proceedings of the 27th International Conference on Computational Linguistics: System Demonstrations*, pages 1–4, Santa Fe, New Mexico. Association for Computational Linguistics.

Dinh-Truong Do, Ha Thanh Nguyen, Thang Ngoc Bui, and Hieu Dinh Vo. 2021. Vsec: Transformer-based model for vietnamese spelling correction. In *PRICAI 2021: Trends in Artificial Intelligence*, pages 259–272, Cham. Springer International Publishing.

Giannis Karamanolakis, Subhabrata Mukherjee, Guoqing Zheng, and Ahmed Hassan Awadallah. 2021. Self-training with weak supervision. In *Proceedings of the 2021 Conference of the North American Chapter of the Association for Computational Linguistics: Human Language Technologies*, pages 845–863, Online. Association for Computational Linguistics.

Benjamin Muller, Benoit Sagot, and Djamé Seddah. 2019. Enhancing BERT for lexical normalization. In *Proceedings of the 5th Workshop on Noisy User-generated Text (W-NUT 2019)*, pages 297–306, Hong Kong, China. Association for Computational Linguistics.

Anh Thi-Hoang Nguyen, Dung Ha Nguyen, Nguyet Thi Nguyen, Khanh Thanh-Duy Ho, and Kiet Van Nguyen. 2024a. Automatic textual normalization for hate speech detection. In *Intelligent Systems Design and Applications*, pages 1–12, Cham. Springer Nature Switzerland.

Dong Nguyen, Laura Rosseel, and Jack Grieve. 2021. On learning and representing social meaning in NLP: a sociolinguistic perspective. In *Proceedings of the 2021 Conference of the North American Chapter of the Association for Computational Linguistics: Human Language Technologies*, pages 603–612, Online. Association for Computational Linguistics.

Dung Ha Nguyen, Anh Thi Hoang Nguyen, and Kiet Van Nguyen. 2024b. A weakly supervised data labeling framework for machine lexical normalization in vietnamese social media. *Preprint*, arXiv:2409.20467.

Nam Nguyen, Thang Phan, Duc-Vu Nguyen, and Kiet Nguyen. 2023. ViSoBERT: A pre-trained language model for Vietnamese social media text processing. In *Proceedings of the 2023 Conference on Empirical Methods in Natural Language Processing*, pages 5191–5207, Singapore. Association for Computational Linguistics.

Thanh-Nhi Nguyen, Thanh-Phong Le, and Kiet Nguyen. 2024c. ViLexNorm: A lexical normalization corpus for Vietnamese social media text. In *Proceedings of the 18th Conference of the European Chapter of the Association for Computational Linguistics (Volume 1: Long Papers)*, pages 1421–1437, St. Julian's, Malta. Association for Computational Linguistics.

Nguyen Luong Tran, Duong Minh Le, and Dat Quoc Nguyen. 2022. Bartpho: Pre-trained sequence-to-sequence models for vietnamese. *Preprint*, arXiv:2109.09701.

Quang-Linh Tran, Gia-Huy Lam, Van-Binh Duong, and Trong-Hop Do. 2021. A study on diacritic restoration problem in vietnamese text using deep learning based models. In *2021 IEEE International Conference on Communication, Networks and Satellite (COMNETSAT)*, pages 306–310.

Rob van der Goot. 2019. MoNoise: A multi-lingual and easy-to-use lexical normalization tool. In *Proceedings of the 57th Annual Meeting of the Association for Computational Linguistics: System Demonstrations*, pages 201–206, Florence, Italy. Association for Computational Linguistics.

CompUGE-Bench: Comparative Understanding and Generation Evaluation Benchmark for Comparative Question Answering

Ahmad Shallouf and **Irina Nikishina** and **Chris Biemann**
University of Hamburg
Germany
{name.surname}@uni-hamburg.de

Abstract

This paper presents CompUGE, a comprehensive benchmark designed to evaluate Comparative Question Answering (CompQA) systems. The benchmark is structured around four core tasks: Comparative Question Identification, Object and Aspect Identification, Stance Classification, and Answer Generation. It unifies multiple datasets and provides a robust evaluation platform to compare various models across these sub-tasks. We also create additional all-encompassing CompUGE datasets by filtering and merging the existing ones. The benchmark for comparative question answering sub-tasks is designed as a web application available on HuggingFace Spaces.[1,2]

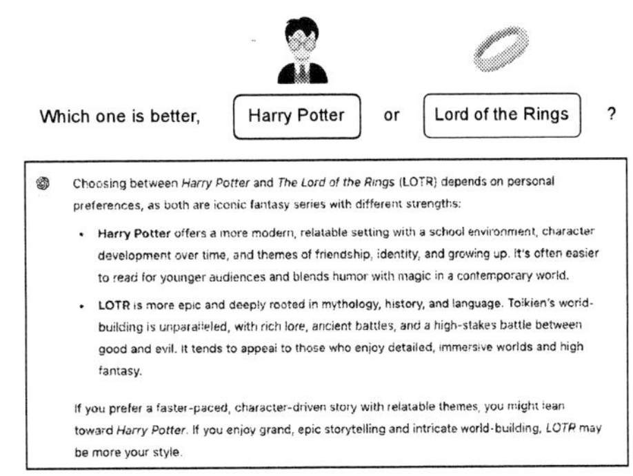

Figure 1: Example of answering comparative questions using ChatGPT.

1 Introduction

Nowadays, people are frequently confronted with a wide array of decisions, ranging from mundane tasks, such as selecting a meal, to more significant choices, such as determining a career path or making investment decisions. For instance, when selecting a movie to watch, many would ask, "Which one is better, *Harry Potter* or *The Lord of the Rings*?" Comparative Question Answering (CompQA) in the field of Natural Language Processing (NLP) aims to address exactly these types of questions. The task involves comparing two or more entities across different aspects and providing an answer backed by logical reasoning and argumentation. CompQA systems (Panchenko et al., 2019; Chekalina et al., 2021; Shallouf et al., 2024) help users make informed decisions by retrieving, processing, and generating comparative information.

In previous work (Bondarenko et al., 2022a; Shallouf et al., 2024), four key tasks are identified as essential for building an effective CompQA system: Comparative Question Identification (CQI), Object and Aspect Identification (OAI), Stance Classification (SC), and Answer Generation (AG). Each of these tasks plays a pivotal role in the system's ability to generate meaningful comparative answers. However, one of the main challenges in developing these systems is the diversity of available datasets (four for CQI, three for OAI, and two for SC). They vary in structure, labels, and coverage, making it challenging to compare models consistently using these datasets separately.

To address this challenge, we introduce **CompUGE-Bench**, a unified benchmark designed to evaluate CompQA systems across these four tasks. **CompUGE-Bench** combines datasets from multiple sources to allow fair model comparison. It is a standardized platform to evaluate their CompQA solutions, promoting progress in the field.

Therefore, we formulate the following research questions: *(RQ1) What datasets should be used for creating CompUGE Bench?* and *(RQ2) How can a web-based benchmark be effectively designed for comparative question answering sub-tasks?*

Our contributions are as follows:

- We design a web-based benchmark, making it publicly available for submitting new results.

[1]https://huggingface.co/spaces/uhhlt/CompUGE-Bench
[2]https://youtu.be/rnf6HW1Y7mc

Proceedings of the 31st International Conference on Computational Linguistics: System Demonstrations, pages 189–198
January 19–24, 2025.

- We select and merge datasets for each task, bringing them into a unified structure.

- We conduct extensive experiments, providing baselines for future research.

CompUGE is available as a web application[3,4]; the source code for the benchmark, experiments, and analysis are available under an MIT License.[5]

2 Related Work

In this section, we do not describe the papers describing the datasets we utilize for constructing our benchmark, but focus on other existing approaches for Comparative QA and the adjacent tasks.

One of the significant contributions to the field is the Touché competition series (Bondarenko et al., 2021, 2022b, 2023), organized as part of the Conference and Labs of the Evaluation Forum (CLEF). It focuses on argument retrieval and comparative argumentation, providing a platform for researchers to develop systems capable of retrieving and ranking arguments on diverse topics, including those requiring comparative reasoning.

Schildwächter et al. (2019) investigate methods for answering comparative questions beyond traditional search results, and present CAM — Comparative Argumentative Machine, a specialized system that can handle the nuances of comparative queries. Chekalina et al. (2021) develop a similar system for answering comparative questions, highlighting the importance of handling predicates and aspects in comparisons. Inspired by CAM, Maslova et al. (2023) develop a comparative question system for Russian, while Nikishina et al. (2024) explore the ability of both CAM and RuCAM to process comparative questions in both languages, addressing the challenge of language diversity in user queries.

Regarding Stance Detection task, Kang et al. (2023) explore how LLMs can classify the stance of comparative sentences. By leveraging the vast knowledge and contextual understanding of LLMs, their approach improves the accuracy of preference predictions derived from natural language inputs.

As for answer generation, comparative opinion summarization is a closely related task. Iso et al. (2022) present a method for generating summaries that encapsulate comparative opinions from multiple sources. Their approach focuses on collaborative decoding to produce summaries that highlight key differences and similarities between entities. This work aligns with our answer generation task, as both aim to distill essential comparative information into concise summaries, however, their dataset tackles summaries for each object separately.

Comparative Question Identification			
Dataset	Total	Comp	Non-Comp
Webis 2020	14100	1431	13569
Webis 2022	9876	4938	4938
Beloucif et al. (2022)	796	387	409
Mintaka	20000	2000	18000
CompUGE	37684	7565	30119

Object and Aspect Identification	
Dataset	Total
Beloucif et al. (2022)	2332
Webis-2022	3530
Chekalina et al. (2021)	3004
CompUGE	5862

Stance Classification					
Dataset	Total	Better	Worse	Neutral	None
CompSent-19	7199	1,364	593	-	5242
Webis-2022	950	69	287	324	276
Webis-2022*	144	14	46	-	84
CompUGE	7343	1378	639	-	5326

Table 1: Datasets statistics for each task. Asterisk (*) stands for the dataset after filtration of unavailable sentences with non-disclosure agreements.

3 Tasks and Datasets

Comparative Question Answering involves several interconnected tasks, each requiring specific datasets for training and evaluation. In this section, we delve deeper into the datasets associated with the primary tasks: Comparative Question Identification (CQI), Object and Aspect Identification (OAI), and Stance Classification (SC). We highlight the internal structures of these datasets, the differences among them, and the challenges faced in merging them into a unified benchmark. The statistics for each dataset is presented in Table 1.

3.1 Comparative Question Identification

Comparative Question Identification (CQI) is a binary classification task aiming to determine whether a given question is comparative or not. Figure 2 presents examples of comparative and non-comparative questions. Existing datasets for CQI include *Webis 2020* (Bondarenko et al., 2020), *Webis 2022* (Bondarenko et al., 2022a), *Beloucif*

[3]https://huggingface.co/spaces/uhhlt/CompUGE-Bench

[4]https://youtu.be/rnf6HW1Y7mc

[5]https://github.com/uhh-lt/compuge

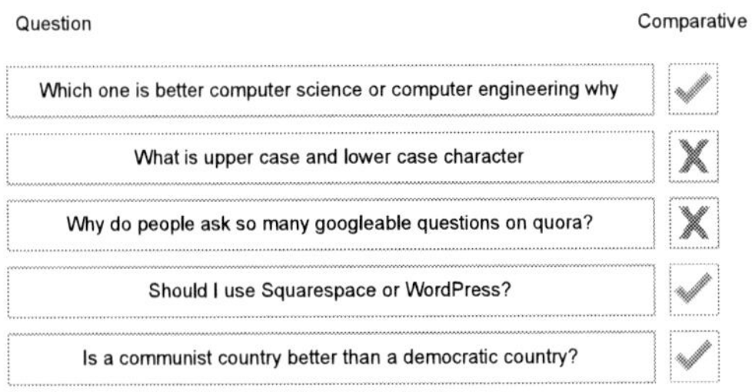

Figure 2: Examples of comparative and non-comparative questions.

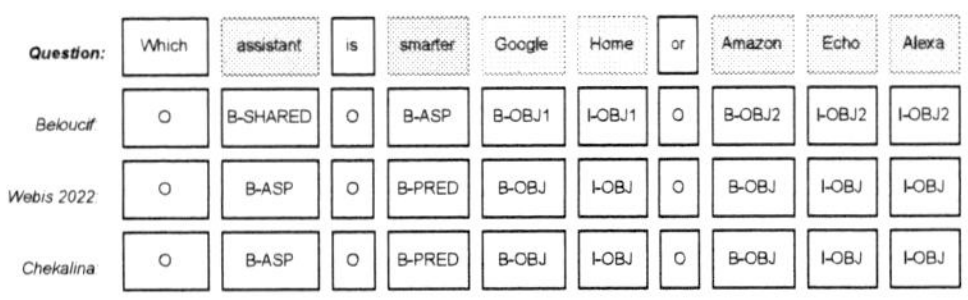

Figure 3: Example of Object and Aspect Identification annotation schemata for different datasets.

Dataset (Beloucif et al., 2022), *Mintaka* (Sen et al., 2022). We describe them in the next paragraphs.

Webis 2020 (Bondarenko et al., 2020): This dataset has significant class imbalance which poses challenges for model training, often requiring techniques like resampling or class weighting to address the skewed distribution. The questions are primarily sourced from web search queries and are short and colloquial. They often lack context and may contain misspellings or abbreviations, reflecting real-world user queries.

Webis 2022 (Bondarenko et al., 2022a): Unlike Webis 2020, the questions in Webis 2022 are more diverse and include additional annotations, such as the objects being compared. The balanced class distribution aids in training models without the need for class balancing techniques. However, there is an overlap of approximately 2,700 questions between Webis 2020 and Webis 2022, which can lead to data leakage if not properly managed.

Beloucif Dataset (Beloucif et al., 2022): Notably, only the test set is publicly available; the training set is not accessible, which complicates direct comparisons with models trained on this dataset. The questions in the Beloucif dataset are carefully curated and may include more complex linguistic structures, making them potentially more challenging for models trained on other datasets.

Mintaka (Sen et al., 2022): The questions are labeled with their respective types and include additional metadata such as language, difficulty level, and domain. Unlike the other datasets, Mintaka is artificially created and designed to cover a wide range of question types. The comparative questions may follow a specific template or structure, which might differ from the more naturally occurring questions in the Webis datasets.

Merging these datasets into a unified benchmark for CQI is non-trivial due to the following factors: class imbalance of Webis 2020 dataset; the overlap of around 2,700 questions between Webis 2020 and Webis 2022; different criteria for what constitutes a comparative question (e.g. Webis 2022 classifies sentence like *"what was highest temperature in nigeria ever"* as comparative); style and complexity of the questions (e.g. Mintaka's artificially created questions are much easier to identify).

3.2 Object and Aspect Identification

Object and Aspect Identification (OAI) is a sequence labelling task focused on identifying the objects and aspects (attributes or features) being compared in a question or sentence. Figure 3 illustrates an example of OAI including different annotation schemata that we also describe below.

Beloucif Dataset (Beloucif et al., 2022) introduces four labels for tokens: *OBJECT-1*, *OBJECT-2 ASPECT*, and *SHARED*. The *SHARED* label is used for tokens that are common to both objects being compared. The annotations are in the BIO (Begin-Inside-Outside) format, sentences are tokenized, and each token is assigned a label.

Webis 2022 (Bondarenko et al., 2022a) uses three entity types: *OBJECT*, *ASPECT*, and *PREDICATE*. The *PREDICATE* label represents comparative predicates or verbs that express the comparison. The annotations may not be compatible with the labels used in Beloucif et al. (2022) due to the different roles assigned to tokens.

Chekalina 2021 (Chekalina et al., 2021) focuses on comparative sentences rather than questions, with annotations for *OBJECT*, *ASPECT*, and *PREDICATE* in BIO-format. It contains sentences from comparative texts, and the annotations include longer texts and more complex linguistic structures.

The main challenge in merging these datasets for OAI is the difference in annotation schemata. The use of *SHARED*, *OBJECT-1* and *OBJECT-2* in the Beloucif dataset versus *PREDICATE* and *OBJECT*

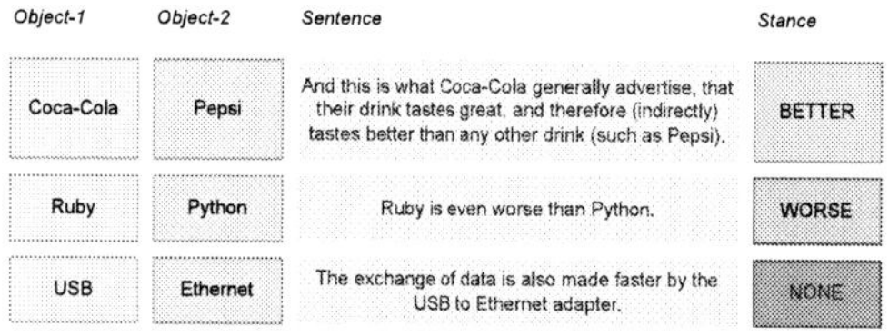

Figure 4: Examples of Stance Classification labels.

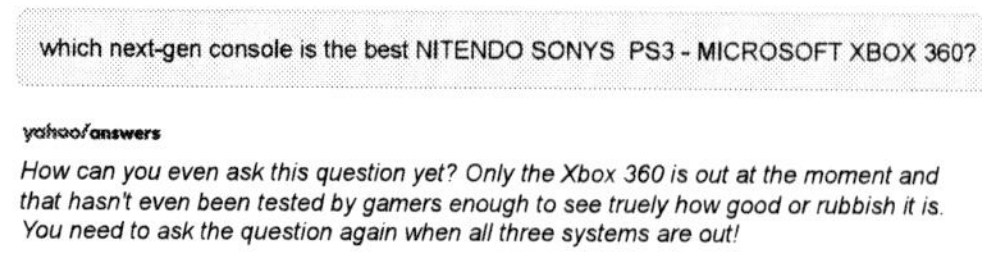

Figure 5: Example of a comparative answer from Chekalina et al. (2021).

in Webis 2022 and Chekalina 2021 creates inconsistency in labels. Another problem is the input type: Beloucif and Webis 2022 focus on questions, while Chekalina 2021 includes sentences from comparative texts. The difference between questions and sentences affects the language structure and the way entities are expressed. Finally, the tokenization differences across datasets can complicate the merging process during the post-processing stage.

3.3 Stance Classification

Stance classification involves determining whether one object is better, worse, or neutral compared to the other in a sentence. Figure 4 provides an example for each label type.

CompSent-19 (Panchenko et al., 2019): contains sentences with *better*, *worse*, or *neutral* labels for each sentence. The dataset focuses on comparative sentences extracted from web, and the objects are explicitly identified as separate columns.

Webis 2022 (Bondarenko et al., 2022a): introduces an additional class, making it a four-class classification problem (*better*, *worse*, *neutral*, *none*). The sentences in this dataset may be longer and more complex, and 806 entries had to be discarded due to non-disclosure agreements or excessive length, resulting in 144 sentences left.

The main challenges in merging these datasets are the inconsistent labels and a large difference between sentence lengths (97 tokens for CompSent-19 and 1624 tokens for Webis 2022).

3.4 Answer Generation

Answer Generation is the task of generating a concise summary or answer that compares two objects based on a set of comparative sentences. Figure 5 illustrates this task with the example from (Chekalina et al., 2021), which includes a human-written answer from Yahoo!Answers[6]. As we have only one dataset for this task, merging datasets is not applicable.

[6]https://en.wikipedia.org/wiki/Yahoo_Answers

4 CompUGE Datasets Creation

For each task, existing datasets are brought into a unified structure. The datasets are merged using all possible permutations to create comprehensive training sets. Then, we then train four Transformer Encoder models on each dataset combination: **DistilBERT-base-uncased fine-tuned on English** (Sanh et al., 2019), **DistilBERT-base-uncased** (Sanh et al., 2019), **RoBERTa-base** (Liu et al., 2019), **DeBERTa-base** (He et al., 2020). These models were chosen for their balance of performance and computational efficiency in (Shallouf et al., 2024). They also represent a variety of Encoder architectures and sizes, which is beneficial for assessing model robustness across tasks.

Each model is then tested on every test set for that task. All model predictions alongside key metrics (accuracy, precision, recall, F1-score) are stored. We averaged the metrics between all four models. Finally, we analyzed the resulting metrics and prediction files alongside the structures of the datasets to select the best dataset combinations.

4.1 Comparative Question Identification

We do seven permutations for training (three individual datasets, three pairwise merges, and one merge of all datasets) and tested on all four datasets (including Beloucif's test set).

Results Table 2 shows the averaged accuracy across models when trained on different dataset combinations and tested on each dataset. When testing on Beloucif et al. (2022), the best performance is achieved by training on all datasets combined, yielding an average accuracy of 0.8, and it is clearly visible that Beloucif et al. (2022) is the most challenging one. Table 3 provides detailed metrics for models tested on this dataset. Based on these results, we decide to merge Mintaka, Webis 2020, and Webis 2022 for training and use Beloucif for testing in the benchmark.

Training Data	Beloucif	Mintaka	Webis 20	Webis 22
All Datasets	0.80	0.99	0.97	0.97
Mintaka	0.63	0.99	0.89	0.68
Mintaka + Webis 20	0.70	0.99	0.97	0.93
Mintaka + Webis 22	0.74	0.99	0.94	0.97
Webis 20	0.72	0.75	0.97	0.88
Webis 20 + Webis 22	0.74	0.97	0.97	0.98
Webis 22	0.72	0.96	0.94	0.97

Table 2: Averaged accuracy across models for CQI.

Training Data	Accuracy	Precision	Recall	F1-Score
All Datasets	0.80	0.85	0.80	0.79
Mintaka	0.63	0.66	0.63	0.60
Mintaka + Webis 20	0.70	0.73	0.70	0.68
Mintaka + Webis 22	0.74	0.82	0.74	0.73
Webis 20	0.72	0.74	0.72	0.71
Webis 20 + Webis 22	0.74	0.82	0.74	0.73
Webis 22	0.72	0.81	0.72	0.70

Table 3: Averaged metrics for models tested on Beloucif et al. (2022).

4.2 Object and Aspect Identification

We conduct experiments with 7 dataset combinations for training and test on all three datasets.

Results Table 4 presents the averaged F1-scores across models when trained on different dataset combinations and tested on each dataset. When excluding Chekalina et al. (2021) from training and testing, we observe better alignment between Webis 2022 and Beloucif datasets. Table 6 in Appendix A shows the averaged F1-scores without training or testing on Chekalina et al. (2021) alone. Based on these observations, we decide to merge the processed version of Webis 2022 with Beloucif and exclude Chekalina 2021 from the main OAI benchmark. The processed version of Webis 2022 relabels all *PREDICATE* entities to *ASPECT*, and in Beloucif, we removed sentences containing the *SHARED* label.

4.3 Stance Classification

For this task, we use two datasets (CompSent-19 and the processed version of Webis 2022) and one merged dataset, resulting in three training permutations. The Webis 2022 dataset required significant preprocessing: entries with non-disclosure agreements were removed, extremely long sentences were discarded, and the four classes were reduced to three by merging *NO-STANCE* and *NEUTRAL* into *NEUTRAL* resulting in 144 sentences.

Results Table 5 shows the averaged F1-scores across models when trained on different dataset combinations and tested on each dataset. Training on the merged dataset improved performance on

Training Data	All	Beloucif	Webis	Chekalina
All Datasets	0.81	0.76	0.82	0.83
Chekalina + Webis	0.75	0.59	0.80	0.84
Webis + Beloucif	0.68	0.76	0.82	0.46
Chekalina + Beloucif	0.65	0.75	0.36	0.84
Webis	0.63	0.61	0.81	0.47
Beloucif	0.51	0.76	0.35	0.45
Chekalina	0.49	0.30	0.21	0.84

Table 4: Averaged F1-scores across models for OAI.

Training Data	CompSent-19	Webis 2022
All Datasets	0.89	0.53
CompSent-19	0.89	0.42
Webis 2022	0.42	0.36

Table 5: Averaged F1-scores for Stance Classification.

Webis 2022, increasing the F1-score from 0.42 to 0.53. However, the performance on CompSent-19 remained high regardless of whether Webis 2022 was included in training. Based on these results, we merge CompSent-19 with the processed version of Webis 2022 for the benchmark.

5 System Design and Architecture

The CompUGE benchmark system is designed with a modular architecture, consisting of three main components.

PostgreSQL Database serves as the central repository for storing datasets, model submissions, evaluation results, and leaderboards. It ensures data integrity and supports concurrent access by multiple users.

FastAPI Backend Server acts as the intermediary between the frontend and the database. It handles API requests from the frontend, processes data, runs evaluation scripts, and communicates with the database. The backend is built using FastAPI[7], a modern, high-performance web framework for building APIs with Python.

Angular Frontend provides an interactive web interface for users to interact with the benchmark. Users can explore available tasks and datasets, submit their model results for evaluation, and view leaderboards. The frontend is developed using Angular[8], a popular web application framework.

Each component is containerized using Docker for ease of deployment and scalability. The database and backend server are deployed on an

[7] `https://fastapi.tiangolo.com`
[8] `https://angular.io`

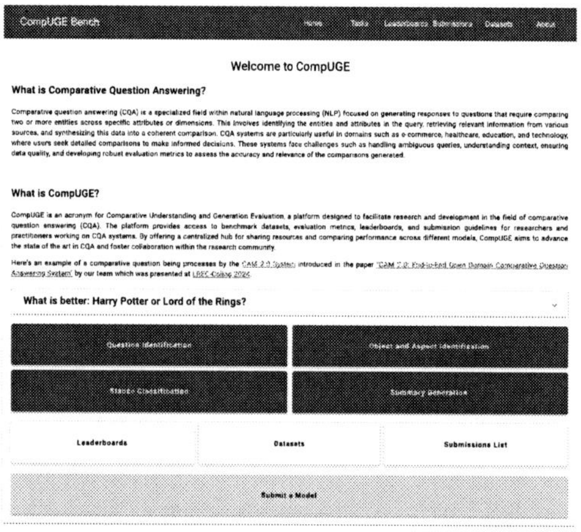

Figure 6: CompUGE Benchmark Start Page.

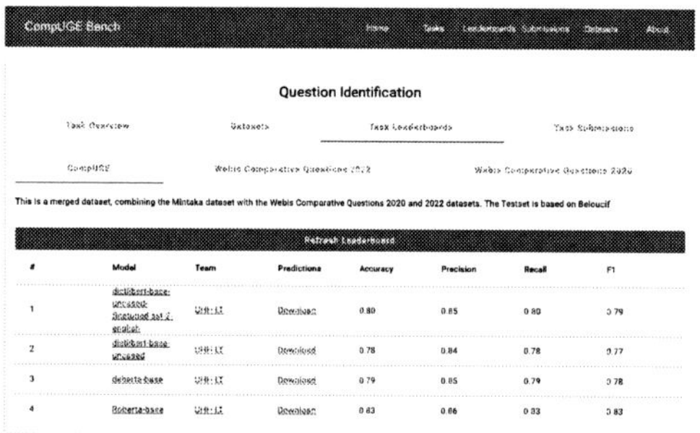

Figure 7: Example of the leaderboard display for the CQI task.

internal server, ensuring data security and compliance with institutional policies. The frontend is hosted on HuggingFace Spaces[9], making the benchmark easily accessible to the research community.

5.1 Modular Design

The system's modular design allows for easy expansion and maintenance. Key features include:

- **Expandable List of Tasks**: More Comparative QA tasks can be added to the system without affecting existing functionalities.
- **Datasets Association**: Each task can have multiple associated datasets, all adhering to the same data format.
- **Leaderboards**: For each task and dataset combination, there is a corresponding leaderboard that tracks model performances using standardized metrics.

[9]https://huggingface.co/spaces

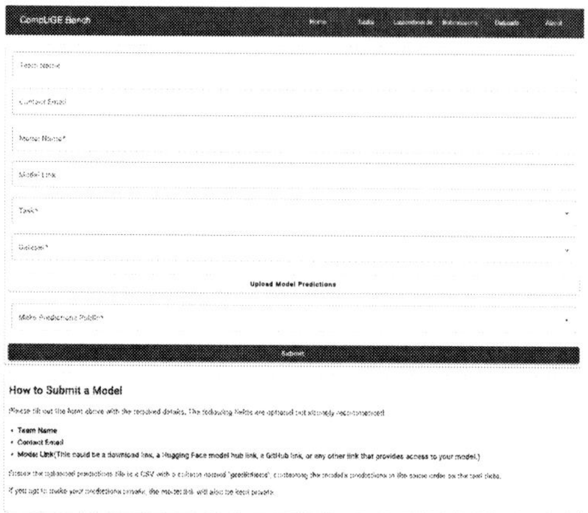

Figure 8: New Submission interface, with a simple guide on how to submit a model to CompUGE

All datasets for a given task share the same data format, and their leaderboards use consistent evaluation metrics. This design choice simplifies the process for researchers to benchmark their models across different datasets and tasks. Figure 6 demonstrates the start page of the benchmark, while 7 showcases a leaderboard for one of the tasks.

The submission page in Figure 8 allows users to submit the results of their models for evaluation. The form requires users to provide key details: team, contact email, model name, etc. The model link could point to a download link, a Hugging Face model hub, a GitHub repository, or any other online location that provides access to the model. The model's predictions are updated as a CSV file, ensuring the predictions are in the same order as the test data and that the file contains a column named "predictions". Users are also asked whether they want to make their predictions public. If users choose to keep their predictions private, the model link will also be kept confidential. After filling in the necessary details, the submission can be finalized by clicking the Submit button. More screenshots can be seen in Appendix B.

6 Conclusion

CompUGE provides a structured and comprehensive benchmark for evaluating comparative question answering systems. By integrating datasets from multiple sources and evaluating models across distinct sub-tasks, it offers a robust platform for future research. The benchmark is available on Hugging Face Spaces, and its source code is open-sourced under the MIT License.

Limitations

The main limitations of the paper are as follows:

- All our experiments with different Comparative Question Answering tasks are done using Encoder Transformer models. We do not run experiments using LLMs, as more time- and resource-consuming models. Our main idea was to provide baselines and select the best datasets for the benchmark, not to test all existing models. However, we leave testing Generative Transformer models for future work.
- Due to limited resources available, our benchmark allows only result file upload to the server. This may lead to unfair and non-reproducible results. We try to approach it by asking the user to provide the path or the name of the used model, leaving server model evaluation for future work.

Ethical Statement

This work was conducted in compliance with ethical standards in AI research. All datasets used in the study are publicly available, and no private data was utilized. The benchmark is designed to support reproducible research and transparent model evaluation.

References

Meriem Beloucif, Seid Muhie Yimam, Sarah Stahlhacke, and Chris Biemann. 2022. Classification and identification of elements in comparative questions. In *Proceedings of the 13th International Conference on Language Resources and Evaluation (LREC 2022)*, pages 3771–3779.

Alexander Bondarenko, Yamen Ajjour, Vivien Dittmar, Niklas Homann, Pavel Braslavski, and Matthias Hagen. 2022a. Towards understanding and answering comparative questions. In *Proceedings of the Fifteenth ACM International Conference on Web Search and Data Mining (WSDM 2022)*, pages 66–74.

Alexander Bondarenko, Pavel Braslavski, Michael Völske, Robin Aly, Maik Fröbe, Alexander Panchenko, Chris Biemann, Benno Stein, and Matthias Hagen. 2020. Comparative web search questions. In *Proceedings of the 13th International Conference on Web Search and Data Mining (WSDM 2020)*, pages 52 60.

Alexander Bondarenko, Maik Fröbe, Johannes Kiesel, Ferdinand Schlatt, Valentin Barriere, Brian Ravenet, Léo Hemamou, Simon Luck, Jan Heinrich Reimer, Benno Stein, Martin Potthast, and Matthias Hagen. 2023. Overview of Touché 2023: Argument and Causal Retrieval. In *Experimental IR Meets Multilinguality, Multimodality, and Interaction. 14th International Conference of the CLEF Association (CLEF 2023)*, volume 14163 of *Lecture Notes in Computer Science*, pages 507–530, Berlin Heidelberg New York. Springer.

Alexander Bondarenko, Maik Fröbe, Johannes Kiesel, Shahbaz Syed, Timon Gurcke, Meriem Beloucif, Alexander Panchenko, Chris Biemann, Benno Stein, Henning Wachsmuth, Martin Potthast, and Matthias Hagen. 2022b. Overview of Touché 2022: Argument Retrieval. In *Experimental IR Meets Multilinguality, Multimodality, and Interaction. 13th International Conference of the CLEF Association (CLEF 2022)*, volume 13390 of *Lecture Notes in Computer Science*, Berlin Heidelberg New York. Springer.

Alexander Bondarenko, Lukas Gienapp, Maik Fröbe, Meriem Beloucif, Yamen Ajjour, Alexander Panchenko, Chris Biemann, Benno Stein, Henning Wachsmuth, Martin Potthast, and Matthias Hagen. 2021. Overview of Touché 2021: Argument Retrieval. In *Experimental IR Meets Multilinguality, Multimodality, and Interaction. 12th International Conference of the CLEF Association (CLEF 2021)*, volume 12880 of *Lecture Notes in Computer Science*, pages 450–467, Berlin Heidelberg New York. Springer.

Valeriya Chekalina, Alexander Bondarenko, Chris Biemann, Meriem Beloucif, Varvara Logacheva, and Alexander Panchenko. 2021. Which is better for deep learning: Python or matlab? answering comparative questions in natural language. In *Proceedings of the 16th Conference of the European Chapter of the Association for Computational Linguistics: System Demonstrations (EACL 2021)*, pages 302–311.

Pengcheng He, Xiaodong Liu, Jianfeng Gao, and Weizhu Chen. 2020. Deberta: Decoding-enhanced bert with disentangled attention. *arXiv preprint arXiv:2006.03654*.

Hayate Iso, Xiaolan Wang, Stefanos Angelidis, and Yoshihiko Suhara. 2022. Comparative opinion summarization via collaborative decoding. In *Findings of the Association for Computational Linguistics: ACL 2022*, pages 3307–3324, Dublin, Ireland. Association for Computational Linguistics.

Inwon Kang, Sikai Ruan, Tyler Ho, Jui-Chien Lin, Farhad Mohsin, Oshani Seneviratne, and Lirong Xia. 2023. Llm-augmented preference learning from natural language. *CoRR*, abs/2310.08523.

Yinhan Liu, Myle Ott, Naman Goyal, Jingfei Du, Mandar Joshi, Danqi Chen, Omer Levy, Mike Lewis, Luke Zettlemoyer, and Veselin Stoyanov. 2019. Roberta: A robustly optimized bert pretraining approach. *arXiv preprint arXiv:1907.11692*.

Maria Maslova, Stefan Rebrikov, Anton Artsishevski, Sebastian Zaczek, Chris Biemann, and Irina Nikishina. 2023. Rucam: Comparative argumentative machine for the russian language. In *AIST*, volume 14486 of *Lecture Notes in Computer Science*, pages 78–91. Springer.

Irina Nikishina, Alexander Bondarenko, Sebastian Zaczek, Onno Lander Haag, Matthias Hagen, and Chris Biemann. 2024. Extending the comparative argumentative machine: Multilingualism and stance detection. In *RATIO*, volume 14638 of *Lecture Notes in Computer Science*, pages 317–334. Springer.

Alexander Panchenko, Alexander Bondarenko, Marc Franzek, Matthias Hagen, and Chris Biemann. 2019. Categorizing comparative sentences. In *Proceedings of the 6th Workshop on Argument Mining (ArgMining 2019)*, pages 136–145.

Victor Sanh, Lysandre Debut, Julien Chaumond, and Thomas Wolf. 2019. Distilbert, a distilled version of bert: smaller, faster, cheaper and lighter. *arXiv preprint arXiv:1910.01108*.

Maike Schildwächter, Alexander Bondarenko, Juliane Zenker, Matthias Hagen, Chris Biemann, and Alexander Panchenko. 2019. Answering comparative questions: Better than ten-blue-links? In *Proceedings of the 2019 Conference on Human Information Interaction and Retrieval*, pages 361–365.

Parth Sen, Alham Fikri Aji, and Amir Saffari. 2022. Mintaka: A complex, natural, and multilingual dataset for end-to-end question answering. In *Proceedings of the 29th International Conference on Computational Linguistics (COLING 2022)*, pages 1604–1619.

Ahmad Shallouf, Irina Nikishina, and Chris Biemann. 2024. Cam 2.0: End-to-end open domain comparative question answering system. In *Proceedings of the 2024 Joint International Conference on Computational Linguistics, Language Resources and Evaluation (LREC-COLING 2024)*.

A Additional Results

Training Data	Tested on	Overall	Object	Aspect
Webis	Webis	0.84	0.82	0.86
All Datasets	Webis	0.84	0.83	0.85
Webis + Beloucif	Webis	0.84	0.82	0.86
Webis + Beloucif	Beloucif	0.79	0.84	0.60
All Datasets	Beloucif	0.78	0.85	0.55
Beloucif	Beloucif	0.77	0.83	0.53

Table 6: Averaged F1-scores for Webis and Beloucif combinations as well as all datasets.

Training Data	Overall	Object	Aspect
Chekalina	0.86	0.92	0.79
Chekalina + Webis	0.86	0.91	0.79
Chekalina + Beloucif	0.86	0.91	0.80
All Datasets	0.85	0.89	0.80
Webis	0.50	0.45	0.56
Webis + Beloucif	0.46	0.41	0.53
Beloucif	0.40	0.49	0.25

Table 7: Averaged F1-scores tested on Chekalina et al. (2021).

B CompUGE Benchmark Details

We include several screenshots of the CompUGE benchmark system to illustrate its user interface and functionalities. Figures 9 to 11 showcase different parts of the system.

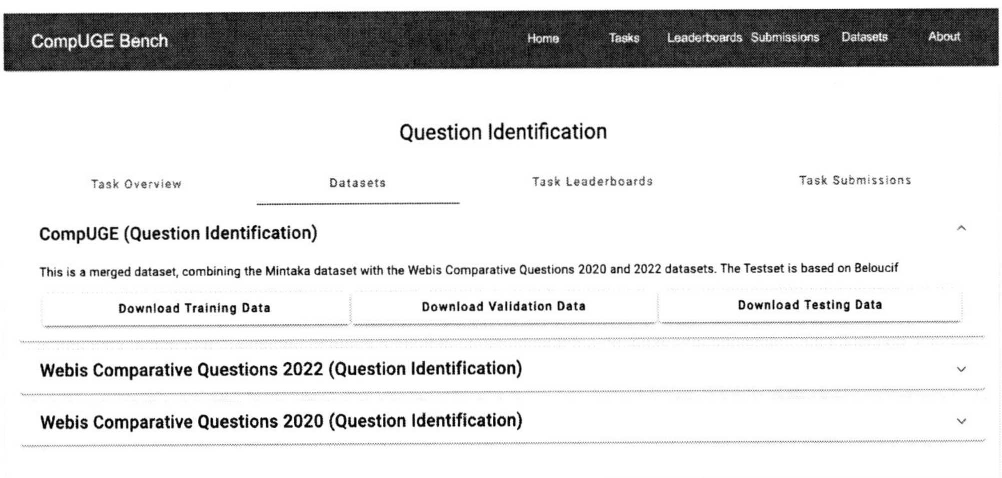

Figure 9: The datasets tab in a Task Page (Question Identification), provides drop down for each dataset, containing description and download buttons for splits

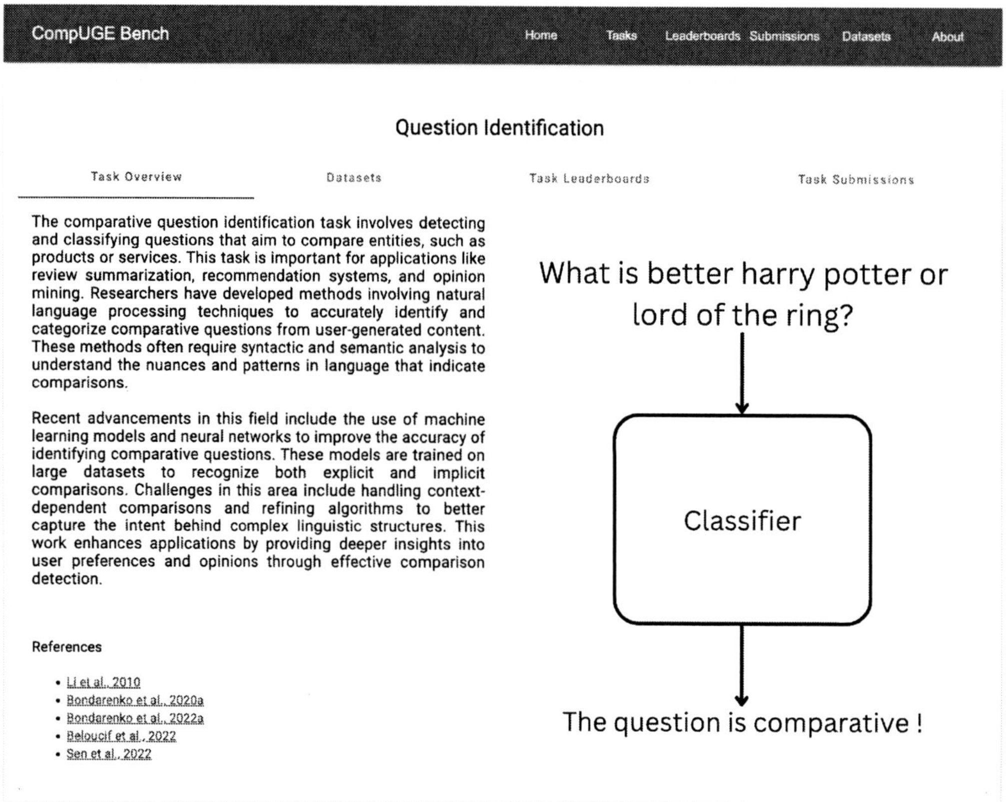

Figure 10: Task Page, which provides access to an overview of the task, Datasets, Task specific leaderboards and Task specific Submissions

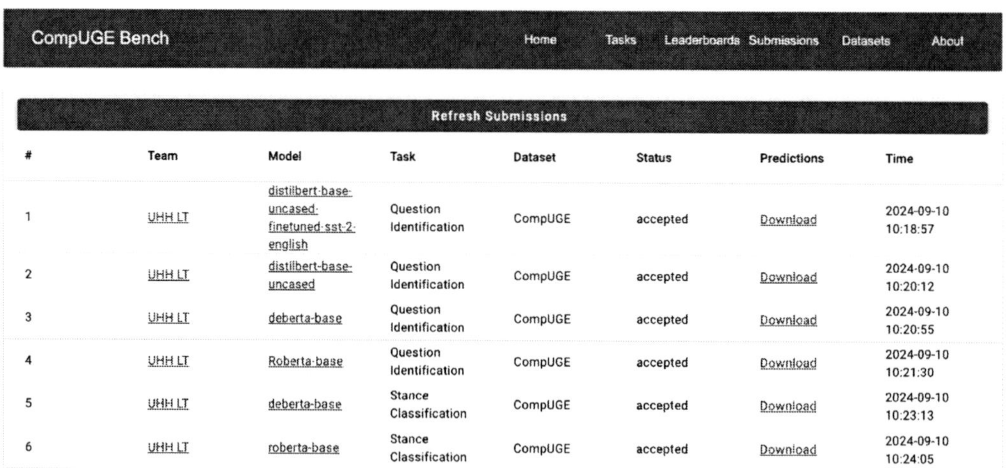

#	Team	Model	Task	Dataset	Status	Predictions	Time
1	UHH LT	distilbert-base-uncased-finetuned-sst-2-english	Question Identification	CompUGE	accepted	Download	2024-09-10 10:18:57
2	UHH LT	distilbert-base-uncased	Question Identification	CompUGE	accepted	Download	2024-09-10 10:20:12
3	UHH LT	deberta-base	Question Identification	CompUGE	accepted	Download	2024-09-10 10:20:55
4	UHH LT	Roberta-base	Question Identification	CompUGE	accepted	Download	2024-09-10 10:21:30
5	UHH LT	deberta-base	Stance Classification	CompUGE	accepted	Download	2024-09-10 10:23:13
6	UHH LT	roberta-base	Stance Classification	CompUGE	accepted	Download	2024-09-10 10:24:05

Figure 11: Overall Submissions list, which provides information on weather a submission was accepted, and for public submissions gives access to submitted predictions, contact email of submitter and model link

Autonomous Machine Learning-Based Peer Reviewer Selection System

Nurmukhammed Aitymbetov, Dimitrios Zorbas
Nazarbayev University, School of Engineering & Digital Sciences, Astana, Kazakhstan
E-mail: {firstname.lastname}@nu.edu.kz

Abstract

The peer review process is essential for academic research, yet it faces challenges such as inefficiencies, biases, and limited access to qualified reviewers. This paper introduces an autonomous peer reviewer selection system that employs the Natural Language Processing (NLP) model to match submitted papers with expert reviewers independently of traditional journals and conferences. Our model performs competitively in comparison with the transformer-based state-of-the-art models while being 10 times faster at inference and 7 times smaller, which makes our platform highly scalable. Additionally, with our paper-reviewer matching model being trained on scientific papers from various academic fields, our system allows scholars from different backgrounds to benefit from this automation.

1 Introduction

Peer review is a major component of the academic publishing process that ensures the integrity and quality of scholarly research. Traditionally, peer review has been a manual and often cumbersome process, hindered by prolonged turnaround times. With the growing volume of paper submissions, manual reviewer selection has become impractical, leading to the development of automated paper-reviewer matching algorithms. However, even with these advancements, authors still face challenges. They are often required to adhere to strict deadlines and wait extended periods for their reviews, leaving them with limited time to respond to peer reviewers' feedback (Huisman and Smits, 2017). This can impede the feedback loop and limit authors' opportunities to improve their work. Furthermore, submitting to specific journals or conferences may introduce conflicts of interest and biases in feedback, as the process can be manipulated to favor or hinder certain submissions (Adler and Stayer, 2017; da Silva et al., 2019).

In response to these issues, we introduce an autonomous peer reviewer selection system designed to function independently of the traditional academic publishing venues, such as conferences and journals. It could be used to provide a flexible and efficient alternative for researchers seeking preliminary review of their papers. This system facilitates rapid reviewer assignment, enabling researchers to receive timely feedback. Importantly, it operates continuously, allowing users to submit their papers at any time without being constrained by traditional deadlines. By decoupling the peer review process from the traditional venues, the platform also aims to minimize the potential for conflicts of interest and biases, as reviewers are less likely to be influenced by the stakes of formal decision-making. The proposed platform aims to democratize and accelerate the peer review process, offering researchers the opportunity to improve their work before formal submission to journals or conferences. By facilitating quick and high-quality peer reviewer assignments from a global pool of experts, the system has the potential to enhance the overall quality of academic publications. Its scalability and efficiency also make it a promising solution for the future, with the capability to support a large database of authors and reviewers.

The core innovation of the system lies in its custom paper-reviewer matching model, which is significantly smaller and faster than existing transformer-based models while maintaining competitive performance. This efficiency allows the system to scale effectively, accommodating the needs of a potentially large number of users without compromising the quality of the reviewer matches. Moreover, unlike many automated matching systems that are typically developed and fine-tuned for specific fields such as computer science or machine learning, the proposed model is trained on a diverse set of academic disciplines. This makes the platform accessible to scholars from a wide range

Proceedings of the 31st International Conference on Computational Linguistics: System Demonstrations, pages 199–207
January 19–24, 2025. ©2025 Association for Computational Linguistics

of fields, ensuring that they can also benefit from rapid and high-quality reviewer assignments.

Overall, the contributions of this work are summarized as follows:

- We develop and implement an open-source prototype of a peer review system that operates independently of traditional journals and conferences, featuring continuous paper submission and automated reviewer assignment[1].

- We introduce an efficient GRU-based paper-reviewer matching model that performs comparably to existing transformer-based approaches, while being significantly smaller and faster at inference.

- We show that classification-based pre-training using subject-area classification can be effective for learning paper representation vectors useful for paper-reviewer matching task. The learned representation vectors capture meaningful topic information and measure paper-reviewer affinity surprisingly well.

The rest of the paper is organized as follows. Section 2 provides an overview of the related research on the paper-reviewer matching problem and the current systems used in practice. Section 3 delves deeper into the technical description of the proposed system, including the details of our paper-reviewer matching model. Section 4 describes the experimental setup used to evaluate the performance of our paper-reviewer matching system. Section 5 concludes the paper by summarizing key findings and offering suggestions for further improvements. Section 6 discusses some limitations of the proposed system.

2 Related Research

The use of automatic paper-reviewer matching systems is not a new trend in the academic world and have been studied for almost a decade (Li and Watanabe, 2013). Modern paper-reviewer assignment systems mainly consist of three components: (1) expertise modeling system, (2) reviewer assignment system and (3) conflict-of-interests (COI) detection system. The first component involves the development of models that accurately represent whether the reviewer has the required topical expertise to review the submitted paper. The second component involves actually assigning reviewers to papers based on the expertise modeling results. The third component involves detecting any relationship reviewers and authors may have and addressing them in order to ensure fair review.

2.1 Expertise modeling

Expertise modeling is essential for aligning papers with reviewers who possess relevant knowledge. Initial approaches in this area relied on keyword matching (Conry et al., 2009) and simple word-based techniques such as TF-IDF to measure similarity between paper content and reviewers' past publications (Yarowsky and Florian, 1999; Hettich and Pazzani, 2006). More advanced approaches introduced topic modeling methods such as Latent Dirichlet Allocation (LDA), which generates topic distributions for both papers and reviewers to calculate a more abstract similarity (Mimno and McCallum, 2007). These models have been widely adopted in conference management systems such as the Toronto Paper Matching System (TPMS) (Charlin and Zemel, 2013) and IEEE INFOCOM Reviewer Assignment System (Li and Hou, 2016).

A more recent approach to expert modeling is based on neural network models, which represent papers and reviewers as dense vectors (document embeddings). These models capture deeper semantic features, making them highly effective for paper-reviewer matching. In particular, scientific paper representation models, such as SciBERT (Beltagy et al., 2019), SPECTER (Cohan et al., 2020), and SciNCL (Ostendorff et al., 2022), have become prominent in the field, and they have been adopted by OpenReview, a platform widely used in major conferences such as NeurIPS and ICLR (OpenReview, 2024). These models represent both papers and reviewers as vector embeddings, allowing for the computation of similarity between them. The similarity score reflects the reviewer's expertise relative to the paper's topic, which can be used to assign the best-suited reviewers. Our system adopts this document embedding approach for representing papers and reviewers' profiles, leveraging these embeddings to compute expertise scores.

2.2 Reviewer assignment

In traditional systems, reviewer assignment is often handled via matching-based approaches, where all papers and reviewers are considered simulta-

[1]The source code and a video demonstration is found in this link: https://github.com/nurmybtw/autonomous-peer-review-platform

neously, and the assignment is determined using optimization algorithms such as Integer Linear Programming or Mixed Integer Programming (Charlin and Zemel, 2013; Leyton-Brown et al., 2022). This optimization is primarily used in batch-processing scenarios, such as conferences that collect all submissions before a deadline and then process them in bulk, matching papers to a set of reviewers. In contrast, our system follows a retrieval-based approach, where papers are served on a rolling basis and assigned to reviewers individually. As an online system, our platform continuously matches papers with the best available reviewers based on their expertise.

2.3 COI detection

Most of the traditional peer review systems also implement COI detection system to minimize the biases (Tang et al., 2010; Wu et al., 2018; Leyton-Brown et al., 2022). However, our system does not incorporate COI detection, as its primary goal is to provide independent feedback rather than formal acceptance into a journal or conference. We prioritize reviewer expertise over potential conflicts, ensuring that authors receive high-quality feedback without being constrained by COI limitations.

3 Proposed System

In this section, we present our system and the paper-reviewer matching model within it. First, we describe how the system operates on a high-level. Then, we describe core technical innovation: efficient paper-reviewer matching model based on bidirectional Gated Recurrent Unit (GRU) and classification-based pre-training.

3.1 System Overview

The core of the platform is a two-part system that analyzes submitted paper abstracts to find the best matching reviewers. It is important to note that all the components within this system focus only on the papers' content and do not consider any identifying information related to the author or potential reviewer. This minimizes biases, while maximizing the quality of matches.

The information flow begins with authors submitting their research papers via the web interface, providing the title and abstract along with the document. As depicted in Figure 1, the proposed system employs a sequential pipeline comprising two interconnected components: topic-based filtering and expertise-based ranking.

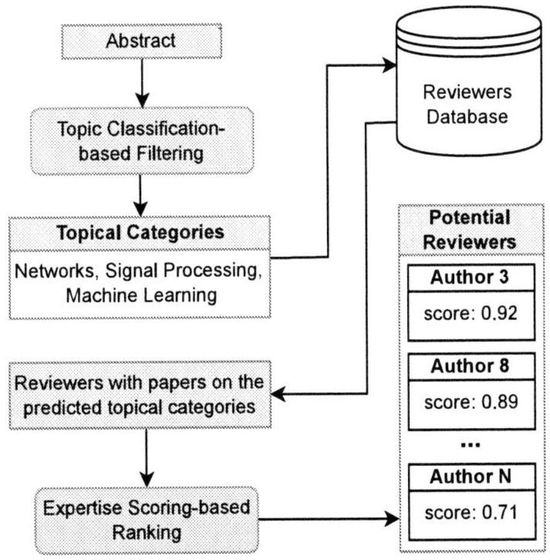

Figure 1: Proposed system flow consisting of two major components: initial filtering based on topic classification and final ranking based on expertise scoring.

The first component of the system involves the classification of the incoming paper abstract into three of the 158 predefined topic domains. After determining the paper topics, only the reviewers who have written a certain amount of papers on those topics are selected for the next step. This greatly reduces the number of reviewers and papers to be analyzed in detail during the expertise scoring process, optimizing the response time of the overall system, as the evaluation of the textual data of possibly thousands of authors is a costly operation. Choosing three categories for each paper abstract reflects the possibility of the paper belonging to multiple topics.

Then, the system transitions to the second stage, where the potential reviewers are assigned expertise scores and ranked accordingly; a higher score represents a closer match between the potential reviewer's expertise and the paper topics. This scoring process is based on cosine similarity, comparing the latent representation of the incoming paper's abstract with candidate reviewers' past publications. This method facilitates fine-grained ranking of reviewers.

The choice of combining topic-based filtering with expertise-based ranking stems from the need to balance efficiency and precision. Topic-based filtering serves as a rapid initial filter, eliminating clearly unqualified reviewers from the pool. Subsequently, expertise-based ranking using the latent representations offers a more detailed and nuanced assessment of each reviewer's expertise, ensuring

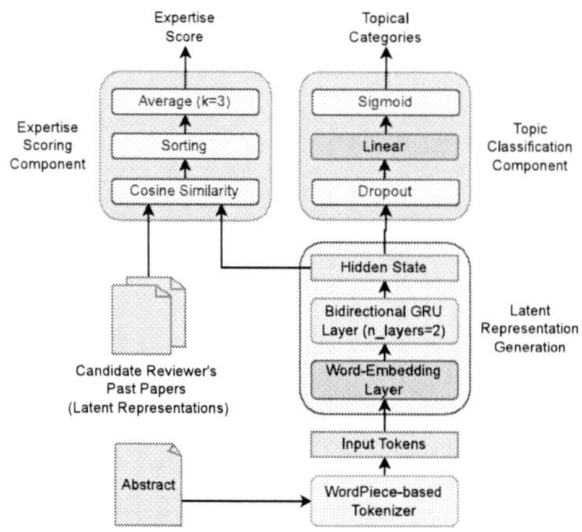

Figure 2: Model Architecture. The model is used for both topic classification and expertise scoring components. The Second GRU layer's hidden state is used as a latent representation vector for papers.

that the final matches are highly relevant.

Finally, after ranking the potential reviewers based on their expertise scores, two of the best available candidates are selected and sent a review request. If the selected reviewer accepts the review request, this reviewer will be officially assigned to the paper for providing feedback. Authors can then utilize this feedback to improve their manuscripts before submitting them to journals or conferences. In case of rejection, a review request is sent to the next available candidate. If the potential reviewer does not respond to the request for a certain amount of time, authors will have the opportunity to initiate the search for a new reviewer via the platform.

3.2 Model

The core of our paper-reviewer matching system is a Gated Recurrent Unit (GRU)-based model that serves a dual purpose: predicting the topical categories of submitted papers and generating latent representations of the abstracts for subsequent expertise scoring (see Figure 2). This dual functionality is achieved using a classification-based pretraining approach that we describe in the next paragraph.

Classification-based pre-training Zhang et al. (2020) interpreted paper-reviewer matching as a multi-label classification task. In their approach, the model was first trained to generate representation vectors of abstracts, which were then used for multi-label classification. The matching was based on the degree of alignment between the predicted labels of the submitted paper and the predicted labels of the reviewer's past papers, demonstrating the effectiveness of classification-based methods for this task. In contrast, our approach first pretrains the GRU model for multi-label classification, then uses the learned representation vectors for matching. Evaluations demonstrate that GRU's hidden state can be surprisingly effective when used as a representation vector of abstracts. The model's ability to generate useful latent representations for paper-reviewer expertise modeling while being trained primarily for classification might be logical and intuitive. When assessing a reviewer's suitability, one naturally examines their research areas. Thus, a model trained to classify topics inherently learns to generate representation vectors that encapsulate these research areas effectively.

Expertise scoring To compute the expertise score, the system first retrieves the latent representations of the abstracts from the most recent papers authored by each reviewer r_i. Let $\mathbf{p}_i^1, \mathbf{p}_i^2, \ldots, \mathbf{p}_i^m$ represent the representation vectors of the m papers authored by r_i, and let s denote the representation vector of the submitted paper. Following Stelmakh et al. (2023), we limit m to the last 10 papers published by each reviewer, as they showed that using more than 10 papers provides minimal additional benefit. The system then computes the cosine similarity $\cos(\mathbf{s}, \mathbf{p}_i^j)$ between the submitted paper's representation vector s and each representation vector $\mathbf{p}_i^j$ of the reviewer's previous papers. Notably, we use only the abstracts of these papers to obtain latent representations, rather than the full text, as Stelmakh et al. (2023) demonstrated that the performance difference between using abstracts and full text is marginal.

For each reviewer r_i, we consider the top three cosine similarity scores, which correspond to the three most related papers the reviewer has authored. The final expertise score E_i for reviewer r_i is computed as the average of these top three scores: $E_i = \frac{1}{3}\sum_{k=1}^{3} \cos(\mathbf{s}, \mathbf{p}_i^k)$. The reason for averaging the top three scores stems from our assumption that reviewers have good expertise for reviewing the submitted paper if they have written at least three related papers. Authors often focus on different topics, and using the top three scores provides a robust measure of a reviewer's expertise. If a reviewer has written fewer than three related papers, their overall score will automatically reduce as a result.

Training The model was trained to classify topics on a subset of the open-source ArXiv dataset from Kaggle (Cornell University, 2020) for 20 epochs with a batch size of 256 using NVIDIA P100 GPU. It contains metadata such as title, abstract, authors, and topical categories for 2.4M academic papers featured in the ArXiv repository. The dataset includes papers spanning 158 categories across 8 academic fields included in ArXiv's official categorical taxonomy. The dataset provides rich categorical labels for each entry, allowing for multi-label classification. For detailed view of these categories, refer to Appendix A.

Dataset pre-processing The ArXiv dataset (Cornell University, 2020) originally contained approximately 2.4 million entries with varying numbers of categories assigned to each entry. Most entries had only one label, followed by those with two and three labels. Instances with more than three labels were much less common. For the purpose of training the model, only multi-label entries with two or three categories were used, as these provide richer context for expertise scoring. This selection process was designed to focus on multi-label instances because papers can naturally belong to multiple fields, offering more informative training data. To address class imbalance issue in the dataset, a cap of 15,000 entries per category was applied, resulting in a balanced subset of 840K entries, 710K of which were used for training. The first category assigned to each paper was used for random stratified splitting into training and test sets; however, all assigned categories were used during training.

Tokenization A custom WordPiece-based tokenizer (Wu et al., 2016) was trained on the ArXiv dataset's training set, resulting in a vocabulary of 50,000 tokens. The tokenizer was implemented using the HuggingFace's BertTokenizer class. The model was configured to accept inputs with a maximum length of 256 tokens, with both padding and truncation applied.

4 Evaluation & Discussion of the results

In this section, we present the evaluation details of our paper-reviewer matching model. First, we start off by defining the experimental settings in terms of the metrics and datasets used in our evaluation. Then, we briefly describe the baseline and state-of-the-art models used for comparison. Finally, we present the results and discuss certain implications.

4.1 Evaluation Datasets

For evaluating topic classification performance, we employed the test set from the previously mentioned arXiv dataset (Cornell University, 2020). Refer to Section 3 for dataset details.

For expertise scoring, we utilized the dataset presented by Stelmakh et al. (2023). OpenReview platform uses this dataset to evaluate its models (OpenReview, 2024), making it an ideal fit for our tests. It contains 477 self-reported expertise scores from 58 researchers evaluating papers they have read recently. Each researcher rated their expertise for a given paper on a scale from 1.0 (not qualified) to 5.0 (fully qualified). These evaluations cover both easy (large difference in expertise scores) and hard (small difference in expertise scores) cases. The dataset is well-suited for evaluating expertise scoring models, with participants' profiles constructed from up to 20 of their most recent publications with titles and abstracts included.

4.2 Evaluation Metrics

For topic classification, we used two metrics: **Single-match Accuracy**, which measures the percentage of cases where at least one of the three predicted topics matches a true topic of the paper, and **Recall@3**, which calculates the proportion of true topics that appear in the top three predicted topics for each paper.

The expertise scoring was evaluated using metrics defined by Stelmakh et al. (2023). The primary metric is a **Loss** based on a modified Kendall's Tau distance, penalizing incorrect ranking of paper pairs by the difference in their true expertise scores. Also, **Easy Triplets Accuracy** and **Hard Triplets Accuracy** are measured as the fraction of correctly ordered paper pairs in terms of researcher's predicted expertise for large differences (easy triplets) and small differences (hard triplets) in true expertise scores, respectively. Lower loss and higher accuracy across triplet categories indicate better performance.

Finally, for model efficiency, we evaluated the system's **Inference Time per 1000 Samples**, and **Model Size** in terms of the number of parameters in the model. Efficiency was evaluated using NVIDIA P100 GPU.

4.3 Comparison Models

We compare our model with scientific representation models featured in OpenReview platform:

SciBERT (Beltagy et al., 2019), SPECTER2 (Singh et al., 2023), SciNCL (Ostendorff et al., 2022). For topic classification comparison, SciBERT and SciNCL were fine-tuned for 2 epochs in a multi-label classification setting. For SPECTER2, since it is an adapter-based model, we fine-tuned it by training a new adapter in a multi-label classification setting for 2 epochs. For expertise scoring comparison, we used the base versions of the models.

SciBERT SciBERT (Beltagy et al., 2019) is a pretrained language model specifically designed for scientific text. It is based on the BERT (Devlin et al., 2019) architecture but trained on a large corpus of scientific papers from the computer science and biomedical domains. SciBERT uses an in-domain vocabulary, making it more effective at processing scientific language compared to general-domain models such as BERT. SciBERT serves as the foundation for many state-of-the-art scientific document representation models, making it an important baseline.

SPECTER2 Building upon SciBERT, Cohan et al. (2020) introduced SPECTER. The key innovation in SPECTER is its use of the citation graph for learning document representations. It leverages contrastive learning by considering papers that cite each other as close in the embedding space, while papers without citation links are placed further apart. This approach improves performance on various document-level tasks such as recommendation and classification. SPECTER2 (Singh et al., 2023) extends this model by introducing task-specific adapters, for tasks such as proximity or regression. Additionally, it uses a larger and more diverse training set, which includes papers from a broader range of scientific fields, further enhancing its robustness across disciplines.

SciNCL SciNCL (Ostendorff et al., 2022) builds upon the idea used in original SPECTER (Cohan et al., 2020), which leverages citation graphs to inform contrastive learning samples. However, unlike SPECTER, which uses a discrete binary relationship (i.e., either papers cite each other or they do not), SciNCL employs a continuous similarity measure to capture more nuanced relationships between papers. It enhances contrastive learning by sampling positive examples not just from directly cited papers, but also from closely related papers within the k-nearest neighbors of the citation graph.

4.4 Results and Discussion

Tables 1 and 2 present the evaluation results of the proposed GRU-based model against state-of-the-art models in the paper-reviewer-expertise modeling field across both topic classification and expertise scoring (modeling) tasks.

Model	**Single-match Accuracy (k=3)**	**Recall@3**
SciBERT (fine-tuned)	96.69	0.794
SPECTER2 (fine-tuned)	95.95	0.771
SciNCL (fine-tuned)	96.51	0.789
Our model	95.32	0.766

Table 1: Performance comparison of different models on topic classification

Model	**Loss**	**Easy Triplets**	**Hard Triplets**
SciBERT (base)	0.30	0.82	0.55
SPECTER2 (base)	0.22	0.89	0.61
SciNCL (base)	0.22	0.91	0.65
Our model	0.26	0.83	0.57

Table 2: Performance comparison of different models on expertise scoring

Our GRU-based model, although slightly outperformed by more complex transformer-based models, demonstrates respectable performance in both tasks. In topic classification, it achieved a single-match accuracy of 95.32% and a Recall@3 of 0.766. In expertise scoring, our GRU-based model achieved a loss of 0.26. The model's accuracy on easy triples was 0.83, and on hard triples, it was 0.57. While these metrics are lower than those of the state-of-the-art transformer-based models (SPECTER2 and SciNCL), our model outperformed SciBERT baseline in expertise scoring.

Despite being mostly inferior to the state-of-the-art models in both tasks, our model offers significant efficiency gains (see Table 3). Our model has a significantly faster inference time (around 1.7 seconds per 1000 samples) compared to the transformer-based models, which require around 16 to 18 seconds. Moreover, our model is much smaller with 15M parameters, compared to 110M parameters of the BERT-based models.

This efficiency makes our model highly suitable for large-scale systems like ours, where thousands of scholars may use the platform. This trade-off between performance and efficiency is critical for the proposed system, ensuring rapid and scalable processing without compromising the overall quality

Model	Model Size (params)	Inference time per 1000 samples (seconds)
SciBERT	110M	16.62
SPECTER2	111M	18.22
SciNCL	110M	16.87
Our model	15M	1.72

Table 3: Efficiency comparison of different models in terms of model size and inference time spent per 1000 samples

of the automation.

Interestingly, in the expertise modeling task, the GRU-based model performs surprisingly well. This result suggests that pre-training models on topic classification can be effective for paper-reviewer expertise modeling. The explanation for this behavior might be intuitive, since topic classification requires the model to learn latent representations that encapsulate the topical areas, which are naturally used for assessing the relevance of a reviewer's expertise. We suggest the further exploration of classification-based pre-training to understand the potential of this approach in paper-reviewer-expertise modeling and more general task of scientific text representation.

5 Conclusion

Our research presented a prototype of an autonomous peer reviewer selection system that effectively leverages NLP techniques to streamline the peer review process. By employing a GRU-based model, our system demonstrates a solid balance between accuracy and efficiency. The continuous and on-demand nature of the system offers researchers rapid access to expert feedback, bypassing the constraints of traditional review cycles tied to specific journals or conferences.

A key area for future improvement is the development of an effective reviewer onboarding system, which is essential for ensuring the platform has a high-quality pool of reviewers. Furthermore, it is important to integrate a feedback mechanism where users can rate the quality of reviewer matches and the usefulness of the feedback. These ratings could be used to iteratively adjust and improve the matching system.

Additionally, wc suggcst further development of the classification-based pre-training, as it shows a potential in paper-reviewer matching and the broader field of scientific text representation.

6 Limitations

While the proposed system demonstrates significant potential, several limitations remain, both at the platform and model levels. The key challenge lies in recruiting and motivating reviewers to visit the platform and perform "out-of-formal" reviews. Since these reviews are independent of traditional academic venues like journals and conferences, encouraging expert reviewers to join and contribute actively remains a limiting factor. A potential solution could involve a system where users must contribute reviews to receive feedback on their own submissions.

Additionally, the current paper-reviewer matching model supports 158 categories across 8 academic fields, which may not capture the full granularity of many specialized fields. However, it should be noted that our model performs well even with this limited number of categories, suggesting that using more fine-grained taxonomies could further improve the model's performance and adaptability to niche topics.

Acknowledgments

This publication has emanated from research conducted with the financial support of the Ministry of Science and Higher Education of the Republic of Kazakhstan for the project “Leveraging IoT Mesh Networks for Machine Learning Knowledge Transfer” (grant No. AP23487072).

References

Adam C. Adler and Stephen A. Stayer. 2017. Bias among peer reviewers. *JAMA*, 318 8:755.

Iz Beltagy, Kyle Lo, and Arman Cohan. 2019. SciBERT: A pretrained language model for scientific text. In *Proceedings of the 2019 Conference on Empirical Methods in Natural Language Processing and the 9th International Joint Conference on Natural Language Processing (EMNLP-IJCNLP)*, pages 3615–3620, Hong Kong, China. Association for Computational Linguistics.

Laurent Charlin and Richard Zemel. 2013. The toronto paper matching system: an automated paper-reviewer assignment system. In *Proceedings of the 2013 ICML workshop on peer reviewing and publishing models*.

Arman Cohan, Sergey Feldman, Iz Beltagy, Doug Downey, and Daniel Weld. 2020. SPECTER: Document-level representation learning using citation-informed transformers. In *Proceedings of the 58th Annual Meeting of the Association for Computational Linguistics*, pages 2270–2282, Online. Association for Computational Linguistics.

Don Conry, Yehuda Koren, and Naren Ramakrishnan. 2009. Recommender systems for the conference paper assignment problem. In *Proceedings of the Third ACM Conference on Recommender Systems*, RecSys '09, page 357–360, New York, NY, USA. Association for Computing Machinery.

Cornell University. 2020. arxiv dataset. Accessed: 2024-09-29.

Jaime A. Teixeira da Silva, Judit Dobránszki, Radha Holla Bhar, and Charles T. Mehlman. 2019. Editors should declare conflicts of interest. *Journal of Bioethical Inquiry*, 16:279 – 298.

Jacob Devlin, Ming-Wei Chang, Kenton Lee, and Kristina Toutanova. 2019. BERT: Pre-training of deep bidirectional transformers for language understanding. In *Proceedings of the 2019 Conference of the North American Chapter of the Association for Computational Linguistics: Human Language Technologies, Volume 1 (Long and Short Papers)*, pages 4171–4186, Minneapolis, Minnesota. Association for Computational Linguistics.

Seth Hettich and Michael J. Pazzani. 2006. Mining for proposal reviewers: lessons learned at the national science foundation. In *Proceedings of the 12th ACM SIGKDD International Conference on Knowledge Discovery and Data Mining*, KDD '06, page 862–871, New York, NY, USA. Association for Computing Machinery.

Janine Huisman and Jeroen Smits. 2017. Duration and quality of the peer review process: the author's perspective. *Scientometrics*, 113(1):633–650.

Kevin Leyton-Brown, Yatin Nandwani, Hedayat Zarkoob, Chris Cameron, Neil Newman, Dinesh Raghu, et al. 2022. Matching papers and reviewers at large conferences. *arXiv preprint arXiv:2202.12273*.

Baochun Li and Y. Thomas Hou. 2016. The new automated ieee infocom review assignment system. *IEEE Network*, 30(5):18–24.

Xinlian Li and Toyohide Watanabe. 2013. Automatic paper-to-reviewer assignment, based on the matching degree of the reviewers. *Procedia Computer Science*, 22:633–642.

David Mimno and Andrew McCallum. 2007. Expertise modeling for matching papers with reviewers. In *Proceedings of the 13th ACM SIGKDD international conference on Knowledge discovery and data mining*, pages 500–509.

OpenReview. 2024. Paper-reviewer affinity modeling for openreview. `https://github.com/openreview/openreview-expertise`. Accessed: 2024-09-24.

Malte Ostendorff, Nils Rethmeier, Isabelle Augenstein, Bela Gipp, and Georg Rehm. 2022. Neighborhood contrastive learning for scientific document representations with citation embeddings. In *Proceedings of the 2022 Conference on Empirical Methods in Natural Language Processing*, pages 11670–11688, Abu Dhabi, United Arab Emirates. Association for Computational Linguistics.

Amanpreet Singh, Mike D'Arcy, Arman Cohan, Doug Downey, and Sergey Feldman. 2023. SciRepEval: A multi-format benchmark for scientific document representations. In *Proceedings of the 2023 Conference on Empirical Methods in Natural Language Processing*, pages 5548–5566, Singapore. Association for Computational Linguistics.

Ivan Stelmakh, John Wieting, Graham Neubig, and Nihar B. Shah. 2023. A gold standard dataset for the reviewer assignment problem. *ArXiv*, abs/2303.16750.

Wenbin Tang, Jie Tang, and Chenhao Tan. 2010. Expertise matching via constraint-based optimization. In *2010 IEEE/WIC/ACM International Conference on Web Intelligence and Intelligent Agent Technology*, volume 1, pages 34–41.

Siyuan Wu, Leong Hou U., Sourav S. Bhowmick, and Wolfgang Gatterbauer. 2018. Pistis: A conflict of interest declaration and detection system for peer review management. In *Proceedings of the 2018 International Conference on Management of Data*, SIGMOD '18, page 1713–1716, New York, NY, USA. Association for Computing Machinery.

Yonghui Wu, Mike Schuster, Z. Chen, Quoc V. Le, Mohammad Norouzi, Wolfgang Macherey, Maxim Krikun, Yuan Cao, Qin Gao, Klaus Macherey, Jeff Klingner, Apurva Shah, Melvin Johnson, Xiaobing Liu, Lukasz Kaiser, Stephan Gouws, Yoshikiyo Kato, Taku Kudo, Hideto Kazawa, Keith Stevens, George Kurian, Nishant Patil, Wei Wang, Cliff Young, Jason R. Smith, Jason Riesa, Alex Rudnick, Oriol Vinyals, Gregory S. Corrado, Macduff Hughes, and Jeffrey Dean. 2016. Google's neural machine translation system: Bridging the gap between human and machine translation. *ArXiv*, abs/1609.08144.

David Yarowsky and Radu Florian. 1999. Taking the load off the conference chairs-towards a digital paper-routing assistant. In *1999 Joint SIGDAT Conference on Empirical Methods in Natural Language Processing and Very Large Corpora*.

Dong Zhang, Shu Zhao, Zhen Duan, Jie Chen, Yanping Zhang, and Jie Tang. 2020. A multi-label classification method using a hierarchical and transparent representation for paper-reviewer recommendation. *ACM Trans. Inf. Syst.*, 38(1).

Appendix A Paper categories used for classification-based pre-training

Field	Categories
Computer Science	Artificial Intelligence; Hardware Architecture; Computational Complexity; Computational Engineering, Finance and Science; Computational Geometry; Computation and Language; Cryptography and Security; Computer Vision and Pattern Recognition; Computers and Society; Databases; Distributed, Parallel, and Cluster Computing; Digital Libraries; Discrete Mathematics; Data Structures and Algorithms; Emerging Technologies; Formal Languages and Automata Theory; General Literature; Graphics; Computer Science and Game Theory; Human-Computer Interaction; Information Retrieval; Information Theory; Machine Learning; Logic in Computer Science; Multiagent Systems; Multimedia; Mathematical Software; Numerical Analysis; Neural and Evolutionary Computing; Networking and Internet Architecture; Other Computer Science; Operating Systems; Performance; Programming Languages; Robotics; Symbolic Computation; Sound; Software Engineering; Social and Information Networks; Systems and Control
Economics	Econometrics; General Economics; Theoretical Economics
Electrical Engineering and Systems Science	Audio and Speech Processing; Image and Video Processing; Signal Processing; Systems and Control
Mathematics	Commutative Algebra; Algebraic Geometry; Analysis of PDEs; Algebraic Topology; Classical Analysis and ODEs; Combinatorics; Category Theory; Complex Variables; Differential Geometry; Dynamical Systems; Functional Analysis; General Mathematics; General Topology; Group Theory; Geometric Topology; History and Overview; Information Theory; K-Theory and Homology; Logic; Metric Geometry; Mathematical Physics; Numerical Analysis; Number Theory; Operator Algebras; Optimization and Control; Probability; Quantum Algebra; Rings and Algebras; Representation Theory; Symplectic Geometry; Spectral Theory; Statistics Theory
Physics	Accelerator Physics; Atmospheric and Oceanic Physics; Applied Physics; Atomic and Molecular Clusters; Atomic Physics; Biological Physics; Chemical Physics; Classical Physics; Computational Physics; Data Analysis, Statistics and Probability; Physics Education; Fluid Dynamics; General Physics; Geophysics; History and Philosophy of Physics; Instrumentation and Detectors; Medical Physics; Optics; Plasma Physics; Popular Physics; Physics and Society; Space Physics; Nuclear Theory; Nuclear Experiment; Exactly Solvable and Integrable Systems; Pattern Formation and Solitons; Cellular Automata and Lattice Gases; Chaotic Dynamics; Adaptation and Self-Organizing Systems; Mathematical Physics; High Energy Physics - Theory; High Energy Physics - Phenomenology; High Energy Physics - Lattice; High Energy Physics - Experiment; General Relativity and Quantum Cosmology; Superconductivity; Strongly Correlated Electrons; Statistical Mechanics; Soft Condensed Matter; Quantum Gases; Other Condensed Matter; Materials Science; Mesoscale and Nanoscale Physics; Disordered Systems and Neural Networks; Condensed Matter; Solar and Stellar Astrophysics; Instrumentation and Methods for Astrophysics; High Energy Astrophysical Phenomena; Astrophysics of Galaxies; Earth and Planetary Astrophysics; Cosmology and Nongalactic Astrophysics; Astrophysics
Quantitative Biology	Biomolecules; Cell Behavior; Genomics; Molecular Networks; Neurons and Cognition; Other Quantitative Biology; Populations and Evolution; Quantitative Methods; Subcellular Processes; Tissues and Organs
Quantitative Finance	Computational Finance; Economics; General Finance; Mathematical Finance; Portfolio Management; Pricing of Securities; Risk Management; Statistical Finance; Trading and Market Microstructure
Statistics	Applications; Computation; Methodology; Machine Learning; Other Statistics; Statistics Theory

Table 4: 158 categories across 8 academic fields used for pre-training our paper-reviewer matching model. These categories are derived from the official categorical taxonomy of the ArXiv repository.

CULTURALLY YOURS: A Reading Assistant for Cross-Cultural Content

Saurabh Kumar Pandey[1], **Harshit Budhiraja**[2], **Sougata Saha**[1], **Monojit Choudhury**[1]
[1]MBZUAI, [2]Wadhwani AI
[1]{saurabh.pandey, sougata.saha, monojit.choudhury}@mbzuai.ac.ae
[2]{hbudhi36@gmail.com}

Abstract

Users from diverse cultural backgrounds frequently face challenges in understanding content from various online sources written by people from different cultures. This paper presents CULTURALLY YOURS (CY), a first-of-its-kind cultural reading assistant tool designed to identify culture-specific items (CSIs) for users from varying cultural contexts. By leveraging principles of relevance feedback and using culture as a prior, our tool personalizes to the user's preferences based on their interaction with the tool. CY can use any LLM capable of reasoning with the user's cultural background in English-based prompts as the back-end. Using culture as part of the prompt, CY iteratively refines the prompt as the user keeps interacting with the system. In this demo, we use GPT-4o as the back-end. We also conducted a user study across 13 users from 8 different geographies. The results demonstrate CY's effectiveness in enhancing user engagement and personalization alongside comprehension of cross-cultural content. The tool can be accessed by following instructions on Github [1].

1 Introduction

With increasing digitization, people frequently encounter text from diverse sources that they find difficult to understand, often due to a lack of common ground between the writer of the text and the reader. For example, people unfamiliar with the Arabic culture might not understand the meaning of the dishes *"Machboos"* and *"Luqaimat"* from the review text *"The Machboos was perfectly spiced, and the Luqaimat was a real treat"*. Or, someone unfamiliar with the Western culture might not understand that *"golden arches"* refers to *"McDonald's"* in the text *"Let's go to the golden arches for a quick bite"*. Thus, communication can get hampered in cross-cultural contexts due to a lack of appropriate common ground between the interlocutors (Meyer, 2014; Korkut et al., 2018), which, in turn, can adversely impact a user in many scenarios that involve decision-making, such as from *user-reviews* on e-commerce platforms like Amazon and travel platforms like Booking.com.

To address this challenge in the cross-cultural understanding of online text, we have developed a cultural reading assistant, **Culturally Yours (CY)**, which acts as a cultural mediator and identifies exotic concepts from an unknown source culture to the user's culture. CY facilitates cross-cultural communication by globalizing local textual articles and enabling users to understand and engage with content they might otherwise struggle to interpret. Thus, it can help businesses improve user engagement and reach broader audiences across diverse cultural markets worldwide.

CY uses the principles of *relevance feedback* (Rui et al., 1998) from information retrieval, which involves iterative refinement of results using user feedback to improve the system's performance. Not understanding the preferences of new users, famously known as the *cold-start problem*, is a well-established issue in collaborative filtering (Hu et al., 2008) that hinders personalization. Using culture as a prior, CY efficiently ameliorates the cold-start problem and gradually adapts to a user's preference, incorporating multiple iterations of relevance feedback. Defining culture by demographic features, the tool initially highlights and explains certain portions of text that the user might find hard to understand due to the cross-cultural gap in common-ground. Users then provide feedback by deselecting the highlighted spans or highlighting new spans missed by the tool. Over time, with multiple such cycles of relevance feedback spanning texts from diverse domains, CY gradually understands and adapts to the user's preferences. Eventually, CY personalizes to users and helps them acquaint themselves with text from different cul-

[1] https://github.com/skp1999/CULTURALLY_YOURS

Proceedings of the 31st International Conference on Computational Linguistics: System Demonstrations, pages 208–216
January 19–24, 2025.

tures.

Using Large Language Models (LLMs) (Achiam et al., 2023; Dubey et al., 2024; Bubeck et al., 2023; Nori et al., 2023; Lai et al., 2023) as the underlying model, CY implements a prompt-based algorithm to identify and explain culture-specific items (CSIs) (Newmark, 2003) based on a user's cultural background and preferences. CSIs are cultural items that people from different backgrounds might not understand and be unfamiliar with. Initially, CY identifies the CSIs from any English text solely based on the user's demographics. Over time, as the user interacts with the tool, CY captures their preferences across diverse domains and algorithmically adjusts its prompt to better align the CSI identification and explication with the user's background and preferences. Currently, the tool uses GPT-4o[2] as the backend LLM, but can be replaced by any other LLM suitable for this task. We also experimented with three prompting-based algorithms and conducted a user study over 13 users to determine the best personalization algorithm for the backend. In summary, the main contributions of our work are as follows.

- We introduce CULTURALLY YOURS, a first-of-its-kind reading assistant tool, to help people from different cultural backgrounds understand online text from unknown cultures. Such a tool facilitates cross-cultural communication and promotes globalizing local content.
- We propose and experiment with three strategies for optimizing CY's backend prompt-based algorithm.
- We demonstrate the usefulness and effectiveness of such a tool through a small-scale user study.

2 Culturally Yours

2.1 Overview

Given a user's cultural background, they might be unfamiliar with many concepts mentioned in online text, such as reviews, news articles, blogs, social media posts, etc. CY is a reading assistant that helps users acquaint themselves with such concepts by highlighting spans of text that a user might be unfamiliar with, given their cultural background. As shown in Figure 1, the tool takes a URL as input and identifies CSIs based on the demographic details of the user. The tool also categorizes the identified spans into *Unfamiliar* and *Somewhat Familiar*, depicting different levels of familiarity of the highlighted spans. To personalize CY, users can interact with the tool and make adjustments by (i) Selecting other text spans they don't understand and assigning a level of familiarity. (ii) Modifying the familiarity levels of the currently highlighted spans. (iii) Removing the highlighted spans. The initial back-end prompt is updated based on these interactions, and the updated prompt subsequently identifies spans in new documents. The spans highlighted in a new document show that the tool, starting from the user's culture, has adjusted to their preferences. Users can iteratively use the tool for multiple documents, where each interaction improves the tool's understanding of the user's preferences and facilitates personalization.

2.2 Features

CY incorporates a range of functionalities designed to assist users in identifying CSIs. Below, we outline the key features of the system:

1. **URL Parsing:** The system inputs URLs of documents and efficiently extracts the relevant textual content from the document.
2. **CSI Identification:** The tool highlights CSIs from the extracted text per the user's demographic background and categorizes the CSIs as "unfamiliar" or "somewhat familiar".
3. **User Interaction:** Users can delete highlighted spans, modify the familiarity level of the highlighted span, or select new spans of text with two levels of familiarity. The interaction window enables a customized and interactive experience for the users.
4. **User Feedback:** The system treats the user interaction as *relevance feedback* and adjusts its prompt to align the CSIs according to the user's preference in a new input URL/document.

2.3 Frontend

The front end of CY uses the `Vue.js`[3] framework. The framework manages user sessions, collects the user's socio-demographic information, and highlights CSIs for the user from a given cultural background. The front end mainly consists of the following two pages.

1. **Homepage:** This page allows users to input a URL and provide their demographic informa-

[2]https://openai.com/index/hello-gpt-4o/

[3]`https://vuejs.org/guide/introduction.html`

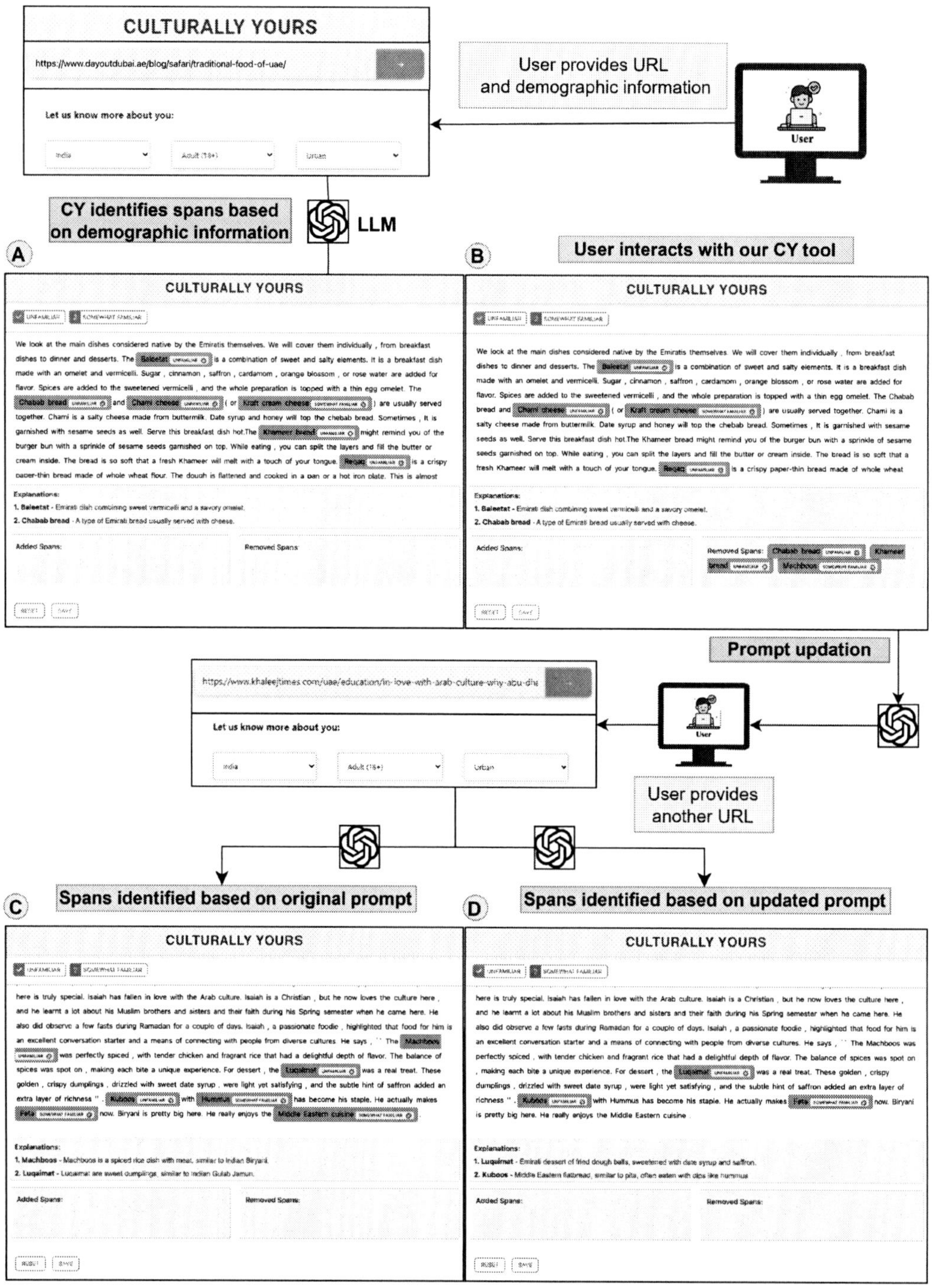

Figure 1: System overview of CULTURALLY YOURS (CY). A user provides a URL and demographic information such as country, age group, and region. (A) CY identifies CSIs based on the user's demographic details. (B) The user interacts with the tool, which updates the user's preferences and the prompt. CSIs are identified in a new text using the updated prompt. (C) Shows the highlighted spans on a new text using the original prompt. (D) Shows the highlighted spans on a new text using the updated prompt.

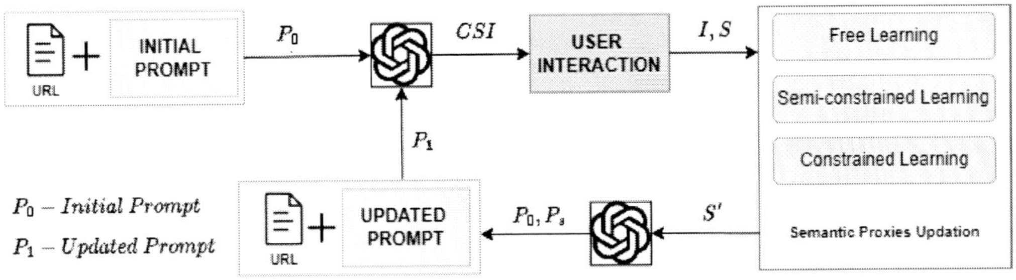

Figure 2: Overview of the prompt refinement in the backend. I represents the list of selected and deselected spans of text. S represents the initial semantic proxies. S' represents the updated semantic proxies based on I.

tion: country, age group, and region.

2. **Interaction page:** Given a URL and demographic information, this page displays the relevant text with CSIs highlighted with different levels of familiarity. This page also allows users to interact with our tool by modifying the familiarity level of the highlighted spans, deleting highlighted spans, and adding spans unfamiliar to the user that were unidentified by the tool. This interaction helps the tool learn user preferences and adjust accordingly.

2.4 Backend

The backend consists of a REST-based web server hosted on an Azure Virtual Machine with 16 GB of RAM. This setup enables scalable and efficient interactions with the APIs of various closed-source and open-source LLMs, supporting the execution of experimental workflows. The backend uses inputs from the user to interact with the LLMs, which generate responses and return the processed output in JSON format. The backend system performs the following tasks:

1. Parses the textual content from the user-provided URL.
2. Given the parsed URL text and the user's demographic information, the backend identifies CSIs for the user. It also categorizes the CSIs into two levels of familiarity - somewhat familiar and unfamiliar.
3. Explains the highlighted CSIs by simplifying them as per the user. It tries to relate them to concepts from the user's culture.
4. Utilizes the interactions to reformulate the prompts and improve alignment with the user's cultural background and preferences. The overview of the prompt refinement in the backend is shown in Figure 2. The prompts used for updating semantic proxies are shown in Figure 6.

2.5 Prompting Strategies for Personalization

We implement three prompting-based learning strategies for personalizing the tool to a user's preferences. (i) **Free learning:** The user's selected and deselected text spans are used directly in the backend LLM's prompt as preferences without explicitly interpreting their meaning. We implement a chat-based system to interact with the LLM. We append the spans to the LLM's prompt history, and the model personalizes to the user's preferences without explicitly interpreting the meaning of highlighting or deselecting a span in terms of preferences. (ii) **Constrained learning:** We introduce four semantic proxies, *political awareness*, *food cuisine*, *education level*, and *literature preference*, to denote user preferences. Semantic proxies refer to deeper representations of a culture and help bridge the gap between various cultural understandings (Thompson et al., 2020; Adilazuarda et al., 2024). We use the user's interaction to update the semantic proxies and reformulate the chat-based prompts to align the LLM with the user's preferences. (iii) **Semi-constrained learning:** This strategy mixes free and constrained learning, where we update only two semantic proxies based on the user's interaction and append the selected or deselected spans for the other two proxies, much like the free learning strategy.

3 User Study

We perform a user study using CY with three different prompting-based settings to evaluate the effectiveness of the CY tool and determine the best-performing setting for personalization to the user's culture.

3.1 Document Samples

We select articles from two domains - political news and food reviews. We consider three online articles each from news related to US elections and the traditional food of UAE. Food reviews contain descriptions of local and global food spanning various cultures. The news articles pertain to global political news that is widely recognized and understood. This choice of articles allows us to analyze how cultural familiarity influences user interactions through localized and universally known content. We limit the number of articles for each domain to three to ensure a focused user study while allowing us to gather meaningful insights across a diverse range of demographics.

3.2 Method

For a domain, the user enters their demography (country, region, and age group) and a URL. Estimating the user's culture by their demography, we prompt GPT-4o to identify CSIs in the text extracted from the URL, using culture as a prior. CY identifies CSIs and categorizes them into different familiarity levels. The user interacts with the tool by deselecting the highlighted CSIs they are already familiar with and selecting new CSIs from the text they are unfamiliar with. Once the user is satisfied with the interaction, they can save their preferences. The user interacts with the tool subsequently with two more URLs and saves their preferences every time. A user repeats this study for both domains (food and politics) under the three learning strategies (free, constrained, and semi-constrained). Lastly, we collect feedback from the user on the following aspects of CY.

- **CSI Identification:** How effective is the tool at identifying CSIs?
- **CSI Explanation:** How accurate is the tool at explaining CSIs?
- **Personalization:** How good is the tool at personalization?

We perform this study across 13 users from 8 diverse demographics of India, Indonesia, China, Mexico, Sri Lanka, Egypt, Uzbekistan, and Kazakhstan.

3.3 Evaluation

We define a metric, Average Interaction Rate (AIR), to measure the effectiveness of CY. The AIR is computed for each domain (S) and overall, and defined as follows.

Strategy	Domain		
	Food ↓	Politics ↓	Overall ↓
Free	0.57	**0.60**	0.58
Semi-constrained	0.53	0.64	0.59
Constrained	**0.52**	0.62	**0.57**

Table 1: Average Interaction Rate for different strategies across 13 users for Food, Politics, and Overall

$$\text{AIR}(S) = \frac{1}{|U| \times |D|} \sum_{u=1}^{U} \sum_{d=1}^{D} \frac{I(u,d)}{HS(u,d)}$$

U is the set of all the users and D is the set of all documents for a domain S. $I(u,d)$ is the total number of interactions for a user u on a document d. $HS(u,d)$ represents the total number of highlighted spans after interaction from a user u on a document d. The fraction represents the percentage of interaction by a user u on a document d.

Lesser selection and deselection by the user yields a lower AIR score and indicates that the tool appropriately highlighted CSIs according to the user's culture and preferences, demonstrating better personalization to the user. A higher AIR score suggests otherwise.

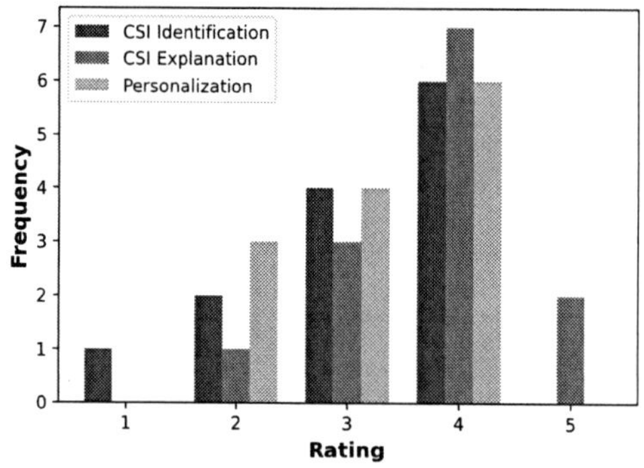

Figure 3: Plot of user ratings on a Likert scale.

3.4 Findings

From Table 1, we observe that **Free Learning** yields a lower average interaction value on Politics (0.60), whereas **Constrained learning** attains the best result for Food domain (0.52) and overall (0.57). We hypothesize that the nature of a domain impacts the performance of a learning strategy, where each domain might implement distinct strategies. We leave testing this hypothesis across multiple domains and more users as future work.

We also collect user feedback on a Likert Scale (1-5) for three different aspects of our tool, namely CSI Identification, CSI Explanation, and Personalization, as described in Section 3.2 and Section 6. From Figure 3, we observe high satisfaction among users for the explanation of CSIs. We also observe positive feedback on CSI Identification and Personalization, with 10 out of 13 users providing ratings of 3 and 4. The absence of ratings of 5 for CSI identification and personalization suggests that while users are generally satisfied, there is still room for further enhancement of the tool's features to reach higher satisfaction levels.

4 Related work

Copilots: The rapid advancement of AI-based copilots has significantly influenced software development and writing assistance. One of the most notable examples is GitHub Copilot, which assists developers by providing code suggestions in real-time. Finnie-Ansley et al. (2022) demonstrates that while copilots enhance workflow efficiency, human oversight is essential for accuracy. Dakhel et al. (2023) also shows that copilot works for almost all fundamental algorithmic problems. However, some solutions are buggy and non-reproducible. An empirical study was carried out by Nguyen and Nadi (2022), which shows some shortcomings of copilots, such as generating complex code that is reducible and code that relies on undefined helper methods.

Writing assistants: Paetzold and Specia (2016) proposed the task of Complex Word Identification (CWI) to learn which words are challenging for non-native English speakers. Recent methods (North et al., 2023) also show that the complexity of words within a given text various for different readers. With the recent advancements of AI technologies, research suggests that digital writing tools can positively impact the quality of English writing (Nobles and Paganucci, 2015). AI-powered writing tools have emerged to support users in their English writing processes (Barrot, 2022; Coenen et al., 2021) and enhance users' writing skills while facilitating their learning (Pokrivcakova, 2019; Nazari et al., 2021). Most writing tools focus on the revision and editing stage (Winans, 2021). Zhao (2023) introduced Wordtune, an AI-powered technology that helps users during the writing process by understanding what they wish to say and helping them formulate their ideas into sentences by offering rephrasing options.

5 Conclusion

We introduce Culturally Yours (CY), a unique cultural reading assistant designed to bridge the gap in cross-cultural understanding of online texts. By leveraging user feedback and relevance feedback techniques, CY captures user preferences and algorithmically adapts its prompt to suit the user's background and preferences. The tool's ability to overcome the cultural cold-start problem and improve personalization based on user interaction under three different experimental settings prove the usefulness of the tool. With its focus on cultural adaptation, CY enhances cross-cultural content understanding and opens up avenues for improving user engagement across global platforms. Thus helping globalize locally written content.

Acknowledgements

This work is supported by the Microsoft Accelerate Foundation Models Research (AFMR) Grant. We thank all the participants involved in the internal ideation workshop of the tool. We also thank all the users involved in the tool's internal pilot study.

References

Josh Achiam, Steven Adler, Sandhini Agarwal, Lama Ahmad, Ilge Akkaya, Florencia Leoni Aleman, Diogo Almeida, Janko Altenschmidt, Sam Altman, Shyamal Anadkat, et al. 2023. Gpt-4 technical report. *arXiv preprint arXiv:2303.08774*.

Muhammad Farid Adilazuarda, Sagnik Mukherjee, Pradhyumna Lavania, Siddhant Singh, Ashutosh Dwivedi, Alham Fikri Aji, Jacki O'Neill, Ashutosh Modi, and Monojit Choudhury. 2024. Towards measuring and modeling" culture" in llms: A survey. *arXiv preprint arXiv:2403.15412*.

Jessie Saraza Barrot. 2022. Integrating technology into esl/efl writing through grammarly. *Relc Journal*, 53(3):764–768.

Sébastien Bubeck, Varun Chandrasekaran, Ronen Eldan, Johannes Gehrke, Eric Horvitz, Ece Kamar, Peter Lee, Yin Tat Lee, Yuanzhi Li, Scott Lundberg, et al. 2023. Sparks of artificial general intelligence: Early experiments with gpt-4. *arXiv preprint arXiv:2303.12712*.

Andy Coenen, Luke Davis, Daphne Ippolito, Emily Reif, and Ann Yuan. 2021. Wordcraft: A human-ai collaborative editor for story writing. *arXiv preprint arXiv:2107.07430*.

Arghavan Moradi Dakhel, Vahid Majdinasab, Amin Nikanjam, Foutse Khomh, Michel C Desmarais, and Zhen Ming Jack Jiang. 2023. Github copilot ai pair programmer: Asset or liability? *Journal of Systems and Software*, 203:111734.

Abhimanyu Dubey, Abhinav Jauhri, Abhinav Pandey, Abhishek Kadian, Ahmad Al-Dahle, Aiesha Letman, Akhil Mathur, Alan Schelten, Amy Yang, Angela Fan, et al. 2024. The llama 3 herd of models. *arXiv preprint arXiv:2407.21783*.

James Finnie-Ansley, Paul Denny, Brett A Becker, Andrew Luxton-Reilly, and James Prather. 2022. The robots are coming: Exploring the implications of openai codex on introductory programming. In *Proceedings of the 24th Australasian Computing Education Conference*, pages 10–19.

Yifan Hu, Yehuda Koren, and Chris Volinsky. 2008. Collaborative filtering for implicit feedback datasets. In *2008 Eighth IEEE international conference on data mining*, pages 263–272. Ieee.

Perihan Korkut, Mustafa Dolmacı, and Burcu Karaca. 2018. A study on communication breakdowns: Sources of misunderstanding in a cross-cultural setting. *Eurasian Journal of Educational Research*, 18(78):139–158.

Jinqi Lai, Wensheng Gan, Jiayang Wu, Zhenlian Qi, and Philip S Yu. 2023. Large language models in law: A survey. *arXiv preprint arXiv:2312.03718*.

Erin Meyer. 2014. *The culture map: Breaking through the invisible boundaries of global business*. Public Affairs.

Nabi Nazari, Muhammad Salman Shabbir, and Roy Setiawan. 2021. Application of artificial intelligence powered digital writing assistant in higher education: randomized controlled trial. *Heliyon*, 7(5).

Peter Newmark. 2003. A textbook of translation.

Nhan Nguyen and Sarah Nadi. 2022. An empirical evaluation of github copilot's code suggestions. In *Proceedings of the 19th International Conference on Mining Software Repositories*, pages 1–5.

Susanne Nobles and Laura Paganucci. 2015. Do digital writing tools deliver? student perceptions of writing quality using digital tools and online writing environments. *Computers and Composition*, 38:16–31.

Harsha Nori, Nicholas King, Scott Mayer McKinney, Dean Carignan, and Eric Horvitz. 2023. Capabilities of gpt-4 on medical challenge problems. *arXiv preprint arXiv:2303.13375*.

Kai North, Marcos Zampieri, and Matthew Shardlow. 2023. Lexical complexity prediction: An overview. *ACM Computing Surveys*, 55(9):1–42.

Gustavo Paetzold and Lucia Specia. 2016. Semeval 2016 task 11: Complex word identification. In *Proceedings of the 10th International Workshop on Semantic Evaluation (SemEval-2016)*, pages 560–569.

Silvia Pokrivcakova. 2019. Preparing teachers for the application of ai-powered technologies in foreign language education. *Journal of Language and Cultural Education*, 7(3):135–153.

Yong Rui, T.S. Huang, M. Ortega, and S. Mehrotra. 1998. Relevance feedback: a power tool for interactive content-based image retrieval. *IEEE Transactions on Circuits and Systems for Video Technology*, 8(5):644–655.

Bill Thompson, Seán G Roberts, and Gary Lupyan. 2020. Cultural influences on word meanings revealed through large-scale semantic alignment. *Nature Human Behaviour*, 4(10):1029–1038.

Michael D Winans. 2021. Grammarly's tone detector: Helping students write pragmatically appropriate texts. *Relc Journal*, 52(2):348–352.

Xin Zhao. 2023. Leveraging artificial intelligence (ai) technology for english writing: Introducing wordtune as a digital writing assistant for efl writers. *RELC Journal*, 54(3):890–894.

6 Appendix

User Study Feedback Tables 2, 3, 4 represent the descriptions of various rating levels used for CSI identification, CSI explanation, and Personalization.

Rating	Description
5	Highlighted all the spans correctly
4	Highlighted most of the spans correctly, missed a few spans
3	Highlighted some of the spans correctly, missed a few spans
2	Higlighted some of the spans incorrectly, missed a lot of spans
1	Higlighted most of the spans incorrectly, missed a few spans

Table 2: Rating description for Identification of Spans

Rating	Description
5	Personalizes perfectly, identifies all spans correctly
4	Personalizes reasonably well, identifies most of the spans correctly
3	Personalizes to a certain extent, some spans were identified incorrectly
2	Does not personalize properly, most of the spans were identified incorrectly
1	Does not personalize at all, all the spans were identified incorrectly

Table 3: Rating description for feedback on personalization

Rating	Description
5	Gave perfect explanations, helped me learn new things
4	Gave reasonably good explanations, helped me understand the text better
3	Some more explanations were needed, some cases it did not help
2	Explanations seem factually correct but did not help me understand the article better
1	Explanations were factually incorrect and confused me a lot

Table 4: Rating description for Explanation of CSIs

Initial Prompt

AI Rules
- Output response in JSON format only
- Do not output any extra text
- Do not wrap the JSON codes in JSON or Python markers
- JSON keys and values in double-quotes

You are a cultural mediator who understands all cultures across the world. As a mediator, your job is to identify and translate culturally exotic concepts from texts from an unknown source culture to my culture. I am a well-educated [age_group] person who grew up in [region] [country], which defines my culture. I came across a piece of text.

Task 1: Identify all culture-specific items (CSIs) from the text that I might find hard to understand due to my cultural background. CSIs are textual spans denoting concepts and items uncommon and not prevalent in my culture, making them difficult to understand.

Task2: For each CSI, identify its familiarity from one of the following three levels: 1. Familiar: Most people from my culture know and relate to the concept as intended. 2. Somewhat familiar: Only some people from my culture know and relate to the concept as intended. 3. Unfamiliar: Most people from my culture do not know or relate to the concept.

Task 3: Within 50 words, detail your reason for highlighting the span as CSI in Task 1 by correlating it with my background.

Task 4: Explain each CSI span within 20 words to make it more understandable to your client. Provide facts, examples, equivalences, analogies, etc, if needed.

Format your response as a valid Python dictionary formatted as: "spans": [List of Python dictionaries where each dictionary item is formatted as: "CSI": <task 1: copy the CSI span from text>, "familiarity": <task 2: familiarity level name>, "reason": <task 3: reason within 50 words>, "explanation": <task 4: explain the span within 20 words>]. Respond with "spans": "None" if you think I will not find anything difficult to understand.

Text: [review_text]

Update Prompt (Free Learning)

AI Rules
- Output response in JSON format only
- Do not output any extra text
- Do not wrap the JSON codes in JSON or Python markers
- JSON keys and values in double-quotes

On further understanding, I observe the following things.

I am familiar with spans of text like [[spans of text]]. I am somewhat familiar with spans of text like [[spans of text]]. I am unfamiliar with spans of text like [[spans of text]].

Update Prompt (Semi-constrained Learning)

AI Rules
- Output response in JSON format only
- Do not output any extra text
- Do not wrap the JSON codes in JSON or Python markers
- JSON keys and values in double-quotes

On further understanding, I observe the following things.

I am familiar with spans of text like [[spans of text]]. I am somewhat familiar with spans of text like [[spans of text]]. I am unfamiliar with spans of text like [[spans of text]].

Based on familiarity with these spans, update my background cultural information. Return them as a valid Python dictionary. {"political-awareness":<yes/no>, "food-cuisine":<japanese/mexican/american/emirati>}

Update Prompt (Constrained Learning)

AI Rules
- Output response in JSON format only
- Do not output any extra text
- Do not wrap the JSON codes in JSON or Python markers
- JSON keys and values in double-quotes

On further understanding, I observe the following things.

I am familiar with spans of text like [[spans of text]]. I am somewhat familiar with spans of text like [[spans of text]]. I am unfamiliar with spans of text like [[spans of text]].

Based on familiarity with these spans, update my background cultural information. Return them as a valid Python dictionary. {"political-awareness":<yes/no>, "education-level":<primary/secondary>, "food-cuisine":<japanese/mexican/american/emirati>, "literature-preference":<bengali/english/hindi>}

FEAT-writing: An Interactive Training System for Argumentative Writing

Yuning Ding[1], **Franziska Wehrhahn**[1], **Andrea Horbach**[1,2,3]
yuning.ding@fernuni-hagen.de | f.wehrhahn@mail.de | horbach@leibniz-ipn.de
[1]CATALPA, FernUniversität in Hagen, Germany
[2]Leibniz Institute for Science and Mathematics Education, Kiel, Germany
[3]University of Kiel, Germany

Abstract

Recent developments in Natural Language Processing (NLP) for argument mining offer new opportunities to analyze the argumentative units (AUs) in student essays. These advancements can be leveraged to provide automatically generated feedback and exercises for students engaging in online argumentative essay writing practice. Writing standards for both native English speakers (L1) and English-as-a-foreign-language (L2) learners require students to understand formal essay structures and different AUs. To address this need, we developed FEAT-writing (Feedback and Exercises for Argumentative Training in writing), an interactive system that provides students with automatically generated exercises and distinct feedback on their argumentative writing. In a preliminary evaluation involving 346 students, we assessed the impact of six different automated feedback types on essay quality, with results showing general improvements in writing after receiving feedback from the system.

1 Introduction

Argumentative writing is a critical skill for academic success, requiring students to construct well-reasoned arguments, link ideas coherently, and support claims with relevant evidence. However, many students struggle to develop these skills (Graham and Perin, 2007). Mastering argumentative writing requires understanding essay structure and organizing ideas based on a clear argumentative framework (Hillocks, 2011).

One widely recognized model for teaching and analyzing argumentation is Toulmin's model (Toulmin, 2003), in which the central argumentative unit (AU) is a *claim* supported by *data* based on a *warrant*. This model has been incorporated into writing standards for L1 students, such as the Common Core State Standards for English Language Arts (CCSSO and NGA, 2010), which require students to introduce *claims* and logically organize the *evidence*. This model is also applied in L2 instruction, for instance, Germany's educational standards for the first foreign language (KMK, 2024) mandate that students express their own *opinions* and substantiate them with factual *reasons*.

Despite the importance of argumentative writing and the established standards, teachers in traditional classroom instruction often cannot provide detailed and individualized feedback due to time and resource constraints (Ferris, 2003). While automated tools exist to help students with grammar and spelling, they generally overlook the deeper aspects of language such as argumentation (Ranalli et al., 2017; Wilson and Roscoe, 2020).

To address these challenges, we developed FEAT-writing, an interactive system designed to help students improve their argumentative writing. The system generates exercises that aimed at supporting students to progressively build a solid argumentative framework, moving from simple tasks (i.e., distinguishing different AUs) to more complex ones (i.e., linking AUs with transitional words and supporting claims with evidence) and finally to writing complete argumentative essays. This approach is grounded in educational psychology, drawing from cognitive constructivism (Kalina and Powell, 2009) and a bottom-up learning approach (Sun et al., 2001). The system also provides students with automatically generated formative, summative, and elaborate feedback (Johnson and Priest, 2014), as well as automatically identified AUs visualized in color-coding (Maldonado-Otto and Ormsbee, 2019), which follows the principles of multimedia learning (Mayer, 2005).

We developed a web-based application (see Figure 1) that offers English writing exercises, aimed at helping students master the AUs and flow of argumentative writing. The final essay writing step in our system, writing an argumentative essay, was evaluated with 346 students in Germany,

Proceedings of the 31st International Conference on Computational Linguistics: System Demonstrations, pages 217–225
January 19–24, 2025. ©2025 Association for Computational Linguistics

and preliminary findings indicate improvements in the completeness of the argument structure after receiving color-coded elaborate feedback.

2 Background and Related Work

In this section, we first introduce the argumentative units types (AUs) used in our system, then review related work in two areas: feedback systems supporting the learning of AUs and exercises that train students to use them in writing.

2.1 AUs and their Effectiveness

The data foundation for our system is the PERSUADE corpus (Crossley et al., 2022, 2024), which contains over 280,000 discourse annotations for over 25,000 argumentative essays. Its annotation of AUs follows Toulmin's model. To focus on the most critical elements of argumentative writing and increase the system's accuracy, we use a simplified version of the original PERSUADE AUs following Ding et al. (2024). They defined AUs as followed:

- *Lead*: an introduction that begins with a statistic, a quotation, a description, or some other device to grab the reader's attention and point toward the thesis.
- *Position*: an opinion or conclusion on the main question.
- *Claim*: a claim that supports the position, refutes another claim or gives an opposing reason to the position.
- *Evidence*: ideas or examples that support claims, counterclaims, or rebuttals.
- *Concluding Statement*: a conclusion that restates the claims

The PERSUADE corpus also provides effectiveness scores for each AU. For the generation of exercises in the first three steps, we only use effective AUs, which are defined as shown in Appendix A.1.

2.2 AU Feedback Systems

With the popularity of online learning platforms, providing automated feedback becomes more and more critical to support teachers (Cavalcanti et al., 2021). With a focus on writing skills, numerous systems have been developed to provide students with automated feedback, primarily in the form of scores, since Page's seminal paper (Page, 1966). Comprehensive overviews of these systems can be found in the literature reviews by Ke and Ng (2019) and Beigman Klebanov and Madnani (2020). Specifically targeting argumentation feedback systems, Kuhn et al. (2017) provide a detailed summary.

This paper focuses on the systems that provide feedback on AUs. Wambsganss et al. (2021) introduced ArgueTutor, an adaptive dialog-based learning system that offers personalized feedback for argumentative texts by analyzing individual argumentative components. Bai and Stede (2022) provide feedback on the similarity between pairs of claims. The most similar work to ours is ALEN App (Wambsganss et al., 2022) and the system developed by Liu et al. (2016), both of which automatically detect claim-premise structures in students' essays and offer visual feedback to help students repair any broken argumentation structures.

However, these systems provide feedback only after students have completed a text or text snippets, whereas the training of argumentative writing benefits from step-by-step guidance. Our system, FEAT-writing, stands out by offering tailored task-specific feedback for exercises throughout the entire argumentative writing training process, addressing various stages of learning and providing the possibility of multiple attempts and revision.

2.3 AU Exercises and Automatic Generation

The automatic generation of language exercises is already a common application of NLP in education, encompassing vocabulary exercises (e.g. Heilman and Eskenazi, 2007; Peng et al., 2023), grammar exercises (e.g. Perez-Beltrachini et al., 2012; Heck et al., 2021) and their combination, such as c-tests (e.g. Haring et al., 2021; Lee et al., 2024). However, to the best of our knowledge, there has been little work on automating exercises specifically designed to train students in argumentative writing, or more specifically, in learning AUs.

Without automated generation, classroom exercises focusing on AUs, however, have demonstrated improvements in students' writing performance (Rafik-Galea et al., 2008; Khodabandeh et al., 2013). To address this gap, we leverage exercises such as distinguishing different AUs, linking AUs with transitional words, and supporting claims with the most effective evidence to enhance students' understanding and applications of AUs.

3 System Design

As introduced above and shown in Figure 1, FEAT-writing is designed to guide students through a

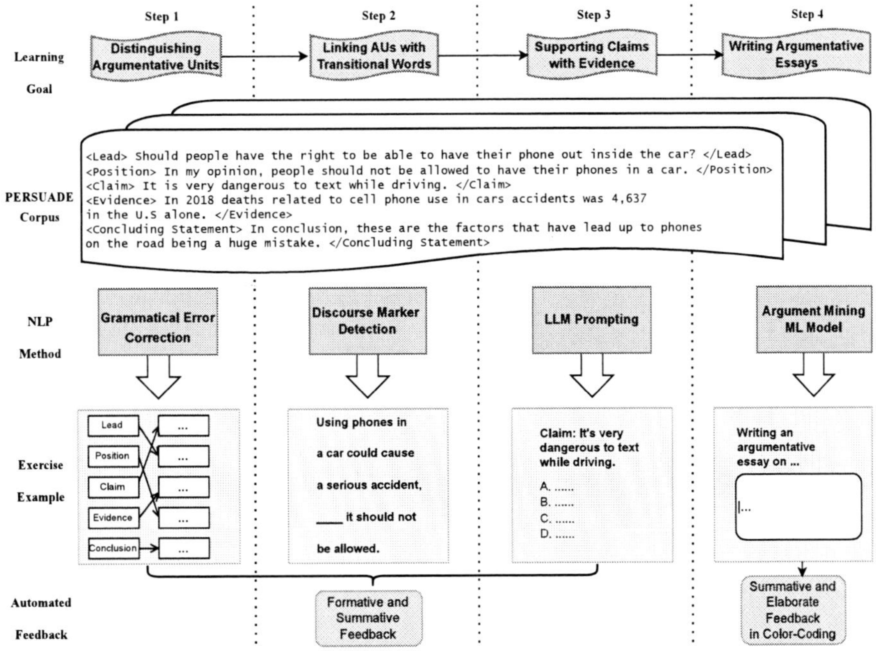

Figure 1: Structure of FEAT-writing.

sequence of exercises aimed at improving their argumentative writing skills. Each step builds upon the previous one, helping students move from basic recognition of AUs to writing full argumentative essays. This section outlines the system's functionality and the technology used in each step.

In alignment with scientific standards and the principles of Open Science, a key part of our plan involves the publication of anonymized datasets in publicly accessible repositories. To address privacy and ethical considerations, we have implemented a consent process. Before using the tool, students will be presented with a consent form allowing them to decide whether they permit the collection and publication of their data after anonymization.

A taskbar, displayed at the bottom of the page allows students to monitor their progress and switch between tasks. Students can easily return to prior exercises, practice further, and refine their skills, making the learning process more interactive and adaptive to individual needs.

3.1 Step 1: Distinguishing AUs

In the first step, students learn to distinguish between leads, positions, claims, evidence, and concluding statement by engaging in interactive linking tasks in a two-sided grid. The system presents definitions of AUs as described in Section 2.1 on the left side. On the right side, essay snippets constituting an AU, are selected from individual essays in the PERSUADE corpus so that all five types of AUs are represented and listed in random order. Using a click-and-link mechanism, students are asked to match each AU definition to its corresponding example. Once the task is completed and the "Check Answer" button is clicked, the system provides formative feedback by retaining the correct links and encouraging students to retry linking any previously incorrect ones. After three attempts with mistakes, the system prompts the student to view the correct answer. Upon finishing the current task correctly, students can either attempt another linking task or proceed to the next step.

To address spelling and grammatical errors in the raw texts from the PERSUADE corpus, we applied Grammatical Error Correction using LanguageTool[1]. This ensures that the example texts students work with are mostly free from distracting errors.

[1]https://languagetool.org

3.2 Step 2: Linking AUs with Transitional Words

In the second step, students practice linking AUs with appropriate transitional words to improve the logical flow of their arguments. Therefore, we filter the AUs used in step 1 for those containing discourse markers from a pre-compiled list. The system presents fill-in-the-blank tasks where students type in the correct transitional words for five different types of transitions: addition, contrast, cause and effect, example, and conclusion. The system allows alternatives with the same meaning.

After each attempt, the system provides formative feedback: following the first incorrect try, it reveals the transition type; after the second incorrect attempt, it suggests example transitional words to encourage further revision. If students enter an incorrect word three times, they are encouraged to click the "Show the Correct Answer" button, which provides summative feedback along with the correct solution.

3.3 Step 3: Supporting Claims with Evidence

In the third step, students focus on providing effective evidence to support claims. This is a multiple-choice exercise where the system presents a claim along with four potential pieces of evidence. Students need to select the evidence that best supports the claim, helping them understand the importance of using facts, statistics, and research to strengthen their arguments. After each selection, the system provides feedback on whether the chosen evidence is appropriate, explaining why certain pieces of evidence are not effective.

The system utilizes claim-evidence pairs from the AUs in Step 1. For the distractor choices, LLM prompting via the OpenAI API[2] is used to generate ineffective evidence. As the prompt shown in Appendix A.2, it also allows the system to provide immediate, detailed feedback on the effectiveness of the chosen evidence, teaching students to critically evaluate the support for their arguments.

3.4 Step 4: Writing Argumentative Essays

In the final step, students apply what they've learned in the previous exercises to write a full argumentative essay. After completing the essay, the system analyzes the text, identifying the AUs.

To achieve this, we utilize a machine learning pipeline for argument mining (Ding et al., 2022). In our process, 80% of the essays from the PERSUADE corpus, with annotated AUs, are preprocessed into tokens labeled with Inside-Outside-Beginning (IOB) tags and used as input for the pretrained Longformer model (longformer-large-4096) (Beltagy et al., 2020) for token classification. After 10 epochs of training with a maximum sequence length of 1024 tokens, the IOB-tagged tokens are transformed into predictions for different AUs during post-processing. The performance of this model is validated and tested on the remaining 10% of the essays, as discussed in Section 4.1.

Based on the AUs identified by this model in the students' essays, FEAT-writing provides two types of feedback as shown in Figure 2:

- **Summative Feedback** presented as a table listing the number of AUs identified in the text. This feedback offers a concise overview of the essay's structural completeness, giving students a clear, quantifiable measure of how well they have included key argumentative components (Tricomi and DePasque, 2016).
- **Elaborate Feedback** includes written text offering positive reinforcement, a list of AUs already present, and suggestions for additional AUs that students could incorporate in revision. The use of elaborate feedback is grounded in educational psychology, as providing detailed, constructive feedback can promote student self-efficacy and foster deeper learning. By offering specific guidance and motivation, this feedback type helps students understand not only what they are missing but also how to improve their writing (Cáceres et al., 2021).

Additionally, AUs are color-coded making it easier for students to understand the feedback and improve their writing (Maldonado-Otto and Ormsbee, 2019). After receiving feedback, students can revise their essays, return to a previous exercise, or write a new essay based on a different prompt.

4 Evaluation

FEAT-writing is evaluated primarily in the final step: writing argumentative essays. While the earlier exercises are crucial for building foundational skills in argumentative writing, their impact is best measured through the student's ability to produce

[2]https://platform.openai.com/docs/api-reference/introduction

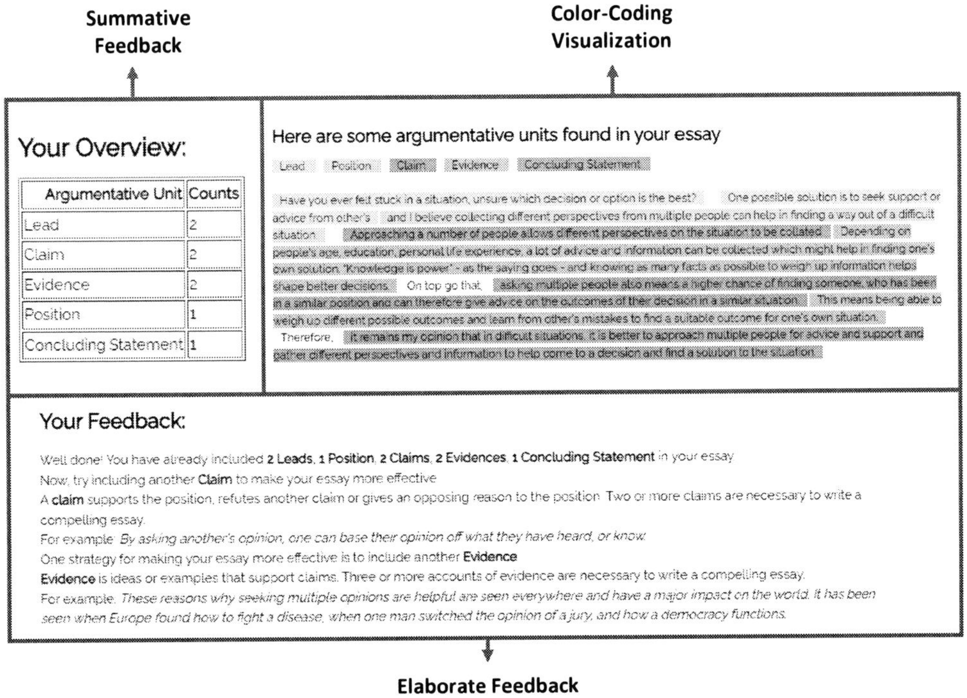

Figure 2: Feedback in Step 4 of FEAT-writing.

well-structured essays. Consequently, we first focus our evaluation on the system's performance in detecting AUs within student essays and the overall effectiveness of the feedback provided to students, leaving the evaluation of early steps in future work.

4.1 Performance of AU Detection

The performance evaluation of our argument mining model was conducted on 10% of the essays in the PERSUADE corpus. We consider a predicted AU to be a true positive if it overlaps with the corresponding ground truth AU by more than 50%. Conversely, predictions that do not match any ground truth units are marked as false positives, and ground truth units without a corresponding prediction are marked as false negatives. Using this approach, our model achieved an overall F1 score of 0.66, with a precision of 0.68 and a recall of 0.64. This indicates a reasonable level of accuracy in detecting AUs within the essays, which is crucial for providing meaningful feedback to students.

However, we acknowledge that assigning equal importance to all tokens in the matching process is a simplification. Methods that assign different weights to content and function words or incorporate token position, as described in (Schmidt et al., 2024), could further refine evaluation metrics and improve precision.

4.2 Effectiveness of Feedback

The evaluation of the effectiveness of automated feedback was structured as an online study with a focus on how different feedback types influence students' revisions and overall writing quality.

4.2.1 Variables and Methods

The independent variables were the use of color-coding in marking AUs within the student text and the feedback types provided by FEAT-writing. The feedback type included three variants:

- **Outcome Feedback**: A percentage score based on the presence of key AUs.
- **Summative Feedback**: A table listing the number of AUs identified, and
- **Elaborate Feedback**: Written feedback, including positive affirmations, a list of AUs already present, and suggestions for additional AUs to include.

Participants were randomly assigned to one of six feedback groups in a 2x3 between-subjects design, based on the presence or absence of color-coding and the feedback type received. After writing an initial draft in response to a given prompt, participants received automated feedback according to their group assignment. They were then asked to revise their essays within a set timeframe (15 minutes).

Different from the description in Section 3.4, we introduced an **Outcome Feedback** score during the evaluation phase to provide a straightforward, quantitative measure of essay completeness. Specifically, students received a score of 100% if their essay contained at least one lead, one position, three claims, three pieces of evidence, and one concluding statement. This scoring method served as an initial, objective measure of the presence of key argumentative elements, which allowed us to compare essays systematically during the evaluation. Consequently, the scores participants received for their first draft (1st score) and their revised draft (2nd score) were used as our first dependent variables to measure Completeness Gain.

However, we recognize that this metric captures only the structural completeness of an essay in a rigid, predefined manner. While it was useful in the evaluation phase to gain insights into how revisions impacted essay structure, its limitations led to its exclusion from the final system, which focuses on more objective and detailed feedback.

Other dependent variables include:

- **Completeness Gain**: The difference between the 1st and 2nd scores.
- **Edit Distance**: The Levenshtein Distance (Levenshtein, 1966) between the original and revised essays, measuring the extent of changes made.
- **Lexical Diversity Gain**: The change in the Type-Token Ratio (TTR) between the original and revised essays, reflecting variations in word usage.

Data was collected through a combination of self-report surveys and log data from the writing tasks. Besides demographic information, participants were also surveyed about their experience with argumentative writing and automated feedback systems.

4.2.2 Results

Feedback is Effective A total of 346 L2 students from various German universities participated in this study. On average, participants were 31.2 years old and enrolled in their 6th semester. This higher-than-usual average age for university students can be attributed to the fact that most participants were enrolled in remote university programs, which typically attract older students balancing studies with professional or personal responsibilities. Notably, 42.2% had no prior experience with argumentative essay writing, and 54.6% had not received automated feedback before this evaluation.

Dependent Variables	Average (M)	Standard Deviation (SD)
1st Score	76.7%	18.0%
2nd Score	81.5%	16.0%
Completeness Gain	4.8%	13.5%
Edit Distance	435.7	531.53
Lexical Diversity Gain	0.02	0.03

Table 1: Average of dependent variables showing essay improvement after feedback.

As shown in Table 1, the average **1st score** for the initial drafts was 76.7%. After receiving feedback and revising their essays, the average **2nd score** increased to 81.5%. The **Completeness Gain** between the drafts averaged 4.8%, with 28.03% participants improving their score by up to 71.8%, while 19.94% showed a decrease. The **Edit Distance** averaged 435.7, indicating a substantial degree of revisions. Only 17.3% of students made no edits after receiving feedback. Additionally, the average TTR improved from 0.53 in the initial draft to 0.55 in the revision, reflecting an improvement in **Lexical Diversity**.

Comparison of Feedback Groups Given that the dependent variables were not normally distributed, we used Kruskal-Wallis tests (Kruskal and Wallis, 1952) to compare six feedback groups. The results, presented in Appendix A.3, show significant differences between groups, but cannot specify between which groups these differences occur.

Therefore, Dunn's tests (Dunn, 1961) for pairwise comparisons were subsequently used to locate the specific differences between groups and revealed several key findings: For **Completeness Gain**, the group receiving outcome feedback with color-coding showed the highest improvement. In terms of **Edit Distance**, the longest changes were observed in the group receiving elaborate feedback with color-coding. This suggests that more elaborate feedback with visual cues encourages more extensive revisions. For **Lexical Diversity Gain**, the most diverse word usage was observed in the group that received elaborate feedback without color-coding.

5 Conclusion and Outlook

We introduced FEAT-writing, an interactive training system designed to enhance student's argumentative writing skills. It guides students through a series of exercises that progressively build their understanding, connecting, supporting, and writing of AUs. In each step, our system provides students with different types of automated feedback.

The results of our evaluation, which focused on the final step, where students wrote and revised full argumentative essays, indicate that FEAT-writing positively impacts students' argumentative writing.

Future work will first focus on extending our evaluation to the earlier steps in the system. These steps are crucial for skill building, but their effectiveness is not as easy to capture as the completeness of the final essay. Additionally, we plan to enhance the natural language processing capabilities of the system, including scoring the general quality of the essays automatically and refining the feedback mechanisms based on usability.

Limitations and Ethical Considerations

While FEAT-writing demonstrates the potential to support students' argumentative writing skills, there are some limitations to consider. First, the NLP models underlying FEAT-writing were trained on the PERSUADE corpus, which may carry inherent biases reflective of the data's sources. This could potentially affect the system's ability to provide equitable feedback across diverse linguistic and cultural backgrounds.

Furthermore, the predefined criteria for scoring, such as the specific requirements for "completeness", may not align perfectly with every educational context, potentially limiting the system's adaptability.

Given that FEAT-writing collects and processes students' written texts for evaluation, data privacy is a primary ethical consideration. In compliance with GDPR[3] and other data protection regulations, all user data, including essay submissions and interaction logs, are anonymized before analysis. The system only stores data necessary for educational purposes and does not retain personal information beyond what is required for feedback generation. Additionally, students' consent is obtained prior to participation, and they are fully informed about how their data will be used. Users have the right to withdraw their consent and request data deletion at any time, ensuring that their privacy and autonomy are respected throughout the writing process.

Acknowledgements

This work was partially conducted at "CATALPA - Center of Advanced Technology for Assisted Learning and Predictive Analytics" of the FernUniversität in Hagen, Germany.

References

Xiaoyu Bai and Manfred Stede. 2022. Argument similarity assessment in german for intelligent tutoring: Crowdsourced dataset and first experiments. In *Proceedings of the Thirteenth Language Resources and Evaluation Conference*, pages 2177–2187.

Beata Beigman Klebanov and Nitin Madnani. 2020. Automated evaluation of writing – 50 years and counting. In *Proceedings of the 58th Annual Meeting of the Association for Computational Linguistics*, pages 7796–7810, Online. Association for Computational Linguistics.

Iz Beltagy, Matthew E Peters, and Arman Cohan. 2020. Longformer: The long-document transformer. *arXiv preprint arXiv:2004.05150*.

Martín Cáceres, Miguel Nussbaum, Fernando González, and Vicente Gardulski. 2021. Is more detailed feedback better for problem-solving? *Interactive Learning Environments*, 29(7):1189–1210.

Anderson Pinheiro Cavalcanti, Arthur Barbosa, Ruan Carvalho, Fred Freitas, Yi-Shan Tsai, Dragan Gašević, and Rafael Ferreira Mello. 2021. Automatic feedback in online learning environments: A systematic literature review. *Computers and Education: Artificial Intelligence*, 2:100027.

CCSSO and NGA. 2010. Common core state standards for english language arts 6-12. *Common core state standards for English language arts literacy in history/social studies, science, and technical subjects.*

S.A. Crossley, Y. Tian, P. Baffour, A. Franklin, M. Benner, and U. Boser. 2024. A large-scale corpus for assessing written argumentation: PERSUADE 2.0. *Assessing Writing*, 61:100865.

Scott A Crossley, Perpetual Baffour, Yu Tian, Aigner Picou, Meg Benner, and Ulrich Boser. 2022. The persuasive essays for rating, selecting, and understanding argumentative and discourse elements (PERSUADE) corpus 1.0. *Assessing Writing*, 54:100667.

Yuning Ding, Marie Bexte, and Andrea Horbach. 2022. Don't drop the topic-the role of the prompt in argument identification in student writing. In *Proceedings of the 17th Workshop on Innovative Use of NLP for Building Educational Applications (BEA 2022)*, pages 124–133.

[3]https://gdpr-info.eu

Yuning Ding, Omid Kashefi, Swapna Somasundaran, and Andrea Horbach. 2024. When argumentation meets cohesion: Enhancing automatic feedback in student writing. In *Proceedings of the 2024 Joint International Conference on Computational Linguistics, Language Resources and Evaluation (LREC-COLING 2024)*, pages 17513–17524.

Olive Jean Dunn. 1961. Multiple comparisons among means. *Journal of the American statistical association*, 56(293):52–64.

Dana R Ferris. 2003. Response to student writing: Implications for second language students. *Lawrence Earlbaum Associates*.

Steve Graham and Dolores Perin. 2007. Writing next-effective strategies to improve writing of adolescents in middle and high schools.

Christian Haring, Rene Lehmann, Andrea Horbach, and Torsten Zesch. 2021. C-test collector: A proficiency testing application to collect training data for C-tests. In *Proceedings of the 16th Workshop on Innovative Use of NLP for Building Educational Applications*, pages 180–184, Online. Association for Computational Linguistics.

Tanja Heck, Detmar Meurers, and Stephen Bodnar. 2021. Automatic generation of form-based grammar exercises from authentic texts.

Michael Heilman and Maxine Eskenazi. 2007. Application of automatic thesaurus extraction for computer generation of vocabulary questions. In *SLaTE*, pages 65–68.

George Hillocks. 2011. Teaching argument writing, grades 6–12. *Portsmouth, NH: Heinemanri*.

Cheryl I Johnson and Heather A Priest. 2014. 19 the feedback principle in multimedia learning. *The Cambridge handbook of multimedia learning*, page 449.

Cody Kalina and KC Powell. 2009. Cognitive and social constructivism: Developing tools for an effective classroom. *Education*, 130(2):241–250.

Zixuan Ke and Vincent Ng. 2019. Automated essay scoring: A survey of the state of the art. In *IJCAI*, volume 19, pages 6300–6308.

Farzaneh Khodabandeh, Manochehre Jafarigohar, Hassan Soleimani, and Fatemeh Hemmati. 2013. The impact of explicit, implicit, and no-formal genre-based instruction on argumentative essay writing. *Linguistics Journal*, 7(1).

KMK. 2024. Bildungsstandards für die erste Fremdsprache (Englisch/Französisch) für den Ersten Schulabschluss und den Mittleren Schulabschluss.

William H Kruskal and W Allen Wallis. 1952. Use of ranks in one-criterion variance analysis. *Journal of the American statistical Association*, 47(260):583–621.

Deanna Kuhn, Laura Hemberger, and Valerie Khait. 2017. *Argue with me: Argument as a path to developing students' thinking and writing*. Routledge.

Ji-Ung Lee, Marc E Pfetsch, and Iryna Gurevych. 2024. Constrained c-test generation via mixed-integer programming. *arXiv preprint arXiv:2404.08821*.

V Levenshtein. 1966. Binary codes capable of correcting deletions, insertions, and reversals. *Proceedings of the Soviet physics doklady*.

Ming Liu, Yi Li, Weiwei Xu, and Li Liu. 2016. Automated essay feedback generation and its impact on revision. *IEEE Transactions on Learning Technologies*, 10(4):502–513.

C Maldonado-Otto and C Ormsbee. 2019. Color-coding affect on writing instruction for students with learning difficulties. In *ICERI2019 Proceedings*, pages 11421–11432. IATED.

RE Mayer. 2005. Cognitive theory of multimedia learning.

Ellis B Page. 1966. The imminence of... grading essays by computer. *The Phi Delta Kappan*, 47(5):238–243.

Zhenhui Peng, Xingbo Wang, Qiushi Han, Junkai Zhu, Xiaojuan Ma, and Huamin Qu. 2023. Storyfier: Exploring vocabulary learning support with text generation models. In *Proceedings of the 36th Annual ACM Symposium on User Interface Software and Technology*, pages 1–16.

Laura Perez-Beltrachini, Claire Gardent, and German Kruszewski. 2012. Generating grammar exercises. In *Proceedings of the Seventh Workshop on Building Educational Applications Using NLP*, pages 147–156.

S Rafik-Galea, Siti Zaidah Zainuddin, and PV Galea. 2008. Learning to think critically the toulmin way. In *13th Seminar International Conference on Thinking*.

Jim Ranalli, Stephanie Link, and Evgeny Chukharev-Hudilainen. 2017. Automated writing evaluation for formative assessment of second language writing: Investigating the accuracy and usefulness of feedback as part of argument-based validation. *Educational Psychology*, 37(1):8–25.

Federico M. Schmidt, Sebastian Gottifredi, and Alejandro J. García. 2024. Identifying arguments within a text: Categorizing errors and their impact in arguments' relation prediction. *International Journal of Approximate Reasoning*, 173:109267.

Ron Sun, Edward Merrill, and Todd Peterson. 2001. From implicit skills to explicit knowledge: A bottom-up model of skill learning. *Cognitive science*, 25(2):203–244.

Stephen E Toulmin. 2003. *The uses of argument*. Cambridge university press.

Elizabeth Tricomi and Samantha DePasque. 2016. The role of feedback in learning and motivation. In *Recent developments in neuroscience research on human motivation*, pages 175–202. Emerald Group Publishing Limited.

Thiemo Wambsganss, Andrew Caines, and Paula Buttery. 2022. Alen app: Persuasive writing support to foster english language learning. *BEA 2022*, page 134.

Thiemo Wambsganss, Tobias Kueng, Matthias Soellner, and Jan Marco Leimeister. 2021. Arguetutor: An adaptive dialog-based learning system for argumentation skills. In *Proceedings of the 2021 CHI conference on human factors in computing systems*, pages 1–13.

Joshua Wilson and Rod D Roscoe. 2020. Automated writing evaluation and feedback: Multiple metrics of efficacy. *Journal of Educational Computing Research*, 58(1):87–125.

A Appendix

A.1 Definitions of Effective AUs

The following definitions of effective AUs come from the scoring rubric of PERSUADE corpus, which can be found at `https://github.com/scrosseye/persuade_corpus_2.0/blob/main/argumentation_effectiveness_rubric.pdf`.

- *Effective Lead*: The lead grabs the reader's attention and strongly points toward the position.
- *Effective Position*: The position states a clear stance closely related to the topic.
- *Effective Claim*: The claim is closely relevant to the position and backs up the position with specific points or perspectives. The claim is valid and acceptable.
- *Effective Evidence*: The evidence is closely relevant to the claim they support and back up the claim objectively with concrete facts, examples, research, statistics, or studies. The reasons in the evidence support the claim and are sound and well substantiated.
- *Effective Concluding Statement*: The concluding summary effectively restates the claims using different wording. It may readdress the claims in light of the evidence provided.

A.2 LLM Prompt for Generation of Ineffective evidence

Given the claim: "$claim", generate three pieces of ineffective evidence, that are irrelevant to the claim, or provide only a few valid examples, making unsubstantiated assumptions. The evidence generated should be used as distractors for effective evidence: "$effective evidence", so they should have similar lengths but significant differences in content. For each ineffective piece of evidence, explain why it is not effective.

A.3 Results of Kruskal-Wallis Tests

Dependent Variables	**Kruskal-Wallis Value** χ^2**(5, 346)**
Completeness Gain	12.11*
Edit Distance	12.25*
Lexical Diversity Gain	11.22*

Table 2: Comparison of six feedback groups measured by Kruskal-Wallis tests. Results with * indicate significant values $p < .05$.

Author Index

Aitymbetov, Nurmukhammed, 199
Androutsopoulos, Ion, 174
Arenas-García, Jerónimo, 151

Baldwin, Timothy, 28
Barbakos, Spiros, 174
Biemann, Chris, 189
Budhiraja, Harshit, 208
Buitelaar, Paul, 104

Calvo Bartolomé, Lorena, 151
Chen, Linqing, 9
Chen, Siming, 63
Choudhury, Monojit, 208

Dikonomaki, Chrysa, 174
Ding, Yuning, 217
Do, Truong Dinh, 1
Dutková, Lucia, 117

El-Haj, Mo, 20
Elmers, Mikey, 136
Everingham, Yvette, 54
Ezeani, Ignatius, 20

Feujio, Loic, 126
Fu, Yahui, 136

Gebeşçe, Ali, 163
Geng, Yilin, 28
Georgiou, Mary, 174

Han, Xudong, 28
Hay, Rachel, 54
Horbach, Andrea, 217
Hou, Yang, 83
Hraška, Peter, 117
Huang, Xuanjing, 63

Inoue, Koji, 136

Karetka, Gregor, 117
Kawahara, Tatsuya, 136
Koutsikakis, John, 174
Kuang, Haoyu, 63
Kyriakakis, Manolis, 174

Lal, Daisy Monika, 20
Lala, Divesh, 136
Lan, Yunshi, 37
Lee, Daniel, 126
Li, Haonan, 28
LI, Yijie, 91
Li, Yunyao, 126
Li, Zhenghua, 83
Liu, Xiawei, 63
Liu, Yufeng, 20
Loukas, Lefteris, 174

Ma, Xi, 83
Maharaj, Akash, 126
Manjunath, Sampritha Hassan, 104
Matsumoto, Yuji, 1

Nakov, Preslav, 28
Naseem, Usman, 54
Negi, Gaurav, 104
Nguyen, Anh Thi-Hoang, 183
Nguyen, Dung Ha, 183
Nguyen, Kiet Van, 183
Nguyen, Minh Le, 1
Nikishina, Irina, 189

Pandey, Saurabh Kumar, 208
Pang, Zi Haur, 136
Pavlopoulos, John, 174
Pérez Fernández, David, 151
Peter, Christopher, 20
Phi, Van-Thuy, 1
Pillai, Devishree, 104

Qian, Weining, 37

Rayson, Paul, 20

Saha, Sougata, 208
Şahin, Gözde Gül, 163
Shallouf, Ahmad, 189
Skottis, Demetris, 117
Smyrnioudis, Nikolaos, 174
Sree Harsha, Sai, 126
Sun, Libo, 63

Sun, Yuan, 91
Suppa, Marek, 117

Toumazatos, Anastasios, 174
Trieu, An Hoang, 1

Ustalov, Dmitry, 46

Vassos, Stavros, 174

Wang, Hao, 28
Wang, Minghan, 28
Wang, Xiaoman, 37
Wang, Xuebin, 83
Wang, Yuxia, 28
Wehrhahn, Franziska, 217
Wei, Zhongyu, 63
Wilson, Carrie-Ann, 54

Xing, Rui, 28

Yang, Shiyue, 63
Yang, Yihang, 63

Zayed, Omnia, 104
Zhai, Zenan, 28
Zhang, Hong, 126
Zhang, Xinnong, 63
Zhang, Zhihao, 54
Zhao, Yike, 37
Zhu, Yafei, 20
Zhu, Zhengyuan, 126
Zorbas, Dimitrios, 199

Association for Computational Linguistics
209 N. Eighth Street
Stroudsburg, Pennsylvania 18360

ISBN 979-8-3313-1357-9

CURRAN ASSOCIATES INC.
proceedings.com